Greetings from BANTAM, CONN.

Greetings from SEYMOUR, CONN.

The
Trout Pool
Paradox

THE
TROUT POOL
PARADOX

THE AMERICAN LIVES
OF THREE RIVERS

George Black

Houghton
Mifflin
Company
BOSTON
NEW YORK
2004

Library of Congress Cataloging-in-Publication Data

Black, George, date.
The trout pool paradox : the American lives of three rivers / George Black.
p. cm.
Includes bibliographical references (p.).
ISBN 0-618-31080-0
1. Stream ecology—Connecticut—History.   2. Human ecology—Connecticut—History.
3. Nature—Effect of human beings on—Connecticut—History.   4. Rivers—Connecticut—
History.   I. Title.
QH105.C8B57 2004
304.2'09746—dc22   2003056898

Book design by Anne Chalmers
Typeface: Miller
Map on page 2 by Jacques Chazaud

Printed in the United States of America

QUM 10 9 8 7 6 5 4 3 2 1

The postcard on page 125 is reprinted by permission of the Gunn Historical Museum,
Washington, Connecticut.

FOR DAVID,

dam builder extraordinary,

FOR JULIA,

who put the bop in the bop shoo bop shoo bop,

AND FOR MY MOTHER,

who always knew where the blaeberries grew

Contents

Book I
WATERSHED

I always feel that I am fishing in some strange, unreal vacuum unless I know the purpose of the people and the meaning of the country around my rivers.

— Roderick Haig-Brown,
Fisherman's Winter, 1954

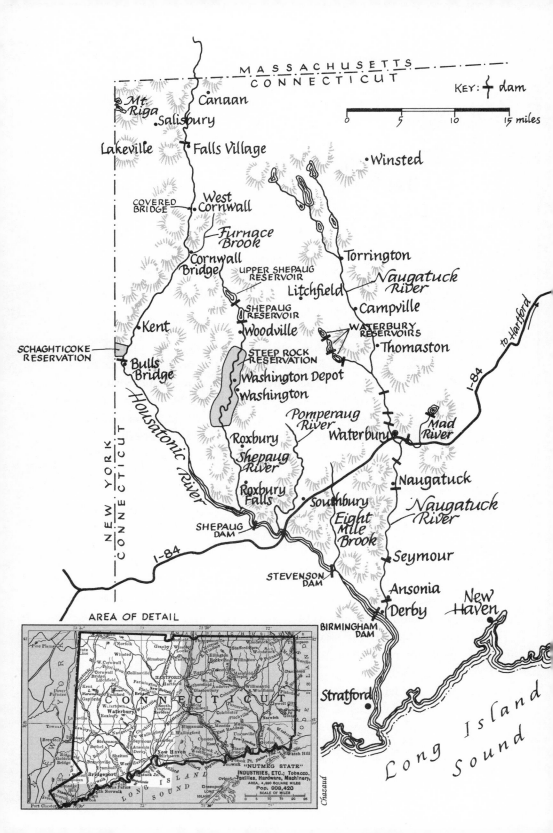

1
The Trout Pool Paradox

THE STATE OF CONNECTICUT covers 4,845 square miles. You could fit it, if you were so minded, about fifty-five times into the state of Texas. If you drove diagonally across the state between its most widely separated points—say, from the New York suburbs of Greenwich, Connecticut, to the northeast corner, on the Massachusetts line—you would, in Texan terms, be making a quick hop from Dallas to Wichita Falls.

Battle Swamp Brook lies in the hilly northwestern part of the state. From my home in Manhattan, the odometer records the journey as eighty-three miles, and with light traffic on the Henry Hudson Parkway, I can be on the stream in ninety minutes flat. Battle Swamp Brook is as wild a place as you can find in the state of Connecticut. Without thinking too much about their choice of words, a lot of people would call it a pristine wilderness. *Pristine:* "remaining in a pure state, uncorrupted by civilization." That's what it says in *The American Heritage Dictionary.*

Less than a mile from here, the brook enters the Shepaug River— "a wilderness gem," according to the Connecticut Fund for the Environment. The Shepaug is the second-largest tributary of the Housatonic, which winds for more than a hundred miles from the Berkshire Hills of Massachusetts before it passes under Interstate 95 and flows sluggishly into Long Island Sound. Next valley over, barely ten miles from here, just across the forested hills, is the Naugatuck—the largest of the Housatonic's tributaries, which joins the big river at tidewater.

I began to fish this watershed ten years ago, when our kids were newborns and we rented a summer place in the town of Southbury, Connecticut. Southbury formed the base point of a triangle. Fifteen miles and twenty-five minutes in one direction took us to the town of Washington, the crown jewel of the Shepaug Valley and a magnet for affluent New Yorkers, a kind of Hamptons-Without-the-Crowds (or the ocean). Fifteen miles and twenty-five minutes in the other direction, most of it on the interstate, and we descended into the valley of the Naugatuck and the town of Waterbury, past the red-brick chimneys of derelict mills, the spires of innumerable Catholic churches, and the Italianate tower of the old railroad depot, an exact replica of the Torre del Mangia in Siena. We went to Washington for riverbank picnics, watching as the kids waded out to net giant crayfish. We went to Waterbury if we wanted to do a big shop at the mall or if the car needed to make a pit stop at Midas Muffler.

I say that I began to fish the Housatonic watershed. To be more accurate, I'd have to say that I fished the Shepaug until Memorial Day. In springtime, the river is like the Platonic ideal of a trout stream, as it rushes through places called Steep Rock and Hidden Valley. Sarah Griswold, the director of the little Gunn Historical Museum in Washington, once told me that during the thirteen years she lived in California, she never stopped thinking about the river for a single day. She told Californians that the Sierras had nothing to compare with Steep Rock. They told Sarah she couldn't be serious, talking that way about some rinky-dink place in Connecticut. She said, "I'm *serious.*"

It isn't hard to see what Sarah Griswold meant. The Shepaug is a river to break your heart. Not just because it's so beautiful, or because of the big brown trout and wild brookies that hide in its tea-colored runs, but because it has spent eighty years on the brink of extinction. In April and May it's the river that nature intended it to be, and watching its hydrology, geology, biology, and hydraulics all pulling in sync is like watching the Guarneri Quartet play Beethoven.

But after Memorial Day the Shepaug becomes a shadow of itself. As the consequence of a 1921 agreement, which the selectmen of Washington signed in a moment of weakness, their industrial neighbor, the city of Waterbury, built a dam on the Shepaug and began to divert the river water for its own needs. So in summertime the rocks bake, the water temperature soars into the eighties, parents are afraid to let their children play in the river because of the risk of infection by *E. coli*, and trout are found floating belly-up below Roxbury Falls.

I'd fish the Shepaug, then, for a month or so each spring, knowing that I could almost always find solitude there, in a landscape of hemlock woods, shaded forest paths, and the scattered estates of gentlemen farmers. For the rest of the year, I joined the community of anglers who stalk fat brown trout in the six-mile stretch of the Housatonic that flanks the town of Cornwall. But I never heard of anyone fishing the Naugatuck. The name alone was a sufficient deterrent. The Naugatuck was to the Northeast what Ohio's Cuyahoga was to the Midwest—a chemical sewer that was chiefly known for catching fire.

Topographically, this didn't make any sense to me. A geological map of northwestern Connecticut showed similar granite hills enclosing two steep, parallel valleys of roughly similar length—the Shepaug and the Naugatuck. It seemed therefore that the two rivers should have followed a similar course of settlement and development. Yet the divide was absolute. The rain that fell on the west side of the Litchfield Hills flowed into a rural idyll. The rain that fell to the east fed an urban nightmare. One river was filled with polished rocks and water the color of Earl Grey tea, home to brown trout and mayflies; the other was filled with car tires and shopping carts. I wondered why this should be so.

From the small fieldstone bridge over Battle Swamp Brook, the trail winds sharply uphill from the dirt road. Off to the right, from a wooded ravine, comes the sound of running water. Through thick stands of hemlock and rhododendron, glints of the stream begin to appear as you walk uphill. It's a small brook, no more than fifteen feet at its widest, its course defined by stairstep shelves of Precambrian bedrock. Each successive set of falls is lipped with white spray; the water drops away into the next short, deep pool, stained amber with tannins from the hemlocks. The pools are studded with sharp-edged boulders, long ago scattered in random patterns by the departing glaciers.

On these small, glaciated New England streams, it's never easy for the angler to maneuver into a good casting position. There are too many obstacles. The sides of the brook rise abruptly, and the dark canopy of hemlock branches waits to snag any careless backcast. But the fish are eager to flash at any morsel that drifts past their feeding stations, and within minutes I've caught and released three. They're wild brook trout, six or eight inches long, with sleek dark sides that harmonize with their surroundings. The single male among them has an intense splash of orange on his belly, advance notice that he will soon be ready for spawning.

The best place to drop a fly is in the quiet back eddy at the foot of the largest waterfall, where helpless insects are funneled into a slow-motion whirlpool. This is where I'd expect to find the largest fish in the pool. Even so, the jolting force of the strike comes as a surprise. The fish is full of muscular strength, and it takes me down over the lip of the pool and into the stony riffle below. In this confined environment, with a short, light rod, I experience the momentary illusion of fighting a tarpon. But it's a brown trout, and a beauty, a quintessence of trout.

Those who write about the trout tend to strain for metaphors to describe its form. Yet it seems redundant to say that it's torpedo-shaped, or football-shaped, or anything-else-shaped. All that really needs to be said is that it's trout-shaped. The form is self-defining, an archetype, an ideal of natural beauty. This particular trout is fully eleven inches long, with strong, thick shoulders. The spots are bright roundels of a color that the English would call pillar-box red. I doubt whether the food supply in this small mountain brook—the sparse hatches of mayflies, stoneflies, and caddis flies; the blacknose dace and creek chub; the crickets, grasshoppers, beetles, and ants that are blown into the stream by summer breezes—could build a larger or healthier specimen.

Even so, the brown trout is an unlikely roommate for the native brookies. It's a European immigrant that came to this country a little over a hundred years ago, at about the same time that millions of other immigrants were pouring in through Ellis Island. In this northwestern Connecticut drainage, in fact, *Salmo trutta* has not even been around that long; the first ones were introduced here only in the 1920s. So my brown is an interloper in a sense, not many generations removed from stocked fish that swam up this tributary from the Shepaug in search of spawning grounds. In this corner of New England—indeed, in most of the American Northeast—this type of wild fish, stream-bred but not native, will have to be enough to satisfy our longings for wildness.

By THE TIME the trout has revived and slid back under its sheltering rock, the morning has grown warm. Time to eat. Crusty sourdough

TUNXIS FALLS, NEAR WINSTED, CONN.

bread, a thick hunk of cheddar cheese, an apple, ice-cold water. At the edge of the pool, there's a serviceable lunch table, a flat rock edged with dark, damp moss. A twenty-foot hemlock, as thick around as my thigh, has somehow contrived to anchor itself here, extracting just sufficient moisture for survival from the dense metamorphic rock. Its trunk arches out over the stream, and its roots snake across the rock face before burrowing into the small pockets of soil trapped in the crevices. The tracery of roots intrigues me, and I follow its path with my finger. Beneath the tangle, the crevices in the rock seem oddly regular, falling in unnaturally straight lines and right angles. Only by standing back a few steps is it possible to apprehend the larger shape—not a table rock at all but the grown-over ruins of a milldam.

Right here at my feet is what I've come to think of as the trout pool paradox. If you are looking for cultural archetypes, look no farther than the trout pool, where wild creatures of astonishing beauty swim free in the limpid currents at the base of a waterfall. The image pervades recorded American history. You'll find it in the first engravings of the colonists and the prints of Currier and Ives, in the hand-colored turn-of-the-century post card and the sentimental Hallmark greeting card. The trout pool is a place for solitary contemplation, for romantic love, for a sense of reconnection with lost wilderness. And yet paradoxically, the pristine trout pools of western Connecticut nurtured the most noisome and alienating developments of the American industrial revolution—factory towns, foundries, mass production, the modern armaments and aerospace industries.

For millennia, before they were displaced and decimated by disease, Pootatuck Indians would have gathered their wigwams seasonally near this spot to intercept American shad and lamprey eels, and perhaps Atlantic salmon, as these creatures made their spawning runs up the Housatonic, into the Shepaug, and up this brook, perhaps as far as the small falls where I'm standing. When European colonists began to populate these rocky hills with their farmsteads in the early eighteenth century, they found that the means of powering waterwheels was close at hand. The building of the mills followed the imperatives of survival—food, shelter, and clothing. First gristmills ground the grain to make bread. Next, sawmills transformed the abundant forests into boards for farmhouses, fences for fields, and waterwheels and gears and dam planking for more mills, such as the fulling mills that would turn coarse woolen yardage into cloth. When these necessities were attended to, a secondary wave of mills made the axes, the barrel staves, the hard cider— an expanding universe of farm tools, household implements, and food and beverage. The raw materials were right there to hand, embedded in the rocks, ready to spawn a growing army of blacksmiths, ironworkers, and other specialized artisans who would turn the agrarian economy of the Housatonic Valley into an industrial one.

WHEN I FIRST chanced upon the ruins on Battle Swamp Brook, there was nothing to tell me what kind of mill had once stood here or why it had failed. But I thought it was a fair bet that the mill owner had stood at the center of the local social web. Given their strategic importance to the economy, millers came to be indispensable sources of information, power brokers, often a community's first bankers and capitalists and politicians. Only years later did curiosity take me to the local archives, in the town of Roxbury, where I found old maps confirming that the ruins on Battle Swamp Brook had once been a sawmill. A map from the 1860s showed the residence of a Colonel Albert L. Hodge next to the mill.

The colonel had left more than his name on a map. In addition to his sawmill interests, he was a "West Point alumnus, farmer, business-man, road commissioner, retailer, saloon keeper, iron mine director, church elder, state legislator, and Roxbury's registrar of voters." He had done enough to merit a biography, and he had kept a daybook, which the public library had preserved. Reading these volumes was like looking into a nineteenth-century stereopticon. They combined to show me a three-dimensional picture of a New England valley at the end of the Civil War, quivering on the brink of a heavy industrial future because of the energies that men like Colonel Hodge applied to the natural conditions they found here.

We tend to think of the Victorians as verbose, but Hodge was laconic in the extreme. The entries in his daybook rarely run to more than ten words. While the Civil War ground on, his main concern was farming.

APRIL 5, 1864   *Plowed my garden today.*
APRIL 11   *Sowed clover seed and rye. Snow and rain.*
MAY 28   *Put manure on my tobacco ground.*
MAY 29   *Sheared my sheep.*

Yet five years after the war, the daybook reflects very different preoc-cupations.

JUNE 21, 1870   *A fine early shower. To the mine and started a shaft.*
AUGUST 1   *Measured the drifts [at the iron mine] and made out the statement.*
AUGUST 4   *Took up the small bridge at the mill. Logan and Perkins came on railroad matters.*

In the boom years that followed the war, Colonel Hodge and his fellow civic leaders were clamoring to use the Shepaug in order to become as filthy rich as the men of affairs of the neighboring Naugatuck Valley, who had turned the city of Waterbury into the world capital of the brass industry. Hodge's days were consumed by the Shepaug Spathic Iron and Steel Company, which he dreamed would produce surgical-grade steel in Roxbury, and the Shepaug Valley Railroad Company, whose tracks would turn the sleepy valley into an industrial powerhouse.

But the dream collapsed. In Waterbury and along the Naugatuck, the boom and the filth lasted for another hundred years. Yet in Roxbury,

Washington, and the other towns of the Shepaug Valley, the idea of an industrial future was dead within three. All that remained was the old abandoned railbed—the forest path that I used to hike from one Shepaug trout pool to the next. I needed to know why, and the first schematic histories I read helped me—up to a point. In this particular corner of Connecticut, I could quickly see, the symmetry between the elements of a healthy trout stream and the ingredients of an industrial sewer was almost uncanny, seemingly invented by someone wanting to make a didactic point about our culture. Over the course of two hundred years, the poverty of the land and the waterpower provided by fast-flowing glaciated rivers made this the cradle of the American industrial revolution. Gristmills mutated into factories, and factories spawned factory towns. Rivers were choked with sawdust and poisoned with industrial waste. The old-growth forests that shaded and cooled the trout streams were cut down to feed the insatiable appetite of industry. People showed me old photographs to prove that a hundred years ago, from the top of Mount Riga, where Connecticut, Massachusetts, and New York meet, you would not have seen a tree in any direction.

ALL OF THIS was true enough as a broad-brush picture, yet it felt too overdetermined. The fact is that some sawmills went one way, and some went another. At the turn of the twenty-first century, here I was, fly-fishing over wild trout in a former mill setting that apparently had reverted to its pristine state. The Naugatuck had gone one way, but the Shepaug had gone another. The Housatonic itself could easily have become another Monongahela or another Ruhr. Falls Village, where the river hurtles over bedrock shelves in a spectacle that the first European travelers could compare only with Niagara, could easily have been overrun by heavy industry, like Pittsburgh or Duisburg. Certainly there was no shortage of entrepreneurs and investors who wanted to make that happen by bending the river to their will. But in the end it didn't, and Falls Village remained a sleepy hamlet with a half-forgotten railroad halt.

As I ran my fingers over the tough roots of the hemlock, it occurred to me that if Colonel Hodge's ruined mill had anything to tell us, it is that nothing is predetermined about the course of history. There are no guarantees, no fixed plan. Any river, and by extension, I suppose, the human society around it, can teeter on the edge as the Shepaug did. Which way it tips is the result of a multitude of factors—natural phenomena, human choices both harmful and benign, economics, timing, and sheer blind chance.

It's hard to achieve intimacy with a river without at least a passing knowledge of many things: geology, hydrology and hydraulics, animal and plant biology, entomology, climate change, land use, economic and political power, human settlement and migration patterns. The list is endless. Each element has its own distinct part to play, and each conditions the others in a ceaseless dynamic of change, every bit as protean as the flow of the river itself. While no one can be expected to master all of these disciplines, it seemed to me that, as a fly-fisherman, I was at least presented with both motive and opportunity to learn something about each of them. Droves of technically adept fishermen, of course, remain blithely ignorant of all these factors, except perhaps for some basic entomology. Conversely, though, it would be hard to think deeply about these things and not emerge a better fisherman—if not in the technical sense, then at least in understanding what needs to be done if our rivers are to remain, or become once again, the kind of place where trout will want to live.

Sometimes the cause and effect of human action is blindingly transparent. Fishing one stream, you may notice that the trout no longer rise to hatches of mayflies because, in accord with local zoning ordinances, a new mall was built, silting up the pool you're standing in with the runoff from its impervious asphalt parking lot. Fishing another river, you may wonder how much the profusion of caddis fly larvae beneath the rocks has to do with the bankruptcy of a nineteenth-century investor, whose failure headed off the assault of industry. These examples are a little simplistic, of course. Most of the time, reading the water is more complicated, and the social, economic, and political food chain of the watershed is every bit as intricate as the ecology that creates the interdependencies of algae, invertebrates, and trout. Often the connections remain obscure, and that's not necessarily a bad thing, since a river without secrets ceases in some fundamental way to be a river.

L ONG BEFORE I was a fisherman, I was a child, of course, and the things that really fascinate me originated in childhood, as they do for all of us. In a Scottish mining town in the 1950s, even in the midst of brown

coal fogs and slag heaps that glowed with methane fires at night, the contested areas, the edgelands between industry and the wild, were never far
away. Wild strawberries grew around the bogs that formed over collapsed
mineshafts, and thick velvet carpets of moss submerged the stones of ruined castle towers, like the hemlocks that rose from the remnants of Colonel Hodge's milldam. On the outskirts of town, the ugly detritus of the
mines gave way abruptly to the rocky seacoast, where seal colonies flourished and Sir Patrick Spens lay buried with the Scots lords at his feet.
Last time we went back, so my children could see where their grandfather
had grown up while he was still alive, the slag heaps had been leveled, the
old pit rail bed looked as if it had been landscaped by Capability Brown,
and there was trout fishing in the loch at the edge of town.

All this may explain why I find it more productive to think about
restoration than preservation. In Europe as in New England, there isn't a
square inch of land that hasn't been picked over and shaped and re-
shaped by human action. Talking about preservation feels like perpetuat-
ing an illusion, and maybe even a dangerous one. Perhaps this piece of
graffiti, which utopian students daubed on the walls of Paris in 1968,
is more accurate: *sous le pavé, une plage*—"under the pavement, there is
a beach."

BEFORE A FISHING TRIP, I used to have one of two recurring night-
mares. The first was a pretty conventional anxiety dream. I would mis-
place my fly rod, lose my car keys, take one wrong turn after another, hit
red lights, slam the car door on my bamboo rod tip, race home, search
frantically for another, drive through unfamiliar urban landscapes where
the one-way systems took me farther away from the river, and end up at
my favorite pool just as the last of the daylight was fading from the sky.

The second dream would take me deeper into these blasted city-
scapes. Cement-lined canals full of debris. A stagnant millpond by a half-
demolished factory full of carrion crows. A scummed-up swimming pool.
Suddenly I'm aware that the biggest trout I've ever seen is finning quietly,
wraithlike, in the water, sipping flies from the surface. Fumbling and
sweating, I fire off a cast, landing the fly like thistledown. The fish turns
to take the fly, but when I set the hook there is no resistance. I reel it in;
it's inert. And when the fish becomes visible, I see that it's not a trout at
all. It's some unknown species, grotesque in form, made of some limp,
rubbery material. And it's dead.

For most of the nineteenth and twentieth centuries, the contest over our rivers was quite one-sided. Happily, that may no longer be the case. Although the battles are still often unequal, people are trying to unravel the trout pool paradox as they strive to save the contested areas of the Housatonic Valley—and other rivers across the postindustrial world. Most labor in anonymity—biologists, hydrologists, land-use planners, elected officials in small communities, litigators, local historians, high school teachers, and just plain fishermen—each in his or her own way having concluded that a river fit for trout is a fine barometer of the general health of a society.

These people reaffirm my wavering faith in a certain notion of democracy, perhaps the kind that Tocqueville had in mind when he wrote, "What most astonishes me about the United States is not so much the marvelous grandeur of some undertakings as the innumerable multitude of small ones." From these undertakings, a picture emerges of the future possibilities of the river.

But I'm getting ahead of myself. It's probably time to start at the beginning.

2
The Edgelands of Alfaro

In the beginning was the word, or, to put it another way, the urge to give things names. My children discovered this principle early in life, on a brook that was all of three feet wide, a tributary of a tributary of the Housatonic River. At first we thought the brook was nameless, nothing more than a thin blue line on the map. Later we discovered it was called Jeremy Brook. Farther down the rocky valley it drained Jeremy Swamp. Some people said this had once been called *Germany* Swamp, though they were at a loss to say why. David and Julia always called the wetland in the hollow Germy Swamp, echoing the concerns of the colonists who steered clear of such places because of their "bad airs."

Two hundred yards of the brook belonged to David and Julia alone, and they called it Alfaro, though no one remembers which of them came up with the name first. A few years later, I asked them why they had chosen that name.

Julia thought the "Al" part was like *all*—"like it was a place that had everything you ever wished for."

David said, "'Faro' sounded like *Pharaoh*—so it sounded like the place where an all-powerful king lived. I thought it had a kind of Egyptian sound—a sort of secret, sneaking-around hiding place."

Male and female answers, I suppose.

For three or four years when they were very small, Alfaro was a private edgeland in their own backyard, a safe encounter with the first principles of wildness and of rivers. The brook flowed down a steep hillside and along the edge of an abandoned, overgrown apple orchard before it turned hard right past the swamp and the ruins of a colonial barn. In the 1920s, a couple had run the place briefly and I think unsuccessfully as a pheasant farm. Later it had been bought by a writer named Gladys Taber, from whose surviving family we rented the place each summer. The main house was a white-painted early colonial, with a picket fence. The old red barn, which had burned down on a winter night in the 1950s, had been the writer's studio.

Despite the fire, it remained very much a writer's home, filled with a writer's associations. The old farmhouse itself had provided the subject, the narrative framework, and, in a way, the leading character for almost a dozen books, which carry its name: *Stillmeadow Sampler, Stillmeadow Daybook, Stillmeadow Seasons,* and so on, all artfully written countrywoman's diaries. I liked their plainspoken sensitivity to the impact on the once-isolated valley of the Pomperaug, the third-largest tributary of the Housatonic, when the new interstate highway came through a couple of miles away. For decades Taber's books had a devoted readership, and one of them even made the *New York Times* bestseller List in 1948, in the same week that George Orwell's *1984* did. She created a comforting world and gave it a brand name, Stillmeadow. If she were writing today, corporate merchandisers would try to turn her into a celebrity along the lines of Martha Stewart. The Stillmeadow logo would be on wallpaper and bed linen and kitchen utensils, and Gladys would have her own TV show.

Just as the books allow readers to live in the house vicariously and become familiar with its smallest details, so the time we spent there drew us irresistibly into a half-century of characters and anecdotes. Things went bump in the night. Visitors preferred not to sleep in one of the upstairs bedrooms, which allowed the kids to spend plenty of time up there, debating whether the dark stain on the floor was really dried blood from the murder-suicide that had taken place there in the 1920s. The Lithuanian farmer's widow who lived across the way had seen the entire thing through a crack in the door of an adjoining room. A jealous man, a beautiful young wife whose infidelities may have existed only in her husband's mind, a drunken rampage that ended when he shot her dead and then turned the gun on himself.

For long stretches, while we adults absorbed the history of the house, the kids created their own associations with the brook. At least at first, it was David's thing more than Julia's. Again, male and female. For her, the brook was a source of sensory delight. She dropped rocks in to see the splashes. She liked the play of its cool water and squealed when creek chub nipped at her ankles. David quickly evinced a desire to colonize the place, to build on it, to reshape its course. She saw a flow, he saw dams, and as we worked to construct them, he was intent on the changes produced by altering the direction and speed of the current. As he worked and issued orders to his crew, we talked in five-year-old's terms about interstitial habitat, how back eddies and standing waves are formed, the suspension of particulate matter, and the process of siltation in the slower reaches where the brook entered a small pond.

David also understood right away the strategic possibilities offered by the terrain and the morphology of the river. One day we found a box filled with hundreds of wine bottle corks, which he conscripted as an army of infantrymen. Working methodically, he placed light contingents on the bends to mount ambushes, heavier reinforcements to guard the narrows, special forces to command the higher rocks and plunge pools, and scouts and spies concealed in the ferns. The remainder of the cork men were drawn back in reserve at a base camp pitched on the miniature alluvial plain beneath a canopy of overhanging alders. He called it the Thorn Fortress.

One day a thunderstorm and a flash flood swept the cork soldiers away. For weeks afterward, we found the dead and wounded in the woods and washed up at the edges of the pond. And we tracked on the map where the majority of casualties had gone, seeing the river system emerge as we did so, as if using an iodine tracer. The contour lines showed that the hill where we stood marked the watershed divide. A drop of rain falling on the other side of the ridge went into the broad, fertile plain of the Pomperaug. On our side lay the steeper drainage area of Eight Mile Brook, with a five-mile interval between the entry point of the two rivers into the Housatonic. The cork army was first carried down the narrow valley of Alfaro, through a neighbor's fields, and into a flatter section of Jeremy Brook. After that, the dead soldiers would have bobbed down through the ravines of Eight Mile Brook and into the Housatonic at the base of the Stevenson Dam. From that point, who could say? Having evaded Stevenson's turbines, did they make it over the last of the dams at Derby and get carried out by the ocean currents into Long Island Sound?

In wintertime, when the pond froze in a sheet eight inches thick, we could see how anchor ice grew in the streambed and how it was different from the jutting shelves of border ice that formed on the rocks. March brought ice-out on the pond, rushing snowmelt in Alfaro, and the first signs of spring. We listened to the ground shifting and cracking as the hard earth readied itself to absorb the rainfall that was now sheeting down the hillside.

We read the portents of the new season together. Its first visible token, skunk cabbage, was hard to miss, with its bilious, purple-green hood, strong enough to poke up through ice in the swamp and along the edges of the brook. *Symplocarpus foetidus* was quickly followed by deep red osier stems, the silver velvet of catkins, and the ooze of sap on the maple trees. By the end of the month there was pollen as well as rain on the wind, and early bees. Coltsfoot, which the colonists used as an herbal remedy for late-season colds, was the first wildflower I could identify. Then liverwort, growing in damp patches of leaf mold. Crocuses, snowdrops. Woodpeckers drummed in the forest. The first tentative songbirds and flocks of red-winged blackbirds were looking for nesting places along the watercourse. Lucky observers might spot the first of the butterflies before the month was out—the purple-brown, yellow, and blue mourning cloak, which the English call the Camberwell Beauty.

As the spring runoff cleared, the brook became more instructive. Even though it only held chub, Alfaro made a fine child-scale diorama of a trout stream. The greatest of all fly-fishing writers, Roderick Haig-Brown, found small brooks absorbing and described them well:

> I can lie for an hour at a time and watch the flow of a little stream, dropping pieces of dry sticks into it to trace the current movements, following the midwater drift of clumps of diatoms or algae torn from the bottom, marking the way sand builds behind a pebble and the current eddies there. It is easy, in the mind, to magnify such a stream to the proportions of a full river, and it is highly profitable for the angler to do so, because the secret vagaries of current are clearly revealed here.

Every piece of running water is uniquely itself, a compound of idiosyncrasies. Yet the basic building blocks are constant. In the early 1990s, state biologists mapped every mile of every stream in Connecticut, using a fixed set of data points that allow you to picture any river behind closed eyes. Breadth, depth, gradient, pool-to-riffle ratio, canopy, in-stream shelter, substrate—from type 1, fine sand, to type 7, solid bedrock, via pebble, cobble, boulder, and so forth. In Alfaro, as on the Housatonic, deep pool gives way to riffle, then to boulder-studded runs, another riffle, and finally to the long slow flat where the brook debouches into the pond.

The Taber family dug the pond in the 1960s. It was nine feet deep in those days, making a cool swimming hole. They drove up to Hartford to pick up a consignment of brown trout from the hatchery. The fish sloshed around in a bucket in the back seat, slunk away into the depths of the pond, and were never heard from again. Now the pond is a textbook ex-ample of siltation, shrunk to less than half its original depth. In summer-time, it's covered with a thick green puree of algae, and the temperature rises into the eighties, well above the lethal range for trout. Ponds are like that. Their owners find them infinitely perverse and fight back with chemicals and clay seals and ultraviolet inhibitors of algae growth. But of course ponds operate entirely according to their own logic. If they needed to be there, they'd be there. This one never did, and never was, and it of-fers an object lesson not only in siltation but also in what happens in the nonnegotiated settlement of a dispute between human actions and natu-ral forces. The artifice doesn't mean that the pond is not beautiful and useful to an ecological system that adapts to its existence. It attracts ducks and salamanders and an occasional great blue heron, and in March the peepers emerge from hibernation and start their chorus.

And in the end, what, other than human fancy, is to say that a trout is a life form superior to a creek chub? Or, for that matter, an eel? We found an eel in the pond one day—or, to be more exact, David found it, beneath a small patio of flagstones on the east side of the pond, a rem-nant of the swimming-hole plan. The previous summer we had seen a school of black bullheads—the small catfish that New Englanders call hornpout—sunning themselves midpond. David was convinced at first that this discovery explained the dark head and the wide mouth he saw protruding from beneath the stones. A rod and a worm were procured, but the putative bullhead tore the worm off the hook and scarfed it down, and the head disappeared into its hole in a puff of silt. After three failed attempts, we escalated to a short, stiff bait-casting rod, armed with sev-enteen-pound-test monofilament. Even with this, it was a struggle. The creature was two feet long, as thick as a fire hose, and tightly wedged into a rock crevice that it was deeply reluctant to leave. But eventually we had it, and it writhed and thrashed on the grass, where, being an eel, it could have survived for several hours without benefit of water.

Since none of us had wide experience in eel sexing, we were unable to determine whether our fish was male or female. The kids wanted some explanations, but I had none to offer. In fact, my puzzlement only betrayed the depth of my ignorance. Gender detection of eels in fresh water proved entirely redundant; they are all females. From the St. Lawrence River to the Gulf of Mexico, young eels of both sexes gather in tidal marshes and estuaries in the spring. The males stay there, and only the females ascend the rivers, taking up residence in fresh water until they reach sexual maturity, which can be anywhere from five to twenty years later. Traveling mainly at night, they drop back to the sea and join the males for the long swim to the Sargasso Sea, a thousand miles east of Florida. There they mingle, but don't mate, with eels that have made the even longer journey from European waters. And that is the end of the eel's story. Spawned out, it dies.

With half-formed fantasies of smoked eel sushi, part of me was tempted to keep the creature. But my wife had a calmer view of things, and under her supervision we introduced the kids to the gentle principles of catch-and-release fishing. I still wonder sometimes if our eel ever made it back to the deep ocean trenches south of Bermuda.

The kids' aquatic education continued on Eight Mile Brook, the nearest river that held reliable numbers of trout and for several years the closest thing I had to a home stream. David and Julia misheard the name the first time, so for a long time it was Empire Brook—not to be confused with the Eight Mile State Building. A map of the town of Southbury after the Civil War shows a long string of paper mills and shingle mills along Eight Mile Brook—particularly dirty little enterprises—culminating in the extensive brick-built complex of the Diamond Match Company. The two iron penstocks from the factory still lie rusting in the riverbed below a small covered bridge.

Already disfigured by its industrial past, the brook now has to contend with an increasingly suburban present. Yet it still has remoter ravine sections with deep pools and quick runs that provide decent early-season fly-fishing, even if you have to clamber over discarded tires, beer cans, and old mattresses to reach them. Most of the trout are stocked, but I've caught a few wild fish, both brookies and browns, and even some that manage to survive into a second season—a couple of fifteen-inch browns and once an emaciated, macrocephalic rainbow that must have pushed eighteen. After I'd fished the brook a few times, it seemed a natural reflex to formalize some sense of affiliation, even of ownership, by naming the pools, if only for my own benefit. Ledgerock Pool and Long Pool were simply descriptive. Skeleton Rock marked the spot where I had found the remains of a whole raccoon, picked clean by scavengers and weather. The Generator Pool took its name from an abandoned piece of electrical equipment that offered the trout an unorthodox holding lie in mid-stream, but just as one flood had brought it, another swept it away, and the pool became anonymous again. The Junkyard Pool, with the rusted carcasses of half a dozen pickup trucks, was my upstream limit. From beyond it came the buzz of chain saws.

My daughter's interest in these developments was limited, but David was willing enough, and the ravine was where I wanted to take him. He was five. He brought his Mickey Mouse rod from K-Mart and a container of pink trout worms, and to keep him company I threw a light spinning rod into the trunk of the car. From the outset the trip was inauspicious. It had rained hard in the night, and a fine drizzle had started up again by the time we reached the stream. The water was high, fast, and murky, and the sides of the ravine were slick. On the way down I slipped on a rock, landed hard on my back, and snapped the wooden frame of a new trout net. At five, David had a tendency to drive himself hard, and I could sense that we were both gearing up for an afternoon of futility and frustration.

But damned if the kid didn't hook a fat rainbow from the fast slick at the head of Ledgerock Pool. Standing a few yards upstream, I found it impossible to get there quickly enough to help him land the fish, and the next few seconds unfolded in a kind of horror-movie slow motion. I saw the trout flopping on the gravel at David's feet, heard his adrenaline-charged cry—"Got one!"—watched powerless as he yanked back hard, too hard, and saw the barbed hook fly out of the trout's mouth like an arrow from a bowstring and embed itself deeply in his thumb.

David's rage was boundless. Groping for words to express it, he screamed, "I wish, I wish . . . I wish I could cut down all the trees in the forest and fill all the rivers with cement." I held him tight and told him it was okay to feel that way, and as we squatted there, enveloped in his anger, it crossed my mind that plenty of adult males had never tran-scended this childhood craving for control and had lived out his fantasy to the letter.

3
Foundation Stones

OPENING DAY IS AN AMERICAN RITUAL, a family affair like Thanksgiving. Get up at an ungodly hour, pile into the car, buy some worms, catch some rainbows, fix a fisherman's breakfast. The pickups are bumper to bumper at every bridge on every stream that the state stocks with rainbows. Most will be gone by Memorial Day. They're easy to raise in hatcheries and easy to catch, the nearest to a sure thing if you've brought a child along. Even if they're not indigenous to the East—they weren't even present in this watershed until the 1930s—they've become a ubiquitous American icon. A hundred years ago, brookies were synonymous with the idea of trout in the East. Today, niche marketers can sell you rainbow doormats, rainbow alarm clocks, rainbow hat stands, rainbow pajamas, rainbow bookends, rainbow wind socks, rainbow salt- and peppershakers. Try finding a brook trout oven mitt.

Predictably, on this third Saturday of April, the Housatonic is running high and chilly. Yet this has its compensations. It means that the Great Falls at Canaan can be seen in their full majesty. The rocky lip of the falls was blasted away with dynamite when the Housatonic was dammed here, but when you stand on the viewing platform below the falls, it's easy to ignore the low concrete apron that holds back the flow of the river to store energy for the hydroelectric plant at Falls Village. With only that small deception, what you see is essentially what Yale president Timothy Dwight saw when he took a coach ride up the Housatonic Valley in 1780 and came upon the falls by accident. He shared the discovery with his friend Dr. Jedidiah Morse, who was at work on his *American Ge-*

ography. But although Morse had made "laborious inquiries" about every part of the country, he hadn't heard of the falls either.

In the second volume of his *Travels in New England and New York,* Dwight wrote:

> The cataract . . . is formed by a vast ledge of limestone, crossing the river obliquely from the northwest to the southeast. The length of this ridge is about 35 rods, its perpendicular height sixty feet, its front, irregular, broken and hanging with a wild magnificence. Here, in a stupendous mass on the western side, and on the eastern in every form and quantity of descending water from the furious torrent to the elegant cascade, this noble stream rushes with astonishing grandeur and the most exquisite beauty. The beauty is unrivaled by any cataract which I have seen except at Glens Falls, and the force when the river is full except by those of Niagara.

Come back here in summer, when the river is running low and the powerhouse is shut down, and it's possible, with a little agility, to walk the streambed from the steel bridge on Water Street all the way to the base of the falls. It's like hiking through an enormous sculpture garden by Barbara Hepworth, with smooth, undulating surfaces of bleached limestone broken by deep holes worn by the ceaseless rotation of rocks and pebbles. Other rocks have been worn into natural bridge formations. The face of the falls, cracked and grooved just as Dwight described it, is pocked with small caverns, and it falls away into an unfathomable scour hole. Legend has it that a boy once drowned here, and his body was never recovered. Below the falls, midstream islands are littered with huge, sun-whitened deadfalls, whole trees swept over the dam by the force of floodwater. Perched on one island are two huge glacial erratics. The larger of the two is balanced precariously on one edge, held up by the other. The walk is a geology primer as simple and eloquent as a road cut.

Geology is one of the first courses in a river education, and limestone is its opening lesson. Limestone is made of ancient sediments: carbonate mud, the pulverized calcium of ancient seashells and fossilized marine creatures. It is the foundation of great trout streams from southern England to New Zealand. Technically, the key to the Housatonic's quality as a trout stream is not limestone but marble—metamorphosed limestone that has been superheated and recrystallized into a harder, less permeable form. But marble, like limestone, dissolves in acid—such as the natural acidity that occurs in rainfall.

One day when he was in fourth grade, my son came home from school, excited about a science experiment his teacher had performed.

"He dropped some sulfuric acid on a piece of chalk," David said.

"What happened?" I asked.

"It fizzed," he said, beaming.

"Did that have a scientific name?"

"Sure," David said, "pH."

These two letters are the key to understanding a river's productivity. The abbreviation stands for "potential of hydrogen," and it is a measure of acidity or alkalinity. A pH reading of 7.0 is neutral. The higher the reading, the harder the water, the richer the aquatic food chain, the greater the total biomass, and the fatter the trout. The calcium in limestone may even benefit the trout physiologically, by shielding them from toxins. If you're equipped with a geological map, you should be able to estimate the pH level of any river with a fair degree of accuracy. Streams that flow into the Housatonic from the high slopes of impervious bedrock will have a low pH, often below 6. The fish in those streams, generally, should be easier to catch, since their sterile environment means they cannot afford to be choosy about feeding. On the other hand, their water will be clearer, so a delicate approach on the part of the fisherman will be necessary. Streams that flow over a limestone bed will usually give a pH reading above 7, and the toughest fishing in the world is on high-pH spring creeks such as those in Pennsylvania, where the trout's nutritional choices are endless. The last time Connecticut fisheries biologists sampled the Sand Hole, one of the most popular pools on the Housatonic, they found a pH of 7.8. This is terrific trout water. By contrast, the Shepaug watershed, which skirts the marble belt, is below 7, and its headwaters, rising in the hemlock forests and acidic upland bogs, are down around 6.

The Housatonic has one distinct geological oddity. After Falls Village, the river ceases to take the course of least resistance and, for reasons that are unclear, begins to hack its way through the more intractable granite and schist of the highlands. The result is the steep-sided Cornwall

Canyon, where I do most of my trout fishing. Below Cornwall Bridge, the river rejoins the bed of the so-called Marble Valley. In the nineteenth century, dozens of marble quarries thrived in the Housatonic Valley, both to the north, beyond the Massachusetts line, and farther south, along the East Aspetuck River. In aesthetic terms, this geological quirk may explain why the Housatonic appeals to me so much. The canyon is bookended by marble and therefore rich in aquatic insects, crayfish, and other organisms, but it is also an obstacle course of large granite boulders that make it look more like a conventional, and more sterile, freestone river.

T IMOTHY DWIGHT, president of Yale, was much more than an amateur geologist; he saw rocks as a readable key to the social and economic circumstances of his time. In contrast to Harvard, with its more rarefied atmosphere, Yale in its early years served as an intellectual portal for practical ideas, social observation, and scientific innovation. Dwight's *Travels* is an absorbing account of New England during a period of rapid social change. It is rich in subtle observations of how human society and the natural world affect each other. Land use, deforestation, and the decline of wildlife populations concerned Dwight as much as the social institutions of New Englanders. Looking outward, he wanted to defend the uniqueness of the American experiment to European skeptics. Looking inward, he wanted New Englanders to better understand their own social and natural history.

Dwight admired the ingenious ways in which mill owners were putting to use the natural features of the Housatonic watershed—fast flows and steep drops. He was especially impressed by an experiment he saw on the Naugatuck, the largest, rockiest, and most flood-prone of the river's tributaries. Just above the present-day town of Seymour, a large eminence known as Rock Rimmon rises seven hundred feet or so above the river. The bedrock extends here to form a natural dam across two thirds of the Naugatuck, concentrating its flow into a fierce, narrow plunge of twenty feet or more. Before the Europeans came, the broad pool below the falls had been one of the finest of the Indian fishing grounds. But by the middle of the eighteenth century, a little cluster of industrial buildings—a gristmill, a sawmill, and a paper mill—had sprung up to appropriate the power of Rimmon Falls. Dwight found the rural-industrial riverscape "in a high degree interesting."

The leading man of the community was its longtime pastor, the Reverend Daniel Humphreys, whose son had made quite a name for himself in the world since leaving rural Connecticut. Colonel David Humphreys was a scholar, historian, soldier, and poet. As personal aide to General George Washington, he had received the English colors from Cornwallis at Yorktown in 1791. As an intimate of Thomas Jefferson, the younger Humphreys had served as secretary of the American Legation in Paris. Now he had come home to become an industrialist. In fact, it's no exaggeration to say that his personal encounter with the trout pool paradox was a seminal episode in the American industrial revolution.

Jefferson, of course, was no lover of industry. On economic, aesthetic, and moral grounds, he had always believed that the country's prosperity should be based on combining human labor with "the spontaneous energies of the earth." In 1787 he wrote to General Washington, "Agriculture is our wisest pursuit, because it will in the end contribute most to real wealth, good morals and happiness." In the global division of labor among "the great family of mankind," the role of the new United States was to trade its agricultural surplus for the manufactured products of Europe. Not that Jefferson had anything against mills per se; for more than thirty years he had busied himself with projects to improve his own cloth-making operation at Rivanna in Virginia, supervising the construction of canals and dams and elevators and conveyor buckets. But he had no wish to see the new country descend into the filth and vice that he associated with the "dark Satanic Mills" of William Blake's England. "Let our workshops remain in Europe," Jefferson wrote; there would be no Manchesters here. The American democratic experiment would not survive the corrupting encounter with such "sinks of voluntary misery," since "the mobs of great cities add just so much to the support of pure government, as sores do to the strength of the human body."

But the gathering conflict with Europe made it hard for Jefferson to sustain his agrarian ideals. By 1807 he had pushed an embargo on foreign trade through Congress. Although its whole point was to punish "the piracies of France and England," Paris and London shrugged off the embargo as a pinprick to their trading economies. What really suffered were the idled seaports of New England, and angry talk of secession rumbled among the Federalist leaders in Boston. Cut off from the supply of finished woolen products from the Lancashire mills, Americans—even the resistant Jefferson—began to conclude that the answer was industrial self-sufficiency, at least in goods manufactured from locally produced raw materials. In 1807, Jefferson wrote in a letter to a Mr. Maury, "The present aspect of our foreign relations has encouraged here a general spirit of encouragement to domestic manufactures. The Merino breed of sheep is well established with us, and fine samples of cloth are sent to us from the North."

From Rimmon Falls, to be exact. Or, as the place was now called, Humphreysville. Using his extensive political connections in Europe and the nineteenth-century equivalent of the diplomatic pouch, Colonel Humphreys had managed to smuggle a flock of merino sheep out of Spain—the first merinos in the New World. In his new factory on the Naugatuck, the colonel's machinery spun and wove the wool into cloth of the finest quality. Americans went mad for the silky merino. Not that Humphreys had any intention of allowing the squalor of the European mill towns to take root in American soil. Like Jefferson, he abhorred the idea. Instead, he recruited his workforce from women and street children in the cities. Far from plunging them into a life of drink, disease, and prostitution, Humphreys was saving them from it, while at the same time assuring himself of a ready pool of cheap labor. A committee appointed by the Connecticut state legislature in October 1808 reported that he had "convert[ed] into an active capital the exertions of persons who otherwise would be idle, and in many instances a burthen to the community." Humphreys housed his workers in clean dormitories, packed them off to church on Sundays, organized his boys into a uniformed militia, and dressed them up for amateur theatricals at Christmas, using scripts that he wrote himself.

To Timothy Dwight, Humphreysville was nothing short of genius. In the factory's first six years of operation, he reported:

> Not an individual belonging to the institution died, and it is believed that among no other equal number of persons has there been less disease. With respect to vice, it may be remarked that every person who is discovered to be openly immoral is discharged. . . . In this manufactory he has, I think, fairly established three points of great

importance. One is that these manufactures can be carried on with success, another that the workmen can be preserved in as good health as that enjoyed by any other class of men in the country, and the third that the deterioration of morals in such institutions, which is so often complained of, is not necessary but incidental, not inherent in the institution itself but the fault of the proprietor.

Jefferson heard of his old friend's success, which kicked his political instincts into high gear. At the end of 1808, he was in the final months of his second term as president. He had rebuffed the pleas of his supporters that he run again, instead anointing Madison, his secretary of state, to succeed him in the White House. As the election approached, Jefferson decided to promote the idea of industrial self-sufficiency as a matter of national principle, propelled by the full force of the bully pulpit. In a letter to Abraham Bishop, a powerful figure in New Haven politics, he wrote:

> Homespun is become the spirit of the times. I think it is an useful one, and, therefore, that it is a duty to encourage it by example. The best fine cloth made in the United States is, I am told, at the manufacture of Colonel Humphreys in your neighborhood. Could I get the favor of you to procure me there as much of his best as would make me a coat? I should prefer a deep blue, but, if not to be had, then a black.

The timing was important. What Jefferson had in mind was the symbolic opportunity provided by the presidential transition. When Bishop wrote back to say that it would take Humphreys four weeks to deliver, Jefferson replied, politely but firmly: "I shall be glad to receive it whenever it can come, but a great desideratum will be lost if not received in time to be made up for our New Year's Day Exhibition when we expect everyone will endeavor to be in homespun, and I should be sorry to be marked as being in default."

Humphreys himself answered the president this time, assuring him in a letter dated December 12 that "a Piece of double milled Casemer made of the pure Merinos" would reach Washington in good time for the New Year's festivities. Jefferson was delighted with the results. His new coat was the talk of the capital, and he wrote to his old friend on January 20, 1809:

> [The cloth] came in good time & does honor to your manufactory, being as good as anyone would wish to wear in any country. Amidst the pressure of evils with which the belligerent edicts have afflicted us, some permanent good will arise, the spring given to manufacturers will have durable effects. Knowing most of my own state, I can affirm with confidence that were free intercourse opened again tomorrow she would never again import half of the coarse goods which she has done to the date of the edicts, these will be made in our families, for finer goods we must resort to the manufactories established in the towns.

The rest of the industrial revolution is, as they say, history.

ONE WEEKEND my wife was asked up to New Haven to talk to a group of student journalists at the *Yale Daily News*. The invitation included accommodation in the guest room at Silliman College, so we decided to take the kids and turn it into a long family weekend. Benjamin Silliman, a scientific polymath, was Timothy Dwight's Yale protégé and literary executor. Very different from his mentor, Silliman was probably the most influential scientist of his time, writing and teaching about geology, chemistry, electromagnetics, water supply, steam heating, and the cultivation of sugarcane. He advised the owners of coal-mining companies in a half-dozen states and Mexico, silver mines in Nevada, and gold mines in California and Nova Scotia. In 1817 Silliman retraced Dwight's steps to the Great Falls of the Housatonic. He pronounced the falls to be "altogether wild and possessed of very considerable grandeur" and studied their rocks closely for the clues they contained about human history.

In the oak-paneled library of Silliman College, I picked up a little book that Silliman had published in 1833, called *Wonders of the Earth and Truths of the Bible: Showing the Consistency of Modern Geology with the Scripture Account of the Creation and Deluge*. It showed the drama of a brilliant intellect struggling to reconcile scientific reason with the prevailing truths of his age, and it kept me reading until two in the morning. When Silliman's geological career began, in the first years of the nineteenth century, he accepted without question the conventional wisdom that the world had been created on October 23, 4004 B.C.—a date that had been calculated by the seventeenth-century Irish archbishop James Ussher, using biblical genealogy. But the discovery in 1802 in the Connecticut River valley of the first fossil evidence of dinosaurs in the New World shook the Irish prelate's elaborate theory to its foundations. Although other religious scholars made determined efforts to prove that the footprints must have been made by the raven of Noah's ark, it quickly became apparent that the world was much older than anyone had thought.

Silliman realized that his countrymen lagged behind the Europeans in these matters but insisted that historical and sociological factors explained their slow start. He wrote:

> In this country the cultivation of scientific geology is of so recent a date that many of our most intelligent and well-educated people are strangers even to its elements, are unacquainted with its amazing store of facts, and are startled when any other geological epochs are spoken of than the Creation and the deluge recorded in the pentateuch. . . . Foreign geologists will do us the justice to remember that our field is vast while our laborers are comparatively few and they are, generally, men occupied by other pursuits. This country is rarely explored by those whom fortune leaves at ease to follow a favorite pursuit. The learned leisure of Europe, and especially of England, is here almost unknown, and our most efficient cultivators of science are also laborers in other fields.

Silliman immersed himself in the revolutionary discoveries being made by European geologists and paleontologists of the time—the *Vindiciae Geologicae* and the *Reliquiae Diluvianae* of William Buckland, the *Geology* of David Ure, the lectures of Baron Georges Cuvier, the writings of Louis Chaubard. These readings made it apparent to Silliman that the earth's crust had not been created in its present form in a single act. Rather, it had been shaped through a slow, gradual process interrupted by cataclysmic upheavals, and fossil evidence showed how successive species of animals and plants had become extinct and entombed in rock. Silliman was contemptuous of those who stuck to the old explanations. How could anyone seriously believe that God had created the mammoth—tusks, hair, and all—and then on a whim buried it under thousands of feet of rock? Did anyone think that God had worked a long series of totally useless miracles, such as inserting plants, seashells, and fish in a mineral mass, just to show that he could do it? "If there are any such persons," Silliman concluded, "we must leave them to their own reflections, since they cannot be influenced by reason and sound argument."

A full quarter-century before *The Origin of Species,* Silliman's view of the creation was an explosive proposition. Yet he set out to show that the dichotomy between science and the scriptural creation myth was a false one. If properly understood, the new scientific data ought to allow all sides to grasp that God had created not only the material world but the physical laws that governed it—the consequences of which had played out over a long period of time. The only question was how long the process had taken. Quite obviously, it was more than the seven days of the creation myth.

Silliman managed to square the circle adroitly. To him only three possible theories could reconcile geological fact with scripture. First option: the present world was created in six days from the ruins and fragments of an earlier one. Dismissed as implausible. Second option: there was a long period between the first act of creation ("in the beginning") and the first day, when God began to arrange proper conditions for the arrival of the first humans. Possible but unconvincing. Silliman reasoned that the problem therefore lay with the phrase "seven days." To solve it, he went back to the theological polemic over the meaning of the Hebrew word *yom,* which is used in Genesis. Though it is usually translated as "day," some scholars argued that it could also mean "epoch" or "period." If this was so, Silliman said, then the contradiction took care of itself. The creation had occurred over six extended periods of time, and the seventh, during which God rested from his labors, was still under way.

Silliman based his argument not just on geological evidence, but also on the internal logic of the biblical text itself. How could the first three "days" of the creation have been literal twenty-four-hour periods, if Genesis said that the concept itself did not arise until the fourth "day," when "God made two great lights to divide the day from the night, and to be for signs and for seasons, and for days and for years"? The seven-day week was to be seen therefore as a human invention, a metaphor for the cycle of creation, in which the Sabbath both mirrors the divine resting period and obliges humankind to reflect on the blessings that God has bestowed. In the end, then, rationalism triumphed in Silliman's argument. But that didn't mean that rationalism trumped faith, since faith could be shown to have a rational basis.

Of course, for all his insights, Silliman remained a man of the early nineteenth century, and like any of us he was defined by the imaginative boundaries of his age. He was no more able than his contemporaries to offer a rational explanation of why the Connecticut mountaintops were strewn with boulders of all shapes and sizes. He could only speculate that they "were once loose and rolling about in the waves of an early ocean, encountering friction and violence in their various modes of action." In fact, the Housatonic Valley was shaped by two forces of which Silliman had no inkling—glaciation, which was not explained for another decade or more, and plate tectonics, which would not be understood for more than a century.

ALTHOUGH THE GENERAL outlines of the story of geological history are familiar, I thought it would be useful to hear them laid out clearly and concisely by someone who understood the local specifics. For that reason, I took myself off one day to the Gunn Library in Washington, Connecticut, to listen to a talk by a man named Curtis Read. As I took my seat, it was giving the president of the Washington Garden Club, a refined Englishwoman, very great pleasure to present the speaker.

"Curtis is a true Renaissance man," she said. Her vowels put me in mind of Queen Elizabeth's televised Christmas address to the nation.

"Child of the sixties," he corrected her quickly, with a self-deprecating smile. Curtis Read has been at various times a photographer in Latin America and Asia, a filmmaker, and a farmer in Virginia. He is a lanky, good-humored man of fifty or so and the chairman of the Litchfield County Soil and Water Conservation District.

Read began his talk by spreading out the *Bedrock Geological Map of Connecticut,* which was completed in the 1980s by John Rodgers of Yale. "This is just a wonderful map," he said. "It shows you graphically what the story of the Shepaug is. The accepted theory at this point is that between 250 and 500 million years ago, Africa, which was much farther south, came up and smacked into North America, or proto–North America. There were some islands in between, in the path of the collision, which geologists call Avalonia. Avalonia was crushed, along with the entire Iapetos Ocean, and geologists think that anywhere from three hundred to five hundred miles of what would be Connecticut were pushed together and squished right along this line, which is called Cameron's Line. Cameron's Line was the point of contact, and one of the places where it blew apart again is the Shepaug watershed."

He picked up a pointer and traced a diagonal from top right to bottom left. "The line comes right down through Litchfield, and it breaks apart right around Woodville, right in here, Bantam Lake, and it comes right down through New Preston, New Milford, along the Housatonic River, and then down through Danbury and the Marble Valley, as they call it. That was a thrust fault, which meant that the ocean floor—limestone and mud—came shooting up, and pushed up a terrane [a rock formation] the size of the Himalayas."

The new megacontinent started to break apart again, about 200 million years ago. The so-called Great Crack became the Connecticut River valley and steadily filled up with soft sediments. The same thing happened on a smaller scale in the Pomperaug Valley. The Marble Valley remained as a relic of the tropical coastal seabed of proto-America, giving the trout and invertebrates of the Housatonic their calcium-rich water and high pH. Around these valleys, the quasi-Himalayan landscape has been slowly ground down from perhaps thirty thousand feet to the present-day Berkshires, which rise to a modest height of 2,380 feet at the point where Connecticut, Massachusetts, and New York converge. High enough to be sometimes startlingly beautiful; low enough that every square foot shows the evidence of human contact. And on every square foot, it seemed to the colonists and farmers, was a boulder.

Curtis Read went on: "In 1825, a fellow named Peter Dobson of Vernon, Connecticut, was digging the foundations for a mill when he found some rounded rocks in the soil, and he thought the only way they could have been formed like that was through the action of ice. Then an English geologist named Charles Lyell proposed that icebergs must have been floating around in Noah's flood. These icebergs were dirty, and when they melted they dropped the soil and rocks they were carrying on the land. So there were all kinds of theories running around about how the land got to be the way it was. Finally a Swiss peasant told a gentleman named Louis Agassiz that it was probably caused by continental glaciers, and that helped to explain why you can find boulders that are perfectly rounded on the tops of mountains." So Agassiz came to New England and explored the Connecticut and Housatonic river valleys to test his theory. "Lo and behold," Curtis Read said, "he found the same thing as he had in Europe. When he proposed this, he was considered outlandish. People laughed at him."

But Agassiz was broadly correct. Glaciation began in the Northern Hemisphere between three and five million years ago, and the glaciers finally began to retreat from Connecticut eighteen thousand years ago. We think of this as the end of the Ice Age, but of course that's an anthropocentric fallacy. The Ice Age is still under way, only it has receded to its last strongholds, at the poles, hastened on its way by our greenhouse gas emissions. The glaciers worked, in the geologist Michael Bell's phrase, "like a great white Brillo pad," dumping ground-up rock, or glacial drift, and whole boulders in their path. The Housatonic Valley contained the promiscuous jumble of soil and rock that geologists call glacial till. Beginning as tundra, it warmed slowly until it could sustain a greater diversity of plant and animal life. Nine thousand years ago the first Indian tribes followed. You can still see the glacial meltwater in a number of large lakes in the Connecticut Highlands, as well as in hundreds of upland swamps and ponds, many of which continue to shrink and revert to forest. But the rocks remain, and if they weigh more than a couple hundred pounds, chances are that they are still lying pretty much where they were dumped by the great melt.

4
Subdue the Earth

I WAS IN PHIL DEMETRI'S FLY SHOP at Cornwall Bridge. I was listening to one of Phil's monologues about bug hatches, most of it conducted in Latin. There were some early Plecoptera, he told me, and the first *Ephemerella subvaria* had appeared earlier in the week; in fact, a disoriented ovipositing female had dropped her eggs right there on the blacktop outside Phil's shop, mistaking its smooth, dark surface for water.

I'd been out on the river for an hour or so, out of sorts with early season rust, and with only a single brown trout to show for my efforts. Phil suggested that if I wasn't in a fishing mood, it would be a nice day to hike up Coltsfoot Mountain to the ghost farming settlement of Dudleytown. He stepped to the door of the fly shop to show me the way.

The path begins just where Furnace Brook runs into the Housatonic, at a place called Dark Entry. Furnace itself looked unfishable. A huge April Fools' Day storm had swept through the valley and left the brook looking as if someone had been playing a game of cosmic pickup sticks. Every pool was blocked with blowdowns, and they included some of the oldest hemlocks in the forest. Their upended root mats formed caves big enough to hide a small symphony orchestra.

If you'd climbed Coltsfoot Mountain a hundred years ago, you would have seen miles of bare slopes dotted with farms, with few trees other than apple orchards and a scattering of isolated, old-growth giants to serve as property markers. Today, pretty much all you will see is the unbroken green of the Housatonic State Forest. But the greenery provides only a rough guide to the makeup of the forests that the colonists knew before they cut them down, even if many of the species are the same.

The guidebooks still try to entice visitors up this forest path by talking about the "Dudleytown curse." They quote an old saw that says of the place, "The grass don't grow, the birds don't sing, and the pictures you take won't turn out." The idea of a curse seems to have originated with the ancestry of the Dudleys. The family who settled here descended from a line of English nobility that lost several heads to the royal executioner's ax. Their most celebrated ancestor was Robert Dudley, Earl of Leicester, the lover of Queen Elizabeth I.

But if this small farming settlement had a curse, it wasn't of supernatural origin. The departing glaciers left most Cornwall land a forbidding mix of rocky upland and swamp, and Dudleytown was about the worst of it. The colonists didn't make it this far north until 1747. The one thing the place had was rocks, which two brothers named Dudley used to build three milldams on Bonney Brook and miles of stone walls that still mark off old property lines that wander through the forests and swamps.

Admittedly, Dudleytown's settled history did have its share of tragic and melodramatic occurrences. One of the two original brothers, Abiel Dudley, grew feeble-minded and became a public charge until he died at ninety. Another villager was killed as the result of a fall during a barn raising. A woman was struck and killed by lightning in an April storm. A family that had recently moved to New York from Dudleytown were attacked by an Indian raiding party, with three killed and three children abducted. The wife of the nineteenth-century journalist Horace Greeley was born in Dudleytown. She hanged herself toward the end of her husband's failed run at the presidency. In the early twentieth century, a New York doctor tried spending summers in the largely abandoned settlement, but his wife suffered a nervous breakdown and committed suicide, and he never came back. It seems like a lot of misfortune, but I wonder whether any township of this size might not be able to come up with a similar list of tragedies over the same 150 years.

The real reasons for Dudleytown's decline aren't hard to see on an early spring day like today, when the landscape is an open book. Though the sun is high in the sky now, almost none of it reaches Dudleytown, which is shaded not only by oak, hickory, and hemlock but also by three surrounding mountains. It's fully ten degrees colder here than in the valley below. Winters must have been brutal in Dudleytown, and local histories tell of times when children froze in their beds and cattle were kept alive with venison broth. The slopes are steep and jagged, with rocks everywhere, and wedges of spongy swamp. The glacial soils were rich in nutrients when the settlers arrived, but they were quickly degraded by overuse, erosion, and an unsustainable growth in population. Eighteenth- and nineteenth-century colonists viewed the soil in much the same way as they did the rivers, the trees, and the minerals they found embedded in the rocks. Farmers were like loggers and miners; they were engaged in an extractive industry. Their historical project was to turn the "howling wilderness" into "a second England for fertilness." When Genesis 1:28 told them to "fill the earth and subdue it," the colonists took this as a literal injunction, with little regard for the consequences.

Yet appearances can be deceptive; both the populated and uninhabited portions of the landscape are full of false clues. What appears to be on offer in the quiet, white-painted villages of the Litchfield Hills is direct acquaintance with the world of the colonists; seemingly these places have been touched by time only in the form of modern conveniences. In fact, nothing could be further from the truth. The white farmhouses, the well-

tended greens, and the even plantings of elm trees are all nineteenth-century innovations, the products of a civic backlash against the squalor of earlier times, when the streets were awash with mud and sewage and fit only for the hogs that wallowed in them. The older colonial farmhouses, many of them now weekend homes for affluent New Yorkers, are an equally unreliable guide to the realities of the colonial landscape. Some have kept their old barns, but most of the other buildings that made up the farming complex disappeared as their functions became obsolete. In the colder elevations of New England, a dozen buildings or more were connected under a single roof, so that the farmers could do all their wintertime chores without exposure to the elements. This "joined architecture" might include a springhouse, an icehouse, a milk house, a wash house, a well house, a chicken house, a woodshed, a wagon shed, a butchering shed, a blacksmith's shop, a dovecote, and an outdoor oven. And there were always two outdoor privies, wallpapered and curtained. The sign for men was a sunburst, providing light and ventilation; ladies had a crescent moon.

Colonial Connecticut was dominated by hardwoods—chestnut, hickory, and red, black, and white oak—interspersed with tall stands of hemlock and white pine. The cutting of these old-growth forests followed the course of the rivers. Farmers began by planting the richer alluvial floodplains and moved relentlessly uphill when these were exhausted. For agricultural purposes, they cut down the maple, hickory, and beech forests to get at the moist black humus in which they grew. Colonists also farmed old beaver swamps that had reverted to meadow when the fur trade wiped out the beaver population. For building materials, they went to the higher elevations, in which hardwoods thrived and agriculture didn't. Chestnut, so hard that it could break the teeth off a saw, was the first choice for homes and fences. In ecological terms, fences may not seem very significant. But the miles of stone walls that snake through Dudleytown's abandoned fields used to be accompanied by wooden fences, which have long since decayed. When rocks were unearthed by plowing, they were flung against the nearest line of fencing, where, over time, they formed Siamese-twin walls. Softer second-growth timber lasted only four or five seasons before it rotted, so a prudent farmer, thinking of the future, always preferred to use old growth. It took a full acre of first-growth forest to provide fencing for ten acres of farmland.

These New England trees were a vital source of trade and profit as well as immediate utility. Since the forests of Old England had disappeared by the seventeenth century, London turned to the colonies for a supply. White pines became the masts of the ships that would expand the reach of the British imperial navy. Oak gave its timbers. Logging practices seemed to strive for the maximum degree of collateral damage. The biggest and oldest-growth timber went first because it was of the highest quality. But the younger trees around it, as well as the neighboring species, were also cut or burned in the process. Tanneries were especially destructive, stripping the hemlock of the acidic bark they required and leaving the rest of the tree to die.

Many years passed before the colonists began to question these practices. They could hardly fail to notice the Indians' habit of firing the forest understory twice a year in controlled blazes that quickly consumed the brush and weeds. But they equated the practice with the specific needs of a nomadic hunting community and made no attempt to imitate it, even though burning created better habitat for both game and predator species and enriched the soil by speeding up the recycling of nutrients. Only much later did they come to appreciate the logic of the practice and the beauty of the landscapes it created. Viewing the result of the controlled burnings, one nineteenth-century revisionist historian wrote:

> The eye roves with delight from ridge to ridge, and from hill to hill; which like the divisions of an immense temple, were crowded with innumerable pillars, the branches of whose shafts interlocking, formed the arch-work of support to that leafy roof, which covered and crowned the whole. But since the white man took possession, the annual fires have been checked, and the woodlands are now filled with shrubs and young trees, obstructing the vision on every side, and converting these once beautiful forests into a rude and tasteless wilderness.

Admittedly this was an aesthetic reaction more than a practical one. Even though Timothy Dwight had warned of the impending dangers of deforestation at the turn of the eighteenth century, it didn't dawn on the European farmers until much later that, in destroying the forests, they had not only removed an impediment to productive agriculture. They had removed the *source* of productive agriculture. Stripped of its vegetation, the soil steadily degraded. Trees, shrubs, and the detritus of the forest floor were no longer there to act as a sponge to absorb rainfall. The land—and the climate in general—became drier and hotter. Winters became colder, and freezes struck harder and deeper. Root systems no longer held the soil together. Corn depleted the nutrients in it. When a field was exhausted, it was not left fallow but given over to cattle, which stamped the earth flat and stripped it of new growth. Starved of oxygen, the land was less productive the next time it was turned over to crops. This ruinous cycle forced farmers to run faster and faster to stay in place. They responded by clearing more and more land, and each newly cleared area was a little poorer than the one before.

The rivers stood at the receiving end of this destructive process. There was no organization like Trout Unlimited to measure fish populations in the eighteenth and nineteenth centuries, but it's only logical to assume that the rivers and their inhabitants suffered grievously. With earlier snowmelt on cleared land and increased runoff throughout the year, cycles of flood and drought became more extreme, washing out habitat and spawning areas and raising summer water temperatures. The loss of the forest canopy left the sun to beat down on the streams as fiercely as it did on the naked land, and older maps show high-country brooks throughout the Housatonic watershed that have dried up and disappeared altogether. Soil erosion had a complementary effect, increasing the silt load, filling in deep pools, and generally making the rivers shallower and slowing their flow. The survival rate of fish eggs and fry would have declined badly under these conditions, and more so as warm-water predators moved into areas formerly occupied by native brook trout. The most perverse impact on fish populations came when farmers responded to the mounting pressure on good grazing land by allowing their livestock to range freely in search of pasture. Their dispersal robbed the farmers of their traditional source of fertilizer, since it was no longer feasible to gather the dung. So they turned to fish—alewives, smelt, shad, and salmon. After the spring spawning runs, the fields must have stunk like an abbatoir.

WALTER LANDGRAF hoists on his L.L.Bean backpack, tucks the tail of his shirt with the Connecticut State Naturalist patch into his green army pants, and heads up the steep trail at a brisk trot, talking all the way. Walt is conducting one of his frequent guided hikes, and I've tagged along to find out more about the changes in the forest. Walt bears a passing resemblance to Sergeant Bilko. It's the mouth, the teeth, the glasses, the monk's tonsure. Like Bilko, Walt Landgraf is never at a loss for words.

For more than thirty years he has been an environmental science and biology teacher at Northwest Regional High School, and he's the kind of whom they write: "Has inspired generations of students." As we gather on the banks of the Farmington River for one of Walt's popular hikes, it's clear that most of our party are loyal regulars. It's all "Do you remember what you were telling us last night at the slide show, Walt?" and "When are we going to do the Algonquin Trail again, Walt?" and "Walt, did you say last time it was pronounced *pie*-le-ated woodpecker, or *pill*-e-ated?"

"*Pie*-le-ated," Walt says. "Flying anteaters."

Some of the hikers seem to have inhaled a prodigious amount of knowledge from Walt, apparently over many years. There's Larry, for instance, a middle-aged hippie with long silvery hair tied back under a head scarf. Larry's eyes dance with a manic glee, like a Merry Prankster on the Grateful Dead bus. Larry is proposing to make the five-and-a-quarter-mile hike in bare feet. His toenails are painted cerise.

"Walt, what's this little mushroom over here about the size of a nickel?" Larry asks.

Walt doesn't miss a beat. "Why, that's commonly known as the nickel-and-dime mushroom, Larry." He pauses for effect, secure in his audience. "Now Larry, you know mycology isn't my field." With every other -ology, however, Walt Landgraf seems entirely at home.

We're standing on the edge of an old glacial lake. Behind us are the remnants of the moraine that blocked the valley. "When the ice sheet melted," Walt says, "it didn't just pack up and move north. The glacier's not running around on wheels, you know. It formed, it oozed, it melted and rotted in place. As the lake drained gradually, right up to about four thousand years ago, the dam wore through as the finer particles washed out, and you were left with the bigger rocks on the surface. Starting about then, a large number of Native American villages were established around the periphery. We've found at least eighteen significant ones, both seasonal and year-round. The people settled mainly on the big gravel terraces across the way because those drained well. The ice melted faster on the east side than on the west, and you'll find that west valley walls tend to be steeper; east valley walls tend to terrace off like these ones here."

Walt is pointing to the east, over the large beaver swamp that lies in the hollow below us. "I have a 1934 aerial photograph of this entire area. If you look at that, you'll see that where the beaver swamp is now, there used to be Mr. Allman's hay field. There were no beavers because they'd all been trapped out and the forests had gone. All around Allman's hay field were big agricultural fields, some areas that were just scrubby brush, with a lot of laurel brush growing in. No canopy of trees anywhere. Then our little flat-tailed engineering friends came back in the 1950s, raised the water level, flooded out the meadow again, and set the stage for what was grassland to become a swamp again. There are sundews out there, some of the insectivorous plants, all types of ferns and rhododendrons that are not common in Connecticut. Great testimony to the regenerative power of the forest."

However, regeneration is not the same thing as restoration or reversion, except in the sense that the forest as a whole comes back, as do many of the same species. But they return in a different order, in different locations, and in different proportions, accompanied by new species of animals, birds, insects, and plants, not all of them welcome. The reasons for these patterns are both ancient and modern, planned and accidental, related to human activity and utterly indifferent to it, and to a large degree unpredictable. There's much more blind chance in Nature's plan than we usually imagine. Right in front of us is an example, a plumed wall of phragmites, marsh reeds that have grown eight feet high.

"For some reason that stuff started to show up about seven hundred years ago in Connecticut," Walt says, following my eye. "Its arrival here is a botanical mystery. One hypothesis is that perhaps like periwinkles, which many people think came in on the hulls of Viking ships, phragmites might have come over in the dirt or the packing material on the ships. Other people hypothesize that they came from Texas. I don't think there's resolution on that yet. What we do know is that it's an invasive species. It spread to our inland wetlands evidently in association with the hurricane of '38. That storm picked up most of the seed from along Long Island Sound and blew it way up here. What concerns us is that it grows above all the native vegetation, as purple loosestrife does, chokes out the cat-o'-nine-tails, the calla lilies, and the arrowroot, and you end up with a monoculture in what was once one of the most diverse ecosystems in our area."

Walt gestures over to the left. "You can't see any water from here, but just below that big hemlock, out in the middle, there's a place where a kayak or a canoe could put in. And you can come up all the way along that little channel, which is anywhere between fifty or sixty feet wide, down to about eight feet wide, and has a fairly good water depth. There's a lot of good native brook trout in there. This is an active brook trout breeding area, right in the middle of the old hay field. There's muskrat, there's mink, there's river otter, lots of waterfowl in wintertime and springtime, lots of wood ducks and mallards. I expect one day to see a big moose standing in there."

When everyone has stopped laughing, he says, "No, I'm serious. The last couple of weeks, we've had a cow and a calf up in Hartland—first time we've seen a reproductive unit in northwestern Connecticut."

The trail begins to wind steadily uphill, and the sun is warm. Walking faster than anyone, back upright and calf muscles flexing and relaxing, Walt fires bite-size missiles of information over his shoulder.

"Sphagnum moss down there in the kettle hole. That's an indicator of very acidic soils, very high organic content, anaerobic. Sphagnum was the original organic diaper. Not only highly absorbent, it also has antiseptic qualities. During World War I, a lot of the women here in town came to these kettle holes, gathered up the sphagnum, washed it, dried it and packaged it, and sent it over to the lines in France.

"See the hand-drill mark on that rock there? We go all over the forest looking for those because they mark the old proprietors' lines. When they were laying out the land in the colonial period, they just went *choonk, choonk, choonk,* in straight lines. Some of these have rock piles at the corners, marked with initials. One day we'll be able to see how all the original property was divided.

"That's laurel right there. The wood was used to make clock gears for the clock factories up and down the Naugatuck Valley. They used it because it's hard, like pear, which they used for clockworks in Europe. Later on they used brass.

"These lichens are edible, you know. They call 'em rock tripe, or toad skin. That's your survival food right there if you ever need it. Combination of an ascomycete, related to the penicillin group of funguses, and a kind of algae. First colonizers after the glaciers moved out. Look at them hanging on to the trees and the rocks for dear life to get themselves up to where there's light. If you're a lichen and you grow on the forest floor, you're doomed."

We're right on Cameron's Line here, where the North American continent and the ocean floor of Iapetos collided. The trail skirts a stack of upended metamorphic rocks thirty feet high, standing on end like books in a library. Walt is silent for once as he looks at them, and you can sense his internal time machine at work. Then he says, half to himself, "When you see the beautiful swirling patterns on those rocks, you can almost feel the force of what happened here, 450 million years ago."

Heading uphill steeply over the last step-shelves of gneiss before the summit, our compact group begins to string out, fifty yards from lead to tail. An older man named Bill has a finely carved walking stick his wife bought him. The stick came from England. Bill mixed up his dates when he looked up the hike on the Internet, and he thought today's was the one-and-a-half-mile stroll around the perimeter of the swamp. But here he is now with the rest of us, only a little winded. At last the whole group assembles on the flat rocks of the overlook and stands to watch ospreys wheeling over the rippled folds of green that stretch away toward Canaan Mountain.

"Oh, my God," one woman cries in horror. "A house."

"Yeah, I know," says another. "It's terrible. We went to the zoning hearing."

The two women stand there, glaring out toward Massachusetts, with the grimness of doctors discovering a cluster of cancer cells in the midst of healthy tissue.

Over the hills to the north, when the breeze blows the topmost branches of the hemlocks aside, it's just possible to see the ribbon of concrete that is the face of the Hogback Dam, on the Farmington River. Slivers of water glitter in the sunlight. It's hard to appreciate at first, up here, that we are standing in a world of rock and fire and disease and accelerated forest succession.

"I suspect we're into adelgid country," Walt says all of a sudden, peering at a tree in front of him. "If you find white stuff on the bottom of some of these hemlock needles, you'll know we've got adelgids." Adelgids are a genus of aphids, closely related to the phylloxerans. They can defoliate a hemlock with the same relentless efficiency as a kid wiping out M&Ms. Walt says, "We're up to thirty, forty, in some places sixty percent canopy defoliation. Adelgids come in with birds, animals, and squirrels moving through the trees. You can see the pattern on the trees where the birds have landed—affected, unaffected, affected, unaffected."

I find this painful, though I'm not sure why. Perhaps it's the association between the hemlock, pure running water, and the brook trout, which some people a century ago called the hemlock trout—my favorite of its many folk names. But there's no running water here. We're seven hundred feet or so above the river and nothing but a blueberry bush or a pitch pine could find water in this rockscape.

"What'll take the place of the hemlock?" I ask Walt.

"Up in this drier area, the chestnut oak has already become the dominant tree," he answers. "It's an extremely fire-resistant species, and it's up on these rock ledges that lightning strikes most often occur. The plants that grow on the rocks are also very well adapted to fire, like blueberries and huckleberries. After the regular burnings during the time of the Indians, these rocky areas would have been literally carpeted with blueberries. There are also white oaks, which have loose, scaly bark. Excellent adaptation for fire protection. When a fire hits a tree like that, it just chars the outer edges, which then have an airfoil effect—the air flowing in behind them protects the tree from the heat. You've also got a lot of black birch regeneration. There's going to be red maple regeneration in here, too.

"Look at this." Walt leans over and pulls back a sapling about eight feet tall, with a long, narrow, serrated leaf. I recognize it at once, though I had no idea that the American chestnut had made a comeback, and the rest of our group seems equally surprised. Chestnut blight broke out in the Brooklyn Botanical Garden in 1904 and spread methodically in all directions over the next twenty years, killing off the species that had been the most highly prized commodity in the colonial forest.

"Was the chestnut killed off by a fungus or by man?" someone asks.

"Both," says Walt, more than happy to make the point. "They were importing Chinese chestnuts for planting. They were careless, the Chinese plants brought in the fungus, and there was no quarantine."

"This one's still alive," Walt says, returning to his specimen. "When I first came here, if you found an American chestnut the size of my thumb, you were doing well. Now we're finding American chestnuts up to eighteen inches in diameter. They are bearing nutlets. People are actually taking the pollen from chestnuts like this one and putting it onto other healthy trees, hoping to create a hybrid that has more and more resistance to the fungus."

I ask Walt if this is a case of regeneration from within or recolonization from the outside.

He answers, "These trees have tremendous root-sprout capability. So when the upper tree is killed off, it's like when you prune a hedge. The lower buds sprout out. This tree was one of the chestnuts decimated in the 1918–1919 period, but fortunately the root system sends up sprouts, they get killed off, it sends up some more sprouts, they get killed off, and it's been doing that for eighty years. This chestnut right next to it has the blight. Here's the fungus coming through the bark, which often splits into these cankers. The trouble is that the stuff remains in the ecosystem—in fact, the oak harbors it as an alternate host—and as soon as you get chestnuts that aren't immune, it goes for them.

"A sad thing happened," he says. "They developed a type of chestnut that was showing great promise, from the South, and a man who was raising them went to Japan, saw a hybrid that he liked, brought it into the United States without passing through quarantine, and brought in a whole new disease. That one is now spreading throughout Georgia and the Carolinas, and it's decimating the Chinese and the Japanese chestnuts, as well as the resistant forms of the American chestnut. We're hoping that we can stop it somehow before it spreads up the Appalachians. Of all the people who should have known not to do it. It just shows you that people are people, you know."

The group mutters disapproval about the incurable ecological recidivism of the human race, and I can see my trail mates making mental catalogues of kudzu and nutria and other unwanted exotics. They seem torn between admiration at the restorative power of the forest, despondency at the enduring ability of human beings to screw it up, and an optimism of the sort that Walt Landgraf's students must have felt, that he and others like him will prevail and make it all come out right in the end.

Then I see another thought forming on Bill's lips, as he leans quietly on his English stick. "Walt, you say that after the hemlocks, this will be mainly chestnut oak, black birch, red maple, and white oak. Those are all deciduous trees."

"That's right," Walt says. "This will no longer be an evergreen forest. It'll be a deciduous forest."

Bill's face clouds over, and in an obscure way I feel something of the same melancholy. Maybe it's an intimation of mortality. Walt Landgraf hoists his backpack a little higher and strides on, up the long staircase of rock.

5
The Cheering Rays
of Civilization

GEOLOGICAL MAPS SHOW one set of facts, and topographical maps another. One thing topographical maps reveal is the extent to
which the urge to cut and dig and dam—all those things my angry five-
year-old had longed to do—has reconfigured and disfigured the land. The
contour lines help you visualize the breadth of each watershed and the
gradient of each stream and track how and where the life of each river begins—from a lake or a pond, a groundwater spring or upland swamp, or
just hilltop rainfall. You can predict with some accuracy which of the
headwaters will hold native populations of brook trout. The first prereq-
uisite is an absence of the small black squares that signify houses.

The Southbury quadrangle in the U.S. Geological Survey's 7.5-min-
ute series has thousands of black squares, and almost as many purple
ones. The basic photogrammetry dates back to 1950, and purple areas on
the map reflect new aerial photographs, taken in 1982. Purple and trout,
people and trout, exist in inverse proportion to each other. The development of the Pomperaug Valley leaps off the folded green page. On a sheet
that covers about fifty-six square miles, I can count the purple crosshatching of more than seventy new ponds, at least one on every minor
brook, as well as five gravel pits or quarries, an eighteen-hole golf course,
and a small airport. The largest purple area of all belongs to Heritage Village, a thousand-acre retirement community down on the floodplain.
Part of this land used to belong to Wallace Nutting, the author-photogra-
pher whose hazy, hand-colored prints of lilac blossoms, stone walls, white

picket fences, and meadow streams created and marketed an image of Connecticut in the 1920s as a timeless rural idyll.

Future editions of the map will show the new mall they call Southbury Green, which was finished a couple of years ago on the old pumpkin patch. Its huge asphalt parking lot now drains road salt, sand, engine oil, and assorted garbage straight into the Pomperaug. Future maps will show dozens of new roads, snaking into the hills, hugging the contour lines, and ending in turning circles. I know these new roads. They're bordered with half-million-dollar faux colonials on acre lots with center halls, cathedral ceilings, two-car garages, and half-inch fiberboard walls. These settlements follow the classic logic of modern exurban growth, fueled by interstate highways with increased speed limits, the corporate tax burden of New York City, and the ease of telecommuting. They provide habitat for managers and programmers and sales executives at Unocal, Uniroyal, or IBM, which has a huge corporate headquarters on Bullet Hill, overlooking I-84. In summertime the families hold tag sales, with trestle tables full of neatly folded and apparently unworn kids' clothes, outgrown plastic toys, board games, jigsaw puzzles, cardboard boxes full of Tom Clancy and Danielle Steel paperbacks, unused exercise machines, single crutches from illnesses long past, sets of Christmas lights with dud bulbs, and rustic ornaments with inspirational mottoes.

Driving these streets today, you wouldn't guess that Southbury was smaller than Cornwall in 1850. Cornwall had a shade over two thousand people in those days, and Southbury fewer than fifteen hundred. That figure is almost exactly the same as the current population of Cornwall, while Southbury has grown to more than twenty-two thousand, if you count the seniors at Heritage Village.

WHAT BROUGHT European settlers to this valley in the first place was not telecommuting or turning circles or retirement communities, but the excellent red earth. In that respect, the Pomperaug Valley is something of an anomaly in the geological formation of western Connecticut. It is a rift valley, a junior twin to the valley of the Connecticut River. Mirroring the Central Valley in every particular, the Mesozoic basin of the Pomperaug was created when sediment and lava from the Appalachian Mountains filled a wedge-shaped trench in the earth. Upwelling lava flows punctuated the valley with a ridge of rust-colored traprock, and the modest but sheer Orenaug Rocks in the town of Woodbury are the local counterpart of the East and West Rocks in New Haven and the Sleeping Giant in Hamden, where Yale students like to go for picnics.

When considering the privations that the first Puritan settlers experienced, it's worth recalling that they did not start off as rugged frontier types, but as comfortably-off burghers, farmers, and gentry who had anticipated living at least as well here as they had in England. Their first years in the New World, filled with disease, starvation, violence, and the death of half the Plymouth colonists during their first winter, remained a fresh and harrowing memory. The colonists had no experience of living richly off the land, as the Indians did, following the food as its availability shifted through the year and storing up a surplus against lean times. It took many decades for the newcomers to adapt the agricultural cycles of the Old World to the seasonal rhythms of the New England ecosystem.

The first settlers to reach the fertile valley of the Pomperaug were a small schismatic group from the Stratford colony, at the mouth of the Housatonic. Stratford had existed since the Great Swamp Fight of 1637, which wiped out the remnant resistance of the Pequots. After the battle, a handful of families from Boston and Concord built a precarious settlement at the mouth of a tidal inlet, erected a palisade around it, mounted a watchtower at each corner, and spent their nights listening to the sounds of the "hideous, howling wilderness" as the wolf packs hunted moose and deer in the surrounding forest. The nearest settlement of any size was New Haven, which was founded in 1638 as a Christian utopia and commercial gateway but still contained only a few hundred souls. New Haven lay twenty miles away, but it must have felt like twenty thousand.

Over the next thirty years, scouting parties from Stratford made several forays up the Housatonic, but they never got farther north than the ten-foot falls near the present-day town of New Milford. In 1673 a group of religious dissidents finally succeeded, under the leadership of the Reverend Zachariah Walker, whose name survives in Walker Brook, a trout-rich feeder stream of the Shepaug.

Initially, at least, Walker's expedition was motivated as much by theology as by the search for food. The crux of the dispute that divided the local Puritans was whether second-generation immigrants should be entitled to the sacrament of communion on the sole basis of what their own conscience dictated, or whether they could enter a state of grace only with the prior authorization of their elders. Since the second generation was itself of childbearing age by now, this was not a negligible issue, for it risked consigning to damnation all the infants who wouldn't be baptizable if their parents weren't members of the church. In the end, the synod of ministers reached a compromise settlement. Such children would be eligible for the sacrament of baptism, but not for that of communion. This "one out of two" solution gave the compromise its name—the Halfway Covenant. Some of the "Halfwayites," such as Zachariah Walker, decided to establish their own settlements, and in 1670 the General Court of Connecticut made it known with a sniff that "it shall not be offensive to this Court if Mr. Walker and his Company doe meet distinctly elsewhere." Those who adhered to the new covenant left a mark of their passage in the name of the small Halfway River, which enters the Housatonic at Newtown. Chard Powers Smith, in his 1946 history *The Housatonic: Puritan River,* called the court's resolution "imperial growth by ecclesiastical cell subdivision."

The classic account of Walker's journey is contained in William Cothren's *History of Ancient Woodbury,* published in two volumes in 1854 and 1872. According to Cothren, the schismatics, consisting of fifteen congregants and their families, learned from earlier scouting missions that they should follow the Pootatuck, or Great River (the name Housatonic had not yet been established), until they reached a good-size stream called the Pomperaug, which entered from the northeast. The tributary took its name from the sachem of the Pootatuck Indians, whose camp lay at the confluence. They were then to follow the Pomperaug upstream for about five miles, at which point they would find themselves on a broad and fertile plain where the Indians cultivated corn, beans, tobacco, and cucumbers. But the Halfway Covenanters became disoriented. They arrived at the mouth of the Pomperaug according to plan but decided that it wasn't big enough to be the river they were looking for. This was an odd reaction because the Pomperaug is a fairly substantial stream at this point and in early springtime would presumably have been further swollen by snowmelt and runoff.

The little party soldiered on between the high forested banks of the Great River, around three more sweeping bends, until they found a second large tributary, which seemed to fit the description better. This one was the Shepaug. They made a painful ascent of the river in their canoes and rafts, past the huge rock outcroppings of Roxbury Falls, over stony flats, deep pools, white-water rapids, and tightly confined meadow sections, until they calculated that the requisite five miles had passed. To their consternation, they found themselves still hemmed in by hills and forests, and the landscape showed no signs of moderating. At this point they seem to have recognized their earlier mistake and struck off overland to the south. They emerged at length onto a flat-topped rise, which is occupied today by a small airstrip. Spread out before them, Cothren says, "they perceived the valley of the Pomperaug, lying below in solitude and silence." The story goes that Deacon John Minor fell to his knees and led a prayer invoking the blessings of heaven on their enterprise and asking "that their posterity might be an upright and godly people to the latest generation." Other versions say that another member of the band, a certain Hinman, prayed that *his* posterity might always be blessed with plenty of "Rum and Military Glory." Without being unduly cynical, you can make the case that both men got their wishes.

In the order of Providence," Cothren wrote, "one race had arisen, another passed away." He continued:

> These pleasant hills and sunny valleys, now teeming with life, intelligence and happiness, were one vast solitude, unvisited by the cheering rays of civilization. Here roamed the savage wild beasts, and untutored men more savage still than they. . . . Everything is now changed. . . . Instead of the wretched orgies of the powwow, and the inhuman sacrifices of the midnight of barbarism, are churches dedicated to the service of the living God. . . . Instead of a race groping in the shadow of dim imaginings, we find one filled with hopes of a rational and glorious immortality. . . . The simple race of the early days has departed—faded from the view, and almost from the memory of men.

We've come a long way from Rousseau here. The Enlightenment view of the noble savage has no place in Cothren's history, and his vision of the Indian as a racial degenerate persisted for the better part of a century. It surfaces again, in a slightly different form, in the writings of Chard Powers Smith. The author of *The Housatonic: Puritan River* takes pains to assure us that it would have been preferable for the Indians to become civilized through proselytization by schools and missions. But he appears resigned to the "natural method" of assimilation, even though this was "by all odds the quickest and surest way of hurrying the natives into degeneracy." The decline of the Indians becomes grist for Smith's larger thesis, which is that the whole history of the Housatonic Valley should be understood as an epic struggle between God and the devil. The Indians were in the devil's army, quite clearly, if only as cannon fodder. In the end—surprise—virtue was rewarded. The Yankee Puritans kept the Shepaug Valley and the upper reaches of the Housatonic pure for the Lord. Moloch, meanwhile, walked off with the Naugatuck.

Cothren was insistent that the ethnic cleansing of Connecticut had come about through benign and peaceful means: "No violence, no conquest, no stain of blood," he wrote, "attached to the hem of the garments of our ancestors." There is some truth to this, certainly in comparison with the slaughter that attended the opening of the western frontier or the sufferings that small and enfeebled tribes like the Pootatuck had endured at the hands of the predatory Mohawks. The word normally used to describe this relationship is *tributary,* but that hardly does it justice. According to the English traveler William Wood, who visited southern New England in 1633, the Mohawks were "a cruell bloody people, which were wont to come downe upon their poore neighbours with more than bruitish savegness, flaying men, ravishing women, yea very canniballs they were, sometimes eating on a man one part after another before his face, and while yet living."

By the time William Wood came to visit, Connecticut's native population was well along the path to extinction. A year later, in 1634, John Winthrop reported that smallpox had largely cleared the way for European settlement. The final decline of the Indians of southern New England was bracketed by two great spasms of violence—the massacre of the Pequots in 1637 and the short-lived revolt known as King Philip's War, which culminated in the slaughter in 1676 of two hundred Indians trying to cross the Housatonic near the present-day town of Great Barrington, Massachusetts. Between these two dates, the dwindling tribes of the Pomperaug and Shepaug valleys traded away what was left of their lands and yielded to the dubious blessings of assimilation.

Technically, the Pomperaug and Shepaug purchases were peaceful, well-mannered transactions. Yet you can hardly say that the two parties met on an equal footing. Over a period of about eighty years, the Pootatucks deeded away their lands in eleven chunks, selling some of them twice and three times over. On July 14, 1673, an extension of the Pomperaug Valley was sold to Mr. Sherman, Lieutenant Joseph Judson, and Mr. John Minor for five shillings in powder, one hatchet worth four shillings, and ten shillings' worth of lead and powder mixed, as well as a gray coat valued at one pound, ten shillings. Kettletown, which is now the site of a popular state park, was sold for a brass kettle. It was later resold, together with a piece of land bounded by the Housatonic and Eight Mile Brook, "in consideration of corn and other goods, as allso of our meer love and Good will." Another tract went for "two pair of trading cloth breeches and one yard of trading cloth." And so on. These purchases squeezed the Pootatucks into a smaller and smaller area around their streamside tepees. By 1758, they had chucked it in altogether, selling off the last of their lands in two parcels, for a total of $200, four shirts, and a gun. The last of the stragglers dispersed into the forests.

MUCH OF THE POOTATUCKS' history has been captured by the Institute for American Indian Studies, which stands on the site of an old Indian settlement above the confluence of Kirby Brook and the Shepaug River, in the town of Washington, Connecticut. Close to the institute, down a steep trail planted with a fragrant mix of sassafras and shadbush, hemlock and witch hazel, white ash and shagbark hickory, you can explore a reconstructed Indian village, with roundhouses and a longhouse and some split-log canoe shells.

I found the institute's bookshop well stocked with the works of William Cronon, an environmental historian, formerly of Yale and now at the University of Wisconsin, whose views on the human relationship to nature have incensed many environmentalists. In a 1995 essay entitled "The Trouble with Wilderness," Cronon argued that the idea of wilderness was an illusion and, worse yet, an illusion that neutralized our capacity for effective environmental action. He wrote: "The flight from history that is very nearly the core of wilderness represents the false hope of an escape from responsibility, the illusion that we can somehow wipe clean the slate of our past and return to the *tabula rasa* that supposedly existed before we began to leave our marks on the world." Instead of posing a false dichotomy between the purity of wilderness and the corrupting impact of humans, he asked, wouldn't it be more fruitful to examine "what an ethical, sustainable, *honorable* place in nature might actually look like"?

Cronon's ideas apply to every square foot of a state that has been as heavily settled as Connecticut, and in an earlier book, *Changes in the Land,* published in 1983, he set out to describe how the choices made concerning land use by both Indians and New England colonists, as well as the conflict between their respective visions of land as property, brought about profound transformations in the ecosystems of New England. In innumerable ways, from their well-known annual burning of the forest to the displacement of hunting by more energy-efficient crop production, Cronon showed convincingly that the Connecticut Indians had been "no more static than the colonists in their activities and organization."

I had to think no further than the case of the infamous Kettletown kettle, which is often cited to show the Pootatucks as a bunch of hapless victims. In fact, as Cronon shows, by the time the colonists reached the Pomperaug Valley, the Indians were deeply immersed in the trading economy. Take deer, for example. The Litchfield Hills are aswarm with deer these days, but by the late eighteenth century the animal was effectively extinct in Connecticut, having gone the way of the moose, the bear, and the lynx. As deerskins grew scarcer, the Indians became reliant on European textiles as an alternative—thus the central part played by cloth and clothing in so many land purchases. Confined to smaller and smaller areas of land, and with deer less and less available as a source of meat and skins, the Indians came to live much more like subsistence peasant farmers in Europe. Their mobility was further limited by the village's reliance on huge wooden kettles, hewn from tree trunks, for cooking. Portable European kettles, Cronon pointed out, "enabled villages to follow animal populations more readily and without the necessity of resorting to base camps." They became, in fact, the single most valuable article of trade that the Europeans had to offer. This is not to say that the Kettletown Purchase was an equitable trade, but it certainly offers a more three-dimensional way of thinking about it.

On one basic fact, however, Cronon would have to accept that Cothren was right. With the exception of the small Schagticoke Reservation, on the west bank of the Housatonic in the town of Kent, the Indians have "faded from view, and almost from the memory of men." There is dispute over whether Schagticoke, or Scatacook, is properly the name of a tribe or just of the traditionally assumed point of entry, via the nearby Tenmile River, for Indian settlement of the Housatonic Valley. It's a melancholy place, with a reputation for rattlesnakes. The river slows to a flat meander here, backed up behind the dam and the power canal at Bull's Bridge, and the reservation occupies a thin waterfront strip along a dirt road, hemmed in by folded rock strata, forced out of the earth by collisions and left at a ninety-degree angle.

When the purchases were complete and the Indians dispossessed, some of the remaining population gathered here as virtual wards of the colonial government, their spiritual welfare entrusted to a Moravian mission. I'd heard stories of an old Moravian chapel in the forest, reputedly with the carving of a fish on its wall, and I pulled over at the reservation office to ask for directions. A knot of young men were standing outside in work clothes, drinking Pepsi. One of them, a thin-faced man in his early twenties with stringy hair tied back in a ponytail, walked over to see what I wanted. He told me that the chapel wasn't there anymore, but I'd see a mound about a mile down the road, past a stand of pines, with a bunch of tumbled stones. His manner was borderline hostile, and he said to me, "You ain't plannin' to steal no stones or nothing?" I wasn't sure why anyone would want to steal stones, but he told me that one of the stones from the chapel had been used to mark his grandfather's grave, which I would see when I passed a small cemetery farther down the road, near the ruins of the old chapel.

It turned out that most of the graves were like that—nothing but a rough, anonymous chunk of schist or granite placed upright in the ground. But others were modern and carried information about who lay beneath them, and the whole cemetery was well kept. The names suggested tangled bloodlines—Kilson, Kelley, Strever, Clinton, Reilly, Kayser, Bishop, Velky, Harris, Lyden. Almost all the graves were decorated with fresh flowers, and Easter lily crosses, and feathers and beads. Some had glass butterflies and figures of angels. Some had small American flags.

THIS EARLY HISTORY made it clear that names, like rocks and water, were a palimpsest on which we could read the past. Kettletown and

Pomperaug. Halfway and IBM. An Indian named Reilly. Cothren knew full well that the act of naming was not a casual matter for the colonists, but a natural and necessary compulsion, ordained by God and intrinsic to ownership. For Cothren, as for the wilderness absolutists who irritate Cronon, nature was a blank slate waiting for human ambitions to be inscribed upon it. As the colonists looked down on the broad valley of the Pomperaug, Cothren wrote:

> Like the land of Canaan to the Israelites of old, the new land was all before them, with its woods and rocks, and hills and streams—nameless as yet. Here were a thousand hills, valleys, streams, and beautiful local objects of every form and style of loveliness, with no names by which they could be called; no appellation by which they might be described. . . . This wilderness must be reclaimed; human habitations must be erected; the church of God, with its accompanying schoolhouse, must be builded from these overarching forest trees, and all objects must receive names and designations. We may imagine the first surveyor, like a second Adam, with every living and inanimate object before him, awaiting the bestowal of an appellation. . . . It was natural that they should then and there name the place whence they had the pleasure of beholding their "land of promise"; their future homes. They called it Good Hill.

The colonists sowed the valleys and hills of Connecticut thickly with references to the promised land—Bethlehem, Goshen, and Sharon; Canaan itself, later the busy intersection of the Housatonic and Connecticut Western railroads; and New Canaan, now eaten up in the urban sprawl of Stamford and Norwalk. At the same time, the devil was given his due, and his name was likely to be invoked wherever a ravine, gorge, cave, or precipice suggested the presence of danger. Since this kind of topography tends to suggest fast-running trout streams, I give more than passing attention to any map that shows a Devil's Den (of which there are five in Connecticut), Devil's Backbone (four), Devil's Kitchen (two), Devil's Pulpit, Devil's Plunge, Devil's Dripping Pan, or Devil's Hopyard. Not to mention Purgatory Brook, Hell Hole, Tophet Hollow (the swamp that presented the final obstacle to Zachariah Walker's party before they reached Good Hill), or Satan's Kingdom (a sheer-sided gorge on the Farmington River with a reputation for giving up big trout).

The choice of town and county names is also redolent of nostalgia for places left behind. The Housatonic flows through Litchfield County, named for an English cathedral town. A couple of miles from the power-house at Falls Village lies Salisbury, named for another. Kent, farther downstream, has the bucolic feel of its English namesake. Cornwall is as rocky as its English counterpart, the last sliver of land tapering into the Atlantic.

Small towns like these tend to wear their colonial history on their highway signs. I need only to think of the various access routes I use to reach the Shepaug. Judd's Bridge and Whittlesey Road are both named for eighteenth-century clergymen. Minor's Bridge, which spans the Shepaug below Roxbury Falls, commemorates the acknowledged leader of the Pomperaug-Shepaug settlers, a man who was, as Cothren puts it, "fore-most in all difficult undertakings." John Minor was town clerk of Stratford for ten years and occupied the same position in Woodbury for another thirty. He was a magistrate, a captain in the militia, and a deacon of the church. But his most notable skill was as a linguist, and Cothren's orthography of Indian names derives from Minor's transliterations. Because of his mastery of their languages, John Minor was asked to preach the gospel to the Indians, since the leaders of the colony had made known their concern for "the everlasting welfare of those poore, lost, naked sonnes of Adam." John also had a redoubtable son named Joseph, who went on to become a colonel and lived to be 101. Cothren tells us that the old man "retained all his physical powers to such an extent, that on his hundredth birthday he rode a horse through the streets of Woodbury. The fame of this feat is, however, marred by the fact that he did not alight, but fell from his horse." Even so.

For the Europeans, who equated land with property and capital, it was an expected thing for a man of influence to leave his stamp on the town he had founded or to be memorialized after his death. One diligent twentieth-century historian counted 141 manufacturing settlements in Connecticut with the suffix *-ville*. A few of these, such as Augerville, Fluteville, and Spoonville, advertised the sole product that came out of their mills. But the vast majority, from Almyville and Amesville to Yalesville and Youngsville, were tributes to the town's founder, not to what his factories produced.

The Indians rarely thought of naming a place after an individual.

Yet to their enduring credit, the colonists also ended up retaining most of the names that the Indians themselves had used, especially for the rivers. Many give a sense of what the rivers must have been like before the mills and malls had their way. The suffix -*aug* denotes "water," -*tuk*, "a tidal river," and -*amaug*, "a fishing place." In this fashion, Shepaug means "rocky river" and Waramaug "the crooked fishing place." Pootatuck is "tidal-river-of-the-falls-place," although Naugatuck, which appears to have the same suffix, may derive from Nau-ko-tunk, or "one large tree," for the giant hemlock that once spread over Rimmon Falls. Lake Quassapaug is "the beautiful clear water," while its outflow stream, the Quassapaug or Kissewaug, "laughing water," inexplicably became Eight Mile Brook, a parallel to the kind of logic that demolishes a historic building and replaces it with a shed with vinyl siding.

The origin of the name Housatonic has always puzzled historians, and Pootatuck is only one of the 120-odd names attached to it at different times. The present name has been rendered variously as Ausotunnoog, Hoooestennuc, Ousetonuck, Ousatonick, and Housatonack, and that's far from a complete list. The Dutch thought it sounded like, and referred to it in land deeds as, Westenhook. Imaginative English colonists heard it as House of Tunnock. To complicate matters further, different stretches of the river had their own names. The lower part was the Pootatuck, the Great River, or the Stratford River; the upper section, the Housatonic or Weantinock. The problem of multiple names persisted at least until the 1750s. But there is no disagreement about what the present name means—Housatonic is "the place beyond the mountains."

More interesting than the romantic allure of these "wild and shaggy names" (as the writer Odell Shepard called them in the 1930s) is the fact that most of them reflect the physical characteristics and ecological function of the place and, often, the human relationship to that function. According to Cronon, "Place-names were used to keep track of beaver dams, the rapids in rivers, oyster banks, egg-gathering spots, cranberry bogs, canoe-repairing places, and so on." The act of naming provided a functional map of the political economy, and no function was more important than fishing, since settlement patterns were dictated by the watercourses and the food resources they offered. The most obvious example of the connection between naming and function is the name of the state itself, which means "land along the long tidal river."

Native Americans were attuned to changes in their environment that signaled the imminent arrival of the spring spawning runs at these natural obstacles, much as some modern trout fishermen bone up on the quasi science of phenology to predict mayfly hatches by the blooming of particular flowers. The abundance that awaited the Indians when they moved their wigwams to the river's edge for the spawning runs was beyond the imaginings of the colonists and is almost incomprehensible from today's perspective. To the point of cliché, colonists' accounts asserted that you could walk across the rivers on the backs of the fish. But these reports may not be that far from the truth, especially when forage fish such as alewives, smelt, and blueback herring were running in shallow water alongside the trout runs.

For a long time, the conventional wisdom was that the colonists were happy enough to harvest the ocean, but oddly negligent of the rich sources of food in their inland waterways. Supposedly they looked down on fishing as something idle Indian males indulged in while the women did all the work; recreational angling (especially fly-fishing) was of limited appeal to rugged individuals hacking out their survival in a hostile environment, and, as stern Puritans, they disdained fishing along with all other forms of recreational activity. In his history of American fly-fishing, Paul Schullery takes issue with these assumptions. The absence of colonial literature on fishing means nothing, Schullery says. After all, no one in the colonial period wrote books about sex, either, but that doesn't mean they were celibate. Perhaps they fished more than they let on.

Excavations such as those at Kirby Brook, on the other hand, have uncovered a record that tells a fair amount about how the Indians caught their fish and prepared it for year-round storage.

In deep water, the Indians used symmetrical plummets of grooved or perforated glacial cobblestone to get their bait down to the fish. Fishhooks were constructed of wood with spear-shaped bone attachments. When the French explorer Champlain saw these in 1605, he wrote: "The whole thing has a fang-shape, and the line attached to it is made of the bark of a tree. In it the bone was fastened on by hemp, like in France, as it seemed to me." To catch larger species, the Indians made harpoons of bone or antler. In tidal estuaries, they employed gill nets with wooden or bark floats and screens woven from hemp or the fiber of the linden tree. Some years ago, when foundations were being dug for the New England

Life Insurance Building in Boston, the construction crews found the remains of a fish weir that was four thousand years old. It was designed so that fish coming inshore with a high tide would be drawn ever more deeply into a complex of pickets from which they could not escape.

During the spring spawning runs, when fish gathered in large numbers to ascend the rapids or climb falls, the main instrument for their capture was a purse net, which could be swung into the water either from the bank or from a canoe. In the latter case, the skilled paddler in the stern kept the boat steady and balanced by pointing it into the fast water. In an even more precarious position, a spear fisherman, or a bowman, might stand in the bow, ready to strike. When the run was over and the fish that had survived this gauntlet were ready to return to the salt, a village might block off the stream's outlet with an improvised fence of branches and then spear or snag the fish at the barrier. The Indians also practiced stream improvement projects of a kind familiar to the modern fly-fisher. With the old-growth forests still intact and with no population pressures, low summer flows would certainly not have been as great an impediment to stream fishing in Connecticut as they are today. But the climatic cycle was essentially the same, and there is evidence that the Indians modified the aquatic habitat by building funnel-shaped stone walls at drops in the streambed, artificially speeding up and oxygenating the summertime flow and creating new rapids and holding water.

Archaeological work has also revealed that fish had religious as well as economic significance. Fish effigies were placed with a dead body to placate the spirits and ensure continued good fishing for the living. In fact, renowned fishing holes, such as Rimmon Falls on the Naugatuck and Roxbury Falls on the Shepaug, were the last Indian lands to be deeded away, and the terms of purchase often included the right to fish in perpetuity. For as long as Indians survived, so did their attachment to fishing and the residual rights that ensured it.

I drove up to Woodbury one evening to talk to Bill Cummings, the author of *A Master's Guide to Atlantic Salmon Fishing,* and his friend Dick Leavenworth. Both men had clear memories of fishing with the last pureblooded Indian in the Pomperaug Valley, who had died some thirty years earlier.

"Joe Capewell was strictly a meat fisherman," Dick said. "He used to have several ways of handling fish. In good weather, he had a holding pond, spring-fed, behind his house, and he kept fish alive there. He and his wife canned fish, smoked and dried fish."

"He and I used to trap snapping turtles," Bill said, laughing.

"Oh yes, he used to sell 'em, too. Thirty-, forty-, fifty-pound turtles."

Bill said, "I remember one time we had emptied the traps, and we were driving back. Joe didn't have a rearview mirror, so he stuck his head out the window to look back at the road. One of the turtles had got loose in back, and as he put his head out it went for him, snapped at his nose."

Dick said, "Yeah, he tied up a big one in his basement one year. He used to feed them water and a special diet of his own, and according to him, that made the meat sweet and tender. In any event, on the Housatonic, anywhere there was a natural impediment, Joe Capewell knew that was a good place to get the migrating fish. Joe had a piece of paper that went back to the original land deeds that he said guaranteed him the right to fish on anybody's property, in any water."

He leaned forward, grinning at Bill. "You remember when he got hauled into court by that New Yorker who had bought a piece of property down at the south end of town, and he built a small dam and had a bass pond down on Transylvania Road there? It was unbelievable. Big largemouth bass. That pond would regularly produce five- and six-pound bass. As far as Joe was concerned, bass, trout, suckers, it didn't make any difference. Whether canned or smoked, it all tasted the same. So he got hauled into court, and he showed his piece of paper that let him go anywhere. 'No Trespassing' signs meant nothing as far as Joe was concerned. It was one of the few privileges his people retained."

Dick went on: "On the Pomperaug, he carried a burlap sack that the fish went into. If he was fishing for his pond, he had a huge bait bucket, which he'd keep refreshing in the river, and he would bring these fish back alive in it. For the most part the fish went into that burlap bag, carried over Joe's back, and it used to drip its juice all down his shirt and into his pants and down his pant leg. Joe was fragrant. He'd come into Buddy Phillips's diner and sit down at the counter, and people would start to move away, and Joe would start talking and never stop. When he caught a really big fish, he'd preserve the head. He used to take it out in the open, hang it up, and let it dry, and the maggots would eat the flesh away, and then he'd have the bones and the skin, and he'd give them a coat of shellac, and he would carry it around in his pocket for weeks. Everywhere he went around Woodbury, he'd pull it out and say, 'Look at this one!'"

Both men smiled at the recollection. Later, smiling myself at the story, I thought the finest part of it was that the author of *A Master's Guide to Atlantic Salmon Fishing* would go out after snapping turtles with old Joe Capewell.

6
Fire on the Mountain

IT COULD HAVE BEEN SO DIFFERENT, I thought, as I stooped to pick up a handful of gleaming rocks from the edge of Furnace Brook, a quarter-mile above its confluence with the Housatonic. I had another thought, too, this one more parochial: these will look good at home in the kids' museum. Something to add to the deer skulls and World War II medals and armadillo shells and fossils and foreign bank notes that had taken over two bookcases in the hallway of our Manhattan apartment. These were no ordinary rocks. While the bedrock boulders along Furnace Brook had been there for half a billion years or more, these rocks had existed for only a nanosecond of geological time. In fact, I learned later, they could be dated quite precisely: they were a byproduct of the Cornwall Bridge Iron Company, which operated here from 1833 to 1897 and gave the brook its name. People with a sense of humor call these rocks Housatonic obsidian, but they are more commonly known as slag.

The squat, tapering tower of the Cornwall Bridge furnace is long gone, but in the high water of spring the brook flows through the remnants of a millrace. Overgrown stone walls still suggest a medieval castle keep in Europe. I'd seen similar ruins, with their three identical gothic arches, on the Blackberry River, on Wachocastinook Brook at the top of Mount Riga, and on the Housatonic itself, down by Kent.

Unimaginable as it seems today, the trout streams of northwestern Connecticut were the epicenter of the American iron and armaments industries from the time of the Revolutionary War to the Civil War. The allure of iron, not farming, in fact, drew the first settlers to this part of Connecticut. Even before 1739, when the first town in the Northwest Corner was incorporated, survey parties from the Hartford colony had found that the rocks of the upper Housatonic Valley were rich in the deposits of reddish brown hematite ore that stretch all the way down along the Appalachians as far south as the steel mills of Birmingham, Alabama. By the early nineteenth century at least fourteen blast furnaces were operating in the Connecticut portion of the Housatonic Valley, with another nine on the Massachusetts side and eight more just over the New York line.

At the heart of this industrial wealth stood the twin towns of Lakeville (known in the nineteenth century as Furnace Village) and Salisbury, which in its heyday was reputed to have the longest bar east of Albany. Salisbury iron masters such as the Barnums and Pettees and Holleys amassed fabulous fortunes. This isn't to say that they were above getting their hands dirty. While some went into the industry as venture capitalists driven by profit, others forged their skills inside the furnaces. Their fortunes mirrored the fortunes of war. It's a history that many American industries share—they may grow to meet the needs of a commercial marketplace, but military procurement contracts drive them to upgrade their quality and their technology and so to dominate their com-

HOUSATONIC FALLS, FALLS VILLAGE, CANAAN, CONN.

petitors. Until 1776, the ironworks in the upper Housatonic watershed turned out pots and pans and locks and latches and hinges. But when the Revolutionary War came, they began to make cannon and cannonballs. Philadelphia may have been the cradle of the Revolution, but Salisbury was its arsenal. Salisbury iron was of legendary quality. In 1798, when Eli Whitney persuaded Congress to give him the contract to produce ten thousand muskets with interchangeable parts, he insisted on Salisbury iron. Iron from the furnaces on Mount Riga was shipped directly to the Springfield Armory in Massachusetts and to the Harpers Ferry arsenal in West Virginia.

The War of 1812 brought even more navy business to the Salisbury ironworks, including the anchors for men-of-war such as the USS *Constitution* and *Constellation.* Local historians tell stories about navy inspectors who would come to town and watch as newly cast anchors were hoisted by means of a wooden tripod on top of Mount Riga and then dropped on the ground. If the anchors survived the fall, the navy officers would shake hands with the iron masters and the spectators would exchange nods of satisfaction, knowing that the handshakes meant continued prosperity for the town of Salisbury.

Although the iron barons were economic competitors, they operated in many respects as a kind of social cartel. They joined the same clubs; they married off their sons and daughters to one another. Considering themselves gentlemen, they fly-fished and cultivated a taste for wilderness, of the not-too-threatening kind. In 1900, Charles W. Burnham, in partnership with a group of white-shoe Manhattan lawyers, opened a fishing and hunting club for his friends on the wooded banks of the Hollenbeck River, close to one of his furnaces. The white colonial clubhouse had once been known as Hunt's Tavern, and Benjamin Silliman of Yale had stayed here during his inspection tour of the northwestern Connecticut iron industry in 1817.

Once a year, if I play my cards right, I manage to wangle an invitation from my friend Whitney Ellsworth to fish the private waters of the Hollenbeck Club. We were sitting on the porch of the clubhouse drinking bourbon one day after fishing the evening hatch. As I peppered Whitney with questions about the arcana of the iron industry, I noticed suddenly that he was giving me the half-quizzical, half-indulgent look of someone who recognizes the grip of obsession. "You know," he said, "if you're really getting into this stuff, I ought to introduce you to Larry Pool."

As we drove over the hills to Cornwall a few days later, Whitney told me that Larry Pool had written a history of the iron and steel industry in Connecticut. He'd also written a slim volume on the Hollenbeck Club, which was privately published in a limited edition for the members in the late 1970s. But calling Larry Pool the historian of the Hollenbeck Club, I discovered, was a bit like saying that Leonardo da Vinci played the lute or designed canal locks; Leonardo is reported to have done both with a high degree of competence, but those talents barely hint at the scope of the man.

We pulled up outside a low, ranch-style house on a hilltop. Behind it the ground fell away sharply and the hills stretched away to the west— first Tarradiddle, then the Housatonic River, and beyond that the hills of Sharon, Red Mountain, Indian Mountain, and the distant Catskills, out across the New York state line. Larry Pool rolled to the door in a wheelchair, a very, very old man—well into his nineties—with dark age spots, deeply sunken cheeks, and bones like a bird's. Behind him, a man a third his age was picking up papers and a tape recorder and preparing to leave.

After the younger man had gone, Larry Pool apologized. "Sorry about all the coming and going. They wanted to interview me for a book on squash. They apparently just realized that my brother Beekman and I are the oldest living U.S. national squash champions." He showed me a photograph—the Harvard squash team and the signature of J. Lawrence Pool, '28; standing behind him was Beekman H. Pool, '32.

His brother's name comes from the mother's side—the New York Beekmans of Mount Pleasant, whose yellow clapboard mansion on the East River served as the British headquarters during the Revolutionary War. Larry's father, Dr. Eugene H. Pool, was president of the American College of Surgeons and a tyrant in the operating theater. Interns quaked in his presence and called him the Iron Duke. Larry himself became a neurosurgeon. He performed lobotomies for as long as they remained in fashion, invented new surgical techniques for treating aneurysms and paraplegia, and ended up as president of the American Academy of Neurosurgery. He came up to the hills of North Cornwall in 1972, after retiring as chairman of the Neurosurgery Department at Columbia.

I asked Larry Pool if he'd written any other books, apart from the two Whitney had mentioned. He thought for a moment and said, "Well, yes." There had been a history of fighting ships of the American Revolution and the origins of the modern navy, a literary-political biography of Izaak Walton, a book on tumors of the auditory nerve, two others on the human brain and nervous system, and perhaps one or two more that he couldn't quite call to mind. And, oh yes, an autobiography. He rolled his wheelchair to the other side of the room to fetch me a copy. "I even had one of the brain books translated into Japanese," he said. "A long time afterward I got a check for the royalties. Forty-seven cents."

I told Larry that my interest in the iron industry had first been piqued by the brightly colored slag that I'd found along Furnace Brook. His face lit up in a smile. "Same thing with me!" he exclaimed. "Interesting the things you find out about while you're fishing."

As Larry talked about the nineteenth-century boom, it occurred to me that the iron industry presented the trout pool paradox in its most extreme form. The production of iron required exactly the same ingredients that make up ideal trout habitat: limestone, fast water, and a cooling forest canopy. On their own, the rocks are useless to industry, since the iron molecules they contain are bound together with oxygen, forming a compound—iron oxide—that could be broken apart only by the application of intense heat. The solution to this problem, however, was right at hand, in the dense forests that provided, when burned to form charcoal, the vast quantities of carbon needed for the smelting process. Those who built the furnaces took advantage of natural falls and existing mill seats, or they dammed the flow to create deep ponds and artificial drops. Waterpower drove the huge bellows of the furnace, and side races provided a secondary flow for the trip hammers of the blacksmith's forge, where pig iron could be converted into useful forms. Late-nineteenth-century photographs show the hillsides denuded of all but stumps, having been clearcut in twenty-five- or thirty-year cycles. The furnaces were so hungry that in the end it became necessary to bring in charcoal from Vermont and the Catskills.

Limestone, meanwhile, was useful to the iron master in a couple of ways. It could be added as an alchemical "flux" to catalyze the smelting process, and it also had the obliging property of fusing with the impurities in the ore—sand, silicates, manganese, sulfur, and phosphorus. As the molten iron flowed from the crucible of the furnace into the hearth, this lighter mixture settled on top, where it could be skimmed off. As this mess solidified, a furnace worker would stick an iron bar into it. When it cooled and hardened, he could yank it free in slabs, and it remained only to pound these into smaller chunks with a sledgehammer and dump the pieces on the riverbanks. The rocks I had brought out of the ruins of the Cornwall Bridge Iron Company were formed in this way.

I mentioned to Larry that I'd seen some old charcoal pits in the forest on my hike with Walt Landgraf, next to an old road that took fuel west to the furnaces and brought finished iron east to Connecticut's old Newgate Prison. Walt had explained, "As soon as the first leaves began to fall in October, all able-bodied folks headed for the hills to cut down any tree with a diameter of more than six or eight inches. They brought the timber to the charcoal hearths in springtime by whatever method was to hand—wheelbarrows, horses, sleds and wagons, shoulders. Each hearth burned thirty cords of wood at a time, and most of them burned four or five times in a season." Do some simple math, and you will be able to reckon how rapidly the forests disappeared.

The colliers came from all over Europe. There were Scots escaping the Highland clearances and Irish fleeing the potato famine. French and Spaniards and Poles came here looking for work. Lithuanians and Letts did it. There were African Americans and Indians from the Schagticoke Reservation down the river. They spent the six-month season, from May to October, in the hills, two men to a hut, living on a diet of squirrels and woodchuck. The most famous of them were the Raggies, who lived on Mount Riga, above Salisbury. Some say the place was named for the colliers' hometown in Latvia.

The collier formed the core of his charcoal hearth by laying in a central chimney of tall timbers, piled up in the form of a triangle. He stacked the structure with meticulous care, large wood on the inside and smaller on the outside, fearful of shifts in the structure of the pile once the fire was started. He left a breathing hole down at the bottom, to allow a small amount of air to enter. Then he threw leaves on top of the pile and covered them with a layer of dirt that might be six inches thick. Once the fire had taken hold inside, the collier had to watch it for the next two weeks to maintain an even temperature. The center needed to be somewhere between seven hundred and nine hundred degrees Fahrenheit; any hotter, and it would consume the wood around it. The collier could regulate the temperature by opening and closing the air hole if he saw the color of the smoke changing or if the fire had the wrong smell. With hundreds of woodpiles burning simultaneously, the Housatonic Valley would have been filled with acrid black smoke and flames that reddened the sky at night.

As the pile burned, it began to shrink in on itself, creating soft spots, the collier's nightmare. The only solution was to climb on top of the pile and tamp solid wood into the hole, with a nine-hundred-degree fire burning away underneath. Walt Landgraf was talking about this one night to a meeting of Housatonic fly-fishermen when someone who had grown up in an iron-producing area of Sweden told how he and his sister had made friends with a collier up in the mountains during World War II. One day, the man was gone. The townspeople said, "You know how those colliers are, he's taken off on a bender, he'll be back." About a week later they decided it was probably time to open up his charcoal pile. All they found was the man's teeth and a piece of his jawbone.

The life of a furnace worker must, if anything, have been worse. The charcoal fire was like a cool spring breeze compared with the two-thousand-degree inferno it took to separate iron from the oxygen and the impurities in the ore. Like the collier's, the ironmaker's life depended on the ability to read danger signs—slag of the wrong color and consistency, suspiciously colored smoke, and the look of the fire itself, monitored through a spy hole covered in fireproof mica. Whereas the collier lay awake at night worrying about soft spots, the furnace worker's worst enemy was the accretion of ore, limestone, and charcoal in a solid mass that blocked the outlet. Furnace workers called this a salamander. At best, the salamander would force a shutdown and a laborious removal operation. At worst, the buildup of toxic gases would cause the entire structure to explode. The cure for a salamander was often as bad as the disease—the remedies included firing a cannon into the mouth of the furnace.

WHITNEY AND LARRY had to discuss some Hollenbeck Club business, so I walked outside to admire the view. Then I sat down and leafed through Larry's autobiography, watching him age through the photographs. A sulky five-year-old in a long smock, at the beach with a nanny. A lean teenager in a dark shirt, bending forward in the saddle in Colorado in 1919. A young man with a modest but knowing smile in a Harvard letterman's sweater, with the crew of the yacht *Mohawk* in the 1928 Fastnet Race. An army officer, balding now, leaning forward over a chess game outside a field hospital tent in North Africa. A handsome man in late middle age, with dark-rimmed glasses and surgical mask, performing aneurysm surgery. A man of eighty at Pulpit Harbor in Maine, in a jersey with the insignia of the Royal Ocean Racing Club; a strong face with fine bones, a long nose, and eyes that have seen a lot.

As a young man Larry Pool thought about a career on Wall Street, but he saw the frenzied greed that grabbed hold of his friends before the crash of '29 and opted for medicine instead. Larry moved in a privileged crowd, the only kind available at Harvard in those days, I suppose, and one day a classmate told him that his father had offered him a choice of gifts—polo ponies or a yacht. They decided on the yacht, reasoning that it was harder to entertain girlfriends on a polo pony. With another friend, a cook, and a one-eyed sea captain from Gloucester, they made a five-day sail from Boston to Halifax, Nova Scotia. On the third day, they ran into a rum runner and took the opportunity to stock up for the winter. At twenty, having mastered the basics of sailing, Larry Pool joined a Harvard crew and made the first of several Atlantic crossings. In Santander, at the end of one of them, he danced with the queen of Spain and her two daughters, the *infantas*.

Fish fascinated Larry Pool. On another Atlantic crossing, he traveled with the crew of a Woods Hole oceanographic research schooner and hauled up weirdly shaped, jet-black, phosphorescent creatures from the deep ocean. He caught his first trout on a fly rod at the age of seven. He fished in Montana, England, France, Kenya, and Chile. He went after steelhead in the Pacific Northwest. He fished for Atlantic salmon in Scotland, Norway, Iceland, Maine, and the Canadian Maritimes. He joined the Anglers' Club of New York. He fished with Benny Goodman. When a patient's cranial veins presented a life-or-death dilemma that had to be solved in less than a minute, Larry Pool imagined them as a tangled fly line.

One day, bored, Larry Pool decided he would learn to fly. So he bought himself a secondhand, two-cylinder, two-seater Aeronca seaplane and for a time flew every weekend to Burlington, Vermont, to perform brain surgery, for which he was paid in apples, eggs, and maple syrup.

Larry decided one weekend that he would fly to Canada. He packed an anchor, a pup tent, and some camping supplies into the Aeronca, consulted the map, and decided the best place to break the journey would be at the north end of Lake George. He rounded a small island at eighty miles an hour, flying into the glare of the setting sun, and slammed straight into a row of black high-tension cables that weren't marked on the map. Blue sparks danced across the floor of the cockpit.

"Well, Pool," he thought, "this is what you see just before you die— blue sparks."

He shut off the ignition to prevent fire, made his body go limp to minimize the risk of a broken neck, and noticed, from his upside-down position, that fish were finning lazily in the water he was about to hit. When he recovered consciousness, he was in waist-deep water. One propeller blade had snapped off, both wings were bent out of shape, and the aluminum floats were crushed beyond recognition. Larry found a rope to tow the plane ashore. As he was securing it, he saw a speedboat racing toward him, with a teenage boy at the wheel.

"He was as pale as a Roman toga," Larry said. "He looked so awful that I said, 'What's the matter, son? Can I help you? I'm a doctor.'"

During World War II, Larry Pool treated brain injuries among frontline troops. This time, after the siege of Montecassino, his dancing partner was Marlene Dietrich; she wore a pale purple dress and matching elbow-length gloves. His field hospital in North Africa was so well appointed that Ernie Pyle, the war correspondent, made a point of staying there when he was in the area. He called it "Pool's Paradise." One day, for want of anything else to do, Larry taught himself to walk on his hands. When he went back to New York after the war, he would entertain guests at black-tie parties by walking downstairs on his hands, with his immaculate patent-leather shoes poised and level, six feet in the air.

My first thought was that I'd never met anyone quite like Larry Pool; but then I thought, well, you find people like him around every corner in the Litchfield Hills. It's one of the things that keep you coming back. Chard Powers Smith had made quite a song and dance about this in writing *The Housatonic: Puritan River.* He had pointed out that (as long as one was willing to overlook inconvenient industrial towns such as Derby, Waterbury, and Pittsfield) the proportion of the population of the Housatonic Valley who could be found in the 1940 edition of

Who's Who in America was higher than for any other single location in the United States, including the intellectual centers of Boston and New Haven. Smith even constructed a neat little table to show that the area had no less than *eleven* times the average national concentration of famous people. He offered this as proof that the forces of godliness were on the march in the Housatonic Valley. Think what you like about Smith's thesis, but the fact remains that understanding how this corner of the country developed means understanding the social, economic, and intellectual vectors that blew people like Larry Pool in from Yale, Harvard, and Manhattan.

WHEN I WAS a college student, I hung on the wall of my room a set of cheap prints of paintings of the English industrial revolution. The most famous of them was probably *Coalbrookdale by Night.* I don't recall the artist's name, since so many of them painted the same scene, all of them fascinated by the contrast between the natural beauty of the river gorge and the red clouds of smoke and flames that billowed from the new industries nestled between its steep, rocky walls.

Beside this painting I hung several by Joseph Wright of Derby, who captured better than any other artist of the eighteenth century the interplay between human activity and the natural environment, and the wild beauty that accompanied the new industrial revolution. Wright painted forges and furnaces, waterwheels and trip hammers, waterfalls and trout streams. A man of the Enlightenment, he befriended the best scientists of the day and took their work as the subject of many of his paintings. Depictions of surgical procedures or experiments with vacuum pumps allowed Wright to explore the interplay of light and darkness. His work no longer reflects the calm, harmonious light of the landscapes of Claude Lorrain, yet it stops short of prefiguring the elemental light of Turner. Human beings are actively at work on Wright's landscapes, bringing an ambiguous kind of loveliness to their endeavor. During Wright's career, a similar process was beginning in America. Timothy Dwight would have been traveling in these hills at about the same time, I thought, wondering in his own fashion at the human transformation of the wild that was under way.

In their most audacious act of renaming, the colonists had entered the wilderness and called it civilization. By the early nineteenth century, those who held economic power in these valleys viewed civilization and industry as interchangeable terms. The Housatonic was a national leader in iron and weapons production; until after the Civil War, the great steel center of Birmingham, Alabama, was, in Larry Pool's phrase, "an unnamed expanse of farms and scruffy fields overrun by rabbits." Over in Waterbury, on the Naugatuck, the old gristmills built by the colonists had given birth to a brass industry that would soon dominate the world. If the Shepaug Valley lagged behind, it was only because no one had yet hit on the magic formula that combined raw materials and market access in the right proportions.

I used to stare at Joseph Wright's paintings for minutes on end, seeing in the red and orange flames and the black smoke of Coalbrookdale the slag heaps and methane fires of my Scottish childhood. Now I looked out over the Litchfield Hills and imagined the black smoke rising from the charcoal pits and the iron span at Coalbrookdale as a bridge over a tributary of the Housatonic, running red with iron oxide.

I gave a start as the door opened behind me and I heard the sound of Larry's wheelchair. "Admiring my salamander?" he asked, smiling. I hadn't noticed it until then, but he pointed at a misshapen chunk of fused rock and silica lying next to the doorstep. "That one came from the hearth of the Mine Hill furnace, down in Roxbury."

The late afternoon light was beginning to fade, and I could see that Larry was getting tired. I said I should probably be getting home. "Any regrets?" I asked him as we stood at his doorstep. "Anything you wish you'd done, but never found time for?"

He thought for a minute. "Well, I miss fishing," he said. "And I always wanted to try skydiving, but I never got around to it. Other than that, no. No regrets."

At home that night, I picked up his autobiography again. As I leafed through the chapters, I noticed that one took as its epigraph a text from the King James Bible, Ecclesiastes 9:10. "Whatsoever thy hand findeth to do, do it with thy might."

A FEW MONTHS LATER I went back to the Hollenbeck Club. This time it was raining hard. Whitney Ellsworth and I fished in a desultory way, dodging the cloudbursts, and neither of us caught much.

After we had eaten lunch, Whitney left me alone to poke around the ruins of the Buena Vista furnace, which Larry Pool had excavated. Buena Vista was named to commemorate Zachary Taylor's victory in 1847, which ended the Mexican War. It wasn't easy to reach the ruins in the sodden forest. But when I finally approached the old structures, I found that they were more extensive than the remains at Cornwall Bridge and told a more literal and graphic story. Here were the stone retaining walls that had once surrounded the casting house. Here was the wheel pit. Here was the archway through which J-shaped metal pipes—*tuyères*—had blasted air into the furnace. And here was the outer wall of the egg-shaped stack itself, lined with yellow pie-wedge firebricks stamped with their maker's name: Newton & Co., Albany, NY. When Larry Pool first explored Buena Vista, he found littered on the ground three generations of brick, distinguishable because stamped with different company names. From this finding he deduced, I'm sure correctly, that the furnace had been rebuilt twice when its lining was worn out by the constant heat and pressure.

When I was done looking around, I scrambled down an unstable bank of colored scree, Housatonic obsidian, to fish for a few minutes at the head of the Slag Pool. I caught a small wild brook trout. The fish had deep green flanks, almost black, with vivid spots of red and blue. I remembered Larry saying that you could read something of the operations of the furnace from the color and texture of the slag, rather like studying the rings on a tree to discover the climate of successive years in the life of the forest. I found one piece that still bore the smooth, rounded imprint of the workman's rod; it had an opaque, blackish gray color and spongy texture, suggesting it had been produced on a poor day for smelting. But I collected other pieces from days that would have been more pleasing to the iron master, pieces that contained shades of dark green, deep milky blue, and jet black. It takes an effort of the mind to associate this kind of beauty with an industrial waste product. Lower down on the scree slope, I saw other chunks of slag that were amethyst and creamy white and the palest aquamarine, and they glistened in the late afternoon light.

7
Ydawaix and Oldphogiz

IN 1863, A RAILROAD ENGINEER from the town of Litch-field called Major Edwin McNeill came home from the war, teamed up with a group of local notables including Colonel Albert Hodge of Roxbury, enlisted an explosives man who went by the name of Glycerine Jack Booth, and announced to the residents of the Shepaug Valley that what they really needed was to turn the little cluster of mills in Factory Hollow into a major industrial center that would rival any in the East. This feat would be accomplished by building a railroad. At least on the upper rungs of the social ladder, the idea held a lot of appeal. The boosters of the railroad, according to the *New Haven Register,* believed they were about to enter "a bright industrial age . . . which they dreamed would rival the neighboring Naugatuck Valley, the world's brass center, in the strength of its manufacturing output."

Brass had been made since the time of the Romans, but it was only in the 1780s that English metalworkers figured out how to extract zinc from ore, add it to molten copper, and mass-produce brass that was strong, malleable, easily polished, attractive, cheap, and infinitely versatile. For two decades, English brass had to be imported into the United States, at the height of the small unpleasantness between London and its former colonies. In 1802, a tinsmith named Abel Porter acquired the old Hopkins gristmill on the Mad River in Waterbury. Porter joined up the dots: waterpower, new technology, a ready mass market, and a patriotic appeal to substitute locally produced goods for imports. Even the ba-

sic infrastructure and know-how were readily on hand in the iron foundries of northwestern Connecticut, whose equipment and workers could
switch to brass making.

With waterpower, skilled niche labor, and a handful of imaginative
entrepreneurs, Waterbury all of a sudden found itself the brass capital
of the world. Like the iron industry, Waterbury's new brass mills cap-
italized on the War of 1812 and the embargo on British imports. By 1858
the city had twenty-five brass factories. By 1896 the number had grown
to thirty-nine. Over time, these were consolidated into the three great
brass empires—Scovill's on the Mad River, on the site of Abel Porter's
old shop; Chase Brass in Waterville; and the American Brass Company.
By 1917, their mills employed twenty-five thousand people. Meanwhile,
brass took the place of hardwoods (such as Walt Landgraf's laurel) as the
raw material for the interchangeable parts needed for the clock industry,
in which the Naugatuck Valley also led the world. The Waterbury Clock
Company and R. H. Ingersoll introduced Americans to the mass-produced "dollar pocket watch." It was said, with reason, that Waterbury
products could be found in any corner of what people then thought of as
the "civilized world."

MEN LIKE Major Edwin McNeill looked at the captains of industry
one valley over and saw themselves becoming the Scovills and the Chases
of the Shepaug. The public record reveals little about Edwin McNeill. But
from a smattering of papers in local archives, I found out that he was a
mathematician, a graduate of the Captain Partridge Military Academy in
Norwich, Vermont, and at one time chief engineer of the Erie Railroad.
He was also a Scotsman ("with all the indomitable energy of his race"),
described as "a progressively minded modern" and "an operations man,
comfortable with blueprints, engineering problems and manpower management." I had the definite sense of a darker side to the man, but if
pressed for evidence, the only thing I could offer would be a little poem,
presumably of McNeill's own composition, which I found inked in the
back of one of his survey notebooks for the Canandaigua and Niagara
Falls Railroad:

> Truth crushed to Earth shall rise again,
> The eternal gems of God are hers,

But lies wounded, writhes in pain
And dies amid His worship.

A hint of the lugubrious and the self-righteous here, I thought, and if so, not the first Scotsman who could be accused of having those qualities.

In the interests of full disclosure, I have to confess here to a weakness not only for eccentric fellow-Scotsmen but also for railroads. Together with the coal mines, they dominated the town in which I grew up, and they occupy a central place in my memories of childhood. Two lines crisscrossed in the town. The smaller of these, a narrow-gauge line, carried a little utility haulage engine—the pug—from pit to pit. Its driver was the father of two of my school friends. Norman and Ken Taylor were my third and fourth best friends, to be exact, sometimes rising to second and third, or even second equal—ten-year-old boys keeping a close accounting of such things. I would watch, fascinated, as Mr. Taylor's pug chugged up the steep sides of the coal bings to dump slag, like a worker ant carrying leaf fragments to its queen.

The second line was altogether more grandiose, and it ran right behind our house. This one carried mainline express trains, even the famed *Flying Scotsman.* These giant locomotives would hurtle with a muffled roar through the deep cutting at the bottom of our garden, out of sight unless we perched on top of the garden fence. As one passed, a dense horizontal plume of smoke would fill the cutting and rise until it enveloped us and made us invisible. In dry summers, the cinders would ignite sudden blazes in the cutting, which would often reach our wooden fence and engulf that, too. It must be forty years since a steam locomotive used this line, but the last time we visited the old house I noticed that some of the fence posts were still charred and blackened. I rubbed them with my finger and thumb and inhaled the smoky residue of the old fires. Proust's madeleine, did someone say?

THE SPECIFIC LOGIC of the Shepaug Valley Railroad was to rescue Litchfield, the county seat, from its commercial isolation, a problem that Major McNeill, as president of the First Litchfield National Bank and founder of the Litchfield Land and Improvement Company, took seriously. Ostensibly the town was serviced by the new Naugatuck Railroad, which had opened in 1849. But Litchfield, an oddly shaped township, sat on an elevated plateau; East Litchfield, the nearest railroad depot, was six miles away and six hundred feet lower in the Naugatuck Valley.

Not that a logical rationale for building a railroad was really necessary in the climate of the times. In May 1869, after a six-year epic of construction, the crews of the Central Pacific engine Jupiter and Union Pacific engine No. 119 met in Utah for the "golden spike" ceremony that marked the completion of the transcontinental railroad. Emulators were everywhere, no matter how obscure the location or how flimsy the rationale. Railroads were to the 1860s, in fact, what dot.coms were to the 1990s: a delirium, a frenzy, often only tenuously grounded in economic reality.

Although local railroads, like those on the Housatonic, the Shepaug, and the Naugatuck, can seem little more than scenic byways of history, the rail lines of northwestern Connecticut ran unusually close to the main arteries of the national railroad boom. The three principal figures in the Union Pacific Railroad all had strong local connections. Thomas Clark "Doc" Durant, known as "the first dictator of the railroad world," had grown up in Lee, Massachusetts, where his father owned a factory on the Housatonic River. More significant than Durant was the Ames family, whose Old Colony shovel had dug up most of the gold in the California gold rush and earned family members the nickname "the Kings of Spades." Oliver Ames was the president of the Union Pacific, and his brother Oakes was a fellow director. A third Ames brother, Horatio, owned one of the largest ironworks in the Housatonic Valley. A lot of Union Pacific business was steered in Horatio's direction, and the ironworkers at Amesville grew to become internationally known specialists in railroad axles, locomotive tires, and railroad car wheels. When the company closed, its huge plant, situated just above the Great Falls at Canaan, became the main manufacturing and repair shop for the Housatonic Railroad Company.

Major Edwin McNeill's prospectus made extravagant claims for his new railroad:

It may be stated: that the aggregate fall from Bantam Lake to the mouth of the Shepaug is, accurately, eight hundred feet; and that the lakes, tributary to this river, furnish natural reservoirs of a capacity of at least two thousand acres. The volume of water, its great fall, and

the command without cost of two thousand acres of flowage, designate this as the best stream in the State for manufacturing purposes.
Again: As compared with other sections of New England, its close
proximity to the coal fields of Pennsylvania, and its nearness to New
York and the coast, is at least, a reasonable guarantee that the establishment of manufactories would follow, immediately upon the opening of the road.

Although the total population of the Shepaug Valley in 1868 was
only about seven thousand, these people had undeniably created the nucleus of a fairly diverse agricultural and industrial economy. A miscel-
lany of small industrial enterprises clustered in Factory Hollow in the
town of Washington. Marble and granite quarries, garnet mines, and silica mines provided raw materials for paint, sandpaper, and grindstones.
A modest hatting industry stood in close proximity to an array of small
foundries, tanneries, cooperages, and of course scores of sawmills, like
those that Colonel Albert Hodge owned on Battle Swamp Brook. The
farms produced a surplus of dairy products and other perishable goods,
including fruit and cigar tobacco. Bantam Lake offered unlimited possibilities for icehouses to keep such produce fresh. Most of all, though,
there was Mine Hill.

Mine Hill isn't much to look at, just a seven-hundred-foot granite
gneiss ridge above the floodplain of the Shepaug at Roxbury. But since
the earliest colonization of the valley, rumors of fabulous mineral wealth
had swirled around the place. In the 1750s, a slanderous story, soon a
folk legend, began to circulate concerning a German goldsmith named
Feuchter, who was accused of spiriting silver from the mine at night in
his horse's saddlebags. But for decades the mine produced nothing but
bankruptcies and litigation to rival *Jarndyce and Jarndyce* in Dickens's
Bleak House.

The vein of iron ore that runs along the Shepaug is not the more
common hematite found around Salisbury. Benjamin Silliman of Yale
visited Mine Hill in 1816 or 1817 and correctly identified it as an intrusion
of siderite, a lighter, yellowish carbonate. Siderite, a top-grade ore, could
produce steel from the cast-iron pig in a single operation, and as the
American industrial revolution gathered steam, it was much in demand
as a raw material for fine machine tools, surgical and other precision in-

struments, and guns produced by Connecticut manufacturers such as Samuel Colt and Pratt and Whitney. The problem was that it rarely occurred in commercially viable concentrations. Most high-grade steel still had to be imported from Europe, particularly from Prussia and Styria (part of present-day Austria).

An elite group of Hartford businessmen founded the Shepaug Spathic Iron and Steel Company in 1864, deciding that the key to its success was to raid the skilled European workforce. They quickly erected an impressive complex of buildings around new roasting and smelting furnaces, on the slopes around the mineshaft. But ill omens seemed to dog the operation. There were steam engine breakdowns and freak summer rains, and the first time the furnace was fired up, it gave birth to a salamander—perhaps the very one that now sat on Larry Pool's doorstep—and had to be immediately shut down again. In 1871 it was belatedly converted from cold to hot blast, scrambling to keep pace with a technology that other furnaces had adopted decades earlier.

M EANWHILE, Major McNeill was running into problems and delays of his own—not that you would have known it from the tone of his fundraising appeals. He estimated that the new line would cost $850,000, and to raise this sum he relied on the business model used by most proponents of new railroad ventures of the Civil War era. This approach was an open invitation, on one hand, to Ponzi schemes and, on the other, to early bankruptcy. Writing in 1890, the railroad historian Thomas Curtis Clarke observed that "one thing which distinguishes the American railway from its English parent . . . is the almost uniform practice of getting the road open for traffic in the cheapest manner and in the least possible time, and then completing it and enlarging its capacity out of its surplus earnings, and from the credit those earnings give it."

McNeill proposed to start with a 5 percent levy on the grand list of the five Shepaug river towns—Litchfield, Morris, Washington, Roxbury, and Bridgewater. These taxes, plus private subscriptions, would raise almost half the construction costs. The remaining half-million dollars or so would come from increased taxable property values in the five towns and from the railroad's future earnings. He blithely claimed, while wooing prospective investors, that these earnings were "fully assured." As proof, he pointed to the Naugatuck Valley towns, which had almost doubled their tax base since the railroad had come through in 1849. The only problem, of course, was that the Naugatuck was now the beating heart of the world's brass industry, while the factories of the Shepaug were still turning out little more than promises.

McNeill also made light of the engineering challenges involved in building the new railroad. He wrote:

> Without encountering expensive works, the great falls at Bantam are overcome at a point five miles west of Litchfield; and the grade line of the road from this point, to the junction of the Shepaug with the Housatonic, 22 miles, is accommodated to the high-water line of that river, and hence generally occupies the alluvial flats lying along it. At the mouth of the Shepaug a most favorable crossing of the Housatonic is effected by a bridge, 250 feet in length, and forty feet in height, the approaches to which are inconsiderable, as no flats on either side of the river exist at this point.

The major's prospectus was a tour de force of selective truth in advertising, I thought, as I knelt over his original survey map of the route of the railroad. The thing was twelve or fifteen feet long. It took two librarians at the Litchfield Historical Society to roll it out on the floor for me, and another to weight it down at the corners with books. The major's survey line twisted and wriggled from one end of the map to the other like an epileptic boa constrictor. Nothing in his engineering survey mentioned the two hundred curves the line would take, the vast amounts of bedrock that would have to be removed, or the unyielding character of the quartzite schist that forced the river to execute two ninety-degree turns around the sheer escarpment known as Steep Rock.

Opposition to McNeill's railroad came in three varieties. Like every locale in the United States, the Shepaug River towns harbored a certain religious constituency who equated the arrival of the fire-breathing steam locomotives with the coming of the devil. Then there were Yankee farmers who feared for their crops, their livestock, and their boundary fences. One day Major McNeill faced down a group of armed and angry farmers along the survey route. "It's all right, boys," he is reported to have said. "I've smelled powder before." But probably the strongest opposition arose from a kind of cultural conservatism, a fear that the remote valley would be invaded by "foreigners and 'smart alecks'" bent on relieving the natives of their cash and their way of life. The German mineworkers who came to chug beer and chase women at Colonel Hodge's Roxbury tavern were bad enough. But perhaps a more ominous threat to the settled order came from the city folk who would gawk at and buy up property in the valley.

The nativists and the forces of progress squared off in furious town meetings. A local satirist named John Champlin waded into the fight with a satirical pamphlet called "The Chronicles of Sirrom" (the inhabitants of Morris, you see, being especially backward). The forces of progress were represented by the Ydawaix. Opponents of the railroad were dubbed the Oldphogiz. Their leaders—easily identifiable to fellow townspeople—were Rawbutt the Pitchite, Inryeguzzle the Swampite, Bilklack the Evertite, and "Aumunstun whose surname is Blowah."

Champlin prophesied financial ruin if the Sirromites ever prevailed:

> And he [Inryeguzzle the Swampite] gathered
> Together all the hosts of the Oldphogiz
> And all the men of the valley of the Naugattog
> And arrayed them on the hill [Litchfield]
> Over and against the Ydawaix and the men of the
> Valley of the Shippog
>
> . . . .
>
> And all the lands on the King's Highway
> Flowed with milk and honey, and the
> People thereof ruled all the nations roundabout.
> But the land of Sirrom was desert and laid waste,
> And there was no habitation of man therein.

One by one, each of the five towns gave their votes to the Ydawaix, but not until December 1869 did the last of them, Roxbury, approve money for the railroad. Construction proceeded by fits and starts, delayed by debt, frost heaves, and assorted petty accidents. Then, as work progressed on the toughest obstacle of all—the 180-foot tunnel through solid rock near the Roxbury-Washington line—the blasting specialist, Glycerine Jack Booth, began to complain of stomach pains and general unwellness, and the work was delayed yet again. By the time the local doctor had finished with him, Glycerine Jack had delivered himself of a tapeworm measuring twenty-four feet and four inches, which for many years after reposed in a glass jar on the doctor's mantel, an object of great fascination to the residents of Washington. When Jack recovered, the work was finally completed, and the first locomotive chugged the thirty-one miles from Hawleyville to Litchfield on January 1, 1872—just in time for the final collapse of the Shepaug Spathic Iron and Steel Company three months later. People began to talk, as they had in earlier years in Dudleytown, of a Mine Hill curse.

The furnace might have had a fighting chance of survival, given the scarcity and value of its high-grade siderite ore. But Benjamin Silliman and the other Yale scientists who had surveyed the site had paid more attention to the quality and potential of the raw material than to the practical difficulty of getting it out of the ground by deep-shaft mining and then converting it into steel. The railroad might have saved it, but the railroad came too late. The two enterprises, in fact, suffered a kind of symbiotic failure. By the time McNeill's first train came through, the Roxbury furnace was in its death throes. By the time the furnace shut down, the Shepaug Valley Railroad couldn't even pay the interest on the second mortgage its directors had been forced to take out within weeks of its inaugural run. The financial panic of 1873 delivered the coup de grâce to both endeavors. The postwar boom was over, steel prices collapsed, and the Shepaug was one of the twenty-five railroads that failed in 1873.

Reconfigured, the Shepaug Valley Railroad managed to limp along for many years, but on the same parish-pump level as the few remaining ironworks. No longer the centerpiece of an industrial dream, it is remembered only for its quaint local charm—the kind of railroad whose engineers might descend from a train to pick wildflowers or return a stray sheep to its fold and then return to the cab, without ever having to break into a run. Instead of taking manufactured goods out, as Major McNeill and his backers had intended, the railroad ended up bringing them in—better-quality marble than was produced in the local quarries, desirable new consumer goods that arrived on the new magic carpet of mail order. But above all, as the Oldphogiz had feared, the railroad brought in people—and not just people, but New Yorkers: weekenders, artists, writers, and sportsmen who flocked to the newly opened inns, lodges, and fishing camps that offered "malaria-free, no mosquito" vaca-

tions among the rushing trout streams and alpine lakes of the Litchfield Hills.

You DON'T HAVE to believe in curses to find Mine Hill a haunted
place today. It's a monument to Victorian gothic architecture, and the
furnace complex—the best preserved of any in Connecticut—appears
half military, half ecclesiastical. The furnaces occupy a series of cleared
terraces on an incline above the narrow floodplain of the river, the abandoned railroad station, and Colonel Hodge's tavern. A hundred and
twenty five years after the last fires went out, the ground is still black with
charcoal, and when the breeze blows across the slopes, I would swear that
it brings with it a smell of burning wood, just as the charred fence posts
do in my Scottish garden.

The path uphill to the mine follows the old haulage road, raised artificially where the forest floor dips, in order to equalize the gradient
for the donkeys. The road is lined with young hemlocks and mountain
laurel. Higher up, deciduous trees—red oak, chestnut oak, black birch,
and red maple—take over, and higher still, around the entrance to the
mineshaft, hemlocks appear again, clinging tenaciously to the moss-
covered rocks. The last portion of the path is strewn with lumps of silvery
quartz, sparkling shards of mica, and chunks of siderite that range in
color from a pale cream to a deep chocolate brown. The mineshaft opens
at the base of a deep, V-shaped notch in the hillside. A sign suspended
over the tunnel mouth says: "DANGER—tunnel has numerous unmarked
vertical shafts—treacherous footing—unstable ceiling rock subject to cave-
ins—standing water up to four feet deep—unmaintained and unsafe iron
ladder and wooden supports—entry into this tunnel presents danger of
death or serious injury from these and other hazards. Entry is forbidden.
Violators will be prosecuted." The entrance is barred with a grille of
heavy, orange-painted iron bars, which deter vandals and reckless spe-
lunkers but allow access for thousands of bats—little brown, big brown,
pipistrelle, and northern long-eared—that winter in the abandoned tun-
nels. Beyond the grating are perpetual darkness, an ice-cold exhalation
from deep inside the hill, and a silence broken only by the steady, echoing
drip of water falling for long distances.

Local histories tell of the men who financed the mine, and owned
the mine, and disputed and litigated its ownership. There's a little about

the skilled furnace workers, who came from Prussia and Styria and were fired after the collapse of 1872, but nothing about the miners—who they were, how they lived, how they died. Staring into the silence of the mineshaft, I can hear old music playing in my head. It's the music of Scottish pipe bands, leading black-faced men with their miners' helmets and Davy lamps and embroidered union banners through the streets of my hometown on Miners' Gala Day. And the verses of an old folk song:

"Oh what will you give me?" say the sad bells of Rhymney.
"And who robbed the miner?" cry the grim bells of Blaina.

It would take a Henry James or an Edith Wharton to do justice to the society that the Ydawaix have built, in and around the town of Washington, in the 130 years since the first locomotive limped into the Shepaug Valley. The new arrivals found that Washington was in reality made up of four separate settlements. The new railroad depot was built by the river, in the place known as Factory Hollow. Above this on the hill, in classic New England fashion, was the Green. The surrounding farms were already in decline, or being turned into residential estates, and the Green was dominated by its two churches, Episcopal and Congregational, and the private Gunnery School, founded by a noted local abolitionist. To the north, the township embraced two more industrial hamlets: New Preston, a huddle of mills along the fast-flowing Aspetuck River, and Marbledale, named for its thriving quarries.

The newcomers, those who created the modern idea of Washington, so to speak, were rich and cultivated people, aristocrats in a country that claimed not to have any, and they set out, quite deliberately, to preserve an idealized vision of America in the Shepaug Valley. They saw themselves, in the words of Alison Gilchrist Picton of the Gunn Museum, as "the torchbearers of a great civilization, imbued with noblesse oblige." Across the hills in the valley of the Naugatuck was everything they despised—not the money, which they had in amounts to rival any of the brass barons, but the vulgarity, avarice, and filth of the mills. The nouveaux riches would not be made welcome in Arcadia.

An 1885 issue of the *Boston Evening Record* offered this appreciation of Washington, Connecticut:

> No hotels, no boarding-houses, no saloons, no unsightly fences, no loafers at street corners . . . a community in which every person is respectable and in which the test of respectability is not the possession of money, but good behavior, intelligence, and right living. . . . Even those who are rich are wholly averse to extravagance or ostentation. . . . Some of them have bought acres upon acres, not with a view to speculation, but to prevent the invasion by opulent barbarians of so tranquil and sterling a community. . . . Here, then, is a kind of Arcadia, peopled by intelligent folk. . . . Nor is this state of things likely to be broken in upon, for any objectionable person whose presence would cause discord would find it difficult to buy a building site here, had he ever so much money.

Embedded in this Arcadian vision were many of the new notions of conservationism that blossomed in the years following the Civil War. Thoreau had died in 1862, the same year as the passage of the Homestead Act, decrying America's "war with the wilderness."

But even as the wild lands were subdued, competing ideals were taking form. Yellowstone became a national park in 1872, and the New York State Constitution was amended in 1885 to ensure that a vast stretch of the Adirondacks would remain "forever wild." Of course, these schemes seem more grandiose than realistic in the narrower confines of Connecticut. As the *Boston Evening Record* makes apparent, what was at stake in Washington was a certain notion of the kind of rural landscape that ought to enfold a classic New England village. Yes, such a landscape should contain elements of wildness; the forests should be large enough, and dark enough, to get lost in. But the whole ensemble—the green, the village, the wooded hinterland—was ultimately well ordered and certainly did not include a threatening sort of wild space. And the conservationist impulse in Washington was not without a hint of—what would we say today?—NIMBYism, "not in my backyard."

VAN INGEN, Van Sinderen, Van Dyke. Some of the newcomers' names suggested where their families belonged in the social register. Edward Hook Van Ingen, a fabulously wealthy wool importer, was the first to fol-

low the railroad to Washington. Van Ingen bought up huge tracts of land
to guarantee a permanently unobstructed view of the Shepaug Valley. On
a hill above the river he built the Holiday House, where parties of young
women from the New York sweatshops were invited each summer for two
weeks of archery, croquet, masked balls, amateur theatricals, and morally
improving novels selected personally by Van Ingen's wife. They were
waited on by young African American men from another of Van Ingen's
philanthropic endeavors, the Hampton Institute in Virginia.

Van Sinderen was William Van Sinderen, another Croesus, who had
made his money importing sugar. Van Sinderen fell in love with a sheltered area of hills and farmland on the east side of the river, below an old
quartz mine. When the Spanish-American War ended in 1898, he heard
that the cavalry horses used by Teddy Roosevelt and his Rough Riders in
Cuba were to be sold at auction. So he went off with a hundred dollars in
his pocket, came back with four horses, and ordered his staff to lay out
forty miles of riding trails in and around his property, which he called
Hidden Valley, after a wild spot in Utah.

Van Dyke was Henry Van Dyke, Renaissance man, pastor of the
Brick Church on Fifth Avenue in Manhattan, profound theologian, renowned preacher, faculty member at Princeton, poet and essayist, president of the National Institute of Arts and Letters, devotee of Woodrow
Wilson, U.S. minister to The Hague during World War I, and one of the
country's most passionate conservationists. In 1906, the *Illustrated Outdoor News* named him as one of the ten greatest living American sportsmen, ranked just behind Teddy Roosevelt.

For their new homes, many Arcadian aristocrats turned to an architect named Ehrick Rossiter, who designed Van Ingen's Holiday House as
well as a score of colonial revival and shingle-style mansions for Washington's new elite. Even though some of the estates could have comfort-
ably rubbed shoulders with any piece of real estate in the country, the
Arcadians called them cottages, which sounded less ostentatious.

Rossiter himself was as ardent a conservationist as any of them. His
father had been an accomplished painter, a minor figure in the Hudson
River school. From him Rossiter inherited a yearning for an idealized
American landscape untouched by human hand, and he searched the
Shepaug Valley for the wildest-looking spot he could find. He chose a
boulder-covered six-acre plot of land near Steep Rock as the site for his

own house, which he called The Rocks. He liked to sit by the window at night and watch the thunderstorms flash their way down the narrow valley. Sometime in the early 1880s he learned that timber companies were preparing to buy up the huge stands of old-growth hemlock that covered Steep Rock. To forestall this disaster, Rossiter bought the land himself, and in 1925, after his retirement, he decided that the Steep Rock property should be preserved forever. You could walk for a week in Steep Rock and never take the same path twice. On the rockier outcrops are isolated patches of mountain laurel and rhododendron, but for the most part the dark hemlock canopy prevents sunlight from reaching the forest floor. Deciduous trees and smaller plants have no chance to thrive here, though young hemlock seedlings will sometimes push their way through in dense clusters where a deadfall opens a keyhole of sky. Otherwise, all that can grow in the shadow of the old hemlocks are moss and fern and ephemeral flowers such as lady's slipper and Indian pipe.

The deed of trust said that Rossiter and the Steep Rock trustees were "desirous of securing its preservation, improvement and maintenance for the use and enjoyment of citizens and residents of Washington and Litchfield County and of their guests and friends and of the general public." This expansive wording is not without later significance, for Litchfield County stretches clear to Waterbury and includes the industrial towns of the upper Naugatuck Valley. Cast a circular net from Steep Rock, with a radius of a hundred miles, and you would catch a tenth of the general public of the United States.

Steep Rock was a precursor of the land trust movement that exploded in New England in the 1980s, in response to the reduction in federal funding for land acquisition and the Reagan administration's threat to develop public land, including wilderness areas. Steep Rock's holdings grew steadily from the nucleus of Ehrick Rossiter's original bequest. The Van Sinderens made a gift of Hidden Valley. The Van Ingens donated the Holiday House property (now demolished) and the forests and fields around it. One parcel at a time, about a dozen other Washington families added properties until the Steep Rock Reservation expanded to its present size of more than fifteen hundred acres. Broken only by the small town of Washington Depot, it is an otherwise continuous ribbon of undeveloped forest land, enfolding a glorious trout stream, which is impaired only by the fact that for close to seventy years it has run dry every summer.

8
There but for Fortune

THERE IS ALWAYS A ROAD TAKEN and a road not taken. At the end of the Civil War, the furnaces of the Monongahela were in about the same shape as those of the Housatonic. Birmingham, Alabama, had a handful of struggling ironworks whose product was so soft, it was known as "rotten iron." By 1872, however, the Mine Hill dream was dead. In 1893, the Buena Vista furnace on the Hollenbeck River went out of blast. The Cornwall Bridge Iron Company fell silent four years later. By the end of the century, though a few straggling furnaces tried to soldier on, the Housatonic's dominance of the U.S. ironmaking industry had run its course.

Looking back on periods of grand historical change, it's always tempting to reduce them to abstractions. But the industrial revolution didn't roll through America on wheels, any more than did one of Walt Landgraf's glaciers, bringing uniform effects to every town, every valley, every river. It's a lot more complicated than that, and at many junctures in the history of the Housatonic, the Shepaug, and the Naugatuck, things could easily have gone the other way, and for many different reasons.

It was not just heavy industry that collapsed in the Housatonic Valley in the years after the Civil War. The farm economy and the traditional mill economy both fell apart as well. In a book of local history called *Empire over the Dam,* by Kenneth T. Howell and Einar W. Carlson, I found an old New England saying: "As a farmer he is a good miller, and as a miller he is a good farmer." In other words, the mill owners of the Housatonic Valley were badly compromised from the start by trying to wear two hats. Most critically, they failed to make the shift from waterpower to steam. In part this reflected a lack of capital and adequate lines of credit. It also had to do with the absence of fuel (whatever Major McNeill might have said to seduce his investors, the Pennsylvania coalfields were most definitely *not* right next door to the Shepaug Valley).

But the failure of the mills also resulted from the cultural conservatism that had led the Oldphogiz to oppose the Shepaug Valley Railroad. Reluctant to move away from the limited range of products that their grandfathers had made, the Housatonic Valley millers failed to develop markets beyond their local communities. To make matters worse, their archaic water-powered mills were at the mercy of fluctuating seasonal flows. Glaciated rivers, fed by precipitation rather than groundwater springs, had been causing a problem since the earliest settlement—in 1740, one Josiah Walker, who built the first gristmill at the Great Falls, had been granted rights to "ye commanding part of ye Stream in scarce time of Water." But after more than a hundred years of farming, deforestation, and soil depletion, summertime water levels had fallen lower than anyone could remember.

A steady rural exodus began after the Civil War, with the population of the Northwest Corner declining by about 20 percent between 1850 and 1920. Half as many people live in Falls Village today as lived there in 1850. Cornwall still has roughly the same number of residents as it had in 1800. Some moved to the cities to find work. Others moved to the West in search of easier farming, joining a frontier population that was more disposed to risk taking. Skilled ironworkers were raided by the new steelworks in Pennsylvania, Ohio, and the Lake Superior ranges.

Any one of a dozen factors might have been enough to cripple the Connecticut iron industry, but all of them together were lethal. The trout pool paradox no longer tilted in the direction of the iron industry. The trout streams were still there, but their flows were diminished. The limestone was still there, but it served an outmoded technology that could not compete with the high-volume production of the new ore fields. The forest canopy had all but disappeared, and with it the charcoal. But charcoal had been supplanted by coal anyway, and of that there was none.

STILL, two men might have bucked the trend. One might plausibly have turned Falls Village into a booming armaments center; the other might single-handedly have stopped the slide and built Pittsburgh on the Housatonic. The potential armaments king was Horatio Ames, a huge, rotund man obsessed with the idea of building a gigantic cannon that could deliver a knockout blow to the Confederacy by sinking its ironclads. He persuaded his friend Abraham Lincoln to commission fifteen of these monsters, each able to fire hundred-pound projectiles. By early 1865, he had completed two and was at work on the remainder, having gone deep into debt in the process. But then, on April 9, the news reached Falls Village that Robert E. Lee had surrendered at Appomattox. And for the Ames ironworks, that was the end of that.

Meanwhile, early in the Civil War, Alexander Lyman Holley of Salisbury had traveled to Europe to refine his ideas about the military applications of iron and steel. In the steel-making city of Sheffield, England, he met a man named Henry Bessemer, who was working to perfect a revolutionary conversion process that would oxidize impurities in iron by blasting air into the furnace under enormous pressure. Holley worked closely with the Englishman to improve the process and eventually acquired the U.S. patents. But rather than introduce the technology in his hometown of Salisbury, he chose to open the first Bessemer process plant in the United States in Troy, New York, thereby helping to kill off the Connecticut industry rather than saving it. This seems a quixotic decision, given the manufacturing infrastructure already in place in Salisbury and Falls Village. But when Holley was asked why he had acted as he did, he is reported to have said, "Because I love Salisbury so much." Again, translated into the contemporary vernacular, it reads, "Not in my backyard."

Did Holley really say that? Or is it just a piece of local apocrypha? After all, no solid primary sources exist to corroborate it. But in a sense, the question misses the point. Since people believed, or chose to believe, that this was what he said, it helped condition their own subsequent decisions about the town and its surroundings. It became, so to speak, part of the self-conscious rural ideology of the place.

As LONG AS the water of the Housatonic continued to tumble over the limestone ledges at Falls Village, the temptation toward new industry never entirely disappeared. Some of the schemes appear simply insane today, such as the aborted plan to open up the entire river to development by blasting a seventy-mile barge canal out of its bed, from tidewater at Derby all the way up to the Great Falls. That never happened.

But a mile-long, three-level diversion canal did get built in the 1840s, in order to drive a triple-decker factory complex, which would in turn make Falls Village "a second Holyoke." This one really belongs in a book of heroic failures. Not that the finished work isn't impressive. You can still see one level of it, in fact. The modern concrete canal is built on the bed of the old one, and some of the massive, original stone walls remain intact. I walked up there one day, across the iron catwalks above the powerhouse. A grizzled old man and his daughter were spin fishing next to their pickup truck. Their lines and bobbers dangled in the dark flow of water that feeds the Falls Village penstocks. They didn't appear to be catching anything. In 1851, to great fanfare, the townspeople assembled on this spot for the inauguration of the canal. The gate above the falls was opened, the diverted water flowed from the river as it was supposed to, and it ran along the trench. The only snag was that it ran straight out again, since the engineers had neglected to seal the bottom of the canal.

For three decades or so the Housatonic flowed past abandoned factories and ruined dam sites, more or less on its own terms. It took a long time for investor confidence to recover from the canal fiasco, and the dream of developing heavy industry in situ was never seriously revived. What happened instead was a kind of industrialization at one remove. Let me explain.

After railroads and steel, the next wave of technological innovation was electrical power, which burst upon the United States in the 1880s. It had a paradoxical effect on the Housatonic, both blighting the natural flow of the river and sparing the landscape of the valley. From the modest size of the five hydropower plants on the river today, nobody would guess that the Housatonic was in fact the birthplace of American hydropower. It was Housatonic water, in fact, that drove the country's first long-distance transmission of electricity over power lines.

By 1904, there was a power plant at Canaan in Connecticut, above the Great Falls, and another at Bull's Bridge. The Berkshire Power Company dam at Canaan was a wee thing, selling enough electricity to be sold by the bulb, and by the month, to small towns within a twelve-mile radius, with no bulb to be illuminated before sunset or after midnight. Falls Village, built a few years later, was a little bigger, but still produced only enough power to illuminate eight small communities in Litchfield County. The Bull's Bridge plant, with its twin smokestacks, was a more robust affair. Indeed, at the time it was built, in 1904, it was one of the largest hydropower plants in the United States.

But the most imposing dams on the Housatonic lie farther downstream. The largest of the five, in fact the largest in the state, is the Shepaug Dam, which impounds the Housatonic for the thirteen miles of Lake Lillinonah, backs up another three miles into the Shepaug Valley, as far as Roxbury Falls, and generates forty-three thousand kilowatts of power. Ten miles farther south is the Stevenson Dam. Even Chard Powers Smith, old Yankee curmudgeon that he was, was forced to admire Stevenson, which was built in 1919 just a few hundred yards above the confluence with Eight Mile Brook. Stevenson had its own kind of beauty, Smith thought, "comparable to that of any valley or mountain or natural waterfall." It was "comparable in height and imperial aspect to the show dams of the West." This is poetic license, to be honest. Stevenson rises seventy feet from the valley floor, less than a tenth of the height of the biggest western dams. But in the cramped surroundings of Connecticut, one has to make some allowance for scale.

These long-distance transmission lines turned out to be the upper river's final salvation from industry. The power that flowed out of the Housatonic hydropower plants didn't spawn adjacent factory towns, not at Falls Village or Bull's Bridge, not at the Shepaug or the Stevenson. Instead, the power marched across the Litchfield Hills on pylons, lighting the urban slums and driving the "Satanic Mills" along the Naugatuck, a fact from which Chard Powers Smith derived great satisfaction.

THE UNEXPECTED traffic jam that prevents someone from catching a doomed flight; the chance encounter with a person on the subway that gives you a cold—these events have their equivalents in the natural world and human political economy. Use of rivers changes with social priorities; an expression of our current philosophy might be that we used to trash rivers, then we learned our lesson, and now we try harder to take care of them. But it's a lot more complicated than that. The question "What if?" clings to nineteenth-century industrial history like mist to a hillside, and it sticks to our contemporary choices in much the same way.

What if Alexander Lyman Holley hadn't said, in effect, "Not in my backyard"? What if the Civil War had started a year earlier, or a year later? What if the canal engineers had not suffered a mental lapse? What

if the litigation over the ownership of Mine Hill hadn't been so pro-
tracted, and the mine and furnace had gone into production earlier?
What if it hadn't rained so much in a particular summer? What if mad
Major McNeill had managed to complete his railroad on schedule? The
laws of economics were at work here, but so were the laws of physical
topography, geology, and glaciation. The Shepaug Valley Railroad, for
instance, was delayed for three years by the difficulty of attracting investment capital and the ambivalence of old Yankee farmers. But its completion was also slowed by the hard gneiss that had to be blasted away and
the narrowness of the Shepaug floodplain and the interminable bends in
the river. And it was also delayed by Glycerine Jack's tapeworm.

How are we to calibrate the relative importance of these things?
How are we to weigh Alexander Lyman Holley's sentimental attachment
to the hills of Salisbury against the cold economic logic of technology?
Whim and accident against nature and intention? And if things had gone
a different way, just fractionally, and at a particular moment, would sophisticated New Yorkers be spending their weekends today in Waterbury,
rather than one valley over in Washington?

9
Dark Satanic Mills

FROM THE BRIDGE OVER THE SHEPAUG at the entrance to Hidden Valley to the old Bray's Buckle Dam at the confluence of the Naugatuck and Mad rivers is about as far as it's possible to travel in the state of Connecticut, even though it's barely fifteen miles as the crow flies. Distance can be measured in other ways.

At the corner of Washington Street, someone has put up a wishful sign that says, "Mad River Industrial Park." At the bottom of the sign, it says, "Site of *Stanley and Iris,* 1989." I'd never seen the movie, but I remembered it vaguely. Jane Fonda, Robert De Niro. Widow meets illiterate factory worker; she teaches him to read; they fall in love. I went to the local video store to rent a copy. It opened with a long panning shot across the Waterbury skyline, the sawtooth roofs of the abandoned mills, the wooden homes of mill workers scaling the hillsides. In the first twenty minutes, we trudged through a mugging, domestic violence, teen pregnancy, homelessness, and unemployment. I could see right away what question and answer had gone through the director's mind: "Where do you set a story like that? Waterbury."

Not that the city had ever been the kind of place that would make the cover of *House and Garden,* at least not for the past two hundred years. In 1938, writers for the Works Progress Administration came to Waterbury. In the WPA guide to the state of Connecticut, they wrote: "Black iron and yellow firebrick stacks tower above the casting shops and rolling mills, throwing off saffron-yellow and greenish clouds of smoke.

. . . The speckled brown and granite-grey hillsides have been stripped of all except third-growth saplings."

Waterbury was the focus of hearings in Washington, D.C., in the early 1980s, chosen to concentrate the minds of Congress on the phenomenon of urban blight. The city government was the object of one federal corruption probe after another. In 1992 Waterbury was ranked at the top in *Money* magazine's survey of the one hundred most unlivable cities in America. Some people associate Waterbury with the phrase "two more hours" because that's all you can find to say when you pass it on the interstate, more or less halfway between Boston and New York.

THE FIRST TIME I ever saw Waterbury was at night. What most caught my attention, as I sped past on I-84, was the gigantic illuminated cross on a hill above the Mad River. The opposite side of the river was occupied in those days by the Scovill Manufacturing Company, one of the "Big Three" Waterbury brass companies, whose plant stretched for fully a mile along the riverbank. Years later, I learned that the windswept eminence where the cross stood was called Pine Hill. Someone told me the local joke: Waterbury kids were the only ones who grew up believing that Jesus Christ was electrocuted for their sins. By then I was spending a lot of time poking around in the neighborhood at the foot of Pine Hill, which seemed to me to encapsulate, in a few blocks, everything that had gone wrong with the city of Waterbury.

Some people still called the neighborhood by its old name, Abrigado. Others called it the Abrigador—to rhyme with *alligator*. It's one of the earliest settled parts of Waterbury, a city of discrete, almost self-contained ethnic neighborhoods. No one quite seems to know where the name came from, although to a Spanish speaker it appears obvious: *abrigado* means "the sheltered place," which makes sense because it sits in the lee of Pine Hill, encircled by the last sweeping bend of the Mad River.

Spanish then and Spanish now. This is the Waterbury barrio nowadays. Access to the Mad River is blocked off with chainlink fences. Signs on the fences say, *"Aquifero del Río Loco—No Basura."* Others say, "Danger Asbestos—Cancer and Lung Disease Hazard—Authorized Personnel Only—Respirators and Protective Clothing Are Required in This Area." On the walls of a half-demolished brass mill there is gang graffiti in

Spanish. Standing on the Washington Street Bridge, I narrow my eyes, filter out the past hundred years, and try to see salmon spawning grounds in the gravel bed of the Mad River.

The Puerto Ricans are recent arrivals in Waterbury. Today they make up more than a tenth of the city's population. They came here after World War II to do the jobs that no one else would touch—hauling eighty-pound lead molds or melting down tires at the Uniroyal plant in Naugatuck. Their dream was *un buen trabajo* on the floor at Scovill's. The Latino migrants concentrated in Waterbury's South End, where they jostled for space with the older generations of European immigrants and built Spanish-language churches, clubs, restaurants, and movie theaters. But the building of the interstate in the 1960s cut off the South End from the rest of the city, and urban renewal devastated most of what remained.

WHILE LOCAL PHILOLOGISTS may quibble about the meaning of Abrigado, the origins of the Indian name for the town of Waterbury—Mattatuck—are less problematic. It means "the place without trees," "the poorly wooded place," which gives you a sense of its rocky geography when the settlers arrived. The English name is even more self-explanatory. There's no real floodplain in much of the Naugatuck Valley except for the lower reaches of the present-day city. Then suddenly there's water everywhere. Waterbury (like the neighboring settlements of Watertown and Waterville) doesn't just refer to the Naugatuck River, but to a whole plethora, one historian noted, of "rivulets, ponds, swamps, boggy meadows and wet lands."

Arriving in the isolated and inhospitable valley in the 1670s, the first scouts from the Hartford colony found six hundred acres of "meadow and plowing land lying on both sides of ye river." That turned out to be a hasty judgment. The "meadows" where the community was supposed to produce its food were a long, steep hike from the plot of land they had set aside for housing. And the hillsides were rocky and unproductive, as they were over to Cornwall. Soon a local saying emerged: "You couldn't grow a nettle in the Naugatuck Valley." The General Assembly of Connecticut determined that the site was capable of supporting thirty families, no more. The settlers started off on the steeper west side of the river but quickly switched banks when they realized that they would have no escape route if hostile Indians chose to attack them during one of the Naugatuck's frequent floods. In a sense, the town had too much water and too little water at the same time. There was water everywhere, but it wasn't *useful* water. The Naugatuck flooded all the time, sometimes disastrously, as in 1691, when the alluvial farmland was ruined. The area chosen for securing the growth of the settlement was full of standing water—bogs and marshes and frog ponds and cattail swamps. Mosquitoes thrived better in these conditions than people did, and in 1712 disease wiped out thirty of the two hundred inhabitants of Waterbury.

If Waterbury and the Naugatuck are cursed today by the ugliness of their industrial past, they were cursed in the first place by the conditions that made them so physically beautiful—another manifestation, if you like, of the trout pool paradox. Timothy Dwight, who came here in 1798 and again in 1802, immediately appreciated the aesthetics of the river, the geological oddities of its steep-sided hills of metamorphic bedrock, its industrial potential, and its hazards.

> Its size is that of the Lower Ammonoosuc [in Maine], its length about fifty miles, its current rapid; and when swollen by freshets, as it often is, very suddenly, violent and destructive. It furnishes a great number of excellent mill seats, and is in many places lined with beautiful intervals. Notwithstanding the roughness of the country through which it passes, its bed is worn so deep and to so uniform a surface that from Waterbury northward one of the smoothest and most level turnpike roads in the state has been formed on its banks.

These quirks of geology gave the town a huge, if unorthodox, competitive advantage. Since it had lots of fast water but no good farmland, nothing distracted the valley's settlers from the business of the mills. Relieved of the "two hats" problem that had undermined the farming-milling economy in the rest of the Housatonic watershed, shrewd industrialists such as Abel Porter quickly developed a skilled and specialized workforce. Porter and his associates were convinced that customers wanted more than the cheap tinware offered by the Yankee peddler and decided that an enormous untapped market existed for goods made of a more durable and attractive metal, such as brass. Nothing pretentious—just mundane, everyday items such as buttons.

Such a simple thing, a button. Everyone needs them, to hold their pants up, to secure the cuffs of their shirts, to keep jackets from blowing open in the wind. Buttons were one of the easiest ways to embellish clothing cheaply or make neighbors aware of your social rank. Great fortunes would be made out of the manufacture of buttons.

The great strength of the brass industry was its stability. An unpretentious, functional industry, it produced, as one writer said, "articles of use rather than luxury," not specialized products that might fall victim to changing fashions. Anything from a small electric motor to a battleship needed components made of brass. Brass could be fashioned into lawn sprays and pipe ferrules, curtain fasteners and light fittings, bedsprings and handcuffs. Brass made upholstery nails, rivets and screws, hinges, washers, and cotter pins. Brass was used for oil cans, belt buckles, and paper clips; for chandelier chains, kerosene burners, and gas mantles; for umbrella spokes, fishing reels, and shell casings. To make all these things, Waterbury needed casting shops, rolling mills, forging shops, extrusion shops, refining mills, and machine shops.

The smaller valley towns made their own specialized contributions to the industrial boom. Thomaston, named after the cantankerous inventor Seth Thomas, was the center of the clock industry. The model factory town of Humphreysville, which had helped Thomas Jefferson overcome his resistance to industry, changed its name to Seymour and produced fountain pens and wire. Union City made castings for guns and pistols. The ironmaker Francis Newman Holley of Salisbury came to Torrington in 1837 and started the Union Hardware Company, which mass-produced tens of thousands of pairs of cheap ice skates and fishing tackle.

The town of Naugatuck, meanwhile, once regarded as one of the prettiest in New England, became the hub of the U.S. rubber industry. The person responsible for the transformation was Charles Goodyear, whose parents had moved to Naugatuck from New Haven when he was a child. It was in Naugatuck that Goodyear vulcanized his first pair of rubber overshoes, in a workshop near the future site of the Goodyear Metallic Rubber Shoe Company and the Goodyear India Rubber Glove Company. Shoes were all that Goodyear made until 1851, when he unleashed a mind-boggling array of rubber goods on an incredulous world at the Crystal Palace Exhibition in London. Goodyear's Vulcanite Court was a complete suite of rooms, with roof, walls, furniture, carpets, and draperies all made out of rubber, as well as rubber combs, buttons, earrings, balloons, and musical instruments. By the time of World War I, Naugatuck

81. NAUGATUCK. CONN. Our Rubber Factories   Perry Press, Publishers

had fifteen thousand people and sixty-six factories and was turning out sixty thousand pairs of rubber shoes and boots every day. The Naugatuck Chemical Company produced sulfuric and hydrochloric acids, and in 1914 it bestowed on the world the dubious gift of that vinyl-covered fabric known as Naugahyde.

WILLIAM PAPE, editor of the Waterbury newspaper and a civic booster, noted in 1918 that his city "had no natural advantages—absolutely none." Yet it had ridden out the Depression of the 1890s, the competitive threat from the Midwest, and the menace of hostile takeovers by the new faceless trusts. With striking prescience, Pape wrote of his fears: "Our industries might be gathered into the grasp of giant corporations whose controlling spirits, destitute alike of local affiliations and decency of sentiment, would cold-bloodedly close down many factories on the ground that Waterbury was not a logical site for an industry."

Something very much like this would happen half a century later, when the brass industry went into its terminal decline. For now, however, Waterbury's dominance was simply so great that it could withstand all challengers. Seventy-five percent of all the country's brass was made in Connecticut, and half of it came from the town of Waterbury.

William Pape's Waterbury reeked of civic pride, and its leading men were determined that their local affiliations and decency of sentiment would be properly memorialized in stone. The results are beautiful, if selectively so. As long as you don't stray more than a couple of blocks into the surrounding neighborhoods, you will probably find the civic heart of Waterbury—the Green, Grand Street, and Library Park—as handsome and harmonious a display of early-twentieth-century monumental architecture as you will find anywhere in New England. Above this, on the hill, the brass men built their mansions, in a riot of gables and turrets and cupolas and Elizabethan chimney stacks.

William Pape's Waterbury was a place where 125,000 people—more than the total population—turned out for the inauguration of a grand new city hall of Vermont marble, flanked by eighteen-foot-tall ornamental brass lamp standards and decorated with bas-relief medallions symbolizing Truth, Prudence, Industry, Commerce, Force, Law, Justice, Wisdom, and Order. The leading men of the city milled around in their Masonic lodges and temples, electing each other chancellor commander, prelate, outer and inner guard, noble grand, patriarch militant, generalissimo, excellent high priest, sentinel, illustrious master, potent master, worshipful master, most puissant grand master, dictator, and vice-dictator.

When the automobile came of age, these dictators and vice-dictators set about marketing Waterbury and the Naugatuck as "the Gateway to New England," the first stop in an "Ideal Tour" that would take the adventurous motorist all the way to New Hampshire's White Mountains. Of course, there were some inconvenient aspects to this, but the leading men of Waterbury breezed right past them. A brochure advertising the tour said, "The Naugatuck Valley is dotted here and there with busy towns—whose factories make most of the brass used in the world—yet for many miles at a time one passes through almost primeval forests. . . . The very nature of these portions of the valley prohibits the despoliation of man, and so lends the valley in all of its wild and rugged beauty to the lover of nature and the motor car."

Motorists could enjoy the scenery but avert their eyes, and hold their noses, as the road wound through sad, noisome places such as Beacon Falls and Naugatuck, and look forward at the end of the day to a hot, relaxing bath, a brandy and soda, and the attentive staff of the luxury Elton Hotel in Waterbury, "a rare combination of city beautiful and manufacturing town."

I STOPPED IN West Cornwall one day to have lunch with Jeremy Brecher at the Wandering Moose Café, next to the red covered bridge. Brecher grew up in Cornwall and still lives in its bucolic hills. But he is the leading modern historian of the Waterbury brass industry and the author of an important history of American labor unions called *Strike!* A bundle of barely contained energy, scarcely able to sit still as he eats, Brecher tugs at his straggly ginger beard and delights in the tumbling flow of his own ideas. According to Brecher, the most striking thing about the brass unions is that they divided not by plant or by production activity but by ethnic origin. The Naugatuck Valley was a multinational, multiethnic, polyglot place, but it was in no sense a melting pot. Largely as a matter of choice, its different nationalities lived in self-imposed linguistic and cultural enclaves. The first immigrants to the mills were the Irish, fleeing the potato famine of 1846–1847. Within twenty years seventy thousand foreign-born Irish resided in the state of Connecticut. Next came the English, then the Germans.

Italians began to settle in Connecticut in the 1870s, when the first hundred arrived in New Haven. The main wave followed between 1900 and 1916, when the state's Italian population swelled to sixty thousand. By World War II, that number had almost quadrupled. After the Italians came large numbers of Poles, and then Lithuanians, more than thirty thousand of them, most to work in the brass industry and then, during World War I, in the mushrooming munitions factories. The town of Naugatuck was, and in many respects still is, a largely Portuguese town, settled originally by migrants from the fishing village of Murtosa, where the traditional source of income had been the collection of seaweed for fertilizer. In 1916, the State Bureau of Labor found that women of fifty-seven different nationalities were working in the valley's munitions plants—Ruthenians and Romanians, Serbs and Croats, Moravians and Albanians, Slovaks and Montenegrins.

It is the Italians—one quarter of the population of modern Waterbury—who have left the most distinct physical stamp on these towns, which are full of churches and front-yard plaster saints and sorrowing Virgins. The urban landscape of rundown towns such as Waterbury, Torrington, and Winsted is still heavy with pizza joints and store signs in red, white, and green. Sad places such as Ansonia and Thomaston have flamboyant opera houses, built with the proceeds of the brass boom.

There was never a single Little Italy in Waterbury. Italians always dominated Town Plot, the section established by the first settlers, but a strong Italian presence also flourished in the South End and along the west bank of the Naugatuck in the neighborhood called Brooklyn. The *piemontesi* and northern Italians lived in the East End, speaking their own dialects and keeping pretty much to themselves. Town Plotters went to mass at Our Lady of Mount Carmel; Brooklynites, Italian and Irish alike, went to St. Patrick and St. Joseph; South Enders attended Our Lady of Lourdes, presided over by Fathers Scoglio and Botticelli. Ortone's pastry shop on South Main was a favorite after mass; afterward, you could stroll past Sabatini's grocery, Carissimi's ice cream parlor, and Crocco's bakery, or maybe take in a movie at the Sirica family's theater, the Lido. There were Bianchini the chicken man and Poggi the egg man, Milano who imported cheese and sausage, Piola who carved headstones. You could buy a cigar at Nardiello's or Varanelli's. If you were still hungry, you could sample one of the legendary grinders at Nardelli's or take in one of the restaurants on Bank Street—Salvatore's, Gallo's, Mecca's, D'Angelo's, or, for a special occasion, Diorio's, the fanciest of them all, with its mahogany bankers' booths and embossed tin ceilings. In summertime, for a few weeks, the stores up and down South Main would sell grapes for homemade wine, to sip of an evening in the backyard arbor— *sotto la pergola*—with a few *paesani*.

The Italians were determinedly organized. In the archives of Waterbury's Mattatuck Museum I found a list of all the Italian American organizations that had ever been established in the city. I was astonished by the number—137, starting in 1891 with the Società Vittorio Emanuele. Most were mutual-aid societies that looked out for newcomers from the same region of the old country—the Circolo Filantropico Toscano, the Società Frigentina di Mutuo Soccorso San Rocco, the Daughters of Abruzzi, the Aviglianese Athletic Club. But it took the Italians many years to climb the slippery pole to city government, and these associations were a reasonable response to their exclusion from the political arena. For years the machine was Irish, and its prerogatives were jealously guarded. Many Italians changed their names in an attempt to get ahead. In the 1920s and 1930s, one Italian resident recalled, "It seemed, as I looked around Waterbury, that every position was held by an Irish or a Yankee—teachers, policemen, firemen—just about every job of importance seemed to be held by the Irish." The mill workers' triple-decker houses of the Abrigador were solidly Irish in those days. "You couldn't cross the Baldwin Street Bridge unless you were Irish," a former resident remembered, "or you'd get stoned to death."

I asked Jeremy Brecher about the city's political system and why it had become such a byword for corruption. He explained that the city had a kind of dual or parallel power structure. "What really mattered to the Waterbury elites was shaping the economic investment strategies. So the real power didn't lie with city hall, but with the boards. The water board was critical, for example, and it was run by the brass magnates, who brought in their own engineers. They regarded city government as very unimportant in comparison. The attitude was, 'If you want a job with a pick and shovel, go see someone else. The Irish can have all that stuff that depends on patronage. But if you want to put in a reservoir or a highway, go see Mr. Chase or Mr. Kingsbury [the Scovill company president].' That was where the real power lay."

Eventually, new generations of Italians began to contest the Irish monopoly on city hall, using their clubs and associations to turn mutual assistance into Republican votes. You scratch my back, I'll scratch yours, *paesano*. Not until the 1980s did they manage to capture city hall, and then not always with the most conventional candidates. In 1985 they came up with Joseph Santopietro, a twenty-six-year-old lawn maintenance man; four years later he was in a federal prison on eighteen counts of conspiracy, embezzlement, bank fraud, bribe taking, and tax evasion. Santopietro's term as mayor briefly interrupted the seven-term mayoralty of Edward D. Bergin Jr., itself a long-running soap opera. But the law finally caught up with Bergin, too. In the end he was acquitted of corruption charges, but his political career ended for good in 1995, when he lost to another brash young Italian American, this one a thirty-two-year-old shoemaker's son named Phil Giordano.

People said many things about Phil Giordano. His friends used adjectives like *charismatic* or *fiercely competitive*. His enemies (and he made plenty of them) preferred *arrogant* or *abrasive*. Even his staunchest supporters would concede that the new mayor was "a colorful character." It was widely known that he had been booted out of Holy Cross High School for spending more time stoned than studying. Under his photograph in the class yearbook, he had written the sentence "Without chemicals, life would be impossible." But putting chemicals behind him, Giordano had joined the marines and gone to law school. He had moved up in the world, marrying a nice Italian girl, the daughter of a construction magnate from Long Island. They lived in an architect-designed ranch house in the hills by the Waterbury Country Club, with a double front door with frosted glass panels and a carriage lamp on a stone pillar outside—a long way from the mean streets of the North End where he had grown up. And if Phil Giordano still had a tendency to head out into the night on his Harley-Davidson and cruise the bars for coeds, well, after all, those were the Clinton years, and the Republicans of Waterbury were more worldly than all those stiff-necked Southern Baptist fanatics down in Washington, D.C. Above all, there was no evidence that Phil Giordano was *corrupt,* and that was a word that had clung to his predecessors in city hall like *white* to *rice.*

A ND WHAT OF the cross on top of Pine Hill? Like those on the Empire State Building, the lights on the cross used to change color. Not for Gay Pride Week or the Fourth of July, however, but following the cycles of the liturgical calendar. Lent was purple, Advent was red. Originally, I discovered, the logic of the color changes had been different, reflecting the wishes of the man who built the cross in 1956, a Waterbury lawyer named John Greco.

I drove up Pine Hill from the barrio to see the cross one day, past a tiny parcel of state land, with a portable toilet on which someone had spray-painted the message "Fuck Yuo," and up to a stucco archway marked "Holy Land U.S.A." These same words—*Holy Land U.S.A.,* I mean—appear on a large Hollywood-style sign on the hillside that was repainted blue by a troop of Eagle Scouts a couple of years ago. Why here? I wondered.

Maybe the hill was no good for anything else. Although it had taken its name from a stand of white pines that had once stood at the summit, little but stunted grasses and bushes grew here now. Pine Hill had been devastated by years of smoke from the chimneys of the Scovill brass plant on the other side of the Mad River. Students from the Yale School of Forestry have for the past thirty years been studying the hill as an object lesson in what heavy metal residues do to soil and plant life. John Greco had decided that he would buy this barren lump of contaminated rock, which he thought bore a striking resemblance to the topography of the Holy Land, and turn it into something useful and uplifting.

Like Phil Giordano, Greco was the son of a shoemaker. He had early thoughts of becoming a priest, but his ambitions were frustrated by poor health. Greco led a group of fervent Waterburians who called themselves Catholic Campaigners for Christ; they wanted to return the world to piety in response to the mortal threat of international communism. Almost all of them were Italian. John Greco was a lawyer, but the others in the group were from humbler professions: a liquor salesman, a brass worker, an electrician, a brakeman on the New Haven Railroad, and a Lithuanian who ran a tire shop. They decided that what Waterbury needed to stiffen its faith was a gigantic Peace Cross made of stainless steel, fifty-two feet tall, and illuminated by neon. It helps to remember the context. In 1954, without opposition, the U.S. Congress added the phrase "under God" to the Pledge of Allegiance. A year later, Disneyland opened. In Holy Land U.S.A. the two impulses came together.

The lights of the cross went on and off in sequence as Catholics gathered around for the inauguration, saying their rosaries and praying for the conversion of godless Russia. White symbolized the innocence of victims behind the Iron Curtain, John Greco told them. Red was the blood they had shed. Purple represented the prayers and penance that the people of Waterbury would offer up for them. Green stood for the hope of Christian victory over the forces of evil.

Though undoubtedly a pious man, John Greco, it seems, was not an especially happy one. I found a hand-lettered sign near the entrance to Holy Land U.S.A. that said, "Measure Suffering in Terms of Heaven and Eternity." Farther along the overgrown path was another: "I will put emnities [*sic*] between thee and the woman, thy seed and her seed, she shall crush thy head and thou shalt lie in wait for her heel (Genesis 3:8)." There were two hundred statues and—what shall I call them?—dioramas made of cement, plasterboard, and chicken wire. Some appeared to be built on a foundation of discarded kitchen appliances. John Greco constructed the place with his own hands, getting what he needed by scavenging or by charitable donations. If people were tearing down a church, he'd ask for the altar rails. If someone was throwing out a desk lamp, he'd turn the metal shade upside down and turn it into a chalice for one of his tableaux. He'd get discarded stick-on gold letters from the hardware store and turn them into biblical quotations. He'd find old mannequins from Waterbury clothing stores and dress them up as the devil and the Virgin Mary, as need dictated.

You can visit Herod's palace here and the tomb of Rachel, and you can walk the Stations of the Cross. You can see a reconstruction of the entire town of Bethlehem, or what remains of it. The wise men's plaster camels have lost their heads, but come to that, so have the great majority of the apostles. There used to be a giant fiberglass Bible, permanently open to the Ten Commandments, but that's gone, too. The catacombs were once reputed to contain a handwritten list of all the popes up to 1978 and an exhibit centered on an "actual photograph of Christ." In the 1960s, they say, forty thousand visitors a year flocked here in tour buses to see John Greco's wonderland of piety. A couple from Columbus, Ohio, wrote him a letter that said: "We have visited forty-four of our states, most of them several times, but have seen very few things that would excell [*sic*] what you have there. That statement includes 'Disneyland,' 'Six Flags over Texas,' 'San Juan Capistrano,' 'Knott's Berry Farm,' 'Wisconsin Dells,' etc."

Nowadays, hardly anyone comes to Holy Land but the drug dealers. I had heard that someone had found two pit bulls chained to a tree near the Peace Cross, with food, water, and kennels nearby, but no other signs of human presence. So I jumped when I heard footsteps behind me, but it was only an old man in Coke-bottle glasses, shuffling along the overgrown path, lost in his thoughts.

10
The High Cost of Brass

On the way back down from Holy Land, I pulled in to buy a couple of things at Brass Mill Commons, the vast new mall that has brought JCPenney and Eddie Bauer and the Gap and Victoria's Secret to the channelized banks of the Mad River, on the old site of the Scovill Manufacturing Company. By chance, I found a photo exhibit on the company displayed in the downstairs walkway. One panel was taken up by a large, undated quotation from Scovill's former president, Frederick J. Kingsbury. It said, "While our present hours of labor are shorter, our work is more intense than formerly. In the modern workroom there is no time or opportunity for discussion or conversation. . . . No play is mingled with the work, nothing that tends to expand the faculties or broaden the mental out-look beyond the thing in hand." It was unclear to me for a moment whether any irony was intended in the exhibit. But then I noticed that it had been organized by Jeremy Brecher, which answered my question.

The shop floor of the brass mill was a dirty, alienating, and dangerous place. In the casting shops, the characteristic occupational hazard was known variously as "metal fume fever," "spelter bends," "spelter shakes," or "brass-founder's ague." It was caused by inhaling metal oxide fumes. The symptoms were similar to those of malaria. In his history of Waterbury, William Pape wrote that "it is never fatal, and temporarily cured by the use of Jamaica ginger." That word *temporarily* bothered me.

In writing his own oral history of the brass industry, Brecher came across recollections of other popular remedies:

"Oatmeal and water was what they used to suck. You got home, warm milk and butter."

"The Negro Al Dolson, who worked seven years in the casting shop, says the best thing for spelter shakes is hot cider and pepper."

To give Pape his due, he does provide details of the work of the Scovill Manufacturing Company Hospital, which show that "the number of accidents for the year 1916 will approximate 16,000." But I can't shake the feeling that he's more concerned to demonstrate Scovill's civic-mindedness and efficient record keeping than to ask how in God's name sixteen thousand industrial injuries could occur in a year in the first place, and be tolerated and reported as business as usual among a total workforce of twenty-five thousand. Steel machine parts flew loose and impaled people. Runaway cranes crushed them. Four-hundred-pound weights fell on them. Rollers sucked in hands and arms. Falling bars of brass severed feet. Acid splashed and spilled. Scovill's printed a chart to show which parts of the body were affected. The sixteen thousand injuries in 1916 included more than a thousand to the head, face, and eyes.

Brecher writes about a song about Scovill's that was written by an Irish fireman named Michael "Faker" Sullivan and sung in later years by police lieutenant Packy Moylan. It went, in part:

The half past ten from Tralee town to Queenstown on its way
Brings thousands of our boys and girls off to America.
They leave the place of their birth and that's against their will
And they labor for their bread in Scovill's rolling mill. . . .
And when you are six months in Ireland, and feeble is your walk,
The friends you knew while in your youth, to them you'll scarcely
    talk.
Your dance is gone, your voice is still, six feet of earth you'll fill
And they'll lay you away in the burying ground due to Scovill's roll-
    ing mill.

WILLIAM PAPE'S WATERBURY had just one problem, and that was water. The city had been blessed with enough water to fuel an industrial revolution, but it didn't have nearly enough to slake the revolution's ongoing thirst. As Pape noted astutely, "The physical development of Waterbury ha[d] been largely an engineering problem"—capturing enough water for the city's needs from the "violent and destructive" flow of the Naugatuck, digging sewer lines through the unforgiving bedrock, pumping water to the new residential areas on the steep slopes, and satisfying the appetites of the brass mills, whose industry demanded large volumes of water for washing, processing, and diluting of wastes. It's no exaggeration to say that water became an obsession, a kind of defining pathology, of the city's political elite.

Their priorities did not, however, include the physical health of the Naugatuck. The brass barons bestrode the river and bent it to their whim. Long stretches were torn up, channelized, and redirected to make room for new factories and railroads. In the Waterbury Public Library, I found a 1914 memorandum from an executive at the Chase Metal Works. It said, "Mr. O'Brien: Please change the location of the Naugatuck River as per enclosed blueprint."

Down in Seymour and Ansonia, if you could bear to look at the river at all, you could tell what the factories had been doing each day by watching the color of the waters change from green to blue to orange to yellow. The smell of the river was even worse than its color, since it also received the untreated municipal sewage of Waterbury and eight other river towns. At the height of the brass boom, in the late nineteenth and early twentieth centuries, the population of Waterbury almost quadrupled in fewer than thirty years, from 28,000 to 100,000. But this brought much more than a fourfold increase in the demand for water. When a city of new immigrants grew like this, its residents evolved new demands and new standards. They moved out of their triple-decker tenements and built houses with gardens that needed watering. They insisted on flush toilets instead of cesspits to dispose of their wastes. They began to take regular baths.

I'd never given much thought to sewage, and it certainly never crossed my mind to write about it. It's one of those things you take for granted or prefer not to think about. So when I casually asked a Waterbury official when the city had opened its first wastewater treatment plant, I was shocked by the answer. I imagined she would say sometime in the early part of the twentieth century, certainly before World War I, around the time that other parts of the urban infrastructure were being laid in place. No, she told me, it was in 1951. This was hard to believe, since I knew the condition of the Naugatuck had worried public officials at least since the 1880s, when people first began to latch on to Louis Pasteur's new theories of germ-borne disease. As early as 1886, the chairman of the Connecticut Board of Agriculture declared that "this diabolical bondage of streams' pollution" was "the most important public question the present generation has before it." As a moral crusade, he compared it with the campaign to end slavery.

Despite this, it was another forty years before Connecticut established a water commission, and even then it was one of the first states in the nation to do so. In its initial report, published in 1925, the commission singled out the Naugatuck for special attention. It found that

> the Naugatuck River . . . has all the characteristics of an open sewer. Beginning at its headwaters in Torrington, that city—and every other city and town throughout its entire length—uses it as an adjunct to its sewerage system. The total daily volume of raw sewage emptied into this small brook [*sic*] is far beyond its capacity to dilute or oxidize. The stream has been strangled by this huge volume of organic matter.

It would probably be unfair to say that Waterbury had done *nothing* in the intervening forty years to clean up the wastewater it was dumping in the river. The city had drawn up plans for a treatment plant down near Platts Mills in the 1890s, and by 1908 it had built outfall sewers from the South End to the proposed site. But World War I shifted budgetary priorities elsewhere, and the work stopped. The state water commissioners were angered by Waterbury's inaction, especially since the other river towns complained that it was pointless for them to treat their wastewater if Waterbury didn't. Based on the nature of airborne and river pollution, any cleanup effort can be held hostage to the intransigence of other nearby—or distant—communities. You can't protect Adirondack ponds from acid rain if smokestacks in Michigan don't cooperate, and you couldn't clean up the Naugatuck if eight of the nine river towns treated their sewage but Waterbury didn't. Why did the leading men of the Brass City refuse to act, when the problem stared them in the face and assaulted them in the nostrils?

I'm sure some of their inaction was born of cynicism: the folks who lived on the hill didn't have to deal with the stench from the river, and only the poor were victimized by waterborne diseases. But reading between the lines of that 1925 report from the state water commission, I wondered if a deeper logic of public policy had been involved. The commission took pains to explain that the real imperative for cleaning up Connecticut's rivers was not aesthetics or public or environmental health. Though these concerns were real enough, the more urgent need was to preserve the small state's dominant position in manufacturing. The condition of rivers in the Northeast had become a particular threat to the textile industry in the old mill towns throughout New England, since companies whose plants faced a shortage of clean running water, which was critical to their operation, were being enticed to pull up stakes and move to the South, where they could take advantage of cheaper labor. The brass mills of Waterbury, however, were not vulnerable to these pressures. While the Naugatuck River might be unsightly, its polluted water was quite adequate for their needs. Waterbury's dominance of the world's brass industry was secure, and the huge investment that the locally owned mills had made in creating the infrastructure for their operations made moving south unthinkable. It appears that devoting a lot of time, money, and energy to treating the city's sewage was simply not seen as a priority. "Sewage disposal," William Pape wrote, "seems an unjust addition to the physical difficulties with which Waterbury has so bravely and successfully contended."

WITH THE BRASS BARONS leading the way, the Naugatuck Valley became, in the words of one historian, "one great factory city with a continuous freightyard covering the fifty miles between Winsted and tidewater." In the process, the Naugatuck River died, choked by bacteria and poisoned by industrial toxins. Brass is an unusually dirty industry; its wastes are much more complex, for example, in terms of chemical composition, than those generated by a steel mill. During the manufacturing process, the various alloys have to be treated with powerful acids to remove scale and with caustic soap solutions to aid in drawing. After this, the metal must be washed in cold and hot water. The byproduct of this process is a highly toxic liquid known as "acid pickle liquor," which contains large amounts of sulfuric and nitric acids as well as salts of iron, copper, lead, tin, zinc, and other metals. For many decades, this hideous brew, flecked with the metal sweepings and shavings that kids called "Naugie trout" (there being no other kind), made its way directly into the brass mills' drains and from there into the Mad River and the Naugatuck. While the acid pickle liquor was flushed straight into the rivers, the solid waste from the mills and the semisolid metal hydroxide sludge ended up strewn, for the most part, along the riverbanks.

During the brass era, Waterbury's mantra was not *"clean* water" but *"more* water." Accordingly, the city chose to invest not in pollution controls or sewage treatment plants but in reservoirs. Before the end of the nineteenth century, the great and the good of Waterbury had decided that they would solve their age-old water problem once and for all. They placed this strategic task in the hands of a man named Robert A. Cairns (another Scottish engineer, like Major Edwin McNeill), who may well be the most important figure in the history of modern Waterbury. Not satisfied with planning for a population of a hundred thousand, Cairns proposed to get the city's hands on enough water to deal with any imaginable future contingency, making the assumption that Waterbury's industrial boom would stretch to the millennium and beyond. Cairns resolved—Pape's words again—that he "must needs take time by the forelock."

Cairns was the son of a celebrated local mechanic, also named Robert, who had invented the eyelet machine. This invention may have coined more profits for the brass industry than any other single piece of technology. The fame of Robert Cairns the elder had spread as far as Washington, D.C., since his machines had run twenty-four hours a day during the Civil War, manufacturing vital brass percussion caps for the Union army. At seventeen, the younger Cairns went to work under his father at the Waterbury Brass Company. He had inherited the old man's genes for mechanical aptitude, and in 1890, after graduating from Rensselaer Polytechnic Institute, he was appointed city engineer of Waterbury. Cairns was just thirty-one. He already had a reputation as a sober-minded workaholic: St. John's Protestant Episcopal Church on Sundays, evenings at the Waterbury Club, bent over drawings of sewer lines, railroad tracks, and reservoir sites with his close friend Henry S. Chase, the brass magnate. He worked forty years without a vacation, and when Mrs. Cairns finally dragged him to Europe in 1927, he spent most of his time looking at municipal engineering projects.

Robert Cairns waited to take his holiday until the last piece of his grand design had fallen into place. In rapid succession he laid out the new civic heart of the city, constructed half a dozen bridges over the Naugatuck, drove miles of new sewers through the bedrock, relocated and widened the railroad lines, straightened and rerouted the river, and built an impressive network of impoundments on the small brooks to the northwest of the city. But he had always known that these would not be enough, and he had made sure, early in his tenure as city engineer, that Waterbury would have the means to act boldly when the time came.

Robert Cairns and his allies formed one of the most influential power blocs in Connecticut politics, and they quickly went to work on the state legislature. In 1893, they were rewarded with the Special Law Authorizing the City of Waterbury to Increase Its Water Supply. The city was "authorized and empowered to take and convey from any and all brooks, rivers, springs, ponds, lakes and reservoirs within the limits of the county of New Haven or of the county of Litchfield, such supply of water as the necessities or convenience of the inhabitants of said city may require." *Necessities or convenience.* Those words would have profound consequences.

Anyone looking at a map of the watershed would assume that one obvious solution to Waterbury's water crisis was to tap the flow of the Mad River, the most substantial of all the tributaries of the Naugatuck. In fact, in 1892 a consultant to the city had advised expanding the water supply in exactly this way. But the Scovill Manufacturing Company to all intents and purposes placed the Mad River off limits. All of the brass companies were powerful, but Scovill's was in a class of its own. It resisted efforts in the 1890s to bring all the city's brass mills together under a single umbrella, and when most of its competitors merged to form the American Brass Company, Scovill's, which proudly traced its history back to Abel Porter's original gristmill on the Mad River, remained defiantly independent. Scovill's had its own auxiliary police force, the Plant Protection Bureau, to keep its workforce in line and put down strike threats. And the company insisted on maintaining its own chain of six private reservoirs on the Mad River, supplemented by a whole series of flumes, races, conduits, and canals. City engineer Robert Cairns advised the company on its construction plans for these modifications of the Mad River— no such thing as a conflict of interest in those days.

Cairns decided that the key to Waterbury's future—the "hundred-year solution"—lay not in the Naugatuck or the Mad River, but one valley over, in the Shepaug. Cairns had had his eye on the Shepaug ever since the passage of the Special Law in 1893, and his friend Chase owned much of the land that the city would need to acquire. Yet Cairns recognized, as he wrote many years later, that "the legal difficulties were formidable, both in prospect and at closer approach; and the physical obstacles were far greater than any the city had ever been faced with." Adding forty million gallons of water a day from the Upper Shepaug would mean blasting one tunnel through more than seven miles of gneiss and schist and diorite as well as blasting another through the rock-hard resistance of the townspeople of nearby Washington.

In 1921, when Cairns invoked the Special Law for authority to dam and divert the Shepaug, the residents of Washington realized that this would leave them with "practically a dry river bed" during the summer months. The small town on the Shepaug took its case to the legislature in Hartford, where it introduced a bill to repeal the 1893 law. But three months of coaxing by the "sparse, shy, hard-working" Robert Cairns turned matters around. In May 1921, Washington announced that it was dropping its repeal bill. Waterbury had agreed to release a guaranteed minimum flow into the river—a miserly 1.5 million gallons a day— through a pipe in the base of the new dam that it would build on the Shepaug. Announcing the agreement, First Selectman Titus of Washington told Waterbury, "We all feel that you have tried to do something for us, and when our river gets low, we will feel that you are giving us what God intended us to have." Yet rather like the old Indian land purchases, this agreement didn't involve two equal contracting parties. Washington was a bucolic village that time had passed by. Its sniffy Brahmin elite was no match for the likes of Chase Brass and Scovill's and Robert Cairns.

Two thousand "mole men" were at work on the Shepaug tunnel by the end of that year. They came from all over, soldiers of fortune who would work in damp, foul-smelling holes in the ground, choked by gas and deafened by explosions, in exchange for twenty cents an hour and a life expectancy of forty. There were West Indians, Greeks, Italians, Poles, and Portuguese. Blacks and whites lived in segregated camps where workers named Keg and Thirsty, Goulash and Whiskey, Dollar Bill and Tomahawk, entertained themselves by shooting craps, drank themselves into fistfights, then splashed cold water on their faces and went back to work the next morning for a fastidious Episcopalian who told them they were heroes, building a dream of the future.

On September 23, 1926, Robert Cairns pulled a switch and a deep rumbling explosion echoed through the Litchfield Hills. Men from the eastern work crew and men from the west reached through the hole and shook hands. The tunnel was finished. Aboveground, someone had a radio. The mole men tuned in to the Tunney-Dempsey fight, broadcast live from Philadelphia. The mole men rooted for Gene Tunney, the underdog. When the bell rang at the end of ten, the Manassa Mauler was finished, the underdog was champion of the world, and Robert Cairns was free at last to take his overdue vacation.

THE NAUGATUCK VALLEY brass industry is long gone now. Vietnam gave it one last artificial jolt of adrenaline, but Scovill's and Chase Brass both shut down in 1976, the year after the war ended, and Anaconda (the successor to American Brass) folded its operations four years after that. In the process, the city of Waterbury slid deeper and deeper into debt, the old logic of its economy and political system shaken. The dual power structure no longer existed; with the brass barons gone, everything was concentrated in city hall, in a vast web of patronage that no longer had the industrial infrastructure to sustain it or restrain its excesses. Waterbury's mayors, when they stayed out of jail long enough, looked to the future. They began to boast that brass would give way to high-tech service industries. "Two more hours" would no longer be an insult, but a competitive advantage. When I drove down from the giant illuminated cross of Holy Land U.S.A. to the 150 new shops of Brass Mill Commons, I saw that the administration of Mayor Phil Giordano had hung banners in the streets. They said, "Waterbury—Renaissance City."

Now, *renaissance* is a big word, and it's hard to say which aspect of Waterbury's rebirth—political, economic, or environmental—will be most painful. Much of the responsibility for cleaning up the physical devastation of the city falls to an energetic public health official, a Lebanese-born chemist in her late forties named Dada Jabbour, whose mandate includes cleanup of hazardous materials and brownfield redevelopment. I spent a day with Dr. Jabbour, touring some of the nastiest relics of the brass industry.

The brass companies didn't trouble themselves to record the locations of their toxic waste dumps. A quarter-century after the last mills closed down, the dumps tend to be found only when someone digs in the backyard and finds discolored soil or when rainfall erodes the topsoil and exposes a rusting drum of chemicals. We visited a thirty-acre parcel on the edge of Great Brook, where Scovill's used to truck its solid industrial waste. The dump is now the object of a mandatory Superfund cleanup—part of the federal program that deals with the nation's most egregious hazardous waste sites. Like most hazardous sites in Waterbury, this one was discovered by accident. By the time its existence became known, several blocks of residential property had been built on top of the old Scovill's dump, including a day-care center and a housing complex for low-income seniors.

We went to see the razed foundations of the International Silver Company's old Factory J, on the banks of the Mad River, where silverware had been electroplated for decades. Locals still call the place Rogers Spoon. In an adjacent field, looking every inch like a megalithic burial mound, was an oblong, rounded hill, punctuated by test bores. The mound contained twenty-seven thousand cubic yards of mixed metal hydroxide sludge, Dada Jabbour told me. The two access gates in the chainlink fence around the site were standing wide open, their locks smashed. "They've broken our gates," she complained. "They've stolen our padlock and chain." It wasn't clear who "they" were—addicts, prostitutes, petty thieves, kids on a lark. In a corner of the field lay a filthy mattress, covered with maps of Australia. "That's new," Dada said.

We visited the old site of Chase Brass in the northern suburb of Waterville. Much of the vast plant, on the east bank of the Naugatuck, is now occupied by a Finnish superconductor company. On the opposite bank of the river, across a small pedestrian bridge, the slopes were freshly landscaped and planted with small trees to prevent erosion. This is where Chase used to dump its solid waste. Like the Scovill's dump, the site was discovered fortuitously. Since this stretch of the river could be reached by a public footpath, some local fishermen had expressed interest in stocking it with trout and sponsoring a fishing derby for local kids. First they needed to know who owned the place. It turned out that the city of Waterbury had acquired title to the property when Chase Brass ceased operations in the late 1970s. When the locals looked more closely, they saw foreign objects poking out of the soil here and there. These included rusting oil drums and pieces of asbestos. A series of riprap drainage channels added the runoff from Route 8, which passed along the top of the hill. A five-acre triangle of the site was heavily contaminated.

We climbed the hill to an abandoned electrical substation that once provided power to the Chase Brass plant. Here, too, the gates were broken open and the locks were gone. "They used to come up here and do target practice," Dada Jabbour said. "They would shoot down the capacitors and smash them. Of course, the capacitors were filled with PCBs, so all that would end up in the soil."

Parting the trees behind the substation, we looked straight down on a long stretch of pocket water and boulder-studded runs. "That would be wonderful trout habitat," I said.

Dada Jabbour turned to look at the freshly planted hillside. "This place is so beautiful," she said. "I love to come up here and walk in the hills. It reminds me of Lebanon." She picked up a sparkling shard of mica from the ground. Held at an angle against the light, it made a solid surface of reflective silver. "Here," she said, "take this home to your wife. It's beautiful."

She leaned for a moment on the railing of the footbridge. "I feel so happy when I look at this," she said, waving a hand at the river. "It's like adopting a baby with a birth defect. You take care of it, you love it. It's your pride and joy."

CHASE METAL WORK, WATERVILLE, CONN.

Book II
BACK TO
NATURE

Is it not a maimed and imperfect nature
that I am conversant with?
—Henry David Thoreau,
March 23, 1856, *Journal* VIII

11
Foundlings of the
Finny Family

A FEW YEARS AGO, when the Connecticut hydropower industry was deregulated, advocates of every stripe flocked to town meetings,
hearings, and rallies to demand that the Housatonic River be restored
to its natural condition. Disconcertingly, no one seemed to disagree with
this proposition. You couldn't get through the first thirty seconds of
anyone's stump speech—state officials, hydropower plant managers, politicians both Democrat and Republican—without enduring a stream of
green-tinted bromides. Natural river, natural flow. Natural this, natural that. My first impulse was a feeling of irritation at all this easy
greenspeak, with its unmistakable scent of self-righteousness. Everyone
claimed to want a return to nature; the only problem is that no one could
have said with any certainty what that might be. In most cases, the natural state they envisioned was something that existed in their minds rather
than in the real external world.

Restoring the Housatonic to its original state was not only impossible, I concluded; its "natural" aquatic environment was to some extent
unknowable because it was long gone and virtually undocumented. I
searched in vain for historical records that would tell me what the
Housatonic had been like before the dams went up. I called the Cornwall
town historian, Michael Gannon. He knew the river intimately, and the
books he recommended told me a lot about Cornwall's families and
churches and agriculture and topography. But nothing discussed the biology of the river as such; it appeared only as a function of other priori-

ties. I tend to think that the main stem of the Housatonic would never have held much of a trout population. At least from the time that farming began and the forests were clear-cut, it would simply have run too warm in summer. To my way of thinking, the river in Cornwall would have mainly held eels, blacknose dace, and the big minnows called fallfish, which locals call "Shepaug salmon."

Somewhat more is known about anadromous species, those that migrate from saltwater. The Housatonic would certainly have had good runs of shad, lamprey and sturgeon, alewife and blueback herring, all of them ascending the river at least as far as the Lovers' Leap falls at New Milford. I called Steve Gephard, a biologist in charge of Connecticut's Atlantic salmon restoration program, to ask what kind of salmon population the river would have had before the dams were built. Gephard told me that Charles Atkins, who pioneered Atlantic salmon biology in Maine in the 1870s, had included the Housatonic on his list of rivers containing salmon. This would make sense, Gephard said, since "the distribution of Atlantic salmon is consistent, in terms of latitudes, on both continents, and the southernmost Atlantic salmon stream in Europe, in mid-Portugal, is at the same latitude as Long Island Sound. It's fairly consistent with the distribution of Pacific salmon, too—basically streams with watersheds that were glaciated." The Housatonic run would have begun as early as March, before ocean temperatures became oppressive. "The challenge to salmon at the southern edge of their range," Gephard went on, "is to adapt to the warm saltwater. They can't tolerate saltwater warmer than eighteen degrees centigrade, which Long Island Sound exceeds in the summer." Gephard believes that some salmon—though maybe not more than a thousand—may have made it all the way upstream to the Great Falls at Canaan, at least in years when the river ran high. But he admits that it's only an educated guess.

In other words, even our best reconstructive science is an approximation, and I wondered if my first reaction to all the greenspeak had been unfair. After all, I thought, we've been pursuing the restoration of our rivers for the better part of 140 years. And over that time, despite frequent fuzziness about what was actually achievable and often misplaced faith in the power of technology-based remedies, we've come a long way.

CHARLES ATKINS was the first superintendent of the Craig Brook Salmon Hatchery, which was opened in 1871 near the mouth of the

Penobscot River in Maine. Sportsmen-scientists such as Atkins were an important part of the conservationist movement that was putting down roots in places like Washington, Connecticut, in the years immediately after the Civil War. Their urtext was *The American Angler's Book,* written in 1864 by Thaddeus Norris—known to his many admirers as "Uncle Thad" and perhaps the closest the United States ever came to producing a homegrown Izaak Walton. Norris understood the trout pool paradox in all its dimensions, and though terms such as *species diversity* had not yet been coined, he had an instinctive ability to take a fish- or bug's-eye view of the rivers he fished—an instinct that underpins, in a sense, the whole discipline of modern aquatic biology.

Uncle Thad and his fellow-conservationists were appalled by the damage being done to their trout streams by the nation's headlong rush into industry. Norris's insight into the reasons for the disappearance of the native brook trout remains as fresh today as it was in 1864. It was the result, he wrote, of

> the clearing up of the forests, exposing the surface of the ground to the sun, which has dried up the sources of sylvan brooks, or increased their temperature, and consequently that of the larger waters which they feed, rendering them less suitable for trout. . . . On trout streams, there are still other agencies at work: the coal mine, poisoning the brook with sulphur; the saw-mill filling it with slabs and sawdust; the factory with its dye-stuff; and the tannery fouling the clear stream, covering the bottom of its pools and the spawn-beds with its leached bark, and killing the fish by hundreds with the noxious discharge of its lime-vat.

Norris went on to observe that "any law against such vandalism in the United States is seldom or but feebly enforced." Of all his observations, this may have been the most significant because it helped prod anglers themselves to fill the regulatory vacuum in a society that was dominated by laissez-faire economics, weak public institutions, and the "subdue the earth" mentality we read about in Genesis. The new angler-conservationists were motivated by remorseful self-criticism as well as by enlightened self-interest. They knew that illegal and unsporting methods of fishing were rampant, destroying the very resource on which their dream of the healthy outdoor life depended. Fish were being snared on their spawning beds and caught in seine nets and eel weirs. Poachers waited until the summer drought forced the trout to congregate in isolated pools and then bailed them dry. By about 1880, in response to these excesses, anglers in northwestern Connecticut had begun to organize private patrols to clamp down on abuse. With a peculiarly American kind of schizophrenia, they formed clubs to protect the threatened waters. On one hand, the new conservationists were wedded to a democratic ideal of public access; after all, England's large private estates, locked-up trout streams, and pernicious game laws were the kind of thing people had come to America to escape. On the other, if the barbarians and the game hogs were at the gates, it was only reasonable to create private enclaves— think of the Hollenbeck Club—where the resource could be enjoyed by those with the means to do so responsibly.

IRONICALLY, it is through the pioneering conservationist periodicals that we know as much as we do about the excesses of the game hogs. Again, a certain schizophrenia was at work. In its inaugural issue, dated August 1873, *Forest and Stream,* perhaps the most important of these publications, announced its mission: "to studiously promote a healthful interest in outdoor recreation, and to cultivate a refined taste for natural objects." Yet consistent with the frontier spirit of the age, the magazine's publisher, Charles Hallock, was also interested in encouraging sportsmen to hop on the train and seek out new destinations in a country that was still teeming with fish. Hallock's 1878 book, *The Sportsman's Gazetteer and General Guide,* was really the first organized guidebook for anglers. Hallock told you where to go, how to get there, and what resorts, hotels, and other facilities waited to serve you.

Hallock also helped put northwest Connecticut on the national vacation map. The northern extension of the Housatonic Railroad had been completed in 1850 (a connection to the canal that never was), and a short ride by stage from one of its station stops at Falls Village, Lime Rock, or Canaan put the river within a comfortable day's journey of Manhattan. The Housatonic Railroad Company billed the Litchfield Hills of Connecticut and the Berkshire Hills of Massachusetts as "the Switzerland of America for summer tourists." Their favorite destination was the old ironmaking town of Salisbury and the nearby lakes of Wononscopomuc and Washining. "The Twin Lakes are fast growing into favor as a camping and picnic resort," Hallock noted. "On the mountain tops near at hand, are lakes as wild and much less frequented than the Adirondacks or Maine Lakes, and abundantly stocked with fish and game." Starting in the 1870s, when both species were stocked for the first time, the Twin Lakes were alive with smallmouth bass and landlocked salmon, freshly imported from Maine.

On the opening day of the 1874 trout fishing season, a young Salisbury lawyer set out to ascend Mount Riga, in the uttermost northwest corner of the state. I imagine him looking like one of those gentlemen anglers in a Currier and Ives print—leather hip boots, wicker creel, and a long, supple fly rod of greenheart or lancewood. He returned home with a heavy creel after a good morning on the stream—good enough, in fact, for a friend, signing himself "Piscator" of Canaan, to write up his exploits in *Forest and Stream.* "You can say (out loud)," Piscator wrote, "that a young Salisbury lawyer, whose initials stand for Donald T. Warner, hooked a big dozen about a month ago—or the instant the law would let him—in Mount Rhiga [*sic*] stream, called 'Wach-o-cast-in-hook' by the aborigines for short."

Admittedly, the Housatonic Valley was never seen as being in quite

Members of the Washington Gun Club, c. 1900.

regularly reported in Piscator's column for *Forest and Stream.* In the strictest sense, the inhabitants of these streams were not true trout at all. Brook trout are actually members of the char family, most of whose species inhabit the icy waters of the northern oceans.

The presence of brook trout is as reliable an indicator of the passage of the glaciers as score lines on exposed rock. Having evolved to thrive in Arctic waters, the brookie moved southward, toward the Gulf of Mexico, as the last great movement of ice descended across New York, New England, and the upper Midwest. When the glaciers retreated, the fish colonized new areas, swimming eastward to the Appalachians across newly created lakes of meltwater and then seeking refuge in the cooler, forested upland streams as the lower altitudes warmed. The mountainous tributaries of the Housatonic would have been ideal habitat, and wherever development has been restrained, they still are. When state biologists completed a seven-year stream survey in 1992, they found that native brookies were thriving in more than two thirds of the streams in the upper Housatonic watershed. On a good day, I think I could go to Battle Swamp Brook and catch as many wild fish as Mr. Warner could.

In Americans' long love affair with the brook trout, the fish has gone by a hundred different names. Canadians still refer to brookies as speckled trout. Others have called them mountain trout, or spotted trout, or New York char, or—my own favorite—hemlock trout. Their proper Latin name is *Salvelinus fontinalis.* Linnaeus himself, the originator of the whole system of Latin species nomenclature, came up with *Salvelinus* as a genus name. For most of the nineteenth century, scientists and anglers alike treated the brookie as a true trout and called it *Salmo fontinalis.* It was not reclassified into the genus *Salvelinus* until the late 1870s, and though the name is often rendered in English as "little salmon of the springs [or fountains]," there is still a great deal of mystery about what Linnaeus actually intended it to mean.

The colors of *Salvelinus fontinalis* are as lovely as its name. The precise shading will vary according to the acidity of the water, the surrounding vegetation, the fish's diet, and myriad other local factors. In a hemlock forest, where the water is dark with tannic acid, the brook trout may have the sleek blackness of an otter. Biologists debate whether it is proper to see such differences as indicators of subspecies or simply of strains. At one end of the spectrum of genetic purity are the brook trout of the southern Appalachians (the fish's range extends as far as southern Georgia). These fish have kept their genetic integrity since the Ice Age, and some scientists regard them as different enough to warrant classification as a separate subspecies. Connecticut fish are at the opposite extreme, their gene pool irreversibly affected by decades of interbreeding with stocked fish.

But all of them share the basic beauty. The back and shoulders are a maze of wormlike markings—vermiculations—in dark green and lighter olive. The flanks are covered with spots of pale yellow and lavender and bright scarlet, often haloed with powder blue. The ventral fins are orange, with a slash of black and a leading edge of snowy white. As if this variegation was not enough, in spawning season the belly of the male turns anything from maple-leaf crimson to oak-leaf russet. Brook trout are an American original, as true a symbol of native wildness as the bald eagle. Winslow Homer loved to paint them. Personally, I'd have put one on the flag.

IN THE 1870s, however, all this postglacial bounty was fast disappearing. The population of *Salvelinus fontinalis* was being wiped out, at the same time and with about the same speed and industrial efficiency as the population of Native Americans in the West. On opening day of 1877, Piscator's successor at *Forest and Stream*, someone going by the byline of "Druid O'Salisbury," reported that, on Moore Brook, "Dan Ashman caught a hundred and fifty, some weighing a half pound, and we can guess what sort of fingerlings the other sum were." On an unnamed brook over by Torrington, Mr. Dolbey of Baltimore and a friend were reported to have "had a good day's trout fishing, and succeeded in filling a large soap box with fine brook trout averaging about 8¾ to the pound. The entire number caught by them that day exceeded four hundred."

Four hundred trout! Eight and three quarters to the pound! This wasn't so much sport as wholesale slaughter. By an arcane formula devised in the 1890s by a Toronto biologist named W. Hodgson Ellis, it takes anything from twelve to fifteen inches of fish to make a pound of brook trout flesh. So these would have been four-inch, five-inch, six-inch fish, whole breeding-year classes wiped out. Phrases such as *nonrenewable resource* were not yet part of the vocabulary.

Yet having decimated the brook trout population, Americans developed an incurable nostalgia for its return. In the optimistic flush of the post–Civil War era, no problem seemed to lack a technical solution. If the problem was depletion of resources, then new resources would be manufactured. If the rivers were empty, they would be repopulated with fish raised from eggs in hatcheries.

The rudiments of fish culture had been known for centuries—a French monk had discovered how to artificially impregnate fish eggs as long ago as the fourteenth century. But the emphasis in Europe (and before that in China) had always been on food production. A man named Seth Green changed all that. Green opened his Caledonia Fish Hatchery in Mumford, New York, in 1864, just as the Austrian monk Gregor Mendel was making his breakthroughs in genetics. Green's explicit purpose was not only to put more food on America's table but also to restore disappearing fish populations and enhance the moral uplift that came from healthful outdoor recreation. He took his Caledonia Fish Hatchery public four years later, becoming head of the newly created New York Fisheries Commission. Within a few years, he had inspired all the New England and Mid-Atlantic states to replicate his model.

W HEN I WENT LOOKING for the documentary record of Connecticut's efforts to replace its missing trout, everyone said the man to call was Jim Moulton, manager of inland fisheries at the Department of Environmental Protection (DEP) in Hartford. Moulton proved to be a short, stocky man close to retirement age, with a confusion of gray hair and a white walrus mustache. He stood up from the untidiest desk I had ever seen and greeted me gruffly. Fisheries reports, academic journals, open books, and unfiled correspondence lay all over the room in sprawling piles a foot high. Taped to the walls were maps and charts and graphs, all in similar disorder. But once we had got the gruff, irascible act out of the way, Jim Moulton showed me infinite courtesy. He opened a ramshackle glass-front bookcase in the corner of his office and pulled out a stack of ancient volumes, which showed that Connecticut—small, industrialized, and heavily populated—had been one of the first states to board the Seth Green Express.

The earliest report came from 1870, the year the state's Fish and Game Commission was founded. At first, Connecticut, with a string of great tidal rivers that had seen their long-established commercial fisheries wiped out by industry and dams, may have been less concerned than some other states with the uplifting qualities of freshwater recreation. Feeding a nation exhausted by war seemed to be the commissioners' first goal. "In a very few years," they predicted, "the people of the State will doubtless have a variety of fish-food abundant and cheap. We have great conviction in the dietary value of the fish, because they are strong in albumenoids."

OF ALL THE FOOD FISH, salmon and shad were the most highly prized. In 1873, the commission's records show that 70,000 salmon fry went into the Housatonic, 4,500 into the Naugatuck, and 115,000 into various tributaries of the Connecticut, the largest of the state's waterways. A little later, salmon eggs from the Penobscot River in Maine were stocked in the same rivers. Without a doubt they were swept away or provided snack food for the fish that were already there.

Some of these early failures can simply be ascribed to inadequate technical knowledge. But on other fronts, the commissioners seemed to be fighting with both hands tied behind their backs. On one hand, public policy (as expressed through the Fish and Game Commission) called for the return of migratory fish stocks. On the other, public policy (as expressed by everyone else) called for every possible impediment to be thrown in their way. Even as the commissioners went on planting salmon eggs and shad fry, new barriers were being built on the rivers in which the fish were supposed to swim.

On the Housatonic, the main culprit was the twenty-two-foot-high Birmingham Dam, which was built in 1877, near the broad, swirling confluence with the Naugatuck, to generate power for the factory towns of Derby and Shelton. The commissioners built a shad hatchery below the dam, modeled on the one that Seth Green had built earlier by the "Million Dollar Dam" at Holyoke, Massachusetts. For a couple of years, as they hunted the shad that ran frantically back and forth at the base of the dam, the local fishermen felt as if they had died and gone to heaven. But in reality it was the shad that had.

The Birmingham Dam is still there today, as is the old power canal, in all their bald functionality. Some old New England mill towns have been resuscitated, their industrial buildings turned into antiques malls, craft workshops, and small museums. Collinsville, on the Farmington River, comes to mind. Then there is the other kind, the Derbys and

Sheltons. A large plaster statue of the Virgin stands at the end of the Derby-Shelton Bridge, near a bar called The Recovery Room. A hand-lettered sign on the statue says, "Mary Speaks." Next to the old canal and the Shelton Locks, one derelict factory has been occupied by the Father McKenna Vincent de Paul Shoppe. Its windows are bricked in and decorated with trompe l'oeil murals. A few other buildings are occupied by low-profit, low-turnover assembly plants, making brake linings, cardboard packaging, and the like. I see factory signs for Spongex, Island Asphalt, the Chromium Process Company. They provide the only company for the many "For Rent" signs, which have faded with age near windows broken methodically by local teens with nothing else to fill their time.

Considering that they faced obstacles as daunting as the Birmingham Dam, the fish commissioners made near-heroic efforts. They were filled with the positivism of their age, giddy with the promise of new technologies. Nothing seemed to discourage them. "The work of restoring salmon to our rivers has progressed so far that it cannot be long before all doubts will be solved," they wrote in 1877, even as the Birmingham Dam was nearing completion. A year later, they were reporting that fifteen-pound salmon were showing up at the foot of the dam. The dam's fish way—built to the best specifications of Mr. Foster of Maine—would allow the spawners to bypass the new obstruction. But technology giveth, and technology taketh away. First, the salmon and shad took one look at the fish way and declined to use it; then, in 1887, the structure was wrecked in a flood. Only then did the commissioners acknowledge that their salmon restoration plan was a failure.

They persisted with the shad, however. Here, too, each imminent sighting of the New Jerusalem only foreshadowed a more bitter disappointment. Thanks to the prodigious output from the Birmingham hatchery, for a while it did seem as if the shad runs were making a comeback. The recorded catch rose from fewer then 20,000 shad in 1892 to more than 175,000 in 1903. But the euphoria didn't last. By 1907, the catch had again fallen below 40,000, and the Birmingham hatchery closed down.

INLAND, on the state's lakes, ponds, and rivers, outcomes were somewhat easier to control. The commissioners built a hatchery at Windsor Locks, where "foundlings of the finny family" were fed chopped liver

three times a day, and they announced a plan to "restock the depleted waters of the state with such fish as had been known to thrive there in earlier times." This mainly meant restoring the brook trout, but in every
town pond, the commissioners placed trout and carp together, although
the two species have entirely different habitat requirements; the bottom-
feeding carp is now widely considered to have created ecological havoc.
Black bass, both smallmouth and largemouth, went into every body of
water in the state where raising them was feasible; landlocked salmon
from Maine were introduced into selected rivers and lakes.

Private citizens flocked to join the great, high-minded project of
stream reclamation. Individuals of means, such as the iron barons of the
Hollenbeck Club, raised trout fry of their own and supplied them to the
state for stocking in public waters. At convenient railroad stations—such
as Mine Hill and Washington Depot on the Shepaug Valley line—local
volunteers would meet trains and take possession of buckets and milk
cans filled with trout, paying simply a share of the three dollars a day it
cost to hire the delivery person.

Not surprisingly, the fishing was better than anyone could remember in years. "Shepaug trout" were a prized delicacy in New York restaurants and a particular favorite of Diamond Jim Brady, the celebrated railroad tycoon and gourmand. One day Brady let it be known to the chef at
the Waldorf that the Shepaug trout, while delicious, were on the small
side. He wanted something bigger, something that measured up to his
gargantuan appetite. The message was conveyed to a prodigiously gifted
local fisherman named Bill Hawley, who cabled back, "Your trout is practically caught." Early the next morning, Hawley went down to the deep
plunge pool below Roxbury Falls, where William Cothren's improbable
trout had been netted, with four dozen half-grown field mice for bait. He
ordered the creamery to have a good supply of ice on hand. At 10:00 A.M.
he returned and sent another telegram to the Waldorf. "Have Oscar
grease up the skillet STOP shipping oversize bull trout for Brady dinner
STOP signed Hawley."

To this point, the story is plausible enough, in a New England sort of
way. Here's the rest of it. The dead bull trout was placed in a box, which
was so heavy that it took two men to load it athwart Hawley's wagon. The
fisherman himself was unable to help, since he had lost two fingers and a
thumb before he finally managed to subdue the trout by hitting it on the
head with an ax.

Bull trout or no bull trout, the fishing was too good to last, and the state found that it had to set some legal restrictions. In quick succession, it passed the Act for the Protection of Salmon, barring the taking of salmon for five years; announced size limits and creel limits on trout; and established a closed season for fishing from July 1 to March 31. The new measures weren't popular, and there's no sign they were widely observed. Not for the first time, market forces proved to be stronger than government regulations, and Litchfield County papers of the 1890s tell of small boys being paid a penny for every trout they could bring to market. "It has been pitiful to see the fingerling trout displayed in our markets this year," the commissioners reported. They concluded that "certain persons" must be staking out the streams that were being stocked and resolved to keep their locations secret in future.

Yet remarkably, the commissioners soldiered on, full of optimism and high moral purpose. "It should be remembered," they wrote in their report for 1898,

> what fish propagation means to us as a state: the cheap, healthful and abundant food for all classes of its people; the livelihood for the hardy fisherman; the industrial prosperity of many sections of our state; mental relaxation for the toiling masses of our cities and our towns. . . . The waters of this state can be stocked as never before since the Revolution. The people from the farm, shop, store, factory, pulpit, studio, counting room and court find a healthy relaxation from their cares in angling.

Teddy Roosevelt would have been proud of them.

12
The Magic Bullet

MY GUESS IS THAT MOST PEOPLE think of fisheries managers—to the degree they think about them at all—as paper pushers, lab rats, science nerds. Yet reading those reports in Jim Moulton's office, I could in a sense see seventy years of our national drama—from the Civil War to World War II—played out in the assumptions, ideals, and conflicts of the fish and game commissioners. It was all there: the constant utopian temptation of new science; the belief that control of genetics could allow a humble hatchery technician to play creator, arbiter, and agent of salvation; the intimations—as yet imperfectly understood and only partly articulated—of the concept of sustainable development; the enlightened struggle to assert the common public interest over the prerogatives of private capital. And beneath the surface of the debate about healthy rivers, as in all aspects of the great American project, the unspoken question of social class throbbed invisibly.

By the beginning of the twentieth century, the federal Bureau of Fisheries was distributing more than three and a half billion eggs and fry each year from a prodigious national production line, more evidence of the national mood that conquered yellow fever and built the Panama Canal. "The fish culturist improves upon nature," the Connecticut commissioners boasted.

> Just look how wasteful nature is. A shad lays 25,000 eggs, but they are beset by thousands of dangers. Many are not fecundated; many

are dropped into places fatal for their development; many are killed by polluted water; some are eaten by fish, snakes, frogs and eels; some are buried by drifting sand or carried away by sudden freshets. It is estimated that one shad in a thousand becomes a marketable fish. The fish culturist improves on this, and ninety percent of his eggs survive.

The commissioners also demanded new regulatory powers to protect the state's rivers from industrial pollution. This meant weighing competing notions of the public interest. "On one hand," they wrote in their annual report for 1912, "we have the peril to which capital may be subjected by regulation. On the other, the rights of the people to have their health safeguarded and their aquatic animal food products maintained. . . . The importance, however, of providing wholesome natural animal food for the people is far greater than is generally conceded to the consideration of capital invested in industrial enterprises." This was radical stuff for its time, and it led to new legislation that barred the dumping of untreated sewage into inland and tidal waters.

World War I, like all wars, generated new pressures, new insights, new experiments. When the heroes came home from the front, they returned to towns and cities whose swelling populations subjected the country's inland waterways to a vicious circle of stresses. Stream flows had never recovered from the dumping, rerouting, and industrial development they had undergone in the nineteenth century. Now the rivers had to provide drinking water for larger urban populations, who created more municipal sewage and worked in industries that discharged greater volumes of pollutants into rivers that held less water to flush them. This was essentially the problem that drove Waterbury to raid the waters of the Shepaug in 1921.

Conservationists told of environmental regulations in Europe that put the United States to shame. "Pollution is not known in France, Belgium, Holland, Germany and other European countries," an editorialist wrote in *Forest and Stream*.

Our Army officers and other investigators abroad found the streams in these countries absolutely free from pollution, with trout and all kinds of fish in streams adjacent to tanneries and other industrial plants living as contentedly as if they were in our Adirondack streams. The tan-bark, chemicals and other deleterious substances which we allow to run into our rivers as waste are used as by-products in European countries, thereby paying over and over again the marginal costs of the disposal and rectifying plants.

I have to wonder whether the writer had ever actually *been* to Europe. But the impulse was a noble one, reflecting a sincere desire to learn more about how America's ruined streams could be restored to health.

In 1921, the year of the Washington-Waterbury contract, the Connecticut legislature set up a state commission to investigate stream pollution, making the diseased condition of the Naugatuck its prime concern. The commission's chief was a former U.S. senator, Frederic C. Walcott, who approached his job with missionary zeal: get the boys out of uniform, get them out of the brass mills and the munitions plants, get them into the fresh air. Aggressive conservation and salubrious recreation were the rallying cries of Walcott and his commissioners. Now that the heroes were home, they could apply to Connecticut's trout streams all the manly purpose they had used to subdue Kaiser Wilhelm. "The real sportsmen of America are our best citizens," Senator Walcott wrote,

> clean of mind and body, resourceful, strong and courageous. The sportsmen of the allied countries rid the world of imperialistic militarism, and the sportsmen of the civilized nations today stand as a solid bulwark against all forms of impractical and destructive radicalism. The love of nature—of clean, vigorous sport in the open—is the antidote to the softening, weakening influences of modern civilization. Our battle then is to recover the lost heritage which our ancestors wasted and failed to protect, and having regained it to protect it for our children, and our children's children.

Though the health of the nation's rivers was also much on the mind of the federal government, it was pretty clear that there were limits to how far Washington would intervene to protect running water. Herbert Hoover, the mining engineer, businessman, and fly-fisherman who had just been appointed to the post of secretary of commerce, told a congressional hearing in 1921 that "I have not the feeling that any general prohibition of pollution . . . is desirable at the present moment without more information. We might be doing some localities infinitely more damage to industry and commerce, imposing infinitely more cost upon municipalities than the value of any fishing that could be established would warrant."

For Hoover, and for generations of later politicians, the calculus was little more than a financial balance sheet. The meaning of a healthy river could be reduced to the dollars and cents generated by angling. For his own recreation, meanwhile, Hoover was always assured of a private idyll. After he became president in 1929, he had the government build him a summer retreat, Camp Hoover, on the Rapidan River in the Shenandoah Forest. As the Depression sank its teeth into America, Hoover decided that the gloriously colored native brook trout of the Rapidan were not big enough to give him satisfactory sport, so he had the government stock the river with fat rainbows.

In trout fishing as in the rest of American society, the 1920s roared. Once they had a more accurate sense of which streams offered the best trout habitat, fish and game commissioners ratcheted up hatchery operations to new levels. Unlike the legendary trout streams of the Catskills, Connecticut waters were not typically locked up in private hands. Taking advantage of this, the legislature authorized the commissioners to acquire fishing rights on a dozen of the best streams in the state, which were soon loaded with improbable numbers of trout. By 1928, the state was planting well over twenty thousand trout a year in the Pomperaug. That's an almost inconceivable number of fish for a stream that is barely twelve miles long and, at most, fifty feet wide. Even larger numbers of trout were crammed into the Shepaug.

Although the basic goal of stream restoration was to replicate the lost past, replacing brookies with brookies, no species was too exotic for the Connecticut commissioners to try. Like Hoover, they looked to the Pacific watersheds and saw their native rainbow trout as the game and food fish of the future. The first sizable stocking of rainbows went into the Blackberry River, even though the stream was badly contaminated by industrial discharges.

The commissioners' sense of adventure led to some very peculiar experiments. Wild giants of the Pacific Northwest took up residence (a very short-lived residence, it must be said) in some of the more decorative corners of Connecticut. Steelhead—enormous seagoing rainbows—exerted themselves in Ivy Mountain Brook, a ten-foot-wide trickle in the township of Goshen. Chinook salmon, the royalty of British Columbia and the Yukon, were asked to flex their muscles in the little Mill River, which meanders through the northern suburbs of New Haven. It never seemed to cross the commissioners' minds that these operations were doomed to failure.

But the most radical and lasting change, riddled with connotations of nationality and social class, was the introduction of the European brown trout, *Salmo trutta*. The first shipment of more than twelve thousand juvenile browns went into the Housatonic in 1924, the beginning of the great brown trout fishery that brings thousands of us flocking to the river today. Connecticut came late to this game. To pursue my earlier analogy, the brook trout had been exterminated like the American Indian, and, also in parallel, much of its habitat had since the 1880s been taken over by new waves of European immigrants. A first shipment of brown trout eggs reached the United States in 1883, a gift from Baron Von Behr of the German Fishery Association. Some called the new arrivals "Von Behrs," but anglers preferred "German browns," and that is still the name they are known by in much of the country.

Two years later, New York's Cold Spring Hatchery—the Ellis Island of this immigration story—received one hundred thousand eggs of an entirely different strain. These came from Scotland, from Loch Leven, and their scientific name is *Salmo trutta levenensis*. I find it hard to think dispassionately about the new Scottish import, since Loch Leven is barely twenty miles from my birthplace. Riding the bus, on our way to visit some dreary second cousin twice removed, was a journey across multiple boundaries of time, class, and geography. It began in the grime of the West Fife coalfields, represented by Britain's last Communist member of Parliament in 1949, the year I was born. It ended in the fourteenth century, which was when the ruined castle on the island in the middle of Loch Leven was built. We would stop on the lakeshore, peer through the mist across the green chop, and read about how Mary Queen of Scots had been imprisoned there in 1567, pregnant with twins, head shaved bare after her defeat and capture at the Battle of Carberry Hill. She spent almost a year on the island, her pregnancy ending in a traumatic miscarriage, before a besotted local teenager rowed her ashore to safety, throwing the keys of her prison into the depths of the lake.

From their appearance, Von Behrs and Loch Levens might as well have been different species. The German fish was marked by widely separated black splotches with light halos as well as small numbers of scarlet spots. The Scottish trout, by contrast, was covered with a mass of black spots on a gray-brown ground. Descended from these two ancestral extremes, modern American brown trout can assume an infinite variety of patterns. I've caught big brown trout on the White River in Arkansas—probably the most beautiful I've seen anywhere—with black and red spots the size of dimes and bellies the color of turmeric. I've caught browns in northeastern rivers that could pass for Atlantic salmon, with the lightest dusting of dark markings on iridescent silver bodies, like ocean fish whose colors are masked by pale, sparkling crystals of guanine.

In Europe, Asia, and North Africa today, across its native range, there are dozens of widely differing strains of *Salmo trutta*. Transplanted brown trout thrive from New Zealand to Patagonia, as well as in the temperate portions of most of Queen Victoria's colonies, where they were introduced by bored British army officers and civil servants looking for something to do on weekends other than sit around at the club, drinking pink gins. So naturalized populations of browns swim in the highland streams of Kenya, India, Pakistan, Zimbabwe, and South Africa. In the United States, there are brown trout in every state but no such thing anymore as a pure Von Behr or Loch Leven. That's too bad, since nineteenth-century prints make it clear that both were lovely fish. But hatchery managers allowed them to breed promiscuously, and the railroad engineers who carried them across the United States in milk cans were quite unaware of the genetic consequences.

The European brown trout brought cultural complications as well as genetic ones. Like all forms of immigration, this one exploded in controversy. In the sporting periodicals of the time, the brown trout was regarded as a harbinger of the apocalypse. Private fishing clubs regarded it as a pest, to be killed and removed from their hallowed waters.

The newcomers were said to be ugly: "In appearance, the brown is scaly, flat, greenish-yellow, irregular in form, bad eye, homely all over." They provided mediocre sport: "The play of the fish is decidedly deficient in muscular power . . . [with] none of the vigor and brilliancy of the electric-like dashes of our own brook beauty." They were fit only to be eaten: "The trout of the restaurant will not cease to be; but he is no more like the trout of the wild river than the fat and songless reed-bird is like the bobo-link. Gross feeding and easy pond life enervate and deprave him."

Brown trout grew to unprecedented sizes and had a reputation for cannibalism. When reports spread that an itinerant Minnesota preacher had netted a six-pound brown trout on New York's legendary Beaverkill, the *American Angler* asked indignantly, "How many American trout were engulfed in the stomach of this big 'Dutchman,' as they call these mon-sters?" Though it persisted in folk myth, the charge of cannibalism faded as a serious topic of debate when it became clear that the only difference between browns and brookies in this respect was that the American fish rarely grew big enough to need this kind of calorific intake. When it did, it behaved in much the same way. One of Druid O'Salisbury's columns in *Forest and Stream* told of a brook trout raised in captivity for seven years in a spring-fed pond near the town of Winsted. "When the fish was fif-teen inches in length," he wrote, "two other brook trout, a male and a fe-male, each ten inches long, were placed in the spring to keep the old fel-low company. He promptly fell in love with the lady trout and killed and swallowed her escort."

Over time, the grumbling diminished, and a calmer editorialist wrote that the nativist prejudice against the brown trout only reflected "the natural tendency of mankind to throw bricks or stones at foreign-ers." It also reflected, perhaps, some resentment that they were much harder to catch than the gullible native brookie. But that objection was soon transmuted into snob appeal. "The European stranger," one convert wrote, "is so cunning, shy and suspicious of everything unusual, that the man who lures him to his death must possess extraordinary intellectual gifts and experienced skill to match against his inherited instincts refined to an extreme in a novel environment." The brown trout was now the pre-ferred fish for Anglophiles, and certainly for gentlemen.

ALTHOUGH IT ISN'T a common occurrence, the native and immi-grant species also began to produce hybrids in the wild. *Salvelinus fontinalis* and *Salmo trutta* both spawn in the fall, and occasionally a male brook trout will fertilize the eggs of a female brown. American hatchery managers quickly figured out how to do the same thing by arti-ficial means. Much like plant geneticists working to improve the food supply, the hatcheries looked for crossbreeds, both within and between species, that would increase the trout's longevity, improve its resistance to disease (especially in overcrowded concrete tanks), and provide anglers with better sport.

Like any other "improvement" upon nature, this one had its Frankenstein aspects. Male brookie × female brown = tiger trout, named both for its coloration and its ferocious personality. The reverse = leopard trout. Brook trout × lake trout = splake. Cutthroat × rainbow = cutbow. Brown × Atlantic salmon = trousal. Brown × rainbow = brownbow. Atlantic salmon × rainbow = sambow, a variant that presumably has some value to geneticists but in other respects is pointless, since the few fish that hatch die within a couple of days.

Tiger trout, which are prized as a sport fish in the few places where they've been stocked, can survive in the wild, but they can't reproduce. Browns and brookies are different species—the brookie is a char, remember, and not a trout at all—and their chromosomes are incompatible. There's a good reason for this, of course, which is the foundation stone for any understanding of the natural order of the species. If this genetic barrier did not exist, hybridization would be rampant, and the differentiation of species would rapidly erode.

I thought I might have found a naturally occurring hybrid population one day as I was fishing upstream along Walker Brook, the secluded tributary that takes its name from the seventeenth-century clergyman Zachariah Walker, leader of the Halfway Covenanters. A couple of miles up from the confluence with the Shepaug, the brook runs beneath the dirt road, through a culvert. Below the culvert, I caught a number of trout with colors I had never seen before. Their bodies had a uniform sheen of burnished silver-gold, and each fish had maybe a dozen pinhead-sized red dots on each side but no other markings. Above the culvert, I caught fish whose coloration was identical—except that they also had pale, yet distinct, dorsal vermiculations. In no other respect did they resemble brook trout, although that is obviously what they were.

I was curious enough about these fish to call Mike Humphreys, a state biologist who grew up in the Housatonic Valley and knows it intimately. Mike was puzzled by my description but said categorically that the fish I'd seen had to be browns and brookies, their odd coloration reflecting some quirk of the brook's topography or food supply, each species occupying separate niches in the stream. In seven years of surveying every stream in the state, Mike and his colleagues had found no more than a dozen naturally occurring tiger trout, all of them isolated specimens. Mike told me that these fish resulted from male brook trout sperm drifting downstream and into the spawning redds of female browns— giving a whole new meaning to the idea of casual sex.

As the fisheries managers assembled better empirical data on local conditions, they gained a sharper understanding of the sources of aquatic pollution, parasites, and disease vectors, the migration of anadromous species, and the reasons for failures in the hatchery system. Fish were tagged to track their seasonal movements and survival rates. One important lesson the biologists learned was that environmental degradation involved more than the visible effluent plumes from mills and factories. Rachel Carson was still forty years away, but these scientists began to grasp the risk that toxins posed to organisms at the lower end of the aquatic food chain, though they used different terminology to describe their findings. They came to understand that some forms of pollution "may be innocuous to the fish themselves, but may kill off the minute plant and animal life on which the food supply of the fish depends."

These insights led scientists to shed some hubris: no more introducing steelhead into mountain rills, no more Pacific salmon released into meadow brooks. More and more streams were managed on an individual basis, according to their own idiosyncrasies. The commissioners acknowledged, in their 1935 report, that "most Connecticut streams can only hold trout for about two months of the year, with combined favorable temperatures and flows. Our philosophy, therefore, pending the addressing of the root causes of the problem, is to simulate as closely as possible the conditions in natural trout streams in wilderness areas."

The state hatchery system embarked on an elaborate simulation of wildness, concocted from a blend of science and nostalgia. Chopped liver became a thing of the past as hatchery managers tried all manner of additives to produce wild-looking fish. Now they fed their inmates on alfalfa meal and shrimp heads, on frozen saltwater mussels and dehydrated gulls' eggs—anything to reproduce the brilliant orange-pink flesh of the native brookie. A touch of paprika added redness to the fins. The science has come a long way since then, but the principles remain much the same.

I visited the state hatchery in Burlington one day, where hundreds of trout milled aimlessly in circular concrete tanks, rainbows in one, browns in the next, brookies in another. No Von Behrs, no Loch Levens, no heritage strains of *Salvelinus fontinalis.* After successive generations of human tinkering, the basic distinction between one Connecticut trout and another is simply the hatchery in which its particular strain originated. My guide, a technician named Doug Barnard, told me that state biologists speak of Romes and Cortlands in exactly the same way that owners of apple orchards do.

When Doug came near to feed them, the fish immediately packed themselves into a dense school at his feet. We cast handfuls of trout chow into the water—stubby Hi Performance Pellets, in the $\frac{5}{32}$-inch size, each one packed with animal and plant protein, processed grain byproducts, fish oil, salt, vitamins (A, C, E, K, D_3, and B_{12}), riboflavin, niacin, folic acid, biotin, thiamin, pyridoxine, pantothenic acid, inositol, antioxidants, and a dozen other additives I couldn't pronounce. The hatchery tank boiled like a piranha pool in a horror movie.

SOME FISHERMEN, just a few, suspected that the hatchery's magic bullet was not entirely to be trusted. I came across a description of fishing in the Konkapot, a pretty tributary of the Housatonic that enters the big river just south of the Massachusetts line, by a writer named Leslie Thomson. He complained that things had begun to deteriorate once large numbers of mature trout from the hatchery were introduced into the Konkapot. In 1938, Thomson encountered a local fisherman who asked him with some bewilderment, "The more we put in, the fewer fish there seem to be—what becomes of them?"

It was an excellent question, but one that would take the biologists many years to answer. Thomson could offer only a couple of mechanical theories. Either the masses of early season fishermen were decimating the native populations as well as the hapless stocked fish, or there wasn't enough food to support the newcomers. Perhaps putting a thousand trout into water that could support only a hundred was a bit like pasturing a thousand head of cattle on a one-acre lot. Biologists weren't yet aware of the negative impact of competition between native and hatchery-bred fish or exotic species. As for the great mass of anglers, they saw no reason to trouble themselves with the small print in the reports of the

Fish and Game Commission—tantalizing phrases like "pending the addressing of the root causes of the problem." That sounded like something that could be put off until tomorrow. As long as the anglers could go home with a creel full of trout for breakfast—their taxes and license fees, after all, paid for the fish—what reason was there to complain about the new arrangements?

13
Are Locusts Kosher?
Adventures in Entomology

IT WOULD BE INTERESTING to hand out those reports from the 1920s and 1930s to a group of contemporary biologists and ask them to write a commentary on that pendent phrase—"the addressing of the root causes of the problem." What lies at the heart of a healthy river? Well, water quality obviously—the relative absence of detectable pollutants, both organic and inorganic. But clean water can be sterile. Clearly we're looking for the key to clean water that is brimming with life. So is it trout we're after? Well, yes and no, since basic deindustrialization, coupled with the magic of the hatchery, means, for example, that these days you can catch trout, at least on a seasonal basis, in all sorts of improbable waters.

Instead, our biologists would probably take their yellow highlighters to the phrase I quoted from the 1924 report—"the minute plant and animal life on which the food supply of the fish depends." Then they'd translate it into contemporary terms. Benthic populations. Bugs, and the microorganisms on which they feed. Those are the heart of the matter. We may not put them there, in the literal and direct way that we stock trout, but their presence, their numbers, and above all their variety and diversity are a function of how humans have used or misused the river, a mirror in which we can read our conduct.

They are also an area in which the observant fly-fisher should have something of a comparative advantage, since an understanding of bugs is so fundamental to the enterprise. Let's be clear that we're talking here about fly-fishing of the classic, traditional sort, which involves fashioning a tiny confection of feather, fur, and steel to create the appearance of a living insect. Other things also pass for fly-fishing in the strange times we inhabit. I've read, for instance, of people who like to catch freshly stocked trout on "flies" that are fashioned from epoxy resin to resemble the kind of feed pellets that Doug Barnard and I had tossed into the cement holding tanks at the Burlington Fish Hatchery. In England, there's a thriving subculture of anglers who target the gigantic hatchery rainbow trout held in large underwater cages in the country's reservoirs. Apparently when these holding tanks get overcrowded, the rainbows begin to attack one another. The water fills with the bloody body parts of the weaker fish, adding to the general feeding frenzy. The specialists make artificial lures to resemble torn-up rainbow guts and dangle them over the cages on fast-sinking fly lines. The pages of British sporting magazines then fill with angry polemics about whether this is really fly-fishing. The capacity of the human race to devise new ethical controversies is a constant source of wonder.

Much of the time, amateurs like me can get away with creating a general impression of the bugs that are on the water by using generic flies like the beadhead prince nymph and the gold-ribbed hare's ear, the parachute Adams and the royal trude (don't ask how they acquired these names). But at other times—say, in late May and early June, when all kinds of mayflies and caddis flies are on the water—you can deceive the trout only with a precise imitation. At this time of year the Housatonic offers an extraordinary graduate-level education in entomology and the web of connections that binds the life of insects to that of humans.

As a trout stream, the Housatonic has some distinct disadvantages—high summer temperatures, fluctuating water levels from the Falls Village hydropower plant, and a shortage of good spawning habitat, which means that little if any natural reproduction of trout occurs. But in other respects, the river has all the advantages that geology and topography can bestow. Above the Massachusetts line, it meanders slowly through farmland, picking up suspended organic particles to feed the lower end of the food chain downstream. The limestone and marble bed of the river contributes mineral wealth of the kind that invertebrates and trout value in the way that humans fancy platinum or diamonds. Below Falls Village, the gradient provides abundant oxygen and a varied streambed of ledge rock, boulders, cobble, gravel, and silt, a sustaining habitat for a broad spectrum of invertebrates. There are mayflies of all kinds—clingers, burrowers, crawlers, and swimmers. There are dozens of species of temperature-tolerant caddis flies, abundant stoneflies of various sizes, chironomids, fat crayfish, and the aquatic version of the roly-poly known as the scud.

The volume and complexity of the insect hatches can make life difficult for the angler. Prolonged observation and experiment may be required to figure out which insect the trout are feeding on and which stage of the insect's life cycle is attracting the trout's attention. If it's a mayfly, is it the nymph, the emerger, or the dun? If it's a caddis, is it the emerging pupa or the winged adult? Go to the Housatonic at, say, 11:00 A.M. on May 27, and the answer can be all of the above, and at the same time.

If things are tough for the fishermen, pity the poor amateur entomologist. A little knowledge can be a dangerous thing, especially when it's in Latin. One morning in late May, a small black caddis landed on my arm. Then I noticed another perched on the caramel-colored shaft of my bamboo fly rod. A few minutes later, a third, this one on the light gray fabric of my shirt. Meanwhile, clouds of gray, green, and brown caddis were hatching all around me, all seeming to keep their distance as if I were wearing industrial-strength bug repellent. Back at the car, I pulled out my notebook and earnestly scribbled, "Why should *Chimarra aterrima* like light-colored surfaces, while other caddis appear to ignore them?" Then I thought, wait a minute: why did I find it necessary to use the term *Chimarra aterrima* instead of just *little black caddis*? For that matter, how could I be sure it was *Chimarra aterrima*, rather than a *Glossosoma* or a *Brachycentrus* of similar appearance, not to mention a *Micrasema*, a *Neophylax*, or an *Amiocentrus*? All I really needed to know was that it was a caddis, it was black, and it was about a size twenty— roughly the size of a grain of rice. Not for the first time, I had stumbled in over my entomological waders. When real scientists hear this stuff, they cringe, knowing that to call my little black caddis *Chimarra aterrima* instead of *Neophylax fuscus* is roughly equivalent to calling me Frank instead of George.

FROM THE BIOLOGIST'S point of view, mayflies are a little simpler than caddis flies. For a start, the species are much more easily identified and classified. There are many more species of caddis flies than of mayflies, and the life cycle of the caddis fly has an extra stage. It starts off as a larva, turns into a pupa, breaks free from the water as a fully formed adult fly, and returns, in the case of the female, as an egg layer. The mayfly, on the other hand, goes straight from the nymphal stage—usually a whole year, spent underwater—to full adulthood. Then, by way of a molt, which turns the fly's wings to a shimmering transparency, it ends with mating, ovipositing, and death.

The stonefly goes through a similar three-stage development, although with a significant difference, from the trout's point of view. Virtually all adult mayflies hatch underwater; after penetrating the meniscus, they typically drift downstream for a while on the surface—some passive, others kicking and struggling—as their new wings dry. This makes them easy prey. Stonefly nymphs, however, clamber out of the water before they turn to adults. Watching them lumber into the air like little helicopters, safe from the jaws of the patrolling trout, is one of the small pleasures of fly-fishing, as is finding the parchmentlike exoskeletons they leave behind on the streamside rocks.

A COUPLE OF YEARS AGO, in late May, I decided that I would apply the limited sum of my amateur entomology to an entire day on the river. From first light to last, I would track each emergence I could and see how many different species I could identify. I was probably suffering from a touch of hubris, since my previous trip had been one of those rare times when it seemed I could do nothing wrong. The foot of Turnip Island had been a mass of snow-white apple blossoms. The first caddis flies were on, mainly of the genus *Brachycentrus* (commonly known as the grannom), and all over the Split Rock Pool were noisy, splashing rises. Every so often, a fish would leap bodily out of the water in hot pursuit, rising through the water column to nail the caddis pupae as they fought their way through the surface film. Using a small caddis imitation, I took seven fine brown trout in an hour—typical Housatonic holdovers, fourteen or fifteen inches long, with deep, heavy bodies and bright red spots. I have to say right away that this is not my typical performance.

Heavy rains had fallen in the middle of the month, but a week of sunshine had brought the river down to a manageable level, and when I pulled up at the Elms at first light, I saw that I could wade out easily on the gravel bottom. Punctually at six, a single small black caddis landed on

HOUSATONIC RIVER,
WEST CORNWALL, CONN

my arm. Soon afterward, a single bedraggled ochre-colored march brown mayfly struggled free of the surface. It sat quivering on my fingertip until its wings had dried and then fluttered away into the streamside bushes. It was 6:15. An old man with a thermos, a bait bucket, and two spinning rods made himself comfortable on the bank. When I raised a hand in greeting, he looked down his nose at my fly rod and announced that he'd taken a thirty-two-inch mirror carp from this spot a few weeks earlier. Clearly I wasn't in that league.

I waded back to the car and drove down to the Spring Hole. It's one of my favorite parts of the river, with long, deep boulder runs that hold lots of fish. Along the hedgerows and picket fences were bursts of white and purple lilac. The skunk cabbages, two months old now, were fat and blowsy on the muddy slope where the springs seep from the hillside. There were violets and trilliums and jack-in-the-pulpits. The woods were still a few days short of lush, but the silent movements of chlorophyll were palpable in every leaf, and the call and response of the early songbirds had already turned into the full polyphony of the dawn chorus.

There were march browns at the Spring Hole, too, and a few minutes after seven, the first gray foxes emerged. The two species of mayfly— *Stenonema fuscum* and *Stenonema vicarium*—are closely related and hard to tell apart. At 7:30 some *Ephemerella dorothea* showed—oddly, because their common name, the pale evening dun, reflects the usual time of their appearance. They were followed by tiny yellow mayflies that filled the air for a few minutes like a cloud of pollen. The real stuff—actual pollen from the stamens of trees in bloom—continued to hang in the air in a fine golden haze long after the mayflies had gone.

The first big wave of caddis came off at eight. Small black ones at first, then browns, and then larger, meatier flies in shades of brown and gray. Aerobatic swifts swooped to pluck them from the air. A few fish began to rise, splashing noisily. At 9:30 I saw small creamy-beige caddis, a size eighteen or thereabouts, circling above the riffles at the head of the pool. Then there was a flurry of green caddis, a size or two larger, and a couple of large two-tailed mayflies that I couldn't identify. It was becoming harder to keep track of the explosion of life from the water. More green caddis, more brown. Two black caddis mating on a leaf, head to tail. The shucks of giant brown stonefly nymphs, *Perla capitata,* bunched together on the rocks. Around noon, clouds of pretty yellow mayflies, sulfurs, rose in unison from the runs below Deadman's Hole. Then black caddis arose in numbers that made me dizzy—first the jet-black kind that I'd seen earlier in the day, and then another with a dark gray body and black filigree wings. All around me now were the splashing and leaping of trout.

After lunch I could feel the water beginning to rise with a power release from the dam. I killed the afternoon with odd jobs and wound up at Falls Village toward dusk. In the gloaming, I wandered down to the battleship-gray iron bridge above the power plant. A pale crescent moon was rising in the sky, and the Great Falls were doing their impersonation of Niagara. Staring upstream at the cascade, I felt as if I were reading Timothy Dwight again for the first time.

I walked out to the middle of the bridge and looked down into the flood. The steel girders rattled and vibrated under my feet each time a car went by, its headlights raking across the retaining wall of the old canal. The bridge needed a fresh coat of paint; the girders were covered with small brown and black flecks where the paint seemed to have chipped away. Then one of the flecks moved and landed on my arm. Then another and another, until the satin blue sky was filled with the whir of caddis flies, rising into the air from their resting places on the bridge. I leapt back and forth across the bridge in the thickening dark like a man with St. Vitus' Dance, trying to catch the flies in my baseball cap. But I could see them clearly only when their silhouettes became visible against the sky, and by then they were out of reach. Whatever species they were, thousands upon thousands of bugs were rising from the river, mayflies now as well as caddis, their biological clocks oblivious to the torrent. As they pressed on through their preordained cycle of mating and death, I realized that it had grown too dark to see, and I headed home.

DESPITE ITS COPIOUS mayfly hatches, the Housatonic is better known as a caddis stream, and I found that there was no better way to read the river's history than through studying the humble caddis fly. I'd read somewhere that about twenty years ago, a Yale graduate student named Rodrigo Andrade had collected thirty-four different species of caddis on the river. The book said that the flies had been catalogued by a "Dr. Downes, an MD and avid amateur entomologist from Branford, Connecticut." I wanted to know more about this man, to talk to him if I could.

Andrade is a Portuguese name, and most of the Rodrigos I found through an Internet search seemed to be in Lisbon or Brazil. But one was listed as a neurobiologist at Wayne State University. This turned out to be the right Andrade, and he replied to my e-mail the same day. I was disappointed when he told me that Wil Downs—no *e*—had died in 1991. He also laughed when he heard Downs described as a small-town M.D. In fact, Wil Downs had one of those Larry Pool–type biographies—same generation, same glittering professional success, similar innovations in medical knowledge, a polymath.

In the days that followed, I called a number of people to find out more about Wil Downs. The telephone seemed to glow in my hand when people talked about him. A forensic entomologist named Bill Krinsky sent me a picture of Downs, who had been his mentor. It was a wonderful face, open and generous, with a bucktoothed smile a mile wide. Downs was a professor of epidemiology and public health at Yale for many years, director of the Yale arbovirus research unit, and one of the world's leading authorities on tropical medicine. He was not only an entomologist and an epidemiologist, but also a malariologist, a virologist, and a parasitologist. He ran the Rockefeller Foundation's malaria control program in Mexico; he was an adviser to the World Health Organization, the State and Defense Departments, the National Academy of Sciences; he was one of the first people to question the use of DDT as a means of insect control; he published more than 150 articles in scholarly journals.

Like too much useful science, most of this work was known only to his peers. But in 1969 Wil Downs wound up on the front page of the *New York Times,* after three American missionary nurses in northern Nigeria fell victim to a virulent and terrifying fever. Two of them died. The third was airlifted home and survived. Wil Downs's particular talent was the identification of hitherto unknown lethal viruses in tropical areas. He worked on Marburg, Machupo, Congo, and Crimean hemorrhagic fever. Now his team isolated the virus that had killed the missionary nurses and named it for the Nigerian village in which the outbreak had occurred—Lassa—but not before a Yale technician named Juan Roman had died after he contracted the disease in the lab.

On the trout stream—did I mention that Downs loved to fish?—Wil Downs and Larry Pool could not have been more different. "Wil was a passionate fisherman," said Dr. Charles Remington, professor emeritus of entomology. "He had a summer place called the Ginger Quill Ranch, out in the mountains of northern Colorado. He used to teach classes in fly-tying in the Yale gym." Wil Downs took his restless intelligence to the river with him; Larry Pool left it behind at Columbia Presbyterian. Larry was a Waltonian angler, Downs a fly-fisher of the aerobic school. He traveled to Patagonia and New Zealand in search of giant brown trout. On a trip to Makarora, on New Zealand's South Island, in the mid-1980s, he ran into the writer and fly-fisherman Thomas McGuane. Downs was there with his son Monte, also a doctor. After Wil Downs's death, McGuane recalled their encounter in a touching essay in *Esquire* magazine. He observed that father and son were engaged in "a great catch-up, devised fairly late in the game. They sang antique harmonies, discussed dengue fever and trout, and fished very hard." Wil Downs drove his guides like mules. He grabbed insects off his bathroom mirror while he was shaving. He pinned them to a sheet of Styrofoam and labeled them. When he left, he presented them as a gift to the owner of the lodge.

As an entomologist-angler, Dr. Remington said, "Wil Downs's special interest was the *Trichoptera* of Connecticut"—the state's caddis flies, that is—"and most of his work was done on the Housatonic. In fact, he was working on a book about Connecticut entomology when he died." Rodrigo Andrade told me that the Downs collection of aquatic insects was still being catalogued, but I would find it in the Peabody Museum at Yale.

Rᴀʏ ᴘᴜᴘᴇᴅɪs, the curator of the Peabody's bug collection, invited me to have lunch with a group of Yale entomologists who got together over sandwiches to discuss whatever topic happened to be on their minds that day. Ray turned out to be a tall, soft-spoken man in his midforties with a graying beard and a wry, self-deprecating sense of humor. He did his graduate work at the University of Connecticut on an order of micro-scopic, parasitic insects that live off freshwater sponges. It was, he told me, "about as exotic and useless a group of insects as you could ever study, but it kept me out in the field a lot because no one knew anything about them." Insect taxonomy never ends, Ray said. "With animals you've basically figured it out. But with insects you can still go out into your backyard and collect something new. The essentials are there. Occa-sionally someone will do some new analysis and rearrange the groups a little bit, but basically it's pretty stable. But at the species level, there's still a lot to be done."

In my imagination, the thirty-four species of Housatonic caddis would be neatly pinned on Styrofoam sheets and precisely labeled at the museum. The reality was far from it. These days all the money goes to mi-crobiology, genetic engineering, and nanobots, and the shortage of funds for traditional organismal biology was painfully apparent in the state of the entomology collection. Ray led me through a labyrinth of basement corridors that felt a little like a hospital morgue, past locked rooms with warning signs about contagion risks, until we swung open a steel door and entered a scene from the nineteenth century, when museums were shrines to the Victorian passion for taxonomy. "A lot of the stuff in here does go back over a hundred years," Ray said. Rows of steel shelving and locked cabinets were packed with what seemed a semi-random assort-ment of ancient Mason jars, rubber-stoppered vials of ethanol, and long wooden trays. Interns and volunteers were hunched over benches in dimly lit corners of the room, trying to make a dent in decades of backlogged samples. When Ray came in, they looked up and cracked jokes about slave labor and the minimum wage.

We stopped in front of a shelf of arachnids. At eye level, nineteenth-century scorpions and poisonous spiders were suspended in yellow fluid. Ray said, "At least the collection is all in one place now, for the first time in forty years. But it's been compressed from nine rooms into two. No faculty and no graduate students are available to do this work." He rooted around on the shelves, pulling out a tray here and a group of vials there. He wasn't sure where Wil Downs's notebooks were, so the samples we found told only a partial story of the insect life of the Housatonic. But they said quite a lot about Wil Downs. Ray identified Downs's spidery India ink notations on vials going as far back as 1938. "Entomologists start young," Ray said. "Once we get going, it's hard to stop us." After ten minutes of searching, he was satisfied that we had found most of the important Downs materials. We carried them back to the lunchroom and set them down next to my laptop.

Two other entomologists were already eating. A poster on the wall above them read, "Entomologists get the bugs out." Bill Krinsky was sitting on one side of the table. On the other was a mosquito specialist named Leonard Munstermann. He had a long old-timer's beard that suggested a surgeon in the Union army. Munstermann grew animated when he heard us talking about the Housatonic and began firing questions at me about the stretches where the river cascades over limestone bedrock. He was excited by the discovery in New England of a species of mosquito that had previously been known only in Japan. Some of the samples had come from limestone pools at Kent Falls on the Housatonic. I told him that the Bull's Bridge gorge and the Great Falls were both heavily pockmarked with small, round indentations where high-water residues collected. He nodded vigorously. "Yeah, that's classic. Limestone is soft and porous. It's notorious for creating those pockets where there are weaknesses in the bedrock formation."

As I laid the trays of Wil Downs's Connecticut caddis-fly samples in neat rows in front of me, I kept one ear cocked to the conversation, curious to know what entomologists talked about when they weren't answering questions by visiting writers. A fourth person entered the room as I made my notes, looking for advice. It appeared that she was preparing a talk on insects as food.

"I hear you can eat pollen cactus larvae."

"Don't the Chinese have a taboo against eating honey? Don't they regard it as being the same as fecal matter?"

"Only insect I ever ate was the *gusano* in a bottle of tequila."

"Apparently every time you eat a pancake, you're ingesting insect parts. You can't avoid it; there's no way to keep bugs out of flour."

"That's why you should always put basmati rice in the freezer, someone told me."

"Apparently cicadas are the best; they taste just like shrimp."

An anxious look passed across the face of the woman who was preparing the talk. She asked, "Are locusts kosher, does anyone know? I guess I should talk to the rabbi."

I HAD MOST of the Housatonic samples organized by now, with the vials arranged before me roughly in alphabetical order. Over to my left was *Arctopsyche,* the great gray spotted sedge; *Brachycentrus,* the American grannom; and *Cheumatopsyche,* the little sister sedge. On my extreme right was *Pycnopsyche,* the great brown autumn sedge. The size variations amazed me. Monstrous *Glyphotaelius* stretched more than an inch long; the micro-caddis, *Psychomyidae,* was smaller than a sesame seed. I counted forty-one species altogether.

A few of them, like the grannom, were tube-case makers. Caddis like this predominate in many of the steeper and less fertile tributaries of the Housatonic. Like countless novice fly-fishers before me, I used to spend hours turning over rocks to peer at the inch-long assemblies of gravel, twigs, and leaf matter that the tube-case makers cemented together and glued tightly to the underside of the stones. I used my thumbnail to break open these cases and extract the plump yellow caddis larvae that lived inside. In the process, I came to admire the tube-case makers as a paradigm of inventiveness.

Their cases are marvels of engineering, precisely designed to serve a larva's every need. They provide, in the words of the entomologist Glenn Wiggins, "streamlining, ballast, buoyancy, structural rigidity, camouflage, internal water circulation, external water resistance, protection from predators that would swallow the case whole and from those that would intrude." Using the tube case as a base of operations, the larvae go about their business of shredding dead wood and leaves, scraping algae and fine organic particles from the rocks, grubbing around for food in the silt, and ambushing other aquatic insects. Perhaps it's ridiculous to have anthropomorphic feelings about an insect larva a half-inch long, but it seemed to me that human beings and the tube-case caddis had a surprising amount in common. Like us, the insect uses the resources around it to provide food and shelter and to guarantee survival in order to reproduce. What sets us apart, I thought, was not our deliberate manipulation of the natural environment or our impact on the life of the river but rather the caddis fly's lack of any ethical sense of the consequences of its actions.

There weren't many tube-case makers among Wil Downs's samples, however. As I tried to arrange the specimens roughly by family, it quickly became clear that most of the bugs laid out in front of me were net-spinning caddis. It was one of those small fly-fishing epiphanies. From everything I had learned about the morphology of the river and the human impacts on its flow over the past three hundred years, the predominance of net spinners made perfect sense. These particular caddis flies occupy a pretty lowly rung on the evolutionary ladder, but they perform a vital ecological function, and the Housatonic demands that they perform it in spades. The purpose of the tiny nets they build is to trap organic particles that drift downstream, then to process the simple organisms at the base of the food chain. Their diet may include algae, bacteria, leaf fragments, and animal matter—its precise composition varies from one species to the next.

Thanks to the action of the glaciers and the human political economy, the Housatonic has become a net spinner's paradise. The slow meanders of the upper river through cleared farmland help load the water with plankton and other microorganisms. Small towns on the Massachusetts side contribute their quota of nitrogen and phosphate wastes— enough to enrich the river, but not enough to trigger bacterial growth on a scale that would deplete its dissolved oxygen levels. The dam at Falls Village flushes this suspended organic material downstream toward Cornwall. Thanks to the failure of nineteenth-century industry, the basic shape of the river in northwestern Connecticut has been left more or less intact. The underlying geology of the Great Falls, meanwhile, made building a high dam and a deep impoundment impracticable. So to generate electricity at Falls Village, the engineers have to release warm water from the top of the pond rather than cold water from its bottom, a process that differs from that of most hydropower dams.

In effect, this warm tail water, which funnels significant but not excessive levels of human pollution from farther upstream, acts as a vast food factory. That's why the trout grow so sleek and fat, and it's also why anglers on the Housatonic are always taking involuntary baths—the rocks in the Cornwall Canyon are slick with organic nutrients. These conditions are ideal for net spinners and provide them with a rich and varied diet. Also, the nooks and crannies of the rocky riverbed offer great interstitial habitat.

As the river grows wider, slowing and warming along the way, the mesh of the caddis nets becomes finer in order to deal with the increasing richness of the organic drift. Farther downstream, then, where the smallmouth bass begin to outnumber the trout, you'll find the most spectacular of the Housatonic caddis—the alder fly, *Macronema zebratum,* whose net has the finest mesh of all. Frankly, many of the caddis are homely creatures, but the alder is downright handsome. Its Latin name refers to its brown-and-black-striped wings. Its body is bluish brown, and it has extraordinarily long antennae. Trout love it, and so do anglers.

In the old days, local boys were paid a quarter to walk along the streamside bushes with a stick, beating the branches to flush out the alders. If you heard a freight train approaching on the Housatonic Railroad, which runs along the east bank of the river, you'd call out to alert your friends because the vibrations would shake the alders loose with similar efficiency. When the alder fly hatches in June, anglers from all over the Northeast congregate on the Housatonic. But if you raise a hand in greeting and call out "Any luck?" don't be surprised if the answer is an angry glare. All that organic drift, all those bugs to choose from, can make a trout picky beyond belief.

14
The Pilgrim Road

PERHAPS IT'S WRONG TO SAY that you can plant a fish directly in a river but only generally influence whether a particular bug will live there. Perhaps you can "stock" a bug, too—as long as it's the right bug, and as long as the person doing the stocking has the requisite degree of passion. If the bug, for example, is the undisputed superstar of mayflies, the green drake, and the person is someone like Bob Fumire, who started off wanting to catch big fish and ended with the kind of bug's-eye view that made him a true believer in species diversity and a toxin-free river.

All sorts of drakes hatch on the Housatonic (the name comes from the Latin *draco*, "dragon"). There are brown ones and yellow ones and golden ones, but the most elusive are the green drakes, *Ephemera guttulata*. Some anglers follow this mayfly hatch each spring as if they were pilgrims traveling the road to Compostela. They may begin in West Virginia in the middle of May, spend Memorial Day weekend hopping from one limestone creek to the next in Pennsylvania, and end up around the beginning of June on the Delaware in New York. Fishing writers say that the green drake "brings out the beast in the trout." But it also tends to bring out the beast in the fisherman, and when the hatch is on, Pennsylvania roadsides are lined with SUVs and overcaffeinated anglers with the newest high-tech gear.

This enthusiasm is understandable. The green drake is a beautiful creature, with its olive and black wings, dark olive body, and lighter-colored underbelly. The female can be well over an inch long. When it returns to the river to die—in a form that anglers call the "coffin fly"—the olive body has turned to a snowy white, the three tails have grown to prodigious length, and the outspread wings are clear and shimmering.

Ephemera guttulata is a burrower, spending its nymphal stage in a tunnel that it constructs in streambed silt or fine gravel. Although you can sometimes find the fly in silted pockets behind fast-water boulders, it generally prefers slower and more even currents, which is why Pennsylvania's stable limestone creeks have become synonymous with the green drake hatch. But these conditions aren't nearly so common on the Housatonic, and that may be one reason for the ongoing, and ultimately unresolvable, difference of opinion about the extent to which the Housatonic ever had a substantial green drake population. Ask the state biologists, and they'll express polite skepticism. For some anglers on the river, memories of green drake hatches in the good old days have become an article of faith. But the evidence is anecdotal at best, and the green drake is so weighed down with the baggage of its reputation that memory may be unreliable. One thing that is clear beyond a doubt is that the great flood of 1955 scoured out the riverbed and destroyed any semblance of habitat where the insect might once have thrived.

The worst New England floods typically happen in one of two circumstances. The first is the spring flood, when snowmelt combines with heavy rain. The second, more unpredictable and often more devastating, is the late summer variety, which follows the intense air disturbances set in motion by Caribbean hurricanes moving north. People talk of hundred-year floods, but the Housatonic watershed suffered three of them in a spell of only twenty years. March 1936 brought snowmelt and heavy rain, aggravated by ice jams. September 1938 served up a hurricane. But the mother and father of them all was the flood, or to be more accurate, the twin floods, of August 1955. First, Hurricane Connie dumped eight inches of rain on northwestern Connecticut, washing out roads and bridges. Less than two weeks later, along came Diane. All through the night of August 18–19, Diane raged, and by the time the furor was finally spent, it had lashed the valleys with another sixteen inches of rain. Throughout the Housatonic watershed—and worst of all along the Naugatuck, with its steep, rock-walled valley—the flood tore out streambeds and took the green drake, billions of other insects, and eighty-seven human lives with it.

Bob fumire was the man who tried to put the green drake back. I found him at home in the old clock-making town of Winsted one bright, mild December morning. He was laid up on a sofa, with his leg elevated, trying to recover from a life-threatening blood clot. There were worse places to be convalescent, I thought. The room was spacious and airy, and a large window looked out over a trout pond that Bob had built on the hilltop next to the house. Big fish were dimpling the water, feeding on insects that were invisible to me. It was the home of a man who had been born dirt-poor, worked all his life with energy and focus, and invested the results in a real but unpretentious level of comfort. I didn't think I'd ever met anyone as inherently good-natured as Bob Fumire; just looking at him made me want to smile.

The Fumires arrived in Waterbury from Salerno in the late nineteenth century. They went by Foo-*mee*-reh then, but somewhere along the way, the name was Anglicized, or Germanicized perhaps, to *Few*-meyer. "After my grandfather came over, the family moved to Woodbury," Bob told me. "He was a shoemaker, didn't know a thing about fishing. But living there, he started to fish the Pomperaug, became an expert worm fisherman. It was the need for food. Then he realized you couldn't catch fish on worms twelve months a year because sometimes they were eating flies. My grandfather was very skilled with his hands."

Bob's leg prevented him from getting up, so he gestured over to a box standing on a small table on the other side of the room. I picked it up and admired it. It was a delicate piece of marquetry, with an almost Shaker simplicity.

"So he started tying up imitations. I've seen some of his flies; they were beautiful. Started selling them out of his house in Woodbury; they were awesome, awesome. Somewhere along the line the family got too big, and my grandfather moved them to Waterbury. And he and my father and my uncle began to fish the Housatonic seriously."

World War II got in the way of their fishing plans, however, since it prevented them from getting to the Housatonic easily. Only essential traffic could use Route 7, which runs along the river and served as a major route for tanks and other military vehicles going south to be loaded onto ships. "So of course the military didn't want to tie it up with traffic, people taking a Sunday ride," Bob explained. "So the Fumires, these crazy fishermen, used to get out with the milk wagon, and the driver would drop them off on the river. They'd fish, then the milkman would pick them up and take them home. And of course the milk truck never got stopped. That was the craziness of the Fumire family and fishing. We were just brain-crazy for fishing. My father and grandfather weren't intellectuals, like you read about in the fishing books. They were just *fishermen*."

I asked Bob when the brain-craziness had first afflicted him.

He grinned. "After the war my grandfather bought himself a little camping trailer, about a twelve-footer, and he'd drive over to the Housatonic, park the trailer, and tie flies and fish. That's what he did. And that's what my father and I did. Every Friday, pack up and drive over from Waterbury to the Housatonic. I started when I was six years old, in 1948.

"We'd fish down at Cornwall Bridge and up as far as the Monument Hole. My father, my uncle, my grandfather, used to catch four- and five-pound trout on nymphs, on a regular basis. I caught a twenty-one-inch brown on a worm when I was just a kid. But that was nothing unusual. The state was stocking the river, but not many people knew how to catch the fish, or even wanted to. The dam releases were unregulated in those days. It was slated as a dirty river; people would say it runs muddy all the time. But what people neglected to see was that the food sources in that river were incredible—they still are—and that they grew these big fish. The way we fished wasn't how people fish now. We didn't use to *leave* at nine o'clock at night, we used to *start* at nine o'clock at night, because these enormous trout would start to feed after dark.

"So my grandfather started a very serious business, selling flies at twenty-five cents apiece. They were just awesome. And when I was in third grade, I started to tie flies also. His flies were very close imitations of the naturals. He tied beautiful nymphs, beautifully shaped and formed. There wasn't a trout he caught that he didn't cut the throat open and look at what it had been eating, lay the natural flies down on his bench to imitate them. And I watched him, and learned, and learned, and learned, and learned. I started to sell my own flies to Orvis. When my grandfather passed away, I got his equipment. We were still kids, and I was holding down two jobs, and going fishing every single night, and camping on the river every single weekend."

A LOCAL OUTDOOR WRITER once said that Bob Fumire knew and loved the Housatonic as a Hindu reveres the Ganges. The disappearance of the green drake after 1955 gnawed at him. It seemed a disruption of the proper order of things, and as the years went by, his reverence crystal-lized into a desire to restore the regal insect to the river. In the early 1970s, he decided it was time to do something about it. Bob had read that fly-fishermen in Pennsylvania had tried to restore the green drake to streams from which it had disappeared, with some degree of success. So the Housatonic Fly Fishermen's Association formed a green drake trans-plant committee and put Bob Fumire in charge.

Bob went to the Housatonic Meadows Fly Shop to talk over the idea with Phil Demetri. "He told me it was a lousy idea," Bob recalled. "He said it wasn't worth diddly-squat. But I told him the point of the experiment was not to catch more fish, but to restore the river to the way it had been when my grandfather and his father had known it."

Reactions like Phil Demetri's did nothing to deter Bob; on the con-trary, they only added to the challenge. He pored over obscure scientific articles in the *Bulletin of the Illinois Natural History Survey* and the *Canadian Entomologist*. He showed me a thick file of all the letters he'd written, looking for suggestions. He tried Trout Unlimited and the Smithsonian. He asked state biologists at the DEP in Hartford and the Agricultural Experiment Station in New Haven. He pestered academics at Cornell and Penn State. Where should you look for nymphs to trans-plant? How would you transport them to the river? How would you get adult females to lay eggs for you? How would you increase their chances of survival? How long before you could expect to see results? And how much would it cost? One of those he contacted was Wil Downs, who en-thusiastically offered him the use of lab facilities at the Yale Medical School.

Most of the replies were friendly enough, though marked by a definite undercurrent of skepticism. The DEP was downright conde-scending, noting stuffily that *Ephemera guttulata* had not appeared in the 1920 checklist of *Insects of Connecticut*. Essentially, the agency was telling Bob Fumire that if nature had intended the green drake to be in the Housatonic, it would be there. I thought a lot about this letter. I wondered what it meant to suggest that nature *intended* things to be a certain way. I wasn't sure nature had intended the Falls Village Dam or the Housatonic Railroad to be built. Yet both projects had undoubtedly helped the silt build up in certain pools to a depth where it could be colonized by green drake nymphs. Had nature in any sense *intended* the '55 flood to scour the riverbed? If nature didn't intend for Bob to restore the insect to the Housatonic, did that mean that it would also prefer the DEP to close down its hatcheries and fire its geneticists? Come to that, were Bob Fumire, the DEP, and the rest of us part of this thing called nature in the first place, or did we stand outside it?

The most thoughtful reply came from Alvin Grove, the author of a wonderful book called *The Lure and Lore of Trout Fishing*. Grove said he'd been involved in a couple of attempts—neither of them entirely successful—to reestablish green drake populations in the trout streams of Pennsylvania. He told Bob, "I'm sure you already know that the nymphs in this case are burrowing nymphs and require stream bottom areas where they might penetrate to depths of a foot." Like the net-spinning caddis, the burrowing green drake nymphs feed by filtration. The substrate had to be fine enough for the nymph to make its burrow but not so fine that it risked collapsing like a cave-in in a mineshaft. That appeared to be the problem with the failed transplant of the green drake nymph into Pennsylvania's legendary spring creek, the Letort. The bottom was just too sandy, the grains too fine. In addition, the eggs of the green drake made a particularly tempting snack for freshwater shrimp and caddis larvae.

Bob's immediate problem was to find a good source of nymphs in each stage of development spanning the insect's three-year progression from egg to adult mayfly. The best prospect seemed to be the Mill River in Hamden, on the northern outskirts of New Haven, which was known for its fantastic hatch of green drakes. So on a cold, raw day at the end of March 1973, Bob and a dozen others waded into the forty-degree water of the Mill River and began poking around in the silt and gravel. They used steel garden rakes and clam rakes and caught in a fine-mesh net any nymphs that surfaced. The next day a larger group made a second pass, sifting what they found in wire-mesh boxes, the kind that gardeners use. When they added up the results of their labors, they found they had collected about two hundred green drake nymphs, easily identifiable by their size, their brownish gray coloring, and their three tails.

None of Bob Fumire's correspondents had said much about what he should do next. Since he had no support from science, Bob relied on common sense. He and his wife, Jan, cut holes in the sides of ten kitchen pails and color-coded them with tape, each color denoting a particular pool on the Housatonic with the right kind of soft substrate. They covered the holes with nylon mesh, which would allow oxygenated water to flow through; divided up the nymphs and the mud, a dozen or more bugs to a bucket; and headed north.

Bob had selected three sites for the experiment—the Carse Pool, the Sand Hole, and the Cellar Hole. Fortunately, the river was running unusually low for early spring, and Bob's little work crew found a number of good-looking spots along the shoreline shallows. They dug holes in the silt and embedded the buckets in them. Bob said, "My theory was that the nymphs would get acclimated to their new environment. As the river rose, the pails would empty of the nymphs and mud by overflowing." After that, he reasoned, some of them might burrow into the silt and take up residence in the Housatonic. Looking at the size of the nymphs, the size of the river, and the generally lay character of the operation, you would be forgiven for thinking Bob Fumire a little mad.

L OOK FOR YOUR HATCH in 1975." That had been Alvin Grove's advice. "You may see a few flies in 1974, but don't assume it to be a significant sign of establishment."

Even under the best of conditions, the green drake hatch is an iffy affair. The Compostela pilgrims often find that a monumental hatch one year can be followed by an inexplicable disappearance the next. Nineteen-seventy-four passed uneventfully on the Housatonic. But in 1975, as Grove had hoped, a few scattered duns were sighted. No more than a couple of dozen, but enough to increase Bob Fumire's pulse rate. A year later, Bob became convinced that his experiment had taken. Upstream and downstream of the Carse Pool, fishermen counted hundreds of drakes, and the hatch was spread out over ten consecutive days. By 1980, Bob wrote in his stream diary, "The spinner fall of coffin flies was indeed a sight to behold."

Yet the green drake remained enigmatic. Some said the hatches continued. Others were less sure. The state biologists declared themselves agnostic. For myself, I never seemed to be on the river at the right time. When I talked to Bill Cummings, the Atlantic salmon expert from Woodbury who had been part of the transplant team, he pursed his lips and shook his head. "I don't think it worked," he said. "I'm not sure what went wrong. Could have been the water. Could have been the habitat. Maybe we did something wrong. But I've never seen them."

I was still puzzling over the enigma of the green drake when, one day in mid-February, I noticed the title line on an e-mail message from a fishing friend. It said "Re: Bob Fumire." The message said that Bob was dead, at fifty-six. Whether or not the green drake had defeated Bob Fumire, the blood clot in his leg had.

I thought about Bob a lot that spring, and I was still thinking about him as the light began to fade at the end of a gorgeous afternoon of fishing in the first week of June. The hatches had been quiet for a while, and I was idly drifting a small nymph near the head of the Carse Pool. The river was taking on the luminous stillness of an early summer evening. I stood quietly in midstream, watching the river roll by and feeling its gentle pulse against my waders.

I didn't recognize the green drake at first. It was just a solitary fly, but then another appeared, and another, unmistakable in their size and outline. Even from five yards away, I could clearly make out the limestone-colored body of the male dun and the latticework of olive and black on its upright wings. I expected a trout to engulf the fly, but nothing broke the surface, and I watched the green drake float downstream until it became a black speck against the sparkling water and at last disappeared from view.

15
Toxic Politics

WHEN BOB FUMIRE WAS LOOKING FOR NYMPHS in the Mill River, the site he chose was right behind the house of a retired furrier and former B-24 crewman with the improbable name of Ed Kluck. Ed had acquired his encyclopedic knowledge of the Housatonic over more than forty years, and one day I asked him if there was one single reason why the fishing had come to be so good on the river. Without skipping a beat, he said, "Oh, toxic waste. PCBs." Of all the dimensions of the trout pool paradox, this may be the strangest.

This part of the story begins not in Connecticut but in the grimy industrial town of Pittsfield, Massachusetts. It wasn't always grimy. Starting in the early nineteenth century, the Greek revival mansions of the Housatonic Valley in Massachusetts gained a well-established place in American literary and intellectual history. Oliver Wendell Holmes, who famously remarked that "the best of all tonics is the Housatonic," started spending his summers at Canoe Meadows in about 1837. Catherine Sedgwick, who wrote half a dozen now-forgotten novels in the 1820s and 1830s, turned her family's homes in Stockbridge and Lenox into a literary salon cum seasonal court. The new Connecticut Western Railroad brought Ralph Waldo Emerson and his friend Louis Agassiz, the great geologist who had uncovered the secrets of glaciation. Harriet Beecher Stowe came, and so did Henry Wadsworth Longfellow (who described the Housatonic as "a shallow brown stream, not very clear"). Jenny Lind came to sing, and Daniel Webster came to fish. Edith Wharton married into a Lenox family and built a mock-English stately home on a hilltop. Nathaniel Hawthorne poked around in the rocky glen below his house in Stockbridge, rather as my kids had explored the stream that coursed down the hillside in Southbury. They called theirs Alfaro; Hawthorne called his Shadowbrook and Tanglewood.

LONGFELLOW WAS RIGHT: while the headwaters of the river were the tannic amber of a mountain brook coursing through hemlock forest, the slow serpentines and oxbows around Stockbridge were tinted with a different shade of brown. The tumbling descent and deeper, slower reaches of the upper river lent themselves ideally to the construction of mills and dams. The Pittsfield area in particular quickly outgrew the usual assortment of gristmills and sawmills. After the War of 1812, Pittsfield took advantage of its position as a garrison town to strengthen its manufacturing base and financial services. As iron was to Salisbury, and as brass was to Waterbury, so paper was to Pittsfield and the neighboring river towns. By 1849 the town of Lee was producing a fifth of all the paper used in the United States. By the end of the Civil War, twenty-eight paper mills were strung along the river between Dalton and Great Barrington, Massachusetts—more than one per mile.

Paper mills are not labor-intensive industries, so they tended not to encourage the growth of cities and slums. But they wreaked havoc on rivers. Chard Powers Smith took a canoe trip downriver from Pittsfield to Stratford in the 1940s to observe firsthand, at water level, how went the battle between the Lord of Ideas and the Devil of Greed. Between Pittsfield and Lee, it went badly. At Pittsfield, he reported that the eelgrass was "darkly coated" with "streaks of iridescent grease" and did his best to keep his free hand out of the water. At New Lenox, he described the river as "a Stygian and unhealthy flood." Woods Pond, behind the Smith Paper Company dam, was "a fetid artery of death."

More than just an industrial town, Pittsfield was a company town. In 1903, the General Electric Company bought a large tract of land on the east side of the Housatonic, and by the end of World War II, GE was employing about sixteen thousand workers in response to the heavy wartime demand for electrical transformers and ordnance. People in Pittsfield referred to their town as the "transformer capital of the world." To lubricate and insulate its transformers, GE used a synthetic chlori-

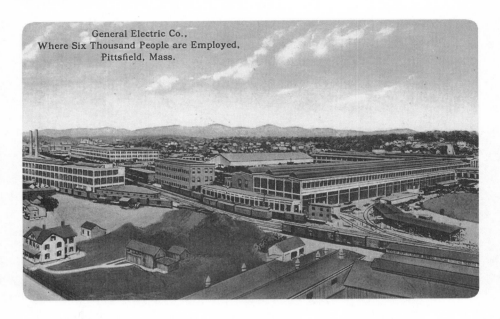

General Electric Co.,
Where Six Thousand People are Employed,
Pittsfield, Mass.

nated organic substance marketed under the name of Pyranol. The Monsanto Chemical Company called it Aroclor. These friendly trade names slipped off the tongue more easily than the cumbersome term the scientists used—polychlorinated biphenyls, or PCBs for short.

The Pittsfield plant is long gone—shut down as a money loser in the mid-1980s—and Aroclor and Pyranol are long forgotten. But for anyone with even a casual interest in modern environmentalism, PCBs have acquired a kind of code-word status. Up and down the Housatonic Valley, when PCBs are mentioned, people take on the panic-stricken expression of Transylvanian villagers in a Dracula movie, looking for garlic to string over their bedposts. Industry defenders of PCBs have protested that such reactions were overcooked. They say that PCBs were unfairly scapegoated, the victims of bad timing and a sinister-sounding acronym, reminiscent of DDT or KGB. They describe PCBs as a case of "political pollution," an issue that had the misfortune to come to public attention just as a wave of new environmental legislation was being introduced.

Although I instinctively mistrusted this as a piece of corporate smoke blowing, I didn't feel comfortable dismissing the argument out of hand. Though we look for simple hero-and-villain narratives that lead to morally comforting conclusions, science is less indulgent. A fact must be a fact. Especially when dealing with something like environmental toxins, accuracy is everything; slogans won't do. The stakes are too high.

PCBs certainly make a lurid villain. But just how villainous are they? What do they do to us? To try to answer those questions, I holed up for a couple of days in an upstairs room of a colonial house in Cornwall Bridge, where the not-for-profit Housatonic Valley Association (HVA) has a whole shelf of scientific studies on PCBs.

Polychlorinated biphenyls had first been synthesized in the latter part of the nineteenth century, but not until 1929 did they go into mass production in the United States. GE began using them in its Large Transformer Plant at Pittsfield three years later. More than two hundred compounds make up the PCB family—congeners, scientists call them—each molecule consisting of two benzene rings and from one to ten chlorine atoms. This makes for remarkable qualities, and GE marketed Pyranol as a miracle invention that would do just about anything but slice your bread in the morning. It didn't dissolve in water. It didn't conduct electricity. Chemicals didn't break down Pyranol. It didn't evaporate. It was uncommonly stable under high temperatures, and it refused to catch fire. For all these reasons, it made an ideal insulator for transformers, capacitors, and heat exchangers. In addition to working well in these "closed" electrical systems, PCBs were also useful in a wide range of "open" applications: copying paper, paints, and varnishes; printing inks, adhesives, and soaps; caulking material and food packaging.

PCB molecules have three additional characteristics. First, they are persistent; they are extremely slow to degrade into a more benign form. The only thing that will break them down effectively is ultraviolet-B radiation. Second, they have a tendency to adhere to silt and soil, which shields them very nicely from the sun's rays. In fact, they have a special affinity for the kind of fine granite, schist, and mica particles that make up much of the sediment in the Housatonic. Being heavier than water, the PCBs that were discharged or spilled from the Pittsfield plant settled in the riverbed—nowhere more than in the reeking black mud of Woods Pond. But they didn't necessarily stay there. Floods or spring runoff could stir up the silt, resuspending the PCB molecules and redistributing them downstream or across the Housatonic floodplain.

The third problem with PCBs, now clearly understood to be their most sinister aspect, is that they become massively concentrated—in the jargon, they "bioaccumulate"—in the fatty tissue of living organisms that ingest them. Brown trout and smallmouth bass in the Housatonic, for example, absorb PCBs through their skin or gills or by eating contaminated benthic insects and crayfish. Rodents, birds, and other small creatures rooting for food in the floodplain offer a second pathway into the food chain.

But for almost forty years, no one used words like *problem* or *contaminated* when talking about PCBs. On the contrary, products like Aroclor and Pyranol promised the synthetic utopia that was to be America's future. Scientific research that suggested PCBs could cause skin lesions and liver damage was brushed aside for years. But then, in 1966, a Swedish scientist named Soren Jensen found PCBs in the feathers of white-tailed eagles that had been collected for a local museum. His work raised serious questions about whether PCBs could indeed be contained in "closed" systems. Two years later, twenty-nine people died in Japan after eating rice-bran oil that was accidentally contaminated with toxic substances associated with Kanechlor 400, a locally produced equivalent of Aroclor.

After the "Yusho incident," scientists began to find PCBs all over the planet: in Australian pelicans, in Baltic seals, and in the milk of cows in West Virginia. The anxiety level peaked in 1975 in response to two almost simultaneous events. New York state authorities warned the public not to eat striped bass from the Hudson River because of unacceptably high levels of PCBs, which they traced to the big GE plant near Albany. Then Dr. Renate Kimbrough of the Centers for Disease Control in Atlanta, who had been feeding high doses of PCBs to laboratory rats, published a landmark study concluding that long-term exposure caused a "tumorigenic response . . . and hepatocellular carcinomas among rodents"—translated into headlines, liver cancer. The federal Environmental Protection Agency declared PCBs a probable human carcinogen.

A year after the Hudson River warnings made the front page of the *New York Times,* the state of Connecticut determined that similar problems were present in the Housatonic. Again, GE was the source. The EPA had set a maximum safety level of 2 parts per million (ppm) for PCBs in the environment. The concentrations in the Housatonic on the Massachusetts side averaged 34 ppm. In some of the hot spots near the GE plant in Pittsfield, concentrations of 54,000 ppm were found in the river sediment and almost twice that amount in the adjacent riverbank. GE calculated that Woods Pond alone contained 95,000 cubic yards of sediment with PCB concentrations in excess of 10 ppm. There were also signs, in both the river and the floodplain, of even nastier toxic compounds, known as polychlorinated dibenzofurans (PCDFs) and poly-chlorinated dibenzodioxins (PCDDs), which are produced when PCBs are heated or burned.

YET NONE OF THIS EVIDENCE was enough to settle the debate. As I continued going through the HVA files, I found reports that Dr. Kimbrough had recanted on some of her original findings, and others that said the real culprit in the Yusho incident had been dibenzofurans, the result of the PCBs passing through a thermal heat exchanger before the rice-bran oil contamination occurred. Too much of the debate had a he-said, she-said quality, which I was still trying to unravel when the long-running skirmish between GE and the federal EPA escalated into full-scale war.

For years, the EPA and state officials from Connecticut and Massachusetts had tried to reach a negotiated settlement with GE over the Housatonic. But the talks fell apart in 1997, and in April of the following year the EPA took the fight to the next level, threatening to designate the old Pittsfield plant and the Housatonic for thirty miles downstream a Superfund site. This move was a little like introducing the threat of nuclear weapons into a conflict being fought with handguns. Superfund designation means, apart from the kind of stigma no corporation wants, that the federal government can step in, use Superfund dollars to clean up a toxic waste site, and then charge the offending party three times the actual cost.

For connoisseurs of corporate misconduct, the PCB fight was a story made in heaven. A *New York Times* columnist wrote that GE's dumping of PCBs "ranks among the most clear-cut and destructive cases of industrial pollution ever recorded." The EPA said that a child playing along the worst stretch of the Housatonic had a one in one thousand chance of contracting cancer. GE called this "fantasy" and "science fiction" and "a polemic calculated to frighten people." But the problem had now grown too big to be left to the corporate public affairs department. Countering force with force, GE decided to send its top man into combat at the shareholders' meeting on April 28.

John F. Welch Jr., chairman and CEO since 1981, had begun his career with the General Electric Company by working for several years at the Pittsfield plant. This gave him a certain degree of authenticity. From those modest beginnings, Welch had built a reputation as America's top corporate guru. I'd seen his face on the jackets of a slew of inspirational business books: polished dome of a forehead, even more highly polished teeth that looked as if they might enjoy taking a bite out of your leg. These books had titles like *Get Better or Get Beaten* and *Control Your Destiny, or Someone Else Will.* The reviews said Jack Welch was "the world's greatest business leader." They said he was "as notorious as he is respected." He was "the toughest boss in America"; he was "Neutron Jack." The reviews did not say whether Jack Welch was the type of man who would lose his cool in public, especially in a debate with a Dominican nun.

In Latin America I'd seen nuns in action who could reduce ambassadors and death squad leaders to a plate of Jell-O, and Sister Patricia Daly, from Newton, New Jersey, was evidently cut from that kind of cloth. Sister Patricia stood up in the GE shareholders' meeting and called on the company to stop sponsoring misleading scientific studies of the impact of PCBs and instead to fund a public education campaign that would warn people along the Hudson and the Housatonic of the dangers they faced.

Neutron Jack lit into her. He said, "PCBs do not pose health risks. Based on the scientific evidence developed since the 1970s, we simply do not believe that there are any significant adverse health effects from PCBs."

He paused, and then went on. "I want to make it very clear to all of you that we, your company, will base our discussion of PCBs, as we have for twenty years, on science, not on bad politics or shouting voices from a few activists. Science will decide this issue. Advocates can shout loudly. They can say anything. They are accountable to no one."

Sister Patricia retorted, "We are all accountable, and you know who I am accountable to."

Welch said, "No, I do not. I would like to . . ."

"I truly think my accountability is ultimately to God, which is why . . ."

"And I think mine is also."

"I am not judging that," Sister Patricia said. "What I am saying, Mr. Welch, is that this is an issue of public education."

Welch shouted, "Sister, why not take public education right to the government, and have them educate the public on the situation? It is not our job to educate."

"It is, however," the nun said. "Let's get this absolutely straight. The EPA continues to list PCBs on its suspected carcinogen list. For you to be saying that PCBs are perfectly harmless is not true. . . . We all remember the image of the CEOs of the tobacco companies swearing that they were telling the truth. Do they have any credibility in the United States today?"

"That is an outrageous comparison!"

"That is an absolutely valid comparison, Mr. Welch."

"It is outrageous."

Sister Patricia bore on relentlessly. "Mr. Welch, I am sorry, but we need to have the independent scientific community decide this, not the GE scientific community."

Welch said, "Twenty-seven studies, twenty-one of them independent, have concluded that there is no correlation between PCB levels and cancer, Sister. You have to stop this conversation. You owe it to God to be on the side of the truth here."

"I am on the side of the truth."

Now, going nose-to-nose with nuns on matters of God and Truth rarely gets you far, and none of this scored GE many points in the court of public opinion. Yet one has to allow Jack Welch his basic point: science had to decide the question, not emotion. Twenty-seven studies were a lot to dismiss, even if Welch did tacitly acknowledge that at least half a dozen of them were tainted by company sponsorship.

What finally settled the debate, as far as I was concerned, was a paper from the Centers for Disease Control, called "Public Health Implications of Exposure to Polychlorinated Biphenyls." This summarized the findings of dozens of studies conducted from 1954 to 1999. It concluded:

> Human health studies discussed in this summary indicate that: (1) reproductive function may be disrupted by exposure to PCBs; (2) neurobehavioral and developmental deficits occur in newborns and continue through school-aged children who had in utero exposure to PCBs; (3) other systemic effects (e.g. self-reported liver disease and diabetes, and effects on the thyroid and immune systems) are associated with elevated serum levels of PCBs; and (4) increased can-

cer risks, e.g. non-Hodgkin's lymphoma, are associated with PCB exposures.

Certain population groups were particularly vulnerable, including the elderly, pregnant women, children, fetuses, nursing infants, members of certain ethnic groups such as the Inuit, and recreational anglers. Consumption of contaminated fish was the most efficient pathway for disease. Capacitor manufacturing workers exposed to commercial PCB mixtures were found to have increased mortality from liver, gallbladder, biliary tract, and gastrointestinal tract cancers and malignant melanoma. Electrical utility workers who handled PCBs had significantly elevated mortality rates from malignant melanoma and brain tumors. I wanted to send a copy of the report to John F. Welch Jr., but I was pretty sure that Sister Daly, or someone like her, would already have taken care of that.

THE READER can be forgiven for wondering what all this has to do with blue-ribbon trout fishing. Ed Kluck told me that part of the story. Like the other hard-core regulars on the river, Ed did not see himself as a political animal, at least at first. The nucleus of the Housatonic Fly Fishermen's Association (of which Ed later became president) was made up of ethnic Italians and Poles from the immigrant cities of Waterbury and New Haven. "My forebears were Polacks," Ed told me. "Came over at the time of World War II. They were farmers who decided it was time to get the hell out and get over here." When Ed joined the HFFA in 1969, the group was eight years old. "It was primarily a blue-collar organization in those days," Ed said. "The Connecticut Fly Fishermen's Association, the CFFA, was white collar, which reflected the area they draw their people from, a bunch of professionals from the Hartford area. Whereas these people, the ones who started the HFFA, were pipe fitters and steamfitters, tradespeople, construction-type people. Very few professionals."

Fly-fishing organizations were beginning to boom in the 1960s, and with their growth came the realization that they had political muscle to flex. At first, Ed told me, "the professional biologists and the fishermen distrusted each other. So they thought they'd get together and form an organization to try to present a unified approach. And it worked, after a while. At least it was the beginning of a process that helped the professionals, the biologists, realize that the river users were not all little gray-haired ladies in tennis shoes or members of the local PTA. Even if they might get overly emotionally involved, they knew what they were talking about. And the reverse started to happen, too. The fishermen began to understand that the professional biologists knew what the hell *they* were talking about—even if they were prohibited from doing the right thing because of the political appointees in Hartford."

In the early days of the HFFA, no one really saw it as a conservationist organization. The main motivation behind it was to catch big fish, and lots of them. But then some of the members began to worry that the state might decide to turn Route 7, the two-lane blacktop that snakes along the riverside, into a superhighway to speed New Yorkers north to Vermont and Canada. A project on that scale would mean tearing up and broadening the valley floor and reshaping the flow of the river.

This wasn't a quixotic fear. By the 1960s, Eisenhower's interstates had been laid in, and now the secondary arteries of the highway system needed to be upgraded. Since river valleys offered the most logical transit corridors, trout fishermen knew very well the threat that the highways could pose. They needed to look no farther than the hallowed streams of the Catskills and the construction of New York's Route 17—the Quickway—which rushed traffic westward from the Hudson Valley, through Elmira and Jamestown, to the shores of Lake Erie. This route cut straight through the inviting valleys of the Beaverkill and the Willowemoc, source of most of the inspirational myths of American fly-fishing. Anglers, valley residents, and environmentalists all fought the Quickway, but they went down to a bitter defeat. Here and there, they succeeded in having the road routed away from the river or minimizing the immediate damage from excavation and blasting. But overall the highway builders prevailed. The Quickway now crisscrosses the Beaverkill and the Willowemoc a dozen times, and fishing there demands a high level of tolerance for the rumble of diesel rigs overhead.

People along the Housatonic worried that they might be next. Interstate 84, which was built in 1961, crosses the river in Southbury, at its confluence with the Pomperaug. Twelve miles and six exits later, it crosses the Naugatuck at Waterbury, in a multilevel tangle of spaghetti, just below the illuminated cross of Holy Land U.S.A. There were two main contenders for the site of a new north-south superhighway to intersect with the interstate. One was Route 7, which runs for more than three hundred miles from Norwalk, Connecticut, to the Canadian border. The other was Route 8, which wound its way through the moribund brass mills of the Naugatuck Valley.

The planners chose the Naugatuck in the end, and in retrospect their choice seems a no-brainer. The same logic that had operated in the building of mills and dams and failed canal schemes now worked for the highways. Once again, geology, economics, the balance of political power, and a certain amount of blind chance determined that not the Housatonic, but rather the endlessly abused Naugatuck, would be torn up. Residents of prosperous small towns along the Housatonic mobilized against the plan to develop Route 7. Naugatuck Valley business leaders and elected officials urged a Route 8 expressway, and the Tri-State Transportation Commission backed them. Waterbury's civic boosters and editorial writers, the spiritual descendants of William Pape, wanted the expressway more than anyone. It might not beautify their blighted town, but with the brass industry in terminal decline, it might be the key to economic renewal. Over on the Housatonic, the fishermen breathed freely again and went back to their fishing. And as Ed Kluck said, "The fishing was pretty darned good."

ED KLUCK had just become president of the HFFA when news broke of the pollution of the river by PCBs. The group was just beginning to dip a toe into environmental politics. It was hard not to: anglers were just as aware as any other group of Americans of the times in which they were living. It's tempting these days to write off the 1970s as a lost decade, remembered only for inflation, gas lines, discos, and orange shag-pile carpeting. But the decade also brought a revolution in environmental consciousness. In some respects, in fact, its flurry of new laws, organizations, and attitudes echoed the birth of the conservationist movement exactly a century earlier, after the Civil War.

Rachel Carson had started it all, of course—or at least brought the environment into public focus—with the publication of *Silent Spring* in 1962. Over a ten-year span, a slew of new federal laws were introduced: the Water Pollution Control Act (1966), the National Environmental Policy Act (1969), the Clean Air Act (1970), the Clean Water Act (1972), the Endangered Species Act (1973), the Safe Drinking Water Act (1974), the

Resource Conservation and Recovery Act (1976), and the Toxic Sub-stances Control Act (1976), which regulated water pollution created by 24 major industries and 126 toxic pollutants.

A new breed of advocacy organizations sprang up, insisting that laws alone were not enough. The Environmental Defense Fund started up on Long Island in 1967, and its slogan—"Sue the Bastards!"—pretty much summed up how many people felt about giant corporate polluters like GE. Three years later, a group of New York lawyers, some of whom had fought the landmark Storm King case opposing a new power plant on the Hudson, formed the Natural Resources Defense Council (NRDC). The first Earth Day, in 1970, was a demand for enforcement. The follow-ing year, the Nixon administration set up the Environmental Protection Agency; a year after that the new EPA ordered a permanent nationwide ban on DDT. A series of events, including the Santa Barbara oil spill of 1969, Three Mile Island in 1979, and Love Canal a year later, defined a decade of public suspicion of the oil industry, nuclear power, and toxic chemicals. All production of PCBs was halted in 1979.

Like hundreds of other local groups, the Housatonic fishermen found that the new environmentalism brought a shift in their membership. The steamfitters and pipe fitters were joined by an influx of lawyers, sci-entists, and academics. Bob Fumire had told me, "When we started, we were just a bunch of guys from over on the Naugatuck. But as the organi-zation grew, a new faction of people came in who really had the right idea. They were very political. They said this isn't sufficient reason to have a club; we need to work to save the river. There was a whole group from the Hamden area, who really didn't know the river, but they wanted to be part of it."

I'd asked Bob if friction had developed between the old guard and the newcomers. "Oh sure," he said with a laugh. "We were suspicious of them at first. We wondered why they wanted to come up from Hamden, sixty miles away, and screw around with our river. There were fights. There were verbal confrontations. The charter of the club then was to stock fish. But that's changed radically. Now it's to make sure no one screws around with our beautiful river. If we saw a state truck dump-ing leftover road salt and sand into the river, we'd pick up the phone and make them stop. When they fixed up the covered bridge at West Cornwall, we told them to make sure they did the construction work in a way that didn't mess up the river. At first they said, 'Who the hell are these guys?' But it worked. That's because more polished people had come in, attorneys, people in the know, people who knew who you had to see in Hartford to get things done, people who could make the right phone call. So we learned. We saw that they could accomplish things that we couldn't. We all grew."

Ed Kluck's predecessor as HFFA president was a Yale professor named Hank Shotwell. During his tenure, the HFFA, like many other local fly-fishing groups, experimented with planting eggs in the river's feeder streams, using mesh-sided Vibert boxes, to see if they could stimulate the natural reproduction of brown trout in the river. The Vibert boxes didn't take, but the experience brought a deeper appreciation of the working processes of the river.

In 1973, the year of the green drake transplant, Shotwell opened up the first serious negotiations with Northeast Utilities about the flow regime from the Falls Village power plant. Ed Kluck remembered it. "Until then, you just had to learn to watch rocks and look for signs that the water was rising. When the plant went onto the Northeast Utilities supply grid, they'd just watch the computer printout. They'd tell the plant operators, when we need power, just kick out. So the timing was totally unpredictable. The rising water trapped a lot of people—didn't do any serious injury to anyone, but it sure gave you an adrenaline rush. After Hank got a dialogue going, we started getting a little more cooperation from the power plant."

A$_T$ THIS POINT, one thing began to lead to another—fish, flows, PCBs, state policies—in interesting and unforeseen ways. As the culture of the HFFA changed, so did its understanding of the reasons for the river's immense productivity. "None of us realized the number of holdover fish that were in the river," Ed said. "At that time, the boys fished for hatchery trout. You heard when the hatchery was doing a stocking, and you came out here with a good supply of black ghost streamers. But after a week or two the hatchery fish stop charging at streamers, and they start reverting to the natural food. So then the cry would go up, 'Jesus, Ed, there ain't no fish in the river! They gotta stock some more!'"

Ed's problem here was, more than anything, an educational one. But in order to educate his membership, he first had to educate himself, not to mention the state biologists, whose own knowledge of the river and its potential was shaky. Ed leaned forward in his seat and grinned, remembering. "I'd become friendly with Larry Banlon, the senior state biologist for the Housatonic. We've always had a good rapport with the fisheries biologists, something that DEP headquarters in Hartford doesn't like. They get very nervous if the professional personnel become friendly with the user groups. But Larry and I got to talking about the holdover fish in the Housatonic. They had no records about this up in Hartford, so they were reluctant to manage the river as a holdover fishery without knowing more. Bottom line is that for three years we used to meet Larry up at the Burlington Fish Hatchery and do various clips—adipose fin clips, left ventral, pectoral, that sort of thing—to identify the year class of the fish that were being planted. And then we kept diaries to show what we were catching. We had forty or fifty people keeping diaries, which is pretty good for a club with two hundred, three hundred members. We identified the fish by size, by where we caught them, the whole schmeer. These diaries began to establish that the holdover population was accounting for at least 20 or 30 percent of the fish caught in the Housatonic. In the fall months, it was even better."

Not only that, the growth rates were equally impressive. An eight-inch juvenile trout grew to a foot from its first summer to its second. Even the older HFFA members, those who had grown up with the "put in big fish" mentality, found themselves drawn in. "Some of the guys created the Rainbow Club as a spinoff," Ed said. "We started tagging the big rainbows that we stocked—with those T-shaped plastic tags that they use to attach labels to your clothes, you know, the kind that won't come out—and we put our name and address on each tag, and a number. The tags were implanted just when the fish were put in the river, so we knew exactly where, for example, number 123 went in. That meant we could tell, when people sent the tags back, what kind of migratory situation was going on. Some of the fish were caught one or two years later, so we had evidence that the rainbows were holding over, as well as the browns. And some of them were migrating. One spring, before opening day, I got an envelope, and I could feel the tag in it. The stamp had a New York cancellation. I opened it, thinking, What the hell is this?—it was the tag from a trout that had been stocked right here, at the Monument Hole. It had gone downstream, passed over the dam at the Bull's Bridge power plant or maybe around it and through the canal, turned right at the Tenmile River, and went up into New York State. You look at the map, that's a twenty-five- or thirty-mile trip."

THIS KIND OF DATA had unforeseen value once the PCB issue erupted in 1977.

"Okay," Ed said, "so as you know, the EPA did its study and found that the PCB concentrations in the Housatonic Valley were pretty damn high. I went to the deputy chief of the DEP and said, 'Look, these PCBs are going to cause a problem. Why don't you reduce the creel limit? That way you're going to cut down the health risk from people keeping and eating too many fish.' They said, 'No way, don't worry about it.' Instead of reducing the catch, the state reduced the stocking levels in 1978, and again in 1979."

Politics now kicked in at a much higher level. Public awareness of environmental toxins was at a high pitch, but understanding of the issue was also quite crude. Today the greatest concern about the impact of PCBs and similar synthetic toxins is the pervasive way in which they take up residence in our tissues. About a third of total world production of PCBs between 1929 and 1977 escaped into the environment, the molecules either entering the food chain directly or rising into the atmosphere on dust particles, returning as rainfall, and infiltrating our lipids that way. By the time a hypothetical PCB molecule from Pittsfield reached the top of the food chain—say, the reproductive organs of an Arctic polar bear—PCB concentrations might be *three billion* times their level at the point of emission. Today, almost all Americans carry PCB molecules in their fatty tissue.

But in 1977, the science on PCBs was rendered in the popular shorthand as "cancer risk." This led, not unnaturally, to what environmentalists call linear responses: don't eat the fish from the Housatonic or you'll get cancer; don't let your kids swim in the Housatonic or their skin will fall off. This kind of reductionism had unfortunate results. For some people it was the equivalent to planting a skull-and-crossbones flag in the river. For others, the fact that the river water didn't eat the flesh off their legs as they waded became proof that the whole business was a false alarm. To this day, whenever the PCB story flares up in the media, you can be sure the reporters will find some bass fisherman who'll say, "Well,

I've been eating the fish for years and look at me—never did me any harm." Even Ed Kluck, who was at the heart of the PCB battle when, as he put it, "the shit hit the fan," was one of those who thought the threat was grossly exaggerated. Ed told me, "I once added it up on a calculator, and I worked out that you would have to keep your limit of five fish, every day, and eat them for something like six months, in order for your system to absorb the amount of PCB-laden fish that the EPA had set as the threshold for residual concentrations in the human body."

Curiously enough, very little militancy on the PCB issue erupted in Massachusetts, where the Housatonic had never been of much recreational interest and those most likely to suffer adverse health effects stayed on the sidelines. When people rely for their livelihood on a single employer, as GE workers did in Pittsfield, it has a way of dampening their instinct to complain. But in Connecticut, the fight galvanized environmentalists, anglers, and savvy, well-funded civic organizations such as the HVA and the Housatonic River Commission, a statutory body set up to represent the interests of seven river towns. Public fears ran at such a pitch that eventually the governor of Connecticut was drawn into the fight, for reasons that may have been as much personal as political.

ELLA GRASSO was the daughter of an Italian family from Essex Locks, on the Connecticut River, and she kept close to her roots. An old-fashioned Democratic Party machine liberal, she had made a name for herself as a vocal opponent of the Vietnam War at the 1968 Chicago convention. In 1974 she became the country's first woman governor. One of her priorities was a landmark solid waste disposal law, to deal with what one official called the "promiscuous discharge of human excrement" into the state's rivers.

Ella Grasso became convinced that the PCBs in the Housatonic were a potentially serious public health problem. It was impossible to separate this from the fact that she herself had just been diagnosed with a terminal case of pancreatic cancer. To this day, state biologists believe that Grasso personally ordered the DEP to cease stocking trout in the Housatonic.

Ed Kluck remembered the situation: "It was a Sunday in April. The state was scheduled to do its stocking the next day, in time for opening day the following Saturday. Then news came over the radio that the commissioner had announced that the Housatonic would not be stocked. So of course things got a little exciting—understatement of the year. Bottom line is, the commissioner, Stanley Pac, said it was his decision—PCBs, bee-dee-bop, bee-dee-bop. Whether Ella Grasso had called Stanley and told him to close the river down, I don't know. That's what they say. I went up to the governor's office one day. She had open house once a week—Wednesdays, Thursdays, whatever damn day it was. She allowed me to come in, and we talked for about fifteen or twenty minutes about the situation. But she was adamant. She was dead a few months after that. I think it's clear that her illness warped her judgment.

"We organized petitions and letter-writing campaigns. And we decided to go to court. So we entered a lawsuit suing Stanley Pac, which didn't make Stanley very happy." Ed chuckled. "But at the same time we had constant interaction with the DEP. I got to know some of the people up there quite well, got to like a lot of them too, like the deputy commissioner, who was a political appointee but also a wildlife biologist. Before the case came to court, the DEP agreed that they would come up with a management plan for the river."

What that plan should be was something of a conundrum. Agreeing that PCBs were toxic was the easy part. But if they were so toxic, how could people be allowed to fish in the river at all? The conventional answer was that the state could ill afford the loss of revenue. All those fishermen, not to mention canoeists, campers, and hikers, brought money into Connecticut. The DEP acknowledged this, but they agonized over what to do about it. If they *didn't* suspend trout stocking, would they be exposing people to an unacceptable health risk? If they *did* halt the stocking, why would anyone continue to fish the river?

The anglers came back with a novel proposal: no-kill management. Let the fishing continue, they said, but on a catch-and-release basis, in accordance with a philosophy that was coming into vogue among American anglers at the time. Their trump card, it turned out, was the holdover studies and stream diaries that Ed Kluck, Bob Fumire, and their friends had been compiling. Ed said, "In 1980, when the DEP was forced to make the decision, they had a fallback. They could tell the governor, and any politician who might be listening to the tree-huggers about stocking fish in a river that was full of PCBs, that this river *did* hold trout year round, and that no-kill would work. Their major fear was that fishermen would stop using the river. They were very upset about no-kill. They worried that there would not be angler support for it on a trout stream of this magnitude. Well, that worry was gone in a year, once word got out that there were lots of trout in this river, even when the stocking was discontinued. The fish were holding over, and they were of a good size. In fact, in May and June of 1980, with no fish stocked in the river, we had some of the best fishing ever. There weren't a lot of smaller fish to bother the feeding habits of the larger ones. It was fun, I mean real fun. Eighteen-inch fish were ho-hum."

The state inaugurated the new trout management area in time for opening day in 1981, with three miles of water above Cornwall Bridge reserved for fly-fishing only. Ed Kluck and his friends vowed to give the DEP holy hell if they allowed other kinds of fishing in that stretch.

ONCE A YEAR, a group of Housatonic regulars get together at the campground, just above the Split Rock Pool, for the HFFA's annual riverbank cleanup and tree planting. Compared with the environmental sagas of the 1970s, the cleanup is small potatoes, simply a small gesture of conscience and a chance to hang out with old friends.

There were a couple of younger men, environmentalists, scientists, advocates of wild fish. With the exception of them, and me, and a young trucker from New Haven, the median age was sixty or sixty-five. There was gray hair, and white hair, and no hair, and lots of wrinkles and stubble, and cheap cigars perfuming the morning air.

"Hey guys, I'm glad I listened to the polka station this morning, or I wouldn't have heard about the cleanup."

"Still eatin' those Drunken Donuts, I see."

"How 'bout you? Not too cold for you to go in the water, huh?"

The audience had heard all the banter before, but it didn't matter. As something of an outsider, I felt as if I was watching a bunch of veteran ethnic comedians—Irish American, Polish American, Italian American— on the standup circuit.

Once they had a couple of garbage sacks filled with soda cans and hamburger wrappers, the men started casting shifty glances around, looking to see who was going to make the first move for his rod and do some fishing. One of the older guys got to his feet, hitched his pants up around his ample stomach, and headed for the pine latrine at the edge of the trees. "Gotta go see Mrs. Murphy," he said.

The group began to disperse. I pulled on my waders and my fishing vest and strung up a nine-foot rod with a six-weight sink-tip line, since the water was running high.

The no-kill philosophy has worked wonderfully well on the Housatonic, just as Ed Kluck predicted. And although eighteen-inch trout are not exactly ho-hum these days, they're still enough of a possibility to keep things interesting. The river was right below me now, broken water glinting in the morning light, and I found myself remembering a local magazine article I'd recently read, written to entice tourists to the valley. It had been full of words like *unspoiled, pristine,* and *wilderness.* I thought of the efforts to build a second Holyoke here and the churning flow from the turbines at Falls Village. I thought of the toxic particles clinging to the quartz and mica silt of the riverbed. But when the magazine writer said the river was pristine, he had certainly intended no irony, and I'm sure none was taken.

With these thoughts running in my head, I turned away from the picnic tables and shimmied down the hillside between the cathedral pines to see what a fly might move in the deep runs below Split Rock. There wasn't a PCB molecule in sight.

16
Row v. Wade

LYNN WERNER IS THE EXECUTIVE DIRECTOR of the
Housatonic Valley Association, for which she has worked for twenty
years. She found her calling to environmentalism as a teenager, when she
had the good fortune to fall into the hands of a gifted high school science
teacher named Walt Landgraf, the everything-ologist who had taken me
hiking in the hills above the Farmington River.

Driving up Route 7 to see Lynn Werner, I found myself thinking
of my own, more modest environmental epiphany. It came, I suppose,
when I was about nine years old. I had grown up in a landscape that had
been raped and despoiled by coal mining. Given these surroundings, my
epiphany might have come in dramatic ways. It might have been trig-
gered by the brown coal fogs that invaded my mother's lungs and almost
took her life. It might have come from watching the methane fires burn
on the slag heaps at night or seeing the stagnant ponds of mine drainage
filled with rusting pit machinery. But in fact it happened in a much more
mundane fashion, on one of the trains that chuffed their way through my
childhood.

It was the middle of the night. I was standing in the third-class toilet
of the *Flying Scotsman,* the dashing, romantic steam locomotive that
whisked us twice a year through the darkness from Edinburgh to visit my
grandparents in London. I had just woken up. Billows of white smoke,
full of sparks and cinders, were swirling past the windows of our com-
partment. The windows were fogged. I cleared a dripping semicircle with

the back of my hand and peered out to see the lights of a station. It was Doncaster, or York, or Crewe, one of those darkened northern towns where the train stopped to take on water. A guard's whistle shrilled. My skin was raw and itchy from sitting on British Rail's rough horsehair seat covers, and the crude and ineffective electric heating was giving me chilblains between my toes. I needed to pee.

As I made my way along the corridor, a voice in my brain was saying, "Heinie Manush—Heinie Manush—Heinie Manush." As far as I knew, Heinie Manush was just a piece of onomatopoeia, coined by my parents to imitate the steady, clacking rhythm of the train wheels. I had no idea that Heinie Manush had been a legendary American League outfielder. Baseball, you understand, was not big in Scotland in the 1950s.

I braced myself with both feet against the lurching of the carriage. As I did so, I looked down into the open toilet bowl and saw the dark gleam of the rails flashing past beneath me. I looked up and saw a metal notice riveted to the wall—fastidiously worded, in the English manner. It said, "Kindly refrain from using toilet while train is standing in station." Although I was bleary with exhaustion, I put two and two together, intuitively understanding a concept that today we would call point-source pollution. I remember being flooded with a sense of connections, a sudden awareness of the impact of my actions—of responsibility, in other words. I buttoned my pants, pushed open the door, and lurched back to my seat through the swaying, sleeping train. The wheels said, "Heinie Manush—Heinie Manush—Heinie Manush."

LYNN WERNER IS A SHORT, dynamic woman in her midforties, with a quick, emphatic manner and the advocate's habit of stressing key words, so that it sounds as if she is speaking partly in italics. I'd wanted to ask her more about PCBs, but she wanted to talk more about the future of the five hydroelectric facilities on the Housatonic. She explained that two things had happened more or less at the same time. Either one would have been enough, on its own, to raise serious questions about the future flow of the river. But both of them together amounted to a revolution of possibilities.

The first event was deregulation, which reached the power industry in the 1990s, with the stated aim of reducing costs through competitive power generation. The true religion swept through one New England state after another and reached the legislature in Hartford in 1998, when

Connecticut Light and Power, after years as a virtual monopoly, was ordered to sell off its generating facilities to the highest bidder.

The second event was the relicensing of the Housatonic hydropower plants by the Federal Energy Regulatory Commission (FERC). Since the last FERC relicensing in the 1970s, a lot had changed. In its early days, FERC had a simple mandate—to promote the development of rivers for hydropower. The environmental movement had gone along with this cheerfully enough, since hydropower (which contributed only about 10 percent of the nation's electricity supply) was thought to be clean energy. No noxious carbon emissions to worry about; no Three Mile Island waiting to happen.

But that benign view had about the same life span as high oil prices. By the mid-1980s, it was hard to ignore the environmental damage done by dams. Even during the height of the Reagan administration, which hardly thought of itself as a friend to the tree-huggers, Congress felt obliged to amend the Federal Power Act. The 1986 law ordered FERC to seek a balance between power generation and other public interests, which were to be given "equal consideration" during the relicensing process. These interests included water quality, wildlife protection, habitat preservation, and recreation.

About twenty-three hundred hydroelectric plants stand on American rivers, and FERC licenses almost half of them. In the first wave of relicensing after 1986, FERC tended to impose limited conditions—such as the installation of fish ladders—to mitigate the worst environmental impact of dams. But environmentalists, sensing the shift in political winds, stepped up pressure for more comprehensive protection measures. Taking advantage of FERC's new mandate, a number of environmentalist and outdoor organizations came together in 1992 to form the Hydropower Reform Commission (HRC). Its mantras were *natural flow, run of the river.*

The centerpiece of the Housatonic relicensing process was a certification of water quality by the state DEP, more commonly known as a "401." The 401 process was an open one, with plenty of room for public hearings, and the environmental lobby had put on a full-court press, urging the natural run of the river as the only responsible "science-based" option.

Of all the voices raised, the loudest belonged to the two most energetic of the user groups, the fly-fishers and the white-water boating enthusiasts. If you took their rhetoric at face value, you'd have thought they were blood kin. Both wanted to "restore the river to its natural state." Both talked a lot about "fragile ecosystems." These are the easy mantras of our time. Who can be against nature, after all? Yet beneath the happy talk, the boaters and the anglers were at war over their respective conceptions—*constructs* might be a better word—of nature. In fact, neither would get what they wanted if they stood back and let "nature"—whatever that might be, after millennia of human interaction with the river—take care of things.

When Connecticut turned on its air conditioners and the engineers at Falls Village cranked up the turbines, the canoeists and kayakers were as happy as clams. Now they could run the river in all its wild and natural grandeur. If any river in the Northeast was capable of stopping the hearts of kayakers, it was the Housatonic. These enthusiasts might be few in number, but they included national and Olympic champions, the kind of elite group who dared to tackle the river's rampaging Class V rapids—the Rattlesnake, the Pencil Sharpener, the Stairway to Hell. Once they realized that their mecca was threatened, they decided to fight hard, and if necessary dirty, to preserve it.

Frame of the powerhouse, Falls Village, Conn.

Anglers accused boaters of distorting the flow of the river to pursue their own selfish interests. Boaters replied that nature never intended brown trout, a nonindigenous species, to be swimming around in this warm-water environment. If the anglers wanted to go on fishing, what was wrong with the indigenous smallmouth bass? This objection was both technically dubious and practically irrelevant. *Salmo trutta,* admittedly, had been here only since 1924. But the smallmouth bass were also non-native—the state of Connecticut had simply introduced them into the river a little earlier, in the 1870s. The truth was that the trout and the bass were both the result of human intervention. And so, of course, was the white water.

L YNN WERNER INSISTED that it was dangerous to rely on the state agency for a full scientific understanding of the river's health. She said, "There are so many political pressures on the DEP. It depends on the year, it depends on the funding, it depends on how much they get from the U.S. Fish and Wildlife Service. We need better scientific data on biodiversity. And it's frustrating to be at the *mercy* of an *agency* that might do it, might not do it. They need to be forced to get the science."

"But surely the science is in, isn't it?" I asked Lynn. "Doesn't everyone agree that artificially high flows, especially in summer, are harmful to—"

"The brown *trout,*" Lynn interrupted, rolling her eyes. She'd heard this tiresome argument from a hundred other fly-fishermen.

"No," I said, a little irritated. "I was going to say harmful to *all* species. Whether it's the trout or the *bass,* or the minnows and *crayfish.*" I found myself unconsciously mimicking the italicized cadences of her speech.

Lynn said, "Okay, sure. The main yardstick for measuring the health of the river is the productivity of the stream, its *native* populations—for example, the fish that normally would survive in a warm-water river. We're now trying to decide whether this should be expanded to include *trout*—brown trout. Even though it's not a native fish, it's really the *fishery.*"

Here was that troublesome distinction again. What did people mean when they talked about "the fish"? When did they really mean "the fishery"? I recalled a statement from Trout Unlimited about the need to restore those rivers "where the ecological and economic value of healthy fisheries outweighs the benefits of dams." But how to measure that value, if not in dollars and cents? When Lynn Werner talked about "the fishery," did she have in mind the contribution that people like me made to the economy of the valley and the tax base of its towns, or was she getting at something larger and more intangible? Thinking about it, I realized that the dollar value of my visits was not negligible. By the time I eat a couple of meals, fill the car with gas, and drop in at the fly shop to pick up some odds and ends, its easy to get rid of a hundred dollars or more. I do this maybe a dozen times a year. Twelve hundred dollars. I wouldn't be making these contributions to the local economy, of course, without the presence of the brown trout. Then multiply my spending by—what—a thousand or fifteen hundred others who share my addiction? We're talking about real money now, the sort the Cornwall selectmen notice when they think about their annual budget.

Yet dollars and cents aren't the whole story. Other values and passions are at stake that are beyond measurement—culturally conditioned ones, of course, and highly subjective. Different people look for different meanings in their relationship with the Housatonic. The river is an escape from reality, a physical challenge to be mastered, an opportunity for reflection, a source of knowledge, or a test of skill. For many, it passes for an encounter with wildness, but there's something alienating in that, a sense that the river is something apart from us, something that can be idealized or, in the old, traditional way, conquered and controlled.

My own feelings are idiosyncratic, I think. I'm reluctant to accept the notion that the river is something apart from me. On the contrary, I'm eager to understand and embrace its artifice, the knowledge that every rock and every riffle has been shaped and worked by humans. Ever since the glaciers retreated and the first humans arrived in the valley, the river has been what we have made it. In the past we used rivers in ignorant, negligent, or misguided ways. At the same time, those uses reflected our priorities, the prevailing state of scientific knowledge, and the social consensus (at least among those powerful enough to be part of it) about the purposes of the river. There is no such rationale for those patterns of conduct to persist in the future. Our expanding knowledge of how rivers work provides a foundation for redefining our relationship with them—for developing a river ethic, so to speak, based on enlightened self-interest.

Breaking in on these rather sententious thoughts, Lynn Werner said, "No one can argue that a river with a dam is better than a river without one. But these rivers have been used for hundreds of years to power industry. The question is not whether the dams are going to have an impact; it's whether they are going to affect the *viability* of the river. Society's been making choices for years. If we suddenly say we're not going to dam any river, well . . . good *luck,* because we're not going to employ our people, we're not going to create power. It's very difficult. I'd prefer not to dam any river, frankly, from a *pure* perspective. But can we say that as a society? Can we reach back for something that may be gone forever? So the question is, how can you operate the dams without undermining the health of the river? Once you've done that, you can figure out how to balance the interests of all those who are *using* the river."

I found myself nodding vigorously in agreement. "Sure," I said. "That makes a lot of sense. But it isn't always easy to get people to see it that way."

Lynn made an angry sound between her teeth. She said, "My real concern in this case is the lack of *willingness* to find a win-win solution. I mean, give me a break, we're adults, there *is* a win-win solution. But they've drawn lines in the sand, they've allowed national organizations to convince them that the only way they can get part of what they want is to go loudly, boldly for *everything* they want, with no compromise at any level. And so you end up in a huge fight. And that's just a huge waste of money and time. I get so *impatient* with the single-issue groups. They need to recognize their common interests, but no—it's my way or the highway."

"I assume you're talking about the fly-fishermen," I said.

Lynn gave an ironic laugh. "Yeah, their attitude seems to be, we're going all the way, we've got the money, we've got the lawyers, see you in court. The fishermen think that we're closet boating supporters. I think we're on their Wall of Shame. On the other hand, the prevailing view among the boaters is that we're closet fishermen. But the fact is, we're not going to align ourselves with either group. They're not interested in what we're interested in, which is a solution to the issue. They're just interested in their own agenda. The point is that one recreational use of the river should not outrank another. Just as wastewater assimilation shouldn't be allowed at the expense of recreation. It's a balancing act.

"Look," she said, leaning across the desk with an urgent look in her eye, "this relicensing is a very big thing. It will affect the face of the Housatonic River for thirty, maybe fifty years. But the danger is that the fishermen may win a battle, or the boaters may win a battle, but we may all lose the war."

Row v. Wade: that was what a clever reporter for the *Waterbury Republican-American* called it. And at times I had to admit that this conflict did have the feel of a full-blown culture war. In a prosperous postindustrial society, fishermen and canoeists found—much to their own surprise—that their competing recreational tastes could affect the flow of America's rivers in ways that had once been reserved for millers and factory owners. They had power, in other words.

For more than sixty years after the Falls Village hydropower plant opened, its engineers had set the river's agenda, and the recreational groups played at the margins. When electricity was required, the engineers opened the gates, the turbines began to spin, and a wall of water headed south. But in the 1970s, Ed Kluck's fly-fishermen managed to negotiate a "pond and release" schedule with the Falls Village engineers. This generally guaranteed safe wading in the early morning hours and during the evening hatch. The boaters got the middle of the day, and during the summer months the local canoe businesses thrived.

Angry words might be exchanged when a paddle and a fly line strayed too close to each other, but basically the two groups rubbed along together. The river seemed big enough for both of them, and no evidence suggested that either activity was doing the river itself any lasting harm. For most of the 1980s the trout seemed to do okay under this regime, and about 40 percent of them held over from one year to the next. But from 1988 on, the summers grew hotter. Bill McKibben wrote *The End of Nature,* and the term *global warming* entered our common vocabulary. Holdover rates fell dramatically. Then, in 1993, no rain fell for weeks, and the air temperature soared into the nineties day after day. Eighty percent of the trout in the Housatonic died from thermal stress.

The drought of '93 ended the uneasy coexistence between the anglers and the white-water boaters. Each side drew a new and more militant set of battle lines. The kayak wizards thrived on the summer weekend surges. So did the college kids, who brought kegs of beer with them, whooped and hollered when they hit a class II riffle, and had only the haziest idea of how to navigate their rented canoes. These people tended not to take a trout's-eye view. Even in normal years, there were plenty of days when a trout might leave the main part of the river with its temperature of seventy-eight degrees Fahrenheit (uncomfortable but survivable), take refuge in the inflow from one of the feeder brooks in a pocket of seventy-four-degree water (warm but bearable), only to have the refuge inundated at midday with a slug of eighty-two-degree water (potentially lethal) from the Falls Village Dam. Brown trout were not genetically equipped to deal with these conditions.

The DEP sent out survey crews in the summer of 1994 with a mandate "to assess the effect of hydropeaking on coldwater refuges, and *to develop flow rates which would be least harmful to trout during adverse temperature periods.*" The italics are mine, and I think they're important, since this wording suggested to the boaters that the DEP had a not-so-hidden agenda, that its science served the economics of recreational angling. The DEP study found that temperatures in the thermal refuges rose by as much as ten degrees after a release, so rapidly that the trout had no time to adjust. Without a change in the patterns of power generation, the trout in the Housatonic might be facing extinction.

The DEP and the power company arrived at a Solomonic solution of sorts. Falls Village would minimize variations in the river's flow when the local air and water temperatures rose above critical levels. On the surface, this "air-water model" seemed to offer something for everyone. The fishermen could fish, the boaters could boat, the trout could survive. But the compromise settled nothing; it only punted the problem. Ironically, Mike Piquette, an active local member of Trout Unlimited, told me that he faulted the model because it protected only the trout. As Mike pointed out, the air-water model guarded against only one-time fish kills. It did nothing to mitigate the day-in, day-out damage that the erratic flows caused to benthic invertebrates and other riverine species.

The more scientifically literate fishermen, people like Mike, were wary of Lynn Werner's "win-win" philosophy. They'd heard similar talk in 1994, when the Deerfield River in northwestern Massachusetts—a serially dammed river that bears some striking similarities to the Housatonic—came up for FERC relicensing. That summer, representatives of the anglers and paddlers, the power company and the local pols, had sat down together under a white canvas tent on the banks of the Deerfield and worked out a compromise that appeared to offer something for everyone. There would be kayak-friendly dam releases in the middle of the day, at times of peak electricity demand and profitability, and low water for fly-fishing at dawn and dusk. The Deerfield compromise made the front page of the *Wall Street Journal,* which hailed it as a national exemplar of responsible cooperation. As far as Mike Piquette was concerned, the deal might have kept the user lobbies happy, but at the expense of the river.

With a stronger scientific basis for determining what was best for the Housatonic, you might suppose that the discussion would become more rational. On the contrary, the nearer we got to the closing date for public comment on the relicensing, the nastier the dispute grew. So many profound issues were at stake, yet the conflict was fast becoming a caricature. The press seized happily on the *Row v. Wade* theme, and the Rowers and the Waders seemed happy to play to the script. Each side polished its sound bites, each worked up statistics to show how much money its activity injected into the local economy, and, to Lynn Werner's chagrin, each brought in the big guns—Trout Unlimited in one corner, American Rivers in the other.

The DEP, to its credit, did all that it could to bring the debate back to what really mattered. Sensitive to the accusations that they were a tool of the fishing lobby, the state biologists took the high road, explicitly leaving the brown trout out of their assessment of the impact of erratic dam releases on aquatic life. Their main interest was the disruption of the river's native species, and they took no position on "exotics" like the trout. But their findings were categorical: "Habitat quality and quantity for immobile species and life stages of other species are greatly reduced as a function of altered flow regimes. . . . The comparisons of species diversity and abundance between river sections affected by flow regulation versus unaffected river sections demonstrate the destructive force of altered flow regimes on riverine communities." In these communities, fluvial specialists were being replaced by more adaptable habitat generalists. For an ecologist, this decline in biodiversity was the worst possible news.

So the DEP recommended run of the river on the Housatonic, in order to restore and improve aquatic habitat and enhance the populations of fish, invertebrates, insects, and freshwater mollusks. The hydropower plants were free to go on making electricity, but only on terms dictated by the natural, unimpeded flow of the river.

Mike piquette e-mailed me one day to tell me that the boaters had decided to organize a mass protest—a flotilla—on the river, in a last-ditch effort to turn the politicians around. I sat on the rocks below the covered bridge and watched them assemble at the rutted gravel parking lot by the Garbage Hole. There were probably two hundred of them: Olympic medalists, people with runners' calves and sweatshirts from New England colleges, a few families with kids. Seeing my fishing vest and waders, a thick-set man in his late forties, with a four-day stubble and a ponytail, bore down on me and yelled, "Release the river! We can coexist, man!" His words said one thing, but his demeanor suggested another.

Classic Old Town canoes and a couple of inflatable rafts had appeared, but kayaks outnumbered them all. Unlike the long, slender kind of kayak I was used to, these stubby, sharp-nosed little numbers were painted in psychedelic designs with primary colors. Their pilots wore crash helmets. Their kayaks had names like Dagger Blast and Sabre and Whiplash. They came across like a tightly disciplined unit of shock troops, navy SEALs perhaps. Some were doing Eskimo rolls in the turbulent water at the head of the pool. I'd been expecting a carnival atmosphere, but there was something grim and purposeful about the kayakers. If they had been NASCAR drivers, they would have been gunning their engines.

I had brought along a thick file of clips on the relicensing dispute, and while the flotilla made ready, I sat on my rock and flipped through it. It contained more invective than science. Fishermen less sophisticated than Mike Piquette accused the canoeists of being willing to kill off the trout in order to indulge their unnatural vices. A spokesperson for the canoeists retorted, "Well, if you want to throw around words like *unnatural*, let's start with the trout. Putting brown trout in the Housatonic was like putting polar bears on a ranch in Texas." A former Olympic bronze medalist from the old iron town of Salisbury told the *Litchfield County Times*, "Once they made a dam and diverted the water around the white water at Rattlesnake Run, it's sort of like saying a fish is natural when you've taken out its heart and lungs. You've ripped the white water out of the river."

As I went on reading, the canards grew loopier. The Adirondack Mountain Club, which ought to have known better, and probably did, said that afternoon dam releases wouldn't harm the fish since fish aren't active at that time of day anyway. A boater stood up at a public meeting and argued that artificial releases were actually *better* than the natural run of the river because they imitated the sharp rise and fall caused by afternoon thunderstorms. The owner of a local outfitter's business was asked what she thought about the DEP's analysis of the benefits of natural flow for aquatic life. She said, "The theory's never been proven." It was a bit like listening to fundamentalist Christians talk about evolution or Republicans talk about global warming.

The weather had put me in a sour and sardonic frame of mind. Here were the boaters, complaining that there was no water in the river. But it had been raining all week, and it was next to impossible to fish. For boating, on the other hand, it seemed ideal. I was suddenly irritated with the boaters' demand for controlled conditions on the Housatonic. They sounded to me like spoiled sports fans whining for a domed stadium so that nature would never rain on their ball game.

By the time the flotilla reached the take-out point, four miles downstream, the paddlers' fire seemed to have burned itself out. People in neoprene wetsuits were lashing kayaks to their roof racks. There was a tent set up, and a trestle table with a six-foot Italian hero sandwich on it. But the crowd was thin, and there was enough left over for seconds. Hand-lettered signs and yellow photocopied leaflets denounced the DEP for wanting to "ban boaters from the Housatonic." A woman told the crowd, "We don't want to see DEP turn the river off." This seemed a bizarre formulation of the problem, since the state agency was proposing just the opposite—to let the river run free.

I heard two young men talking about the dams. One of them was saying, "Jesus, if you want to be ecological about it, tear the damn things down." The other one replied, "Hey, any time. My brother works in high explosives. Let's do it, man."

The handful of boaters who remained were milling around the giant sandwich. They held the food in yellow leaflets that had been discarded. Strands of iceberg lettuce trailed from their mouths, and their fingers were sticky with mayonnaise. Behind them, car doors slammed, engines started up, and the river roared, swollen with natural rain.

17
Reading the Water

ALL THE REST OF THAT SUMMER the Cornwall Canyon baked, the river fell, and the boaters grumbled. The heat wave was relentless, the worst in memory. July turned to August, and the mercury rose into the nineties, day after day. The Housatonic was in pain.

The state biologists spent these weeks in a state of anxiety. High summer is normally the time when they take advantage of low flows to survey the rivers, gathering the empirical data that gives meaning to the abstract language of biodiversity. With their arsenal of canoes and dip nets and low-voltage electroshocking probes, the biologists count the fish—which species, how many of each, grouped by size and age.

I'd been planning to join the survey crews when they headed out on the Housatonic, but Bob Orciari called one morning to say that the survey was on hold until things cooled down. Bob is the senior fisheries biologist for western Connecticut. In practice this means that he knows as much about the ecology of the Housatonic watershed as anyone alive. The trout were too stressed, Bob explained, and it would be irresponsible to disturb them. If they didn't succumb to the heat, or the fungal and bacterial infections to which it left them vulnerable, the electroshocking might well kill them. The DEP was debating whether to close the river to fishing until Labor Day.

This suggestion was probably academic, since there was hardly a soul on the water. I'd driven up to Cornwall a couple of times in July. The first time, I caught a couple of small trout in the early morning mists and quit as soon as the sun hit the water. By my second visit, the water temperature by early afternoon was above eighty degrees Fahrenheit. In this kind of heat, a fish that is stressed will quickly suffer a dangerous buildup of lactic acid in its muscle tissue, and I didn't want to risk hooking one by mistake. But in the slack water below the Carse Pool, I knew that the smallmouth bass would be feeding and that the chances of a trout taking a fly were remote. In the fading evening light, the bass hit a small, bushy white Wulff as predictably as fish taking pellets in a hatchery.

Next morning, I walked from the mouth of one feeder stream to the next, to see what shape the trout were in. Some of the smaller brooks were almost dry. The flow from Pine Swamp Brook, which cascades down the vertical hillside into the Horse Hole, the deepest pool in the Housatonic, was about what you would expect from a garden hose. Even so, it was enough to aerate a patch of water the size of a pool table. Leaning over the guard rail on Route 7, twenty feet above the river, I could see dorsal fins thrashing in distress. They were the biggest fish I'd ever seen in the river, with several over twenty inches in length. A few had white patches of fungus on their backs and flanks. Sometimes a head and shoulders would break water, and I could see the mouth open wide as the trout gasped for air.

Under the covered bridge in West Cornwall, my stream thermometer gave a reading of eighty-one degrees. A few yards upstream, it was two degrees lower, and at least thirty trout were bunched together, shoulder to shoulder, to suck up the extra oxygen where the water tumbled over a rock into a small side channel. These, too, were good-sized fish, with many two-pounders and a couple that would have pushed three. Up a little farther, a boy and his younger sister were playing on the rocks to the north of the bridge. Here, where Mill Brook flows in over the remnants of a nineteenth-century diversion weir, the water temperature was down to seventy-four. The children were close in age to David and Julia, who were spending the month with their grandparents, and suddenly I missed my own children with a painful intensity. I walked the brother and sister over to the edge of the river, bent down to their eye level, and asked them if they could see the fish. They peered intently into the shallow current from Mill Brook, but they said all they could see was the waving mat of weed that had sprouted during the heat wave.

"Stay *very* still, as still as you can," I said to the girl. She made herself a statue. "Now jump up and wave your arms in the air."

Like cockroaches scattering from the light, the mat of weed became a flurry of fifty, sixty, seventy trout, smaller than those that were lying in the side channel. They milled around in circles, their dorsal fins breaking the surface now.

"Wow," the girl said. "That's awesome." I wished she could have been Julia.

We sat there quietly until the fish regrouped. They were all browns, lying in no more than six inches of water, and I could clearly see the variations in their markings. Some had large dark spots on silvery sides. These looked like Romes, I thought, remembering my visit to the Burlington Fish Hatchery. Others had red spots and buttery flanks. They were beautiful fish, with a wild look, and I thought they were probably Cortlands.

To while away the dog days of early August, I occupied myself with a pile of scientific literature that Bob Orciari had been sending me over the past year or so. This pleasurable reading put me in mind of something Roderick Haig-Brown had once written. Haig-Brown liked to read papers on aquatic biology in wintertime, while the Campbell River flowed black and silent past his study window. Even though I was in an air-conditioned room in Manhattan, and not in front of a log fire on Vancouver Island, I understood what he had felt when he wrote, "Scientific papers are the bare bones of natural history, but it is the prerogative of the angler's imagination to cover them with the flesh of his experience and so give them life." This vicarious fishing of the mind kept me going until I could once again do the real thing.

I was halfway through a paper about the growth patterns of smallmouth bass one day when the phone rang. It was Bob. The heat wave had broken, the water temperature had dropped back to the upper sixties, and the survey crew was ready to go.

We met at the Sand Hole. I was there by sunrise, wanting to squeeze in an hour of fishing before the crew arrived. It was a crisp, clear dawn, and deer were foraging in the fields as I drove down from North Cornwall. The first rays of sunlight were just striking the hills above Cornwall Bridge, illuminating them in discrete bands of red, green, and gold until they looked like the flag of Ethiopia. The water was so clear, and the weed beds at the foot of the Sand Hole so thick, that I felt as if I was fishing in a limestone creek in Pennsylvania. At 7:30, the morning freight clanked and grated its way along the railroad track past Turnip Island, half-concealed behind the trees on the east bank.

Neal Hagstrom was the first to arrive, dressed in a khaki shirt, camo waders, and dark shades. Neal is a senior biologist for the state of Connecticut and one of the leaders in developing its trout management plans. One after another, cars and pickup trucks began pulling up on the gravel shoulder of Route 7. The DEP guys unloaded their Old Town canoes, which were loaded to the gunwales with equipment—the control box that regulates voltage and amperage, the live well, sample-collecting buckets, two-foot-long measuring boards, long-handled nets, short-handled dip nets, and low-voltage electrical probes, which look like devices for detecting land mines.

About two dozen of us had assembled by the time Neal gathered us for a safety briefing—how to avoid electric shock from the probes, a reminder that we were taking part in this exercise at our own risk, what to do if you were swept off your feet by the current. Bob Orciari stood off to one side, a dark, slightly built man in his forties in a polo shirt. His diffident manner suggested that, like me, he was only tagging along to watch and hoped he wasn't getting in the way. Our departure was attended by a modest media circus. A man from the Danbury paper took notes. Someone else had brought along a shoulder-mounted video camera. Off we went.

The first pass was a fiasco. The flats below Turnip Island are the shallowest section of the river, and we were about as likely to be knocked off our feet by the current as we were to be hit by a falling meteorite. We found a single trout, with a clipped adipose fin that identified it as one of the fish stocked that spring. In the deeper pockets were large numbers of fallfish—the large, silvery minnow that some people in the valley call Shepaug salmon—and smallmouth bass.

"The fish come back from this pretty good, actually," Bob said, noticing my look of concern. "The current stuns them for three minutes, maybe five. There's very little mortality. There's some evidence that the larger fish may sometimes get microfractures of their vertebrae, especially rainbows, but we don't think it causes them any lasting damage."

Bob pointed out that the prolonged drought had some hidden benefits. He was excited by how many of these fish were young of the year. He said, "That's totally attributable to the low, stable flows we've been having. Conditions like that are conducive to healthy spawning."

I wondered why the bass we were finding varied so much in coloration. We'd net some that were a pure greenish gold, and then, from under the next rock, we'd take others that were mottled heavily with patterns of dark olive and black. I asked Bob if these markings indicated different strains, or the fish's age, or if they were the result of variations in diet.

"None of the above," he replied. "It actually comes from their rapid adaptation to a particular microhabitat. They'll blend in with whatever surroundings they find themselves in. A bass that's sheltering under a rock will quickly develop dark, blackish side markings. One that's lying over sand or cobble will be very pale-colored, so that it can blend in."

A biologist named Tim Barry joined us. He was carrying a white plastic bucket to use for sampling. He said, "Put a smallmouth bass in a bucket like this, and within a matter of minutes you'll see that its pigmentation will change to a blondish gold color."

Bob asked, "Have you ever seen a blind bass? It's almost completely white because it never knows that it has to hide."

After an hour and a half of pulling and probing, netting and measuring, we reached the head of the riffle, at the base of the elliptical Turnip Island, which broke the current like the prow of a ship. We took the right-hand channel, which was the better holding water, studded with large boulders and deep pockets. The probe went down three feet under the first of the rocks, and the dip net came up bulging with fish, like the net on a herring trawler. There must have been fifteen smallmouth podded up under this single rock, good-sized fish of a pound or so each. Out came our measuring boards, marked in centimeters.

Someone called out, "Smallmouth thirty-four, twenty-seven, thirty-two, thirty, twenty-nine, thirty-six."

"Those bigger fish are probably at least eight years old now," Tim said to me. "Down at Swift's Bridge, we'll see some that are even older."

For many years the age of the fish was calculated by examining its scales, which show annual growth in much the same way as the rings of a tree. A more recent—and more accurate—yardstick is to analyze the growth rings on the otolith, a free-floating calcareous growth that builds up in the chambers of a fish's inner ear. For an aquatic biologist, the new technique was a revelation. Otolith analysis showed that the Housatonic smallmouth were positively Methuselahs, living to an age of thirteen or more.

Bob had put me in charge of the live cart on this stretch, a six-foot-long wooden scow with an open mesh bottom. It was filled with a squirming mass of larger fish. One thirteen-inch smallmouth had an eight-inch relative lodged in its throat, partly digested. The sun was high overhead now and had begun to shine with a fierce Saharan glare. The back of my neck was reddened and chafing. I wetted a bandana and draped it over my head, but it was dry again in seconds. When the shallower riffles forced me to pull the heavy live cart over the rocks, bumping and grating along the bottom, it felt like dragging a sack full of corpses with lead weights in their pockets. This was real work, and no one spoke much. The hard manual labor immersed us in the physicality of the river. This was what men felt when they hauled rocks to build dams. Perhaps they despoiled the river, but they also came to know it with an intense intimacy, and if they exalted it, it was as a real living force, for good and for ill, and not as an abstraction.

"Thirty-one, thirty-two, twenty-five, thirty, thirty-four, thirty-nine, twenty-eight."

We measured the last of the smallmouth, tabulated our results on clipboards, and returned the fish to the water. Bob pointed upstream, to the riffles at the head of the deep channel. He said, "If we work through this channel to the top of the island and get fewer than, oh, twenty-five trout, let's call it a day here and move down to the mouth of Furnace Brook." We found two.

The pool where Furnace debouches into the big river, in the shadow of St. Bridget's Church, proved to be little better. The good news was that the water had cooled so much that the trout had abandoned their thermal refuges. The bad news was that we had seen only a half-dozen trout after a morning's work, all browns except for a single brookie, and that meant we had collected too little data to draw any conclusions. Bob recalled the old scientist's dictum: "I know this is frustrating," he said, "but no data is better than bad data. We've got such a small window of time every year to look at the thermal refuges, only about two weeks each summer when the water is warm enough for the trout to be in the refuges, but not so warm that they'll be overstressed by the electroshocking. This year I guess we missed them."

I imagined the fish finning in the deep run below St. Bridget's, out of reach of our probes, luxuriating in the coolness of the water. I imagined myself in a cool shower when our day's work in the sun was over.

The last trout we found was a small one, no more than eight inches in length and heavily spotted. Bob turned it over thoughtfully between his fingers. "Hard to tell if this is a wild fish or not," he said. "With a wild fish, you expect to see that yellow belly, like this one has, and that bluish halo around the red spots. On the other hand, this may be one of the *Seeforellen* browns that were stocked in Furnace last year."

I looked at him in surprise. This was a puzzle to me. *Seeforellen* are natives of the deep alpine lakes of Europe, where they grow to a prodigious size. The name literally means "lake trout" in German. The fingerling program in Furnace Brook had been intended to strengthen a naturally reproducing population of wild fish, but Bob couldn't explain how the *Seeforellen* had been chosen to shoulder that responsibility.

Among many aquatic biologists, the focus on stocking particular strains of trout has become outmoded. "After the PCB scare and the decision to restock the river," Bob told me, "we started off with Bitterroots from Montana. The original thinking was that the Bitterroots were a wilder fish, and that they would do better than other strains. But they didn't. So these days the Housatonic is pretty much of a mix." I wondered if the fish I had seen at the covered bridge were really Romes and Cortlands, or just indeterminate hybrids.

In some quarters, the new buzzword is *survivor strain*. The idea is to single out fish that do well in a particular river environment and encourage the process of natural selection that will lead, over time, to a more self-sustaining population. But Bob Orciari is skeptical about this effort. "You can call them survivors, but they're really not," he said. "These fish are first generation, and so there isn't going to be a great deal of selection. If you're going to develop survivor fish, it's going to take years and years of selection, taking the prime fish out of the river and spawning them, then restocking the progeny. It's a natural selection process."

Bob folded his arms, looking on as his survey crew began to pack up their gear. "Natural selection can occur rapidly," he went on, "but if you're trying to isolate a genetic trait, you have to be able to select the individuals who have that trait most strongly. The tendency is, when you come to a stream, you deal with maybe a hundred fish, but there's another ten thousand still in the river, so you're really taking a very small sample.

Those hundred fish you sample—are they the ones that have the trait you want? When natural selection occurs, you have a bell curve. You have normal individuals, which is most of them, and then you have some with a particular set of traits and others with a completely different set. Then something comes along like a change of climate. Bang—most can't take the temperature, so they're wiped out. But a few survive, those with the right genetic trait, the one-percenters that will carry on and reproduce that trait."

Bob continued talking as we waded back to our cars. He said, "The emphasis now is not only on getting survivors but also mixing in some wild fish to try to develop certain characteristics. That also creates a larger genetic pool to select from. You can't really mix survivors from different rivers. Each river will have its own strain. A survivor fish from the Farmington will do very poorly in the Housatonic because Farmington fish are in constantly cool temperatures." This is because of a simple difference in dam engineering. The Falls Village hydropower plant releases warm water from the top of the pond; the Hogback Dam on the Farmington releases icy water from the bottom of the West Branch Reservoir.

"It's like the rabbit and the tortoise," Bob explained. "Farmington fish grow slowly and steadily. In the Housatonic, the fish grow very rapidly in the springtime, but they metabolize their food very fast during the summer and get very skinny. Then they feed happily again in the fall, but before they gain in length they first have to replenish their losses. This year, with the low rainfall and the moderation of the hydro flows, we saw a real increase in the growth rates of the trout in the Housatonic. Natural flows are just great for a river, even if it's warm water."

This is really the biologists' main point when they try to deflect the charge that they are closet supporters of the fly-fishing lobby. It's not only the trout that suffer from unstable flows; it's the aquatic biota as a whole. In low water with a steady flow, all species thrive. Absolute numbers, population density, and growth rates all rise. That's why we had spent all morning tripping over baby fallfish and young-of-the-year bass.

From our original assembly point, Ed Machowski had brought us here in his pickup truck, which he had left outside the park ranger's house. We piled into the back, in there among the dip nets and probes and sample buckets. The wind whipped our faces as we swung onto Route 7. It felt good. It was the first time in years I had sat in the back of an open pickup. When I closed my eyes, the sensation brought back images from half a lifetime ago—bumping along dirt roads with soldiers going into combat in Central America, riding bareback across an Andean hillside.

I picked up one of the measuring boards. Its scale ran to sixty-five centimeters.

I asked, "Ever had a fish that went off the scale?"

Someone said, "Not a salmonid."

One of our group who had been quiet until now, a taciturn Marlboro Man with a lined, weather-beaten face, said, "I caught a half-dozen trout that size last week."

"Not here?" someone asked dutifully, knowing in advance that the answer was no.

"Nah," Marlboro Man said, "Beaverhead River in Montana." The Beaverhead drains the slopes of the Bitterroot Mountains, in the southwestern corner of the most famous trout-fishing state in the country.

"Well, okay, they were twenty-one, twenty-three inches on the Beaverhead, and then we went on to a chain of lakes and ponds and we had rainbows and cutthroats of twenty-five, twenty-six." He gave a self-deprecating shrug and said, for our benefit perhaps, "But they didn't fight as hard as the trout in the Housatonic."

We pulled over to let the man out near his car, and he walked away with a rolling gait that looked as if he'd just dismounted from his horse. Ed Machowski watched him go with a smile. He said, "Get natural flows into this river, and we'll see who still thinks they need to go to Montana for great fishing."

18
The Call of the Wild

MAYBE IT WAS THOSE ALPINE LAKE TROUT in Furnace Brook, or maybe it was Ed Machowski's vision of trout in the Housatonic to rival those in Montana. Whatever it was, it drove me to the bookshelf in search of William Cronon, looking for this passage: "What we mean when we use the word 'nature' says as much about ourselves as about the things we label with that word." If we called something "nature," did we see ourselves as part of it or place it at a distance? And if we spoke of "natural resources," did that term carry the same connotations that it had for earlier generations—a commodity that was primarily there for our use and gratification?

My conversations with the biologists seemed to have a complicated subtext. Was restoring the river a scientific end in itself? Or was it a means of bringing us closer to a set of cultural values that we saw affirmed in a healthy river, some of which could be defined only by the value—in economic terms—that we expected to extract from it? Were we even justified in talking about *restoring* the river? Was *reengineering* perhaps a better word?

Bob Orciari's team had spent the better part of a decade conducting an unprecedented statewide stream survey, and the outcome was not a scholarly thesis or a cultural essay but a trout management plan. There was no way to get around that word *management*. It acknowledged that the intent of the exercise was to use human artifice to manipulate—literally, to *control*—the environment in which we live. The fact that this manipulation had benign rather than malicious motives seemed to me to be a separate matter.

The stream survey was possible in the first place, of course, only because public funds were available to finance it. And the bulk of those funds came, in the form of taxes and license fees, from citizens to whom the biologists were ultimately accountable. As a result, the scientists faced a dilemma that may well be insoluble. Bob Orciari and his colleagues had been schooled in the midst of an environmental revolution, and their work made no sense unless they subscribed to the accompanying ideology, which sent them forth as stewards of the wild, undoers of the folly of earlier generations. But did those who paid the piper get to call the tune? What if the players knew how to perform Bach, but the payers demanded heavy metal?

THERE ARE SOMETHING LIKE 6,500 miles of running water in the state of Connecticut. To their amazement, the DEP biologists found that 668 of the 800 streams they studied—about 4,000 miles—were inhabited by wild trout. Another 900 miles had habitat that begged for trout to be reintroduced. All this in a state no part of which lies more than three hours from New York City or Boston. The DEP estimated that Connecticut's population of wild trout was at least three million. Almost 90 percent were *Salvelinus fontinalis*. The densest concentrations of wild fish were in the higher elevations and steeper gradients of Litchfield County. Yet they remained secret fish. I had fished over them for years, hiking in through hemlock groves and tangles of rhododendron, fern, and mountain laurel, and I had never once seen another angler on these wild trout waters.

The fishing was happening somewhere else, and as natural science led toward one set of conclusions, the sociological dimension of the stream survey led to another. Six out of every seven Connecticut trout were wild, stream-bred from eggs deposited there by their mothers. Only one in seven came from the two state hatcheries, but they accounted for virtually all the fishing. The vast majority of angling was "harvest-oriented." The state hatcheries churned out half a million "catchable" trout a year, and four out of five of them ended up on someone's dinner table. Most bait anglers kept their catch; most fly-fishers released theirs—but they accounted for only 15 percent of those who fished.

I'd been to a meeting earlier in the summer at which the fisheries biologists had briefed a roomful of skeptical Trout Unlimited types about the draft management plan. The first half-hour had been warm and fuzzy, with softball questions and expressions of enthusiasm for the state's emphasis on wild fish. But then it degenerated into name-calling about the murderous activities of bait fishers and their unseemly influence over the budget, until, after an hour, the awkward PR man who had opened the proceedings suddenly said, "Golly, will you look at the time, guys? Genuinely appreciate your input, work in progress, guess it's probably time to wind things up for tonight."

Fly-fishers tend to look at hatcheries rather as opponents of capital punishment look at the death chamber. They are an unnatural abomination, an icon of our infatuation with quick fixes. Yet the persistence of the hatchery system also says a lot about how hard it is to decommission an entrenched institution, even when many of the assumptions on which it was founded have long since ceased to apply. Think of how hard it was to close down military bases at the end of the cold war.

Seth Green, who had started the modern fish-culture movement in the 1860s, knew nothing of the biological predicates that determined the proper size of natural populations or the "carrying capacity" of streams. Religion taught that the bounty of the earth existed so that humans, standing at the pinnacle of creation, could exploit it. Science and technology were tools to make this exploitation more efficient, since nature itself was so chaotic and disordered. Not coincidentally, the first hatcheries in the Pacific Northwest opened at exactly the same time as the first salmon canneries.

This pattern of behavior has been referred to as the spoil-and-mitigate syndrome. Destroy the habitat, overharvest the fish, but get off the hook, in practical and moral terms, by building hatcheries to put back the depleted resource—indeed, put back even more than we took out in the first place. Like junk food, hatcheries create a cycle of dependency and addiction. The biologists I talked to are no fools, and they clearly see the trap that the hatchery system has set for them. They also know how difficult it is to avoid it. In that sense, they are rather like modern doctors, who may know more than their predecessors about saturated fats, obesity, and anorexia, yet remain largely powerless to reduce the problems. Despite advances in our understanding of the environment, the logic that drives the hatchery system does not—and probably *cannot*—stray far from the imperatives that created the system in the first place.

This is because the entire hatchery enterprise is predicated on overturning the logic of nature, principally by reducing its inherent mortality rates. Ninety-five percent of wild trout will die before they become yearlings, in a selection process that culls those least equipped to survive. Genetic selection in the hatchery ensures the exact reverse. It breeds fish for their tameness, their adaptation to overcrowded conditions, and their resistance to disease. It would be economic lunacy to do otherwise. Why would anyone breed trout for their survival skills in the wild, when four out of every five are going to end up in someone's frying pan by Memorial Day? So fisheries managers have no real alternative but to measure their effectiveness, and secure their funding, by much the same criteria that Seth Green used—employing science to become more efficient than nature, creating a system that is simplified where nature is complex, actuarial where nature is profligate.

It takes a lot of political courage to walk away from this kind of dependency. The Canadians were the first to break ranks, in the 1930s. Yellowstone National Park ceased stocking its streams in 1956. Then the state of Michigan stopped stocking streams where trout were reproducing naturally in significant numbers. Wisconsin quickly followed suit. Montana halted all stocking in its rivers in the mid-1970s. The East, where population pressures were greater and trout habitat scarcer, took a long time to catch up with this trend. Pennsylvania was the pioneer, beginning a program in 1983 to restore degraded habitat and place viable wild trout streams off limits to hatchery fish.

By then, biologists had punctured most of the myths about the hatchery "miracle." Their predecessors had been baffled by the contradictory results of their work—how could it be, for example, that if a thousand hatchery fish went into a stream that held a thousand wild fish, the total population a year later might tally five hundred? By observing trout behavior closely, biologists found the answers to these conundrums. I had to think no further than the trout boiling like a school of piranhas in the cement tanks at the Burlington Fish Hatchery.

This kind of frenzy reflects adaptation to prevailing conditions: population density many times greater than that of a natural setting, lack of cover, and cohabitation with hundreds of other fish of exactly the same

2111 – A True Fish Story.

size, with no seniority system. These trout, you could say, lack even the most rudimentary social skills. Planted in a stream, they become erratic and hyperactive. They rush around aimlessly, wasting calories that wild trout know how to conserve. They compete for food, space, and shelter, displacing wild fish, forcing them to expend energy on territorial defense and disrupting their reproduction. The hatchery fish attack other fish and eat their young. By attracting armies of fishermen in the early season, they contribute to higher mortality among the wild fish population.

Although fisheries managers were as affected as anyone else by the greening of America in the 1970s, the consequences haven't always been benign or enlightened. On one hand, it's hard to find fault with the decision to stop stocking nonindigenous trout in waters that are capable of sustaining the real thing. On the other, you have to wonder whether the impulse to return things to their "natural" state hasn't sometimes amounted to a kind of biological warfare. Take the use of rotenone, for example. Rotenone is a poison extracted from the roots of certain Asian and South American vines. It is extraordinarily efficient at wiping out all the fish in a given body of water. You might use rotenone, for example, to remove unwelcome predators or to get rid of an exploding population of forage fish that is depleting the food supply. When everything is dead, then you can put in your trout. It's a sort of aquatic version of destroying the village in order to save it. You can almost imagine a fisheries manager squatting on his haunches by the water's edge, like Robert Duvall in *Apocalypse Now*—"I love the smell of rotenone in the morning."

Benign or not, efforts like these are based on an underlying illusion: that the hatchery genie can be put back in the bottle. This type of dilemma is not unique to aquatic biologists. Whether their founding father was Seth Green or J. Robert Oppenheimer, professionals from every scientific discipline spend an inordinate amount of time trying to put the lid back on escaped genies—or, come to that, escaped genes. It can't be done.

Meanwhile, the hatchery machine grinds on relentlessly. Nationwide, hatchery production had reached fifty million in 1958. Twenty-five years later, with the environmental revolution in full swing, the figure was up to seventy-eight million. Connecticut essentially followed this national orthodoxy. "What can you do?" Doug Barnard had asked me with a helpless shrug, as we stood over his piranha pool. "It's what the anglers want, and you want to give them satisfaction."

JUST AFTER LABOR DAY, I went with Mike Piquette to help electroshock Furnace Brook. Mike is an analytical chemist by profession. He is also the conservation officer for the Housatonic Fly Fishermen's Association, and Furnace Brook and its wild brown trout are one of his pet projects. This is good news for the brook. Meeting Mike for the first time, you take in the close-cropped beard, the easy movements, and the thoughtful, low-key manner of speaking, and you feel that Furnace is in capable hands. When I picture an environmentalist, I think of someone who looks like Mike Piquette.

Earlier in the year, Mike and I had gone out together to plant hemlocks in the upland meadow section of the brook, up toward the Cornwall post office. The hemlocks had been shockingly green, I remembered, a gray-emerald tone that stood out against the sandy riverbanks and the brown tangle of last year's grasses. With trowels, we had dug holes nine inches deep and placed seedlings in them, arranging their feathery root mats carefully in the damp soil. Those that survived and grew would one day shade and cool the brook. Even if we succeeded in lowering the temperature by only half a degree, we knew that this difference might be critical for the trout downstream.

In April, as usual, the state had planted a couple of thousand trout in Furnace, rainbows mostly. Clustered around the ruins of the old Cornwall Bridge Iron Company are a half-dozen streamside pull-ins. From opening day to Memorial Day, these become busy parking lots. At intervals, the drivers emerge from the ravine, carrying spinning rods and stringers of ten-inch rainbow trout for a fisherman's breakfast. Now, in the fading of summer, the riverbank was deserted, with no competition for the shaded picnic tables where Mike and I met. The word was out that this year's stocking of rainbows was to be the last. Furnace was on a shortlist of streams that the state proposed to manage for wild trout.

Mike Piquette and his friend Steve Grover, who owns a company called Steve's Bagels, have put together what Mike calls a "wild trout road show," which they present to local anglers' groups. Steve does the science, and Mike shows the slides. They also try to reach out to environmental activists who believe that animal rights should extend all the way to hatchery fish and regard anglers, like hunters, as the enemy. Steve expresses a lot of frustration at the inability of anglers and environmentalists to make common cause. If the hostilities are to be dispelled, Steve thinks, the burden of proof must be on the anglers. So when he and Mike make their presentations, they don't even touch the fishing issue. Instead, they talk about the restoration of *habitat,* thereby creating a platform of shared goals.

The first misconception Mike and Steve have to debunk is that *wild* is not the same thing as *native.* "A wild fish is a free-living fish, hatched and reared in a stream, lake, or sea from an egg spawned and deposited there by its mother." That's a well-known definition, popularized by Dr. Ray J. White in an article that is Mike Piquette's standard handout at these meetings.

"You know," Mike said, as we laced up our wading boots, "there's almost no such thing as wild *native* trout anymore, at least not in this part of the country. What you have is actually a large genetic and behavioral spectrum."

At one end of this spectrum are the ancestral native fish, the kind that still hold on in some remote Appalachian streams but are long gone from Connecticut. Somewhere in the middle are the brown trout like those Mike and I are going to look for in Furnace Brook. If you could pick apart the DNA of these wild fish, you'd find Scottish and German accents and distant traces of Seth Green's Caledonia Fish Hatchery. At the other extreme are the hatchery strains, a whole spectrum in themselves, bred to meet specific recreational needs and conditions. The most genetically compromised of these are the rainbow trout planted in quick-turnover, put-and-take fisheries. These poor abraded creatures must technically be classified as "wildlife" or "natural resources," I suppose, although doing so puts me in mind of Ronald Reagan's famous definition of school cafeteria tomato ketchup as a vegetable.

You can catch these rainbows nowadays in all fifty states of the Union, and for all I know in every country of the world, with the possible exception of North Korea. I've fished over them a few times during family vacations. The last time I went to the Mar-Val Trout Camp ("Have a Mar-Val-ous Stay with Us!") in Gore, a town that bills itself as the little-contested "Trout Capital of Oklahoma," the woman at the desk looked at me sympathetically as I signed in. "Too bad you come too late, honey," she said. "You should have been here yesterday. Truck came by and dumped a mess of fish. Don't think he'll be back again till the weekend." The riverbank below us was littered with the pallid intestines and air bladders of rainbows that had been gutted and cleaned on the spot, moments after being caught, hours after being planted.

It's easy to sneer at the goings-on at this end of the trout spectrum, but the other end has its problems, too. Too often, a crude dualism is used to distinguish wild trout from hatchery trout, whereby the wild fish—make that Wild Fish—become an idealized abstraction signifying a wilderness experience that no longer exists. On Furnace Brook, all the fault lines of modern trout management run hard together, and the relationship between humans and trout habitat poses scientific and ethical choices of considerable subtlety.

THE WELL-TRODDEN DIRT fisherman's path led us steeply downhill, past the overgrown millrace of the old ironworks, where a separate diversion channel still flows under a heavy masonry arch, which looks as if it belongs in the Inca ruins at Machu Picchu. At the bottom of the hill, we met a second DEP crew. They were carrying an Old Town canoe, which they had been using to explore the deep, overgrown pools farther upstream. They called out to us excitedly about the size of the brown trout they had found there—sixteen- and seventeen-inch fish, tucked away in reaches of the brook that no one ever penetrated on foot.

They had a canoe; we had a backpack. To be more exact, we had a Coffelt BP-4 dual electrode apparatus. This was less arduous, and more intimate, than the electroshocking we had done a mile away, on the Housatonic itself. In fact, it was uncannily like fishing. The stream was no more than fifteen feet wide here, with room for only one person with the electrode probe and another two moving behind to collect the stunned fish.

Although the wildness of Furnace Brook was in part artificial, its structure, seen at these close quarters, reveal in every particular how wild trout adapt to their stream environment. Early in their lives, trout learn two things, failure to do so being fatal. They learn that most food drifts in a thread of fast current and that the best way to intercept it with the minimum expenditure of energy is to station themselves nearby in quiet water. They also learn that predators operate by sight and usually strike from above; therefore, they prefer slow water close to an undercut rock or some other overhead cover.

Once we got the measure of the stream, it was possible to predict with striking accuracy where the probe should go, like a well-placed fly, and what size of trout it would find, the trout being not only strongly individuated but also subject to a rigid social hierarchy. Under the prime rock at the head of each small pool, there was a good chance of surprising a thick-bodied two- or three-year-old fish that might run to twelve or thirteen inches; the belly and side seams of the pool typically held yearlings of seven or eight inches. The young of the year, with dark vertical parr marks on their flanks, were more randomly distributed.

Later, back at the picnic table, Mike said, "I think the most striking thing about today was the broad range of sizes. I'm not used to seeing that. Also the condition of the fish after such a long, hot summer—I mean, they weren't *snaky*. Normally when you do this, you can tell the year classes apart pretty easily. But today there was a real mix."

Mike continued: "The other thing is, it's still a marvel to me that these streams are stocked so heavily with adult-sized fish, and yet when you shock the stream they're just not there."

This hadn't struck me earlier, but I realized it was true. In a couple of hundred yards of stream, we had found well over a hundred wild browns, thriving in a friendly environment. Almost two thousand rainbows had been stocked in Furnace Brook four months earlier, but we hadn't found a single one. From the findings of the stream survey, I knew that this could be ascribed 80 percent to the methodical assault of the bait fishermen and 20 percent to the adaptational incompetence of the hatchery fish.

THE DEINDUSTRIALIZATION of the United States makes many things possible, and one of them is the expansion of wild trout populations. Stocking fish to provide instant gratification may be an ingrained habit—practically a "tradition"—but in the larger scheme of things it is a short-term anomaly, developed in response to conditions that no longer exist. This argument will probably seem like small potatoes to most people. But I find it indicative of something much larger and more important: how we overcome the alienating duality that exists between humans and the natural environment. I can't find a better way to pose the question than to turn to Cronon again. "What would a more historically and culturally minded way of understanding nature look like," he asks, "which would take seriously not just the natural world but the human cultures that lend meaning and moral imperatives to that world?"

Today we have a fighting chance to bridge the divide, by applying to rivers an ethic derived from our increasing biological understanding of how natural processes work and a better grasp of how social, economic, and cultural choices affect them. But it's a chance we could easily squander. How we work through this kind of cultural transition is in the end a matter of politics and economics, and since rivers stir fierce passions in people, there is every chance that the politics will turn ugly, mirroring the volatile shifts in population, income, and power that are under way in this small corner of America.

"It's pretty basic stuff," Mike Piquette said, interrupting these cosmic musings. "The hatchery system is so embedded, you're not going to get rid of it. But you stop putting hatchery fish in here, and then you put the fish that you save in places that are more accessible, that don't have the same habitat—and that will satisfy that constituency."

But this approach is likely to encourage a kind of segregation, both biological and social, which to some extent is already happening. Where the trout habitat is marginal, the emphasis will be on rainbows, which are easier to catch and aren't expected to live long. In streams where trout can thrive, hold over, and breed, the emphasis will be on browns. Ironically, this will tend to reinforce the kind of class divisions that came over from Britain with the brown trout in the 1870s. Browns for the nobs, rainbows for the hoi polloi.

But this demarcation of habitats and breeds is far from static. What will happen if we manage to reclaim not only the sparkling jewels like Furnace Brook, but also our urban and suburban streams—when they, too, regain the kind of habitat that wild trout need? On the Housatonic, Bob Orciari had said to me, "We're trying to put that kind of fishing within reach of more people. At present, most of those streams are in the northwest part of the state. But if we can produce that kind of fishing closer to urban areas and spread it out throughout the state, then we're really diversifying it."

I said, "That's a terrific goal. At the same time, the more rivers you bring back, the more you're going to get fly-fishers moving in on streams that used to be put-and-take. And the more you restore wild trout to urban areas, the more they may tempt the bait fishermen."

"You may be right," Bob said. "But you don't just want to exclude people. What about fathers and kids? Kids can't start off with fly-fishing. They're not going to be successful, and if they're not successful, they're going to lose interest in fishing."

I had to agree, remembering my own miserable attempt to teach David, at eight, to handle a fly rod on an English chalk stream.

As their environment changes, trout adapt. The concepts of adaptation and adaptive diversity, in fact, are cornerstones of biology. Ray White's article, the one Mike and Steve hand out at their road show, discusses how trout adapt in three different ways. The first is evolutionary, a process affecting whole populations, altering their inherited capacity to survive and reproduce in a changing environment. The second is physiological, taking place in the body of each individual trout. And the third is cultural and behavioral, which, according to the cancer researcher Van R. Potter, "seems to impinge on evolutionary adaptation and physiological adaptation in virtually every instance that can be imagined."

This is what trout do. The issue now, I suppose, is what kind of cultural and behavioral adaptation we humans will manage to accomplish.

Book III
LISTENING
TO THE
RIVER

The thinking of the Enlightenment and the industrial era represented the culmination of an approach to knowledge that goes back to the Greeks. This approach assumed a knowable world, about whose constitution and rules all reasonable people would ultimately agree. . . . The Twentieth Century saw the most noble and the most catastrophic attempts to act on this assumption. Dam-building, space travel and totalitarianism all presuppose that it is possible to understand the world in its essence and to prescribe a right course for the future from that understanding.

—Brian Eno,
"The Big Market Years,"
Foreign Policy, Summer 2000

19
Stakeholders

BACK IN 1940 the *Waterbury Republican-American* had won
a Pulitzer Prize for its exposé of the city's first great corruption scandal,
which brought down the administration of Mayor Frank Hayes. But
those were different times. As Phil Giordano won his third mayoral term
in November 1999, the newspaper's relationship to city hall could most
politely be described as cozy. On the eve of the election, the newspaper
ran a puff piece on the mayor that made my teeth ache. The reporter felt
moved to share with us that Giordano had "stood watch over an era future generations may well consider Waterbury's renaissance." For his
part, Giordano confided that being mayor was "an experience that makes
you a well-rounded individual in all aspects of life." He promised that
"the best is yet to come."

Getting with the program, an editor added the headline "Mayor Says
Exciting Times Just Around the Corner." This, you might say, was putting
it mildly. For in personal, economic, and political terms, Phil Giordano
had embarked on a spectacular meltdown.

The warning signs were not exactly difficult to spot. As Election Day
approached, the mayor and his wife had a third baby on the way, and he
was campaigning on a platform of family values. Yet as a Waterbury
firefighter would later tell the *Hartford Courant*, Giordano increasingly
"viewed the world through his zipper." He was often to be found cruising
for women at the Crossroads Cantina, which must be all of two hundred
yards from the editorial offices of the *Republican-American*. But the peo-

ple of Waterbury were shielded from these facts by what, in less ironic times, might have been called a "gentlemen's agreement."

At the same time, the city was stumbling deeper into the fiscal crisis that had confronted every mayor since the collapse of the brass industry. Hamstrung by its archaic political system, Waterbury had squandered its opportunities to find a seat at the great economic banquet of the 1990s. Phil Giordano swore that the city was solvent, but according to private estimates it was anywhere from $30 million to $70 million in debt. Giordano was reportedly concealing the extent of the problem—much as his predecessors had done—by means of a fiscal shell game, shifting money out of the city employees' pension fund to shore up the general budget.

At the same time, like every mayor before him, Phil Giordano had water on the brain. In essence, Waterbury's long era of prosperity, now no more than a fading memory, had been purchased on the credit drawn from two rivers. As the price of its growth, the city had mortally wounded the Shepaug and killed off the Naugatuck altogether. But now the debts were being called in—and on both rivers at once—by new and powerful forces that Mayor Giordano found it difficult to withstand. In the good old days of Chase and Cairns and Scovill's, public policy had followed the diktats of the Brass City elites. But that was no longer the case. The demographics of political power had shifted radically in northwestern Connecticut, and as Giordano approached his third term in city hall, he was sandwiched between two quite different adversaries, both of them apparently implacable.

On one front, Giordano had to contend with the affluent and legally sophisticated conservationists of Washington and Roxbury, who had decided that it was time to take a fresh look at the agreement that allowed Waterbury to help itself to most of the water from the Shepaug River. Back in 1921, First Selectman Titus of Washington might have felt that 1.5 million gallons a day was "what God intended us to have." But that was fifty years before Connecticut had its state Environmental Protection Act. The challenge over the Shepaug visibly drove Giordano nuts; you don't have to be a psychologist to imagine his resentment of these snooty weekenders who were insisting that the city change the way it had done business for the past eighty years.

The Shepaug campaign was fueled by local residents, but the second squeeze on Mayor Giordano came from an entirely different direction—

the state bureaucracy in Hartford: specifically, the Department of Environmental Protection. The special privileges that Waterbury had traditionally enjoyed in Hartford were steadily eroding. Even Connecticut's Republican governor, John Rowland, a native of Waterbury who always referred to the city as "the center of the universe," could hardly second-guess his environmental experts when they demanded an end to a century of official inertia concerning the condition of the Naugatuck River.

I N T H E T H I R T Y Y E A R S since the beginning of the modern environmentalist movement, a lot of people had come to realize that they had a stake in the health of their rivers and developed the means and the muscle to assert their claims. The new river advocates came from many different sectors. If they were entomologists, they worried about bugs; if they were anglers, they wanted trout; if they were professional biologists, they knew that habitat was the key. Among both public officials and ordinary residents, rivers had become more central to the concept of quality of life. Like nothing else, they expressed a consciousness of place, defining the genius loci of a community.

All citizens who cared about the appearance, the smell, the sound of the rivers that ran through their towns and villages and open lands coalesced around a single core principle. And that was the river's *flow*—full, natural, and unimpeded by what the DEP's scientific studies called "anthropogenic manipulation."

What will the past look like? This odd, Zen-like question seemed to motivate Mike Piquette as he nurtured wild trout in Furnace Brook, Bob Fumire as he tried to turn the Housatonic back into the river his grandfather had known, and the Washington activists as they questioned how God had intended their beloved Shepaug to run. Each was involved in an attempt to re-create, if not a literal copy, then at least an approximation of the past, based on sound science. Although documented history gave them only a few guideposts, the body of environmental law and science that had taken shape since 1970 had added new layers of understanding about how rivers work, and in the process, a new capacity to reimagine the past. In turn, this knowledge and vision could be used as a basis for constructing the future that respected each river as a unique entity, with its own distinct pulse and its own community of species—what the biologists call fluvial specialists.

Each small, local effort, I realized, was part of an infinitely larger agenda of restoration. It came with a heavy price tag. The cleanup of the Naugatuck, for example, would cost $250 million, making it the single most ambitious remediation effort ever undertaken by the state of Connecticut. It included the removal of dams to allow fish to follow their historical migration paths without hindrance; controls on pollution of all kinds; the upgrade of obsolete sewage treatment plants; the preservation and expansion of wetlands and estuaries; the remediation of contaminated industrial sites; and, most fundamental of all, a concerted effort to recover the essence of each river's identity—the in-stream flow that defined its size and its course, its natural meanders, its riffles and pools and back eddies, its unique configuration of habitat and vegetation. In a context of drought summers, freak heat waves, melting polar icecaps, and declining water tables, the river battles I was observing in the Housatonic Valley—Tocqueville's "innumerable multitude of small [undertakings]"—felt less like trivial local dramas than a harbinger of some larger enlightenment.

L YNN WERNER, perhaps because of her infuriating run-ins with the single-issue activists, was less sure. She seemed to believe that too many river advocates continued to operate as if still living in the 1970s. "In the beginning," she said, "the environmental movement created a lot of *linear* programs, and it all fell in linear parallel lines—*stream* protection, *land* protection, *water* protection, *air* protection." As she enumerated each one, she thumped the table with the side of her hand.

She was quick to contrast this with the strategies of the Housatonic Valley Association. The HVA was founded in 1941; in other words, it long predates what we think of as the modern environmentalist movement. "We were always linked to the towns along the river," Lynn told me. "Not just the river, but its *valley,* the land alongside it. The HVA was founded by planners and architects who recognized the real need to balance the imperatives of growth and conservation. That word *balance* flows through everything we do. Preserve what needs to be preserved, then balance the rest. When issues come up that affect the river, we have to figure out *scientifically,* on the basis of *facts,* not *anecdotes,* what's actually going on. It's only after you've figured out what's *happening* that you can figure out what can be *done.*"

From the very start, Lynn Werner said, "our concept has been integral watershed management—the idea of managing in tune with nature, where you are and what's going on around you. It's just very *simple*. It's basic earth science, the water cycle."

Simple though the concept may be, it's extraordinarily difficult to get people to change the way they do business. Lynn said, "We know now that a system is a living thing that is constantly in motion, and we're a piece of the system, not above it. But you have to *educate* people, starting with a map for each town, to show where it lies in each sub-basin. My town, Kent, for example—do people there know they depend on Warren for their water? You need to show those *dependencies*. At least get people thinking about the water they *drink*, if nothing else. Don't put pesticides into your septic tank. Realize that the water you drink may depend on the kindness of your neighbors. I mean, I'm two-thirds water. I *am* a product of this water cycle, so that makes me dependent on thousands of people."

The hardest part, Lynn said, was convincing public agencies that watershed management was actually the smart way to implement a regulatory program. In this regard, she explained, Massachusetts had been the pioneering state in New England, defining the boundaries of every one of the state's major watersheds and then appointing someone with responsibility for each. Lynn explained, "That person's job was to pull together all the *stakeholders* who had an interest in the management of the watershed. Not just the environmentalists, but people with real economic *interests*."

When I asked how the disputes over the Shepaug and the Naugatuck fit into this schema, she wrinkled her nose in frustration. "You're not going to see the watershed management approach on the *Shepaug*," she replied. "It's a linear issue there. You're not going to see it on the *Naugatuck*—it's a linear issue there, too."

How about the work that Mike Piquette was doing on Furnace Brook?

"That's how you really want to protect a river," she answered, perking up a little at my question. "You protect its *feeder* streams—the Furnace Brooks. That's a basic watershed concept. That's where I want to put my money and my resources. If you want to save rivers and streams, you've got to go to these little creeks and feeders and give them a two-hundred-foot vegetative buffer. Or you can pretty much *forget* it down the road, downstream."

That vegetative buffer, needless to say, with its backyard access to running water, is real estate that makes the developers salivate. Lynn said morosely, "We tried to get buffer legislation a few years ago, just ran it up the flagpole briefly, and it was shot down *immediately.* The science showed clearly that two hundred feet is what you need, but *politically* we knew it wasn't going to happen. So we came up with a hundred-foot buffer on major rivers and streams. Anything above a creek would have that much protection. It was completely at odds with what the science demonstrated, but for political reasons we knew it was *necessary.* So public education is really *urgent,* because if we don't take steps now, then in twenty-five years we're not going to have those steps to take. It'll be too late. So you need to bring the stakeholders around the same table to solve problems, in the way the HVA has tried to do for years."

$S_{TAKEHOLDER}$ is a word you hear a lot in nongovernmental politics these days. In essence, the idea is that complex problems can't be solved by any one party trying to impose its will, that confrontation often turns out to be unproductive, and that reasonable people can reach a broader understanding of their common interests—even with those they have thought of as adversaries. The stakeholder idea has made more headway in environmental politics than in other areas, perhaps because the definitions of many problems arising from our engineering of nature have been altered by advances in scientific knowledge.

This is basically the lens through which Lynn Werner looks at an issue such as PCB contamination of the Housatonic. She said to me with conviction, "You can't go anywhere on the *planet* to get away from PCBs. One reason there are so many shades of *gray* in the environmental movement may be how much this has changed. You're not dealing with raw *sewage* coming down the river anymore. You're dealing with things that may not by themselves be such a big deal, but in combination, over *time,* they may be one reason why we're seeing increased incidences of cancer. This makes it very frustrating. It's not as easy as it was twenty years ago to identify the enemy. We know that PCBs have a half-life of, what, five hundred years, so we *know* they're a problem. But the question is, how big a problem, at what levels, over how many years? We just don't know."

Personally, I'm sympathetic to the stakeholder approach to politics. At the same time, if accurate science is to be the benchmark, at times compromise won't make sense; decisions have to be made case by case. I had trouble with the hundred-foot stream buffer compromise, for example, since in this case science seemed to say that half a loaf was, in effect, much the same as no loaf at all. At best it seemed a beachhead of sorts, potentially leading people to the next level of understanding.

The problem for groups like the HVA is that their reluctance to define anyone as an adversary makes some people start to see *them* as the enemy. Talk of compromise, invoke the words *stakeholders* and *shades of gray,* and plenty of critics will scream "Sellout!" and "Corporate shill!" Balancing the imperatives of growth with the imperatives of conservation translates into a search for common ground between valley towns, with an interest in their tax base, and corporations, with investments in the valley, up to and including General Electric, which plenty of people along the Housatonic regard as the antichrist.

What irks the HVA's critics most is that the organization has accepted funding for several years now from GE's charitable foundation. I could see what Lynn Werner was getting at in a general way when she talked about the evolving nature of scientific knowledge—after all, current understanding of how PCBs accumulate in the environment means that power and wealth are no shield against their ill effects: the reproductive systems of Neutron Jack Welch's family are as much at risk as those of my own kids. Yet for all that, it was hard for me to see how the HVA could avoid the appearance of a conflict of interest, and I said so.

Lynn had little patience with this argument. The important thing, she said, was for the HVA to raise the money to build up its own capacity for objective scientific analysis. "Just get the *science,*" she said in exasperation, "without political overtones."

I COULDN'T HELP but think that this position was a little disingenuous. The various river wars seemed to suggest that, for good or for ill, not all stakeholders are created equal. I put this to Ed Kluck one day, as we sat in the front seat of his van, watching the rain sheet down over the Housatonic and wipe out a planned day of fishing. Ed gave me a sardonic look. "Listen," he said, "my people were Polack farmers. I know about class war, believe me. This thing between Washington and Waterbury, that's what it is: class war pure and simple."

Ed was overstating the case, but his words had a grain of truth. Certainly it was hard to look at the cast of characters—on the Naugatuck, along the Shepaug, and between the two—and not have the c-word rear its ugly head.

No matter what your politics (and I thought Ed Kluck's were probably pretty conservative), it was hard to see the ruin of the Naugatuck, for instance, as anything but a parable of economic inequality and power without accountability. The scandal of the Naugatuck was not its poisoning by heavy metals and suffocation by bacteria. It was the fact that everyone had known this for a hundred years, yet no one had done anything about it.

The official chroniclers had worked hard to rationalize this state of affairs. For William Pape and Robert Cairns, cleaning up the river had been just one headache too many; the filth just had to be accepted as the cost of progress. For Chard Powers Smith, fixated on the Manichean struggle for the soul of the Housatonic Valley, it was clear that "the plain motive of the original settlement [of the Naugatuck] was the Devil's." The devil had taken the river, "clanking and reeking with progress," and stirred it into one of his hellish stews. Good riddance, as far as the author of *The Housatonic: Puritan Valley* was concerned. Smith simply decided that he would omit all discussion of the Naugatuck from his book, declaring, in his lordly Yankee way, that to pay attention to the river would force him to "sacrifice continuity."

In legislative terms the first serious attempt to do anything about the clank and reek of progress came in 1967, with the Connecticut Clean Water Act, which mandated the secondary treatment of urban sewage and set new standards for industrial discharges. Federal legislation followed five years later. It stipulated that, wherever obtainable, water-quality goals must provide for the protection and propagation of fish, shellfish, and wildlife and for recreation in and on the water—in the popular shorthand, "fishable/swimmable" conditions.

Yet in 1980, although each river town had installed secondary treatment plants, the New England River Basins Commission found that the Naugatuck still contained "high ammonia, total organic carbon, BOD [biochemical oxygen demand], phosphorus, iron, copper, zinc, low dissolved oxygen from numerous sources, high coliforms from urban runoff and continued sewer overflows." Of all Connecticut's rivers, the Naugatuck was the most worrisome. The geology that had discouraged farming and fostered the growth of industry made the river unusually hard to clean up. With so few tributaries and such steep, impermeable banks, the Naugatuck flushed too quickly. The resultant low summer flows that resulted led to dangerous concentrations of toxins. The citizens of Waterbury contribute as much as eighty million gallons to the Naugatuck River every day, and from July to September fully three quarters of the water in the Naugatuck consists of treated sewage.

The pressure on Waterbury mounted in 1986, when the federal EPA and the state of Connecticut instituted stringent new toxicity controls on industrial effluent. Two years later, having mapped the full extent of the Naugatuck's contribution to the nitrogen overload in Long Island Sound, the state DEP laid down a complementary set of standards for organic pollutants. Then, even as these regulatory screws were tightened, the guys at inland fisheries threw a wild card into the mix. A memorandum from Jim Moulton's office declared that, of all the rivers in Connecticut, the Naugatuck had perhaps the best natural conditions for the restoration of Atlantic salmon—if only the string of dams that blocked the river's flow could be torn down. Unlikely as it might sound, the idea would have tremendous ramifications, since there is nothing like the promise of salmon to bring advocates—and not just local ones—sniffing around a river.

First, though, the water had to be clean. Once again, I found myself immersed in the murky scientific literature on modern wastewater treatment. The first thing you do with eighty million gallons of raw sewage, I discovered, is undertake the three *S*'s—screening, skimming, and settling. When the Waterbury treatment plant finally went on line in 1951, this is all it was set up to do. The next stage—"secondary treatment"—consists of biological action to break down and remove the solids that remain. Waterbury made this upgrade in 1972 to comply with the federal Clean Water Act. The 1988 standards raised the bar again, mandating "tertiary treatment"—denitrification in anoxic tanks and ultraviolet disinfection to kill any remaining harmful microorganisms.

The wastewater saga also bears on our story in another way. The state-mandated upgrade of the Waterbury plant would cost $170 million, making it the most expensive project of its kind ever undertaken in Connecticut. Mayor Phil Giordano had no single bigger headache. In 1996,

Giordano received a letter from Sidney Holbrook, who was DEP commissioner at the time. It made a sound like bailiffs pounding at the door. Beneath the polite bureaucratese lay this message: The pollution of the Naugatuck is intolerable, and so is your foot-dragging. What's the point of every other town on the river complying with our standards if Waterbury decides to ignore them? Waterbury isn't being singled out for special treatment, for heaven's sake—we've been warning you for almost twenty years that your current plant is out-of-date. It doesn't even meet the *old* standards, let alone the new ones. It's now more than *six years* since we issued you an abatement order, but nothing has been done. Any more delays, and we'll have no option but enforcement.

Giordano blinked. In truth, he had no alternative.

When the wastewater plant upgrade was put out to tender, people in city hall were surprised by the direct personal role that the mayor took in the proceedings. Giordano lobbied hard, and in the end successfully, for the $100 million contract to be awarded to the Worth Construction Corporation, which was based in the nearby town of Bethel. Once this agreement was in the bag, the mayor began to press for Worth to be given a second huge contract for the demolition and redevelopment of East Main Street, a depressed section of downtown Waterbury.

The mayor and the company's president, Joseph Pontoriero, were seen more and more in each other's company. Joe Pontoriero had fine taste in clothes, restaurants, cars, and secretaries, and he liked to invite his friends to share his box seats on the fifty-yard line at Giants Stadium in the New Jersey Meadowlands. As Phil Giordano's ambition and vanity grew, the names Pontoriero and Svengali began to be heard in the same sentence. Under Pontoriero's influence, Giordano seemed to spend more time working out at the gym, or getting facials and manicures, than he did on the mundane business of running the city government. His clothes became sharper, his shoes got shinier, and his hair began to look like a Grecian 2000 commercial. He also began to drop hints of running for higher office—the U.S. Senate, for starters. Too bad he had been born in Venezuela, Giordano told one reporter, since that ruled out the presidency.

The only little awkwardness was the FBI's close interest in Joe Pontoriero. The bureau was concerned, for instance, that Pontoriero had been a frequent guest at the Palma Boys Social Club in Manhattan, which was run by Anthony "Fat Tony" Salerno, the crime boss of the Genovese family. Also, Pontoriero's name had often surfaced during the so-called Commission Case—the 1987 trial of Salerno and other top Mafia figures. Phil Giordano knew that the Worth Corporation had been barred from New York City school construction contracts in 1998 because of continuing suspicions about its ties to organized crime. But he decided that the Waterbury board of aldermen need not worry their heads about this, since his friend Joe Pontoriero had never actually been found guilty of any crime.

For the people in the Shepaug Valley, fifteen miles away across the Litchfield Hills, all this might have been happening on another planet. It certainly didn't take up much column space in their local newspaper. The modern-day successors of Van Ingen, Van Sinderen, and Van Dyke take the *New York Times* and the *Wall Street Journal* on weekdays, but on weekends they curl up with the real estate pages, the celebrity profiles, and the militantly conservationist editorials of the *Litchfield County Times*. In the 1980s, the paper was acquired by a new publisher named Arthur Carter, who redesigned it as a clone of the *New York Times*. Carter also bought himself a sprawling farm property on the banks of the Shepaug, close to where Battle Swamp Brook enters the river.

Carter's readers were not to be trifled with when it came to protecting the natural environment. One battle against a giant California energy company named Sempra, which had the temerity to propose building a power plant on the Housatonic in New Milford, produced a classic *LCT* headline: "Styron, Stern, Sondheim, Doctors Look Askance at Sempra's Plan."

We're talking here about the novelist William Styron, the violinist Isaac Stern, and the composer and lyricist Stephen Sondheim, all of them residents of Litchfield County. The Litchfield Hills pullulate with celebrities, especially if you count the weekenders, who make up between a quarter and a half of the population of many small towns. There are poets and painters, screenwriters and movie actors, opera singers and novelists, critics and publishers, cartoonists and sculptors, entire colonies of *New Yorker* writers and *New York Times* reporters. Many of them, of course, are exactly the kind of upstart nouveaux riches that the old money would have fought tooth and nail to keep outside the invisible gates of Arcadia.

These people are enthusiastic supporters of the Housatonic Valley Association. They love the HVA, and it loves them back. The association's annual benefit auction, for example, is one of the plum dates on the Litchfield County social calendar: live jazz, champagne supper, a black-tie auctioneer. In a noble cause, the great and the good of the valley offer themselves and their possessions as prizes. The last time I looked, the high-ticket items included a week in fashion designer Diane Von Furstenberg's Paris apartment and a private tour of Oscar de la Renta's "superbly fabulous grounds." Someone had coughed up $5,000 for a power breakfast at the Regency Hotel—or lunch at the Four Seasons— with Dr. Henry Kissinger. ("Amusing as well as informative," the HVA newsletter promised. "*Herr Doktor* has a great sense of humor!")

Kissinger lives in the town of Kent. For those who find power an aphrodisiac, no other town can touch the place. This is where Oscar de la Renta has his superbly fabulous grounds. Anne Bass lives in Kent. So does Candace Bushnell, author of *Sex and the City*. They value its discretion, the owner of a local real estate firm told the *Hartford Courant*. "We don't have paparazzi on Main Street."

Some years ago, the former national security adviser, known to some of the more uppity locals as Henry Kiss of Death, purchased the old Henderson place, a 350-acre spread off Route 341. When a friend of mine was poking around the country lanes with his daughter a couple of years ago, he strayed innocently onto the dirt road to the Kissinger estate. Before he had gone more than a few yards, stern men in dark glasses materialized and told him to beat it. For years, the previous owner had the custom of allowing local people to visit his land every summer to pick the wild blueberries. Herr Doktor ordered them torn up, all fifty acres. He has, however, been a generous contributor to local environmental causes.

Roxbury probably has more celebrity per capita than any other town. It certainly has a higher median household income—almost $88,000, according to the 2000 census. It all started, people say, when Arthur Miller bought a property in the sleepy village (for one dollar "and other considerations") where he could hide out with Marilyn Monroe. In addition to Styron, Sondheim, and Miller, Roxbury has Dustin Hoffman and Frank McCourt. At various times in the past, it has had Sylvia Sidney and Alexander Calder, Rex Reed and Richard Widmark, Ellery Queen and Walter Matthau. New Milford (where Mr. Blandings built his dream house in the 1948 movie), has Ms. Von Furstenberg (who lives in Leopold Stokowski's old home) and had Vladimir Horowitz. Salisbury has Meryl Streep. Cornwall has the single most expensive property in the Litchfield Hills. This is the $7.1 million estate that belongs to the tennis champion Ivan Lendl. If you had nosed around the back roads of Cornwall during the 1990s, you might also have caught a glimpse of Whoopi Goldberg, or Tom Brokaw, or James Taylor.

Yet these days, when all is said and done, no place touches the town of Washington. Bill Blass and Ralph Lauren both have houses here; so does Graydon Carter, the editor of *Vanity Fair*, and Conan O'Brien, the late-night talk-show host. Washington is where you'll see the greatest number of white-tent parties and even the occasional stretch limo. If your guest house isn't big enough, the overflow can always be put up at the Mayflower Inn, where a room goes for $400 to $600. The real estate agents say that Washington homes have everything a celebrity could want. People love the place because it is so, well . . . *understated.* So unlike the vulgarity of the Hamptons. The landscapes are calendar-perfect and "having your own stream or lake is also a bonus." Large acreages guarantee privacy and can always be deeded over to the Steep Rock Reservation to be protected in perpetuity from development. As for the homes themselves, they offer the best of both worlds: white colonial clapboard and picket fences on the outside, but designer interiors—"large kitchens equipped with upscale appliances, master bathrooms with whirlpool tubs, and media rooms with enough seats for the entire family."

"So what's up with Washington?" the *Litchfield County Times* asked in a recent editorial.

> Many good things, it appears. Washington, as a town and as a state of consciousness, works hard to keep itself in great shape. It preserves its scenic beauty, while keeping the reins tight on residential and business growth. Policing and other public safety services are polished and diligent, the roads are a joy to drive, and amenities for gracious country living are plentiful.

What was it that Boston newspaper had said in 1885? "Here, then, is a kind of Arcadia . . ."

20
Fer Fightin' Over

PERHAPS I WAS BEING UNFAIR, though. Perhaps I was succumbing to my own clichés of class. There was righteous anger in the town of Washington, Connecticut, but it wasn't Ralph Lauren or Bill Blass who was leading the charge. It was, for the most part, another kind of Washingtonian who packed the town meetings to discuss how to force the city of Waterbury to restore a decent flow of water to the Shepaug River. These people were not celebrities or weekenders. If you were to tell these folks, right to their faces, that they were nothing but a bunch of cussed, independent, rock-ribbed, stiff-necked, cantankerous damned New England swamp Yankees, they'd probably chew it over for a moment, nod slowly, and take it as a compliment.

One such person is Bill Bader, who functions as a kind of unofficial historian, storyteller, and keeper of the public memory of the town of Washington. Bill Bader was born here, eighty or so years ago. He has seen Washington go, he says, "from cow town to parlor town." His grandfather, a master butcher from Alsace-Lorraine, came here in 1882, soon after the Shepaug Valley Railroad opened. Bader's Market in Washington Depot—the old Factory Hollow—thrived on the summer business and eventually became one of the largest retail stores in Connecticut. As a child, Bill Bader watched as "the cosmopolitan population brought their money to the hilltops and came to the Depot for their supplies." In those days, the social divide between the Depot and the Green was absolute and unbreachable.

So I assumed I knew exactly what Bill Bader would think about the nouveaux riches who had come flocking to town in the 1990s, and I called him, looking for what a journalist friend of mine used to call a GQ—a good quote. It took him about thirty seconds, however, to dispel my preconceptions. "I like a lot of the new people," he said. "There's a family who just moved in. Young couple in their thirties, paid millions for one of the old Rossiter houses. But they act just like anyone else." The clincher for Bill Bader seemed to be that they did their own grocery shopping. "In the old days, that would never happen," he told me. "Old Harry Van Sinderen would send his chauffeur in to shop at the market while he sat outside in the car. He was the closest thing we ever had to a Bourbon king. So the town's much more democratic now."

Dimitri Rimsky has known Bill Bader since childhood and a few years ago helped him publish an illustrated history of the town. Like Bader, Dimitri Rimsky is a Washingtonian, born and bred. He lives in a converted carriage house just off the Green, which his father, a White Russian émigré painter morbidly obsessed with themes of death, bought in 1950 when one of Washington's old baronial estates was being broken up and sold.

STEEP ROCK PARK – SHEPAUG RIVER, WASHINGTON, CONN.

I had lunch with Dimitri one day at the Deli on the Green to see if I could get any closer to understanding the ghost in the Washington machine. He agreed right away that there is a certain Brigadoon quality to the place. There is no paint-by-numbers way of entering what he sees as the inner Washington, and the challenge of gaining entrée is replete with paradoxes. As in 1885, all the money in the world isn't enough to buy admission. Yet at the same time, being one of the nouveaux riches or being a newcomer is not in itself the bar that it used to be. It all depends on how you carry yourself—on whether, as Bill Bader said, you do your own shopping.

Dimitri tried to illustrate this with a couple of stories. The first concerned something the violinist Yehudi Menuhin had said in a speech at the Congregational Church. (Washington is the kind of place, you note for starters, where the likes of Yehudi Menuhin give speeches at the Congregational Church.) He'd said, "It's comforting to come to a place where your forebears were so convinced of their aesthetic that they imprinted it on everything they built and did."

To Dimitri, the apparent compliment contained a subtle barb. The Washington aesthetic could be summed up, he said, as "clarity, symmetry, balance, simplicity, restraint, proportionality." But fidelity to that aesthetic, he said, "is based on a total hypocrisy of culture."

I must have looked a little puzzled by this, for he tried to explain by telling me a second anecdote. Some years ago Dimitri had a neighbor who was a financial adviser to the Haitian dictator Baby Doc Duvalier. One day the man put in a perfect, instant rolled-turf lawn in front of his house. The lawn extended into an area where people were accustomed to parking their cars, and they continued to do so. Dimitri ran into his neighbor outside the house one morning and complimented him on the appearance of his new lawn. The man snorted and said, "Well, people don't seem to appreciate it." Dimitri said to him, "Well, I think perhaps that's because most of them have to work so hard to achieve the same effect." The barb was more lethal than Menuhin's, but it went right over the man's head. It was a classic Washington exchange.

Dimitri went on. "What we have to sell here is quality of life. Real estate is our only industry. When people buy homes here, they think they're buying something else—that aesthetic of balance and restraint." But the real charm of the Washington community, Dimitri said, is neither readily apparent nor automatically available. "It's a cooperative covenant," he said, "unspoken and intuitive. For example, there may be someone you've never spoken to except to say hello when you pass in the street. But that casual acquaintance will show up at your house to help if there's a fire. Or you'll turn up at his house to help him pick up the debris after a flood. That's not something you can buy from the real estate agent."

Yet the wealthy newcomers are welcome to join, if they learn how to play by Washington rules. According to Dimitri Rimsky, the key is participation. "Do you turn up at the bake sale? If you want to alter the picket fence around your two-million-dollar house, that's fine—as long as you come to the zoning meeting to discuss the issue yourself. But don't send in your lawyer with alligator loafers."

EDWIN MATTHEWS does his own grocery shopping. His passion, the area in which he decided he could make his own particular contribution to the town's unspoken covenant, is the Shepaug River. By virtue of his marriage, Ed straddles the Washington divide between locals and weekenders. Ed is a corporate lawyer with Coudert Brothers in Manhattan. His wife, Patricia, is a filmmaker who grew up in Washington. Ed and Patricia bought a house in Hidden Valley in 1991, and when they went shopping in the Depot, the storekeepers said, "Well, my oh my, hello, Patricia. Welcome back. You've been gone a long time."

I drove to Hidden Valley to see Ed Matthews one Sunday morning. On the way, I stopped at Jack's, the fancy new grocery store in the Depot, to buy the makings of a lunch, thinking there might be time later to get in a couple of hours on the river. I bought bread at Jack's, choosing a Levain Bâtard over a Pugliese or a Fruited Seeded Torpedo. The cheese counter was more challenging. Roucoulons or Eppoisses? Pavé d'Affinois or Tête de Moine? Raclette? Pyrennean Etorki? On the other side of the cooler, I weighed the relative merits of Estribeiro, Appenzeller, and Raw Milk Taleggio. There was Majoreo and Marzolino; there was Sheep's Milk Istara and Catalan Garrotxa. I felt as if I was in the old Monty Python cheese-shop sketch. Venezuelan Beaver Cheese?

I found Ed Matthews outside his house, in blue jeans and a denim work shirt. Open fields swept away to the north; on the other side of a deep gully lay Seymour's Farm. Across the river was the old Van Sinderen estate. We struck out along a path through the hemlocks. Below us, invisible through the trees but just audible, were stretches of the river where I liked to fish—the Flume, the Barn Hole, Bert's Rock.

Like many environmentalists, Ed Matthews walks fast and stops often. He bends down to examine an anthill. He finds the signs of hawks scratching for field mice in the freshly cut stubble. He points to a flock of wild turkeys on the slope and counts them. Nine. He sees a wasps' nest in a tree, deer marks on a trunk, green showing through the shredded bark. He freezes when a fawn emerges at the tree line a full second before I become aware of its presence.

Although I'd known Ed Matthews for several years, I'd never quite been able to place his accent. There was an overlay of Harvard and hints of Europe, where I knew he'd lived for fifteen years. But underneath these, inflections flickered from somewhere farther west. This impression is reinforced by the way Ed carries himself. He is lean and rangy, slightly stooped, and looks as if he'd be comfortable on the back of a horse.

I asked him where he had spent his childhood, and he said Spokane, Washington, where he was born in 1934. He said, "I grew up there and in northern Idaho, where my father and mother had a cabin on a lake at Coeur d'Alene, which was six miles down the lake by boat from the town. I spent every summer of my life there, from the age of two months on. Growing up on that lake was a privileged existence. I loved the wilderness there. We had no road until 1954. We had no phone. We had to generate our own electricity until the Rural Electrification Authority (REA) came in during the war. It was totally free. I could get in a boat, with a sleeping bag, and go around the lake, and sleep and camp. I'd go off on my own when I was eleven or twelve. Even when I was ten years old, I'd go across the lake to go fishing. I'd go off for a week and camp.

"The lake has about eighty miles of navigable river. There were huge areas of shoreline that were uninhabited and unclaimed. I remember one man who lived on a barge on the lake. It was a steam barge powered with wood, and he would go up and down the lake, and put in and cut wood for his barge, and then move on."

Ed made it sound as if the man's life was one that any sensible Manhattan corporate lawyer would envy.

He hunted and fished a lot with his father. They never thought of getting home on time or worried about getting lost or having to sleep out. They were happy just going outdoors and seeing what would happen. Ed said, "I think that gave me an appreciation of nature, and the natural world, which I've kept. It's not something I was taught. It just sort of soaked in, and for me, untrammeled nature was just perfectly normal. I had a taste of what this planet was like before man got here and what this continent was like before the whites arrived. We would up and go off, my father and I, and explore places where people hadn't gone. We were not discovering new continents. But we would find places, little places, where no one had ever been before. We never seemed to follow trails. We often got lost. Sometimes we'd walk all night. I sort of thought that was par for the outdoor course."

That was half a century ago, of course, and Coeur d'Alene has changed. "Today," Ed said, "what with UPS, and rescue systems, you can't even get lost anymore. The lake is still an extraordinary place, but it's been overrun by houses and airplanes and motorboats. As they say, it's been Californicated. I find that sad. North Idaho is one of the fastest-growing areas in the country. The town of Coeur d'Alene had barely ten thousand people then. It's thirty-five thousand now. It has its own high-rise."

After Idaho came boarding school in Seattle. Then east to college. There was never any question it would be Harvard. Ed's father had gone there, and in those days, you applied to only one school. Then Harvard Law School and a stint in the army in France, going to college in the daytime and working nights in a military hospital in Chinon, in the Loire Valley, that was set up to receive casualties when Russian tanks came storming through the Fulda Gap. A little art history at the École du Louvre; a spell on the assembly line at the Renault car factory.

By this time, Ed Matthews felt a little uncomfortable in Coeur d'Alene. Harvard and Europe had created a distance. So he joined Coudert Brothers in New York, as a first-year associate in corporate law. But Ed was never happy for long doing only one thing with his life. He read a lot of Lewis Mumford and worried about the loss of green space in American cities. In 1963, a baby lawyer only a year out of school, Ed persuaded the firm to let him work on a lawsuit to block construction of a sidewalk café that would have required paving over the lake in Central Park.

In those days, there was no real environmental movement to speak of. But there was the Sierra Club, and Ed Matthews wondered if it might be willing to act as a friend of the court in the case. So he called David Brower, who at that time was still the club's president. Brower made a lasting impression on Ed Matthews, an effect he had on almost everyone. More remarkably, it appears that the aspiring young environmentalist lawyer from Coudert Brothers, who was still not quite thirty years old, stuck in David Brower's mind also.

Posted to Coudert's Paris office, where he could use his fluent French, Ed realized that Europe was even further behind than the United States in environmental protection. There wasn't even a local equivalent of the Sierra Club. Economic growth at any cost was the rule of the day. So Ed wrote to David Brower, outlining a plan to make the Sierra Club an international organization.

He heard nothing for a long time, but one day, out of the blue, Brower called. By now, he'd been kicked out of the Sierra Club, after the tumultuous rebellion against his leadership that is recounted in John McPhee's book *Encounters with the Archdruid*. Brower flew to Paris and told Ed he'd decided to start a new organization, called Friends of the Earth. He asked if Ed would help. Ed said yes. He joined the board of Friends of the Earth in 1969 and set about launching groups in England, and Holland, and France, and Italy, and Australia, and Japan, and South Africa. Friends of the Earth has affiliates today in about sixty countries.

"It was all about finding good people," Ed continued. "You talked to them about the importance of doing something and then they'd get addicted. You'd get them around a table, and one guy would say he had an office, and somebody else would say, you know, he had a book he would work on. Within weeks you'd have a Friends of the Earth group. They just took the idea and ran with it. My idea was to set up groups that would have the same name but be autonomous, and be different in each country. Together, they would form some sort of partnership that we would call Friends of the Earth International. So environmental activism would not be something run from the United States or dominated by certain countries. As we know now, environmental problems cut across boundaries. They exist on a planetwide scale, and it is simply not sufficient to attack them in one place."

This was a time when a new environmental organization, a new piece of legislation, was popping up every time you blinked. The Environmental Defense Fund (EDF) wanted to bring science to environmental protection. The Natural Resources Defense Council (NRDC) wanted to use the law as well as science. I asked Ed what set Friends of the Earth apart from the other new organizations.

"Well," he answered, "Friends of the Earth was much more idealistic. It was an activist organization. Our message was that you had to learn new ways to live and behave. It was about more than law and science. You also had to take it into the political sphere. Friends of the Earth prided itself on being more radical, more cutting-edge, more grass-roots, than the others. It wasn't so interested in working with the establishment."

I assumed that this style had a lot to do with the personality of Brower, the Archdruid. I'd recently been rereading the parts of McPhee's book that dealt with Brower's spectacular fall from grace. "Did McPhee capture the personality of the man?" I asked.

"O-o-o-o-h yes," Ed said, nodding and smiling. "Oh yes."

"Actually," he said after a moment, "David gave me a copy of that book. He inscribed it to me, 'To Edwin, who was sacrificed. The Archdruid.'"

"What did he mean by that?" I asked.

"Oh, I was very close to him," Ed answered. "I worked well with him—at a distance. He was running Friends of the Earth in the United States, and I was basically worried about Europe, and I was given total freedom to do what I thought should be done. Several times, David asked me to come to San Francisco and take over Friends of the Earth, but I turned him down. But then in 1979, my firm needed a partner to take charge of our San Francisco office. I had the idea that maybe I could go there and work part-time with my law firm and part-time with Friends of the Earth."

Ed Matthews was forty-five and ready to take stock of his life at the midway point. He and Patricia had just met. Together, they took a month-long kayak trip down the Noatak River in Alaska, all the way from the Brooks Range to the Bering Strait. The trip changed his life, Ed said. "It gave me a lot of time to really think. It also perhaps gave me the courage to think about doing something different with my life, so that it would have more purpose. So I took over from David as president of Friends of the Earth. David was to retire."

He left a long pause, and then said: "Except he didn't retire."

"What happened?" I asked.

Ed replied, "Well, David kept his office, the big one, and I had a smaller one. He had a very complex relationship to the organization, and to the people. Notwithstanding any decision I made, or any recommendation I made, it was David who would ultimately decide. Even if I had reviewed something with him in advance, I would find that it was criticized. It was a very difficult situation."

It sounded like a nightmare to me. I'd been in situations myself where a boss second-guessed everything I did. But Ed, characteristically, seemed to fault himself. "It was part of the arrogance of youth, maybe, that led me to believe that I could do two jobs at once. I was in two different worlds, which weren't easily compatible. Friends of the Earth was impatient with my spending time with the office. I was in a corporate world there, surrounded with people who . . . well, you can't expect everyone to attach the same importance to environmental issues that I did. In addition to that, I found myself in conflict with David."

It wasn't *policy* that was the problem, Ed explained. It wasn't as if one man said, "Let's protect the bowfin whale," and the other man said, "No, let's not." Instead, they might decide to publish a book on whales and agree to publish ten thousand copies. Then Ed would find that Brower had gone ahead and ordered twenty-five thousand—and this in an organization that operated on a shoestring. Basically, Ed said, "He went off and did what he thought needed to be done, irrespective of any decision that the board made or that I had made. I couldn't run the organization. It was an impossible situation. So after a year and a half I resigned."

After fifteen years, Ed was exasperated with the intrigues of not-for-profits. So in the early 1980s, he joined the board of the Sierra Club Legal Defense Fund, now the Earth Justice Legal Defense Fund. LDF operates as a public interest law firm, with fifty lawyers and an annual budget of $20 million. Ed serves on the committee that reviews and approves litigation. Most of the suits brought by LDF are against the government, and the group wins about 90 percent of them.

Ed said, "I appreciate it because it's a law firm, after working with a not-for-profit, where people are volunteers, where nobody is accountable, where the issues are intangible. I mean, changing the way you look at the planet. Where do you start? How do you measure success? Or failure? How do you change an entire society? By comparison, a law firm is a real luxury. If there's a motion, you have to act by Monday. People are accountable. A judge has to make a decision. You win. Or you lose."

AFTER EDWIN AND PATRICIA MATTHEWS arrived in Washington in 1991, it seemed to Ed that this philosophy might usefully be applied to the Shepaug River. Resentment at the dewatering of the river had been simmering for years, but Ed Matthews thought the fight to protect it needed to be taken to a new level. Anyone could see that the Shepaug was running dry, but you needed to be able to prove two things to the satisfaction of outside arbiters. First of all, you had to show that the river was being materially impaired and that Waterbury's diversions were to blame. Second, and harder, was to show that the city had more efficient ways of operating its water supply system, of meeting its legitimate needs without causing undue harm to the Shepaug. You couldn't accomplish this by having biologists measure the river's dissolved oxygen content or its population of blacknose dace. It would mean bringing in hydrologists and hydraulic engineers, gaining access to technical data that Waterbury was reluctant to divulge, and running computer models to estimate what the river's flow would be in the absence of the dam. It would also mean a willingness to play political, and if necessary legal, hardball.

The state of Connecticut formed a task force to try to mediate the dispute, but it had no enforcement powers. All it could do was urge the two sides to negotiate. Sometimes they met, sometimes they didn't. Sometimes Waterbury canceled the meetings. Sometimes Phil Giordano promised to attend and then didn't show up. On the one occasion he appeared, Ed Matthews found himself staring at the soles of the mayor's expensive shoes. "He came in and put his feet on the table," Ed said, "as if to say, 'We control the river and there's not a damn thing you can do about it.'"

"It was Waterbury's arrogance, the way they were just blowing us off, that drove the issue," Dimitri Rimsky had told me. "But two things really pushed our buttons—they were selling our water to other towns and they were using *our* hydraulic force to solve *their* problems. There was this growing resentment that someone else was coveting what was ours. And we took that as an insult to the community as much as to the environment."

On two successive nights in July 1997, Ed Matthews spoke at town meetings in Washington and Roxbury. He told them the talks were going nowhere, that Waterbury was only using them as a stalling device. The meetings were emotional. People stood to pour out their feelings about the river, not always coherently. It was hard to put into words and numbers what the river meant to them. Attorneys for the city of Waterbury sat in the back of the room and took notes.

Ed Matthews said the Shepaug River Association felt it was time for litigation. Each meeting took a vote. In Washington, the vote was 350–0; in Roxbury, 150–0. No one present could recall this kind of unanimity on any other issue. The general mood was, if they want war, let us give them war—a war between two civic cultures, between two views of the meaning and value of running water.

The intensity of feeling may seem surprising in the green hills of Connecticut, the Land of Steady Habits. Thinking of the ornamental fountains of Las Vegas, the irrigated orange groves in the San Fernando Valley, *Chinatown,* you would think that water wars were something peculiar to the arid West. In New England, you might suppose, to paraphrase Mark Twain, that both whiskey and water were "fer drinkin' and not fer fightin' over." But as the suburban and exurban population grows, and the water table drops, this contest for water is moving eastward in the United States at a rate few people yet acknowledge. "You have to realize," Dimitri Rimsky had told me, "that there's a lot of righteousness about water; it's almost like religion. It's the same god, but we all argue about how to divide it."

ED AND I had reached a steeply descending path through the hemlocks, one of the old roads that used to bring milk from the outlying dairy farms to Borden's Creamery in the Depot. Notices on the trees warned of attacks by nesting goshawks. A pair of them had once swooped down on a friend of Ed's while they were walking here, tearing deep claw holes in his bald head. On the slope below us was a glint of aluminum. Although Ed is fifteen years older than I, he shinned quickly down the sixty-degree slope to retrieve the discarded can. Coors Light.

We began to talk about the price of justice, a frequent topic of conversation between us. Ed likes to quote Mark Twain on the subject, to the effect that "justice in this country must be bought." Twain may have meant this cynically, but that isn't why Ed quotes him. He's simply being realistic about the material resources that are needed to bring a case to court and win. Marshal those resources, get the best experts, produce the best evidence—conduct, in other words, what Ed Matthews calls a "fully fought case"—and the system can work for you. If you can't do these things, justice is unlikely to be done.

Patricia Matthews had been urging me to read *A Civil Action,* Jonathan Harr's best-selling account of an environmental lawsuit over contaminated groundwater in Massachusetts, which she saw as a paradigm for what now lay ahead for the Shepaug. I hadn't read the book, but I'd seen the movie starring John Travolta.

I said to Ed, "Do you remember the part where the lawyer has bankrupted himself, and he's wondering how he can possibly continue with the case? He's at the toxic waste site, and he's looking down from a high window at some workers who are tampering with soil samples, or concealing evidence, or whatever. And he says to himself that there are 780,000 civil actions every year, but only 12,000 of them ever reach a verdict. And he says, 'Trials are a corruption of the entire process, and only fools with something to prove end up ensnared in them.'"

Ed cocked his head to one side and thought about it, then answered evenly. "Well, the lawyer destroyed himself because he didn't have the resources to pursue the case, and he was facing formidable opponents who knew that and used everything they could to make it more expensive, to drag it out." He paused and gave me the driest of smiles. "I have not had that disadvantage."

"Would you have taken the *Civil Action* case?" I asked.

Ed thought for a second, then said, "Yes, probably. If you can bear the cost in human and financial terms, if you are determined, you can ultimately get relief. This battle of ours for the river is something that a citizen, or a group of citizens, can wage. And if you do it right, you can win."

We were standing together now on the dirt trail by the river, under the hemlocks. The water in the Shepaug was running clear and amber. I asked Ed if he could estimate the flow, just by looking. He squinted at a rock and said, "Eleven point five million gallons per day." We knelt down by the edge of the water and turned over some football-sized rocks, looking for bugs. There was nothing under the first few, but then we found some stick caddis cases. A plump, dark-colored pupa emerged from a loose assembly of quartz grains under the pressure of my fingernail. It looked to me like *Helicopsyche.*

21
Floodwaters

E DWIN MATTHEWS CALLED ONE DAY to say that two town meetings had been scheduled at the Gunn Library in Washington to discuss the lawsuit. Would I like to come?

I reached the library just as the first meeting was beginning. It was standing room only. Somebody had thought astutely about the purpose of the gathering: to brief the troops for combat. To that end, charts and maps and pointers had been assembled. The scene was reminiscent of one of those World War II movies in which the bomber pilots are given the targets for that night's raid.

Ed Matthews stepped to the podium to open the proceedings. He came to the microphone diffidently, as if public speaking made him uncomfortable. Then he laid out his vision.

"One of the best things we have in this country is access to the courts," he said. "No other country has opened up its government, its legislature, to judicial review. That's a great privilege we enjoy. Imagine where we'd have been without the Supreme Court in the fight to end school segregation. Through the courts, anyone has the standing to call any government agency to task. Even the city of Waterbury."

The meeting covered a lot of ground: part legal briefing, part history lesson, a *Cliff Notes* chronology of the dispute. It walked the people of Washington all the way from the great continental collision that formed Pangaea, and the fault thrust of Cameron's Line, through the advance and retreat of the glaciers, and thence all the way to the completion of the

Shepaug Dam in 1933. Since then, Ed Matthews said, "everything we've learned demonstrates that there is ample water to save the river and that Waterbury is not managing the system as it should. We have just learned, in fact, that Waterbury doesn't have a management plan at all. So we're going to require the city to manage the system so that it preserves the Shepaug and provides it with the water it needs."

Everyone smiled and nodded and applauded and then listened intently as Ed Matthews explained the significance and the complexities of the lawsuit, which would amount to a landmark environmental case. The state of Connecticut was taking a close interest in the outcome, without having openly taken sides. The court's decision would establish a precedent that could affect dozens of other dewatered rivers, and it would show whether ordinary citizens could give substance to the state's Environmental Protection Act (CEPA), passed in 1971 to protect the public trust "in the air, water and other natural resources of the state from unreasonable pollution, impairment or destruction."

But CEPA was not the only standard that bore on the Shepaug case. Multiple pieces of legislation, reflecting other times and other priorities, created anomalies. The law is never a linear affair. It moves rather like a Slinky toy going down stairs, one part moving ahead, then another catching up and leapfrogging over the first. In addition to the standards set forth by CEPA, the court would have to take into account the priorities of 1893, when the state of Connecticut had granted Waterbury carte blanche to appropriate the waters of Litchfield County, and those of 1921, when the town of Washington was sweet-talked into surrender by Robert Cairns and Henry Chase. Since diversions of river water threatened precisely the sort of impairment that CEPA sought to prevent, another piece of legislation was created—the 1982 Water Diversion Act, which imposed more stringent limits on the use of public water. But that in turn created problems. What about preexisting diversions, such as Waterbury's from the Shepaug, which had passed unchallenged for half a century? These were grandfathered, shielding them from environmental impact review.

On a tactical level, too, the case was complicated. Although Washington and Roxbury had set the legal ball rolling, Waterbury had actually been the first to file suit, in a preemptive move that gave the city a favorable venue—the complex litigation division of the Waterbury Superior Court—and left the river advocates in the odd position of appearing as defendants. Judge Beverly Hodgson would be considering *Waterbury v. Washington,* not *Washington v. Waterbury.* On the other hand, Judge Hodgson had something of a reputation as an environmentalist, and the Shepaug forces drew encouragement from this fact.

THE SECOND MEETING at the Gunn Library, a couple of weeks later, was different. It focused on reinforcing morale and a sense of common purpose. With no formal speeches and no fixed program, fifty or sixty people had simply gathered to share their memories of the Shepaug. They were an older crowd, few of them under sixty. A young reporter from the *Litchfield County Times* acted as moderator, prowling the library like the host of a TV talk show.

Immediately an irony surfaced. Here we were, brought together by a shared fear that the river was dying for lack of water. Yet the main thing that people wanted to talk about was the traumatic day in August 1955 when the volume of water in the river had been so great that it changed the face of Washington Depot.

It had rained heavily earlier in July that year, but the end of the month was hot and dry. The rain began in earnest on August 5, and a week later Hurricane Connie swept through, dropping eight inches of rain. The ground was still saturated on August 18 when Diane, an even bigger storm, followed. Sixteen inches of rain fell in a thirty-hour period.

On the night of August 18, a Thursday, the Dramalites opened their production of *Green Grow the Lilacs* at the Washington Club House. The noise of the rain on the roof was so loud that the packed house couldn't hear the actors' lines. By eleven that night, there were two inches of water on Main Street. Yet no one seemed greatly concerned; the Shepaug had flooded often enough in the past.

Six miles north of the Depot, at Woodville, drivers had grumbled for years about a dangerous curve and a narrow bridge where Route 25 crossed the river, a mile south of the Shepaug Dam. For their greater convenience, the state highway engineers had removed the curve and the bridge and filled the hundred-foot-deep ravine with thousands of tons of rubble, which resembled a large earthen dam. Since the Shepaug was a small stream at this point, a bridge seemed superfluous. The engineers decided a culvert would be enough, cut through the base of the landfill, with four concrete pipes to carry the river's modest flow.

As the rain continued through the night, it uprooted shrubs and bushes, and eventually larger trees. One by one, these obstacles stacked up against the mouth of the culvert until they formed an impenetrable barrier. Since it was not a night to be outside, no one was on hand to apprehend the danger as the floodwaters rose behind the new impoundment. By first light, the wall of water was sixty feet high. At 6:30 A.M. the highway and the mountain of fill collapsed with a thunderous roar, and a wave of water, six feet tall and traveling at forty-five miles an hour, descended on Washington Depot, where it hit the Green Hill Bridge at exactly 7:00 A.M.

Mr. Ingersol Townsend, head of the English department at the Gunnery School, six feet five inches tall and built like a stick insect, looked down on the scene and exclaimed, "Great Caesar's ghost! What a catastrophe!"

A herd of cattle hurtled downstream on the flood, bellowing in terror. Like a battering ram, a huge tree trunk hit the home of the Foulois family, right next to the bridge, severing it from its foundation. The imposing three-story house floated off drunkenly down the Shepaug, like a large, ungainly riverboat, with Mr. and Mrs. William Foulois aboard. Half a mile downstream, the house smashed into Moody Bridge, killing the couple and taking the iron bridge along.

Over the weekend, there was looting in town, and the National Guard moved in to keep order. The people of Washington Depot went to church on Sunday, in remembrance of the Foulois family, but the organ was too wet to be played. Mrs. West was heard to remark to Mr. Seabrook, "A little disaster is good for us once in a while."

That seemed to mirror the feelings of the meeting at the Gunn Library. A warm nostalgia was shared among those who had experienced the flood, rather like Londoners who had survived the Blitz together.

"Chet Curtis was the postflood hero," someone said. "He told the Red Cross to go away, we could take care of ourselves." Chet Curtis, I recalled, had been in charge of the town's civil defense, trained to cope with the aftermath of a nuclear attack by the Russians.

Several people jumped to contrast this proud Yankee self-sufficiency with the helpless passivity of people in the mill towns along the Naugatuck. One older man in a brown-check sport jacket said, "Down in Seymour, everyone was just sitting around on the sidewalks looking devastated, with no idea of what to do. In Washington, everyone had their sleeves rolled up; we were fixing the problem by ourselves."

People nodded with satisfaction, agreeing. I appreciated the effort to rally the town against the corrupt and greedy politicians of Waterbury, but we seemed to have crossed some ethical line separating pride and spite. This had been the worst flood ever recorded on the chronically flood-prone Naugatuck. The river towns suffered on a scale much worse than anything that the Shepaug or the Housatonic Valley experienced. The *Waterbury Republican-American* described the river as "a madman in surgeon's clothes, shearing here, breaking there." Entire city blocks came down under the knife. Seventeen houses were swept away on North Riverside Street, a modest neighborhood that housed the families of Lithuanian immigrant brass workers, people whose names were Alisauskas, Garbukas, Gervickas, Padaigis, Seredinskas.

The flood snatched up trucks, buses, railroad engines, and freight cars. It tore out thirty-six miles of track along the New Haven line. The Seymour Public Library disappeared. Local heavy industry never fully recovered from the '55 flood, which inundated the American Brass Company in Ansonia and the old U.S. Rubber plant, now Naugatuck Chemical. It wrecked the Chase Metal Works in Waterville. Chase executives had once ordered engineers to reroute the river here, to accommodate their needs, but the river insisted on having the last word.

The August 19 flood made the cover of *Newsweek*. In all, 191 people were killed in the state of Connecticut, and the material damages were estimated at almost $1.7 billion. The flood left twenty-four dead in Waterbury, ten in Naugatuck, seven in Winsted, six in Torrington. Headstones, vaults, caskets, and human remains found that their last resting place was not in Seymour's Union Cemetery, but in Long Island Sound.

It didn't surprise me that people in Seymour had been shell-shocked. I found myself suddenly irritated by the discussion, wondering whether people in Washington might not have reacted to the flood differently if the Shepaug Spathic Iron Company had turned a profit, if Major McNeill's railroad had prospered, if the inhabitants of the Shepaug Valley, too, had spent a hundred years being industrialized into submission.

But the tone of the meeting had been kindled now, and it blazed away cheerfully. After the flood, someone recalled, the Army Corps of Engineers had gone up and down the Shepaug, blasting away large boulders and tearing out the remains of old dams and bridges. But given the Shepaug's more generous floodplain, they did not need (and perhaps would not have dared) to disfigure the river as they had the Naugatuck, channelizing it and straightening it and lining it with retaining walls and riprap.

Later, someone else remembered, in the 1960s, the corps had poked its nose into the Shepaug Valley again as it cast around for alternative sources of drinking water for southern Connecticut. The engineers thought that Roxbury Falls and the Clam Shell would make fine sites for two additional dams, which would have created an artificial lake lapping at the steps of the Washington town hall. But Washington rose up against the plan, and the corps backed down. "The Army Corps of Engineers found it wasn't worth their while to mess with the town of Washington," a middle-aged man chimed in from the back of the room, and everyone chuckled appreciatively.

THE ARMY CORPS OF ENGINEERS, however, was just one of the many forces that had messed with the Naugatuck. Even now, when there was finally a plan to clean up the river, the impetus seemed to be coming from the top down, from Hartford, rather than from the bottom up. I knew that if the local activists in dismal places like Seymour and Ansonia were to call a town meeting, they might well find themselves talking to an empty room.

By common acclaim, the most notable of these activists was Bob Gregorski, a high school teacher from the town of Middlebury. Bob Gregorski was Mr. Naugatuck. I arranged to meet him at the Seymour town hall, where the enlightened first selectman had just donated office space to the Naugatuck restoration effort. In advance of our meeting, Bob Gregorski sent me a letter outlining his philosophy. It said: "I learned quickly that I could not rely on adults (except those who worked with students and scouts) to do the conservation work that needed to be done. Being an educator, it was obvious—show the students what needed to be done and why, and they will put their brains and brawn to work to get the job done. They have never let me down."

Bob blanketed the local Boy Scout troops and high school ecology clubs with little leaflets on "litter longevity"—cigarette filters take fifteen years to degrade, Styrofoam cups ten, that sort of thing. His teenage volunteers combed the riverbank, armed with his leaflets and a good supply of garbage sacks, which they filled methodically. A lot of Styrofoam cups and cigarette filters grace the banks of the Naugatuck, as well as innumerable aluminum cans (life span one hundred years). From my own unscientific observation, it appears that Budweiser and Bud Light are the preferred brands.

Other things on the banks of the Naugatuck River do not fit so easily into garbage sacks. They include shopping carts, fifty-five-gallon oil drums, and the occasional Chevrolet transmission.

The Boy Scouts and high school students removed these things. In their place they erected bluebird and wood-duck nesting houses, and they stocked trout. They planted trees, bushes, and wildflowers to reduce bankside erosion and siltation, thereby increasing shade, wildlife habitat, and food sources. The species they planted were willows, alders, white pine, white spruce, red cedar, silky dogwood, elderberry, juneberry, cranberry, bulrushes, cattails, sedges, switchgrass, millet, reed grass, and water iris.

I wasn't surprised that Bob Gregorski should rely so heavily on teenagers and Boy Scouts as his foot soldiers, and not just because he was a schoolteacher, with a natural affinity for kids. The dearth of adult volunteers seemed a logical consequence of the valley's history. The Naugatuck itself had of course been devastated by the heavy industry of the nineteenth and twentieth centuries; however, the people had sustained a blow that was more than physical (meaning dangerous working conditions and a polluted environment)—they had also absorbed a mindset that made it hard to generate an effective citizens' movement. I remembered that remark by the president of Scovill's, Frederick Kingsbury—encourage "nothing that tends to expand the faculties or broaden the mental out-look beyond the thing in hand."

The larger industrial philosophy behind this comment was the brainchild of Frederick Winslow Taylor. A pernicious creed, Taylorism was also known as "scientific management." For decades, it was not held to be incompatible with American democracy (or, for that matter, with Soviet communism). Indeed, it formed the backbone of the industrial economy in places like the Naugatuck Valley. Experts in "motion-time analysis" paced around the brass-mill shop floor with clipboards and charts that said things like "The time required for the Start and Stop of a

13″ SHOULDER movement is .00180 Minute." Taylorism treated human beings as if they could be dammed and channeled and disciplined into maximum productivity in much the same fashion as running water.

The Naugatuck mills robbed their workers of all control over the production process. Knowledge and responsibility were concentrated in a small elite of managers; work on the factory floor was subdivided to make each task as repetitive as possible, requiring little skill or thought. At first, this setup had a certain appeal to the European immigrants who streamed into the valley, since they were largely unskilled people escaping from rural poverty. But it locked them into a terrible bargain, from which it was hard to escape when the brass economy eventually collapsed.

The historian Jeremy Brecher has written that Taylorism in the Naugatuck Valley

> had impacts far beyond the realm of production. It shaped motivations, expectations, time horizons, personal "investment" decisions, and ways of life. For many workers in the Valley economic security based on stable employment in a major factory became a central life strategy. Responsibility beyond the family level—whether at work or

"SPOOLERS IN A FALL RIVER COTTON MILL."

in the community—was neither encouraged nor regarded as necessary. For many, this pattern generated ingrained motivations and
habits that militated against responding proactively to the Valley's
economic decline.

Ethnic divisions only made things worse. For all the rhetoric
about the American melting pot, not much melting took place in the
Naugatuck Valley. Lithuanians, Poles, Italians, and Portuguese largely
stuck to their own enclaves, their own churches and clubs and music,
keeping cultural traditions alive but in the process isolating themselves
from the larger community.

I SWUNG THE CAR off the Route 8 ramp and down into the town of
Seymour. The river was green, shallow, and scummy. The largest building
I could see was the pawnshop. Its inventory was heavy on guitars and
guns, suggesting a town of frustrated young men. Next door to it was
Vinnie's Café, and even through the closed car windows I could smell the
heavy, sour odor of last night's beer. Across the river, under the spaghetti
of the Route 8 interchange, backhoes were removing the last remnants of
the huge red brick factory that had housed the Seymour Specialty Wire
Company (SSW).

I had read a little of the company's history. Built in the late nineteenth century, this factory had once been a brass mill that had employed
250 people. Whatever their other shortcomings, factories like this had a
long history of local ownership and management. But then, when the
brass industry began to decline, the failing plants became the target of
speculative buying and selling by much larger corporations, strictly a
short-term investment strategy that Gordon Gecko would have been
proud of. The new absentee owners milked the factories of their assets,
took whatever profits they were capable of yielding, and then resold or
closed them. The plant closings rippled through the valley, destroying not
only the mills themselves but hundreds of small businesses that depended on the mill workers' incomes.

In 1984 the workers got wind of the fact that SSW's new owners,
National Distillers, were planning to lop off their unprofitable metals
division. Desperate to preserve their jobs, they decided to buy the plant,
take a pay cut, and run it themselves. For a time, in fact, SSW was

the largest employee buyout of an industrial company anywhere in the country. But the legacy of Taylorism was too much to overcome. The workforce lacked skills and motivation. They still spoke of the factory floor as "downstairs" and the management as "upstairs." By 1990 the plant was in crisis; in 1993 it declared bankruptcy; now the buildings were being torn down, and a Stop & Shop supermarket was to occupy the brownfield.

B OB GREGORSKI was waiting to meet me on the steps of the Seymour town hall. He looked like everyone's favorite high school science teacher. Early to middle fifties, I guessed, short-sleeved madras shirt, graying mustache, articulate, full of facts, maybe a little didactic, although that was hardly surprising in someone who feels he has spent the better part of twenty years pursuing a one-man crusade.

Bob introduced me to a young man with close-cropped blond hair, who was standing next to him. "This is Jonathan Ploski," he said.

Gregorski, Ploski: I didn't need to ask where their families had come from, or why. But Jon told me anyway. His ancestors had come over from Poland a hundred years ago to work in the American Brass Company mills in Ansonia, a few miles downstream. Jon had grown up in Seymour. "I used to look out of the window at school to see what color the river was running that day," he said, "depending on what color they were dying the sneakers up at the Uniroyal plant in Naugatuck. Later on, when I was in college in Maine and friends were coming to visit, I'd give them complicated, roundabout directions, so they could drive here without having to see or smell the river. It used to embarrass me."

Before coming back to Seymour, Jon had a number of jobs, none of them far from the sound of running water. He'd been a fly-fishing guide in Vermont. He'd worked for a spell for the Regional Water Authority in New Haven and then for a year with a new Audubon Society project on the Pomperaug. Now he had taken the newly created post of Trout Unlimited Naugatuck River steward. The position had been funded for three years by the MacDermid Corporation of Waterbury, a $450 million business that manufactures specialized industrial chemicals and is the only Connecticut company listed on the New York Stock Exchange.

"It took us years to reach this point," Bob said, as the three of us sat around a trestle table in the town hall basement. The work had begun in the mid-1980s, he told me, under the leadership of Trout Unlimited, the national advocacy organization founded in 1959 with the mission of protecting North American trout and salmon rivers. "No one was doing anything about the river back then. We went and testified at hearings. We kept hammering away at the state and federal governments, the EPA and the DEP." They encountered a certain amount of suspicion. Was Trout Unlimited broadly interested in the river or narrowly interested in the fishing? "When they heard the name," Bob said, "they figured this was just an expensive way to get trout into the Naugatuck. But we said no, the fish are the canary in the coal mine. All we're trying to do is restore a very sick river to health."

In the mid-1990s, the Trout Unlimited activists realized that they couldn't accomplish what they wanted without building a broader base of support. But clearly this had been an uphill battle. "People were skeptical about our plantings," Bob complained. "They'd say, why bother? You're losing fifty, sixty percent of them. When Jon's job was announced, we got great publicity. But then we got hit by a terrible drought, and people look at the river and turn round to you and ask what's been accomplished." He sighed. "It's still an open question whether you can get a voluntary riverkeeper system going. We'd like to create a grass-roots movement in each of the towns up and down the river. But there's a big problem of how to break out of the closed circle of activists wearing multiple hats—all the usual faces."

I asked Bob how much support they were getting from the town authorities.

He answered indirectly. "Well, one way you get the politicians' attention is to talk about the impact of the urban wastewater that goes into the river. Tell them that all this organic waste is going to end up on the beaches on Long Island Sound. Tell them that, and they listen."

I remarked to Jon Ploski that it was encouraging to see a local corporation put up the money to pay his salary—and not just any corporation, but one belonging to an industry that didn't exactly have a reputation for environmental responsibility.

Bob answered for him. In fact, his protégé was having a hard time getting a word in. I thought it must be hard to delegate after being a one-man band for so long.

"Jon works under the aegis of Trout Unlimited," Bob said, "but he's actually accountable to MacDermid. Historically they were one of the worst polluters on the river, responsible for a tremendous discharge of copper sulfate two or three years ago, which killed all life in the river for a mile and a half, two miles. But they've been good neighbors since then. And after a lot of pushing and shoving and cajoling"—much of it from Bob Gregorski, I inferred—"they agreed to come up with the money for this position."

"What about the other corporations along the river?" I asked.

Bob frowned. "Fair at best," he said. "Uniroyal in Naugatuck is good, but they're really the exception. Otherwise you have to pound on the doors, write lots of letters. One or two will send you a check for a hundred bucks, but there's very little response really. All those companies had used the river as an open sewer, but maybe one tenth of one percent of them show any interest in it now. There are no meaningful regulations. There are certain things you're not allowed to do within fifty feet of the stream bank, but there's absolutely no enforcement. The state stockpiles road salt and sand along the Mad River. Midas Muffler has piles of old mufflers lying right there on the riverbank. But the companies' attitude is, screw you, you're costing me hundreds of dollars that I don't want to spend."

I asked Jon how he spent his days, trying again to draw him into the conversation. What does a river keeper actually do?

"I'm out on the river two or three times a week," he said, "doing site inspections, checking effluent discharges with the guys from the DEP. We try to be useful to them. We do dissolved oxygen tests every day at three locations: above the Waterbury Wastewater Treatment Plant, below the plant, and below the falls at Seymour. I handle lots of phone calls every day, usually from people asking why the river smells so bad. We do slide shows, meetings with land trusts, rod and gun clubs, Earth Day events, that kind of thing."

He looked glum. But I suppose that if I spent my days dealing with indifferent public officials, hostile muffler dumpers, and Taylorized residents complaining about foul smells and wilting wildflowers, I'd feel the same way that Jon Ploski and Bob Gregorski do. A little martyred.

22
Zero Discharge

TALKING TO JON PLOSKI ABOUT HIS DAYS on the river, checking effluent discharges and dissolved oxygen levels, I started thinking again about Bob Fumire. Before Bob died, we'd talked mainly about the Housatonic. I knew the big river was Bob's passion, but he'd also told me that the poor, battered Naugatuck had become his avocation. I wished I'd had time to ask him more, although he had told me the basics.

At sixteen, Bob Fumire realized he couldn't spend his whole life fishing and tying flies. He found a job sweeping floors at a small electroplating factory called the Summit Corporation of America (SCA). The company had been founded after the war in a one-room shed in Waterbury by a man named Len Foster, who shared the Fumires' brain-craziness about fishing. Bob was a hard worker, not to mention a charmer, and Foster took a liking to him. Bob went from sweeping floors to working on the plating line, and then to driving a delivery truck. Before long, he was crisscrossing the Northeast as a salesman. Foster continued to push him up the corporate ladder, and in the end he became president of SCA, which today is the largest privately owned metal-finishing enterprise in the United States. SCA remained defiantly local, resisting the wave of takeovers of valley industries by the big multinationals. The surnames of its directors—Fumire, Besozzi, Brazauskas—suggested great-grandfathers who had come over from Italy and Lithuania to toil in the brass mills.

Thinking about our conversation again now, I picked up one of the

SCA corporate brochures that Bob Fumire had given me. One paragraph in particular caught my eye: "Our concern for responsible environmental management has led us to meet or exceed federal and state regulations for conserving, reclamation, and recycling of resources with spill containment and a complete emergency back-up power system. Our toxicology program has the ultimate goal of zero discharge."

Zero discharge. It was the kind of thing Bob would have got excited about. I could imagine his eyes lighting up as they had when we talked about restoring the green drake. I was intrigued enough to know how a dirty factory achieved zero discharge to pick up the phone and call Brint Ostrander, SCA's corporate facilities manager. Ostrander said he'd be delighted to give me a tour of the plant.

SCA sits hard on the east bank of the Naugatuck. In fact, the huge asphalt lot where I parked was built over the original bed of the river, after the Army Corps of Engineers straightened the Naugatuck in the aftermath of the 1955 flood. Above and below the effluent plume from SCA, the corps had dug two enormous silt traps, the larger of them ninety feet deep.

Brint Ostrander turned out to be a towering man of about my own age, with a thick mustache and a bone-crushing handshake. I wondered if Ostrander was a Swedish name. He said no, his ancestors were emigrants from Lithuania and Germany, who had come to Waterbury to work at Scovill's. In 1986, when Brint arrived at SCA as an environmental scientist, the company was the largest corporate discharger of pollutants into the Naugatuck. "The DEP knew we were polluters," he said, "for the simple reason that we had a license to pollute. And they knew the toxic effects that our effluent had on the aquatic life of the river. But with new state regulations, we started to reduce the toxicity levels."

In an electroplating plant, heavy metals are as intrinsic to the operation as yeast is to a bakery. It was hard for me to follow a lot of the language of electroplating technology—autographic tensile texture, electrographic porosity definition, energy dispersive X-ray analysis, and so forth. But it was clear that these processes were not only essential to many of the everyday products I took for granted—things like gold wire for telephone lines and lead-free components for Duracell batteries. They were also absolutely germane to the ecology of the river.

Toxicity control is not a straightforward task. Ostrander showed me how it's done by walking me around a series of concrete tanks outside the plant—the same tanks Len Foster had once used to raise trout for stocking in the Housatonic. Although SCA's production has greatly increased since Ostrander joined the company, the volume of effluent has been better than halved. Even so, SCA still has to get rid of a couple of hundred tons of mixed metal hydroxide sludge each day. It has to go somewhere, and these days the law says that place can't be the Naugatuck River.

Ostrander explained that through a series of operations that successively spin and filter and steam it, the toxic sludge is compacted into a form in which it can be exported for recycling. I'd been listening intently to his explanation, trying not to get lost in the labyrinth of technical jargon. When he said "exported," I jumped.

"What do you mean?" I asked him. "Don't you dispose of it in the United States?"

He said, "No. It goes to Canada."

I said, "Canada? Surely Canada's environmental regulations are just as stringent as this country's. What do the Canadians do with it, anyway?"

"They slurry it with cement and form it into what they call 'cells,' which are the size of two football fields," Brint said with a grin. "Then they reexport it to Europe, where it's used to make housing foundations."

I was aware that a look of horror was crossing my face, and he laughed.

"The toxicity isn't a danger," he said. "It's just that in the United States, there's such a fear of litigation and liability that people worry about the smallest chance that a health risk might ever be linked to toxic leaching of this stuff. So it goes to make housing in Europe."

Three-acre pools of toxic slurry are, like swine lagoons, something that seems to exist in a parallel reality. It's easier not to think about it. When a window opens to that other world, it can be deeply unsettling. For the rest of the day, I felt weirdly off balance. Looking at everyday objects and processes felt like an out-of-body experience. How do they make Scotch tape, anyway? Or cat food, for that matter? The next time I picked up a bottle of Elmer's Glue, one of the kids asked me why the company's logo was a cow's head with horns. I realized that I hadn't a clue—and certainly couldn't explain to them—how a rendering plant works.

Rachel Carson used to say that the problem with environmental hazards is not that we don't know, but that we become habituated. Historians and psychologists know that habituation is a social and psychological necessity. Without it, we cease to function; we go mad. But habituation is also how we learn to accept the unacceptable. If environmentalism is about anything, it is about breaking the chains of habituation. The determination to do this may explain why many environmentalists are so hard to be around.

Brint Ostrander led me back to the main building, and we walked over to the toxicology lab. It was a surprisingly modest affair—just a windowless cinder-block room, no more than fifteen by eight feet, with two banks of glass tanks and instruments. A soft-spoken young African American scientist named Reggie Taylor showed me how the lab uses two species from the lower levels of the aquatic food chain to test for toxicity in SCA's effluent. *Daphnia pulex* is a tiny crustacean, and *Pimephales promelas* is a small, olive-colored, algae-eating fish with a slightly bulbous snout, which gives it its common name, the fathead minnow. Both are highly sensitive to water quality. Taylor explained that the daphnia has a life cycle of about fifty days and molts every two weeks or so. Throughout this period, he said, he regularly tests the little creature for its tolerance of immersion in varying concentrations of chlorine. The fathead minnow is especially intolerant of toxins when it's young. That's why SCA conducts most of its tests on specimens that are less than two weeks old.

As we left the lab, Brint Ostrander said to me, "We're already way ahead of federal and state standards. We haven't failed a test since 1988. Connecticut now uses our effluent treatment program as a model for the whole state. But we're not done yet. Bob Fumire's target was zero toxicity, and we intend to reach it."

Next day, I called Bob Orciari at the DEP. "So how clean is the Naugatuck these days?" I asked him. "Come and see," Bob said. "We're about to do the survey."

I т's нот, and no one could accuse us of traveling light. Ed Machowski has hold of one end of the first Old Town canoe, and Jerry Leonard has the other. The path down to the river is a foot wide. It's rough and steep, and thorns catch at our bare arms and score them with thin tracks of blood. Ed grunts with discomfort, Jerry counts one-two-three, and they lift the canoe over an obstructive rock. Behind us, with the second canoe, are Bob Orciari and Mike Humphreys. Neal Hagstrom brings up the rear, followed by a gaggle of summer interns.

The Naugatuck is still low, dead low, after the summer-long drought, and the canoes have to be dragged over the cobble until we can reach a channel deep enough to float them. For a moment there, coming down the steep slope through the enveloping brush, this could have been a portage in Maine. But now that we're in the open, the illusion quickly vanishes. We can see the traffic rumbling over the ugly cement bridge up ahead and the dilapidated industrial buildings beyond. It's clear that we're not in the North Woods but in the crumbling environs of downtown Torrington, Connecticut.

There are three tasks planned for today, Bob tells me. The first is to survey a stretch of the river targeted for reclamation; the state plans to haul 350 boulders in here to provide cover for trout. Farther upstream, our second test will assess the impact of an oil spill on the West Branch last winter. And where the East Branch and the West Branch of the Naugatuck come together, the DEP crew is charged with conducting one of the department's periodic inspections of water quality.

Jerry sets the controls of the generators so that the probes will deliver a mild alternating current. With the machines throbbing loudly, six of us to each canoe, we begin to move slowly upstream toward the bridge. Two of the biologists take the lead, moving the long probes, like windshield blades, in rhythmic arcs, to achieve maximum coverage. A third person pulls the heavy canoe by a rope fastened to the bow. Two more work the long nets, sweeping up the stunned fish and transferring them to the live well. That leaves me to bring up the rear, to pick off any stray fish that elude the lead netters.

But first you have to find the fish. Industrial abuse seems to have left this reach barren, like much of the Naugatuck. In the first hundred yards, all that we find is a computer keyboard encrusted with green algae, a blue plastic child's sled, and a disconsolate Spiderman doll. A thin cord paying out from the stern of the canoe shows how much ground we've covered.

In the fast riffles under the bridge, small silvery shapes begin to flash around our feet. Some leap clear of the water, as baitfish will do in the ocean when they're being pursued by a predator. The netters start transferring their catch into the live well with unhurried concentration. When they've collected enough to calculate population density with some accuracy, we beach the canoes. Neal and Ed lean over and pull out the measuring trays. They look a little like backgammon boards, with a centimeter rule painted along one side.

"Three white suckers, five, six, five."

"Sucker, five."

"Blacknose dace, four."

There's a kind of rough poetry in the count and the easy teamwork.

"Common shiner, seven."

"Blacknose, three, three, and two."

"Sucker six, sucker six, sucker five, seven, four."

"Cutlips minnow, four."

"Why cutlips?" I ask Bob. He points to the fish's mouth. It looks as if it has a cleft palate. Someone else calls over, "If you read the old textbooks, you'll see that the biologists used to believe it used its lips to suck the eyeballs out of other fish."

One way in which fisheries biologists learn to distinguish between minnow species is by putting on scuba gear and observing them underwater. Each minnow has a characteristic swimming motion. But somebody finds a minnow that no one can identify, so it's passed back to Bob for inspection.

"Can't be a blunthead because its head is pointed. Can't be a creek chub because it doesn't have a dark spot on its dorsal fin."

Bob turns it over in his hand.

"Fathead," he says, softly but without hesitation.

I take the tiny fish from Bob. I recognize it now, as the barometer species in the toxicity lab at the Summit Corporation, and its presence here is a good sign.

Half an hour, and we haven't a fish more than three inches in length to show for it. In the next section, a long, slow, silty pool, there's no sign of life at all. We pass the time counting debris. A shopping cart. A truck tire. A soccer ball. A bicycle, royal blue. Two Styrofoam cups with the Dunkin' Donuts logo. Jerry recalls the time a big ugly sucker got its head trapped in one of these, and the sampling crew watched as a Styrofoam cup went swimming in circles around the pool. Everyone laughs.

A radiator grille. An automobile fuel tank. More tires, and some three-foot lengths of thick cement piping. And then, abruptly, two, three, a whole pod of big white suckers—*Catostomus commersoni*—which have taken up residence among the trash. Jerry's canoe is taking five suckers to every one of ours because they're plunging their probes like gardening spades into the deeper water along the east bank. Mixed in with the suckers are a few muddy-green largemouth bass and one or two black bullheads, runty members of the catfish family whose dorsal spine can give you a painful flesh wound. The fish are hiding out in a shopping cart graveyard. There are so many carts—at least twenty that I can see—that they begin to constitute a wading hazard. When one of them takes root in the mud, its metal ribbing first attracts algae growth, then snags stray leaves, twigs, and branches, then larger tree limbs, and pretty soon you have a holding lie that the oldest and most circumspect brown trout would be proud to call home.

"Sucker, twenty."

"Suckers, twenty-two, thirty, twenty-six."

"Largemouth, twenty-three."

"Bullhead, nineteen."

"Suckers, forty-three, forty-four."

A couple of the summer interns crane their necks to take a look at these two—fat olive-white-purple-sided fish of seventeen or eighteen inches, with broad, rubbery, downward-pointing lips that snuffle food off the bottom like a vacuum cleaner.

Someone sets the group to musing on the cultural meaning of the shopping carts. What accounts for the fact that this artifact is most often chosen to dump in rivers? Why not car batteries and hubcaps? Or toaster ovens and microwaves? "Shop till you drop," I suggest. "It's our national credo."

Unfortunately, the carts can't be explained, like PCBs, as an unsavory reminder of a less environmentally enlightened time. Here's a blue one with a plaque riveted to its frame that says "Family Dollar 2/98." This is fresh damage. There's a mall upstream, behind the next road bridge.

"Yeah," one of the crew says, "the shopping cart spawning ground, we call it."

Jerry folds his arms contemplatively. "Maybe the carts will be buried in the silt eventually and fossilized. Then scientists sixty million years from now will speculate about how this race of small creatures was made extinct while they were trying to cross the river in a catastrophic flood, and these primitive wheeled vehicles were their mode of transportation."

Like much of what Jerry says, this makes the rest of us smile. But there's a serious point to the joke. As archaeologists and paleontologists know well, it's always dangerous to leap to conclusions and make broad generalizations about the past on the basis of isolated findings.

As the warmth of the day builds, counting minnows becomes increasingly tedious. We're doing it by gross numbers now, not individual length. It's clear by eleven o'clock that the species balance is pretty close to what it was last time this stretch of river was sampled, except that this year we haven't found a single trout. Normally Bob would expect to find a few surviving stocked fish around the feeder mouths, but the last one we passed was almost dry, leaving no cooling inflow to attract the trout. The fear of a drastic summer fish kill is always present, although Bob says these are harder to detect than you might think. You don't look for schools of dead trout floating downstream, he says, but for subtler signs—more herons perching on the rocks, or a greater density of raccoon tracks in the streamside mud.

When we've finished stowing the gear, I wade with Bob into the shallow riffles of the East Branch. The water is perceptibly cooler here. Finding a flat rock to sit on, I peel off my sticky waders, dip my baseball cap in the flow, and let the water cascade over my hair and inside my shirt. The undersides of the stones here are teeming with caddis, and I reach down to pick up a free-living *Rhyacophila* larva a half-inch long. Its body is a deep grass green, and its head is jet-black. On the back of my hand, it moves like an inchworm, contracting and expanding its body to advance, bobbing and probing with its head as it carefully negotiates each individual hair. Then it retraces its steps, moving backward now.

Bob looks back at the main stem of the Naugatuck, toward the shopping carts and the rest of the detritus of Torrington, the walls of concrete riprap along the bank, and the suspended black silt we've kicked up from the bottom. He sees something the rest of us don't. Bob has the same look in his eye that I've seen in Dada Jabbour's, when we stood on the hill looking down on the ruins of Chase Brass. He says: "It's coming around, you know. This is going to be a good river someday. Once the dams are gone."

23
Old and in the Way

I'VE ALWAYS BEEN A BIG ALFRED HITCHCOCK FAN, and I don't think I like any of his movies better than *Saboteur*. In the second reel, Robert Cummings and Priscilla Lane pass an uncomfortable night hiding from the cops in a circus trailer, in the company of a thin man, a bearded lady, and a pair of argumentative Siamese twins. At dawn, the freak show lets them off on the outskirts of the ghost town of Soda City, in the Nevada desert. They are pursuing a weasel-faced Nazi spy who is bent on striking at the heart of the American war effort.

The scene that follows is as meticulously choreographed as the more famous shower scene in *Psycho*. Our heroes enter an abandoned shack. Mysteriously, a telephone is ringing in the silence of Soda City. Concealed inside the stove is a radio transmitter. They stumble across a tripod, which proves to be just the height of a round hole in the door. Over in another corner, Priscilla Lane finds a telescope. Robert Cummings assembles it on its tripod, points it through the hole in the door, and squints to focus. We follow his line of sight through the telescope, past a blur of sky and mountains, until it settles on the Nazi's target . . . a dam. And not just any dam, but the newly completed Boulder Dam, known today as the Hoover Dam: American pride expressed in 727 feet of sheer concrete, impounding 115 miles of Lake Mead, enough water to cover not only the state of Connecticut, but also the total landmass of Massachusetts, New Hampshire, Vermont, and New Jersey. Robert Cummings says, "Uh oh."

In the three centuries after the first gristmill went up on the first trout pool of the first freestone stream in Connecticut, American dams rose higher and higher, in their physical dimensions and in patriotic esteem. Dams were America's pyramids. They could control floods, irrigate fields, hoard drinking water, generate cheap electricity to power factories, and illuminate farmsteads. Free-flowing water was a wasted opportunity, an affront. As a result, more than 85 percent of American waterways are artificially managed today, and dams have altered the flow and the aquatic ecology of more than 620,000 miles of river.

The rage to plug up rivers was not unique to American capitalism. It was a centerpiece of twentieth-century rationalism and technology. Stalin's Five-Year Plans were filled with impoundments, and so was Mao Zedong's Great Leap Forward, tens of thousands of peasants leaving their farm tools behind to labor on these icons of national purpose, with their promises of affluence and ease and dominion over the hostile forces of the natural world.

Saboteur may be due for a remake. But the plot line would present some problems. More than likely the enemies of freedom would not be blowing up a dam today. They would be building one. For dams, much like communism, are a modern god that has failed, and social attitudes have turned against them with a vengeance.

In the early years of the movement, thanks to the OPEC oil crisis and Three Mile Island, dams and hydropower were in good odor with many environmentalists, who saw them as cheap, clean energy alternatives. Others had their minds made up from the beginning. David Brower, for example, whose opinions were never much known for nuance, used to declare, "I hate all dams, large and small." This view gained traction as the dislike of fossil fuels and nuclear power, and the immediate concern for human health and safety, broadened into a clearer understanding of how dams distorted the function of rivers and impaired ecosystems as a whole.

The first problem with dams is that they raise the temperature and lower the dissolved oxygen content of the water they impound. Temperature is an absolutely critical variable in the character of an aquatic environment. A shift of one or two degrees is all it takes to affect radically the breeding and hatching, or the feeding and migration, of many aquatic species. Dams also distort the river's natural ability to transport and disperse sediment. Downstream areas are starved of it; impoundments are full of it. And when the dams exist for industrial purposes, the sediment load will coat the river bottom with a concentrated charge of pollutants. The PCB-infested Woods Pond on the Housatonic in Pittsfield is a good example.

One striking feature of public policy in the 1970s and 1980s was the trend toward conditionality—such as building mandatory environmental-impact assessments into construction projects and dam relicensing applications, or attaching human rights provisions to foreign assistance programs. In such cases, those making the cost-benefit analysis, or advocating the conditionalities, ran up against the difficulty of quantifying costs in dollar terms. In the case of dams, it was easy to assess the dollar value of benefits—the units of electricity generated or the contribution of a recreational fishery to the local economy. But who could put a dollar value to sediment dispersal, let alone to aesthetics and quality of life?

In the bitter fights that ensued concerning dams, one side fought by counting apples and the other by counting oranges. Not surprisingly, the passions were most inflamed in the West. In what had once been known as the Great American Desert, dams had always been a precondition of life. To a westerner, rearranging rocks and sand into a dam in order to create habitat for humans was every bit as natural and reasonable as a caddis larva constructing its stick case out of elements provided by its environment. The most emotional fights of all have centered on the campaigns against the monstrous dams on the Columbia and Snake River systems in the Pacific Northwest. Again, this isn't surprising, since the prime issue at stake is the well-being of the salmon—a cultural symbol of great complexity and uncertain dollar value.

Surfing the Internet one night, I came across a fairly typical exchange. The debate was stoked by people with screen names like Liberaliarwatch, Mr. Truly Know-It-All, Blue Collar, and Damproud. Few of these people seemed to live east of the Mississippi, and even fewer of them were women. What they appeared to have in common was a lot of naked anger, concealed under a fig leaf of science as confused as my own. Here is a sampling.

> "Studies show that bypassing the Snake River dams will create jobs."
> "Other studies show that bypassing the Snake River dams will destroy jobs."
> "There will be countless benefits to Native American tribes."
> "I've seen rivers where the Indians string their nets two thirds of the way across, alternately from each side, and clean the river of migrating fish. But who does a study of that?"
> "Seventy percent of domestic energy use is for keeping homes at a comfortable temperature. The use of passive solar design and micro-climate control through landscaping could cut that amount down appreciably. I don't use air conditioning and my house stays comfortable because of large shade trees."
> "The real cost of maintaining your shade trees in L.A. is substantial, mostly attributed to the water required to sustain them in the desert. Where do you think that comes from?"
> "On Lake Powell, water is wasted as several hundred thousand acre feet of water per year seeps into the sandstone. In addition, almost a million acre feet of water evaporates every year. That's enough to meet the annual domestic needs of four million people."
> "Why is it any worse for it to evaporate than flow to the sea? Nobody thinks millions of acre feet mixing with saltwater is a waste."
> "Tear them down? You are talking depopulation, tens of millions

of people have to move. Turn 85 percent of Nevada into roadless areas."

"Maybe that's not such a bad thing."

I decided that screen name Call Me Ishmael deserved the last word. "Surely this is a debate where extremism is not necessary. A decent cost-benefit analysis of a particular dam should determine whether that dam is critical to human habitation, or whether it has outlived its usefulness. 'Tear them all down!' is as mindless a strategy as 'Dam up every stream!' apparently was in the WPA years."

The exchange seemed to suggest that we are impaled on the dilemma of knowing too much and too little, and as a result we have equal difficulty sorting out our science, our lifestyle choices, and our ethics. Call Me Ishmael was right, I was sure, but could we even agree on his terms of reference? How, in the end, were we to measure a dam's usefulness?

As in most fields of inquiry, it's best to start small and leave the monsters, the Columbias and the Hoovers, until another day. Nationally, small dams are now being removed at the rate of about one a month. Perhaps the most publicized has been the removal of the Edwards Dam on the Kennebec River in Maine, which was built in 1837 and stood for 162 years until interior secretary Bruce Babbitt came to preside over its breaching, which he said was "the beginning of something that is going to affect the entire nation."

According to Trout Unlimited, the United States has, give or take a few, seventy-five thousand dams taller than six feet. Most of the smaller ones date back to the nineteenth century, at which time they were designed to last forty or fifty years. The big guys came later, beginning with the public works ebullition of the New Deal. Connecticut was a pioneer of small-dam construction. Gristmills, sawmills, cider mills, fulling mills tamed every trout stream in the state. After the Civil War, when legislation and regulation became more systematic, Connecticut was again in the forefront of providing incentives for dam builders. With the Connecticut Mill and Dam Act of 1878, anyone damming a stream acquired the authority to condemn the property of any upstream landowner whose lands might be inundated.

Today, about thirty-eight hundred small dams stand in the state of Connecticut—more than one for every two stream miles. Most are now obsolete and have fallen into disrepair. A decaying dam is an accident waiting to happen, a potential failure in times of flood, a risk to the life and limb of reckless teenagers and picnic parties. In a society whose wheels are lubricated with the oil of litigation, this makes owners worry about liability, giving a new source of leverage to those who would like the nation's rivers to run free once more.

These small, useless dams are what American Rivers, Friends of the Earth, and Trout Unlimited had in mind when they joined forces on a campaign called "Dams That Don't Make Sense." The first state they highlighted was Wisconsin. The second was Connecticut, and its poster child was the Naugatuck, the most grievously abused of all the state's rivers.

The Naugatuck was first dammed in 1706 at Beacon Falls, in one of the wildest stretches of the valley. By 1880 a score of dams dotted the thirty-nine miles of the main stem and the principal tributaries. The key to restoring the river's flow was to remove eight of these dams, all long defunct. They were "low-head" structures used for mechanical power, cooling water, rinse water, boiler water. There's nothing more old and in the way than an ancient dam. It just sits there, like a crutch kept in the corner of a bedroom long after an injury has healed. The river towns were only too happy to see the dams go, Bob Gregorski said. "Their attitude was, get rid of the goddamn things, especially if it won't cost anything."

Of the eight superannuated dams, the largest was the Tingue Dam at Rimmon Falls in Seymour, which had once powered Colonel David Humphreys's experiments with merino wool and persuaded Thomas Jefferson to take a second look at the virtues of industry. I went back to Seymour to take a closer look at Tingue, stopping on the way at the Union City Dam, which had once been owned by the Naugatuck Chemical Company and was another of the seven slated for removal. I thought it was about time I overcame my qualms about fishing the Naugatuck.

It was a cold and rainy day in early fall. I parked at the eastern end of the Union City Dam and contemplated the structure. It was a wreck, frankly, breached once by the great flood of 1955 and subsequently repaired. Now it showed gaping holes in at least two places. Much of the timber cribbing had rotted away, and the rock fill had tumbled into the river. The spillway was leaking badly, and water was escaping through the toe of the dam, creating fast, swirling currents along the far bank. The rocks underfoot were coated with slippery brown filamentous algae.

The smell of the river was not pleasant. Graffiti covered the training wall on the west side of the pool below the dam. One of the spray-painted symbols appeared to be a swastika. I fished for twenty minutes, shivering in the late afternoon chill, and caught a lively bronze-backed smallmouth bass of about a pound and a half.

Over in Seymour, I pulled up in the parking lot behind the town hall and walked to Rimmon Falls. The six-foot-thick concrete pilings of the Route 8 overpass were planted in the riverbed behind the dam like a twentieth-century Stonehenge. But seen narrowly, the west side of the river still looked much as it must have before the colonists arrived, when the Paugussett Indians congregated here for the spring runs of shad and salmon and blueback herring. The masonry structures on the east bank were built on foundations laid for Humphreysville. Given this weight of history, there could be no question of actually tearing down the Tingue Dam or blasting out the bedrock at Rimmon Falls. Instead, the state had agreed to build a bypass channel that would allow migrating fish and canoeists alike to negotiate the falls.

No date had yet been set for the groundbreaking. But it was scheduled to begin with the demolition of a small urban park, which I found tucked away behind a cluster of nondescript industrial buildings. A boy of fourteen or fifteen, with baggy cargo pants and parti-colored hair, was showing off his moves on the skateboard ramp. I couldn't take my eyes off the kid as he flew up one side and down the other. He planted his front foot in the center of the board and his back foot on the edge of the tail and inclined his body forward like a skier. At the lip of the wall, he swung his back foot free of the board, kicked outward, and spun the board in the air, in a move that is called a 180 Kickflip. His friends clapped and whistled. The skateboard ramp had the scooped-out shape of a glaciated river valley.

Two things struck me about the Naugatuck restoration plan. The first was that it was *affirmative;* it sought to achieve a positive good, rather than react under compulsion to some external demand such as hydropower relicensing or an imminent threat to public safety. The second was that it proposed to remove not a single dam, but an entire string of them. The plan bluntly redefined the use value that society assigned to the river. We valued the Naugatuck not because we could confine it and extract power from it but because it offered us, in its unfettered state, something that we valued more. The plan was turning back the clock in the best way, as if the trout pool paradox could, at last, be resolved.

However, no dam removal is simple. When I read over the engineers' site inspection reports, I was amazed at the multitude of factors taken into account in the cost-benefit analysis, no matter how small and insignificant the dam. There are legal questions to consider: who owns the property and who are the abutters? There are economic, aesthetic, cultural, historical, and political issues—all of them, to some degree, subjective intangibles. One person's eyesore may be another's historical marker, and I found out that each dam site had to be reviewed by two separate state bodies for its potential archaeological value, whether pre-Columbian, colonial, or industrial.

Innumerable issues require fine judgments of hydraulics and hydrology. How will the river channel be altered by taking out the dam? Will downstream habitat be degraded? Will there be any effect on the integrity of upstream structures built with the existing character of the river in mind—railroad lines, sewer lines, highway embankments? What soils will be exposed, and what will it take to revegetate them?

And then the big questions of sediment and pollution must be addressed. How much sediment is there in each impoundment? What will happen to it when the dam goes? Will the river be able to transport it downstream, or is the silt load more than the natural flow can bear? Should it be dredged and disposed of? If so, how and where—in gravel ponds, or as landfill or construction aggregate? Most important of all, what toxins lie buried in the sediment after a century and a half of unchecked industrial abuse? To determine this, the engineers carried out site borings at each of the Naugatuck dams scheduled for removal. They tested for fifteen scheduled heavy metals, for petroleum hydrocarbons, for semivolatile and volatile organic compounds, for pesticides and herbicides, and for PCBs.

Six dams harbored concentrations of industrial pollutants above state remediation standards. Only the two-foot-high Freight Street Dam, more a sleeping policeman than a true obstruction, was found to be clean. You could have hit the Freight Street Dam with a paper airplane launched from the windows of MacDermid's sleek corporate headquarters. Elsewhere, four of the fifteen listed heavy metals showed up in excessive concentrations: copper and lead at the Bray's Buckle Dam on the Mad River; cadmium, lead, and nickel at Platts Mills. Platts Mills, the most bucolic site of all to the naked eye, turned out in fact to be the nastiest. In addition to its charge of heavy metals, its gorgeous pocket water contained high levels of dieldrin and PCBs. Dieldrin was a pesticide—a persistent chlorinated hydrocarbon—widely used in agriculture from the 1950s until 1975, when it was banned by the federal government as a probable carcinogen. At other dams, the borings also found excessive levels of benzo[k]fluoranthene, benzo[a]pyrene, and benzo[a]anthracene, all closely related polycyclic aromatic hydrocarbon (PAH) compounds. Some sediment contained bis(2-ethyl hexyl)phthalate, an oily, colorless liquid used in vacuum pumps and plastics.

AT THE 10-FOOT-HIGH, 330-foot-long Anaconda Dam all the issues came together in one place. When I looked at the property records, I couldn't imagine a clearer example of the trout pool paradox, a better metaphor for a century and a half of industrial growth and decline. Anaconda had begun life as Brown's Farm Dam. Around 1909, the dam, gatehouse, and diversion canal were deeded to the Waterbury Brass Company. Within a short time, this had become part of the American Brass Company. Through merger or buyout, ABC became the Anaconda Corporation, and that was the name that stuck. With another corporate takeover, the dam and water rights passed into the hands of the giant Atlantic Richfield Delaware Corporation (ARCO). Then, in April 2000, BP-Amoco, the second-biggest publicly traded oil producer in the world and number nineteen on the Fortune 500, announced that it had bought ARCO for $27 billion. In the meantime, the three parcels that made up the Anaconda Dam and adjoining properties were broken up. ARCO kept one; the other two were sold to a Peter Vileisis Jr. I guessed the name was Lithuanian, visualizing another family of immigrant brass workers. Vileisis in turn sold his parcels to the Waterbury House Wrecking Company.

The river runs slow and flat at Anaconda, over a gentle gradient. It's about the closest the Naugatuck comes to having an alluvial floodplain. As a result, the sediment buildup behind the dam was heavier than at any other targeted site. At the bottom of the Anaconda pond were almost sixteen thousand cubic yards of contaminated silt, enough to cover a football field to a depth of six or seven feet. The worst of the contaminants were benzo[b]fluoranthene and benzo[a]anthracene, toxic compounds found in smoke, soot, coal-tar pitch, and creosote. This was one reason why the engineers had recommended leaving most of the dam in place and taking out only the timber crib spillway. The other reason was the wishes of fishermen, who worried that removing Anaconda altogether might leave this stretch of the Naugatuck too low and warm for trout.

In the winter of 1999, the engineers were waiting for the weather to improve so that a date could be set for the backhoes to move in and start work on the Anaconda Dam. It was cold and miserable, and the river was thick with ice and high from freezing rain. Then, in February, a big winter storm swept down the valley.

"Nature took care of Anaconda for us," Bob Gregorski told me disconsolately. "The dam was on the verge of breaking apart when the storm came through and the high water and ice opened up a thirty- or forty-foot breach below the surface. The flood surge that came through the hole ripped out the riverbank and threatened the sewer line. What was left of the dam was removed within a week."

I said that, for an environmentalist, he seemed bitter about the natural event that had occurred. It appeared that Trout Unlimited was committed to the natural flow of the river—but only up to a point.

He thought about it for a moment. "Well, I guess maybe I am bitter," he said. "Certainly I have mixed feelings about dam removal after Anaconda. When Anaconda went, it took out three miles of trout habitat. It used to be great fishing water, four to six feet deep. But look at it now—it's a disaster area. There used to be a thirty- or forty-foot-deep scour hole in front of the dam, but it's filled in and created massive thermal pollution. Look at our plantings now; they're pathetic. The area was supposed to become a wildlife refuge. We'd been planning to plant bulrushes and cattails. Now it's totally barren. It looks horrible."

I suppose that barrenness, like beauty, exists in the eye of the beholder. To my eye, the river channel below the old dam site was in a state of transition. Granted, it wasn't pretty, but it was full of possibilities, even if, for the moment, these didn't include trout. The silt load had been too much for even the winter flood to carry, and the river had redistributed it in long sandbars, dividing the Naugatuck into a number of distinct braided channels. The name Anaconda seemed well chosen now, for the river twisted and curled around these new sandbars like a giant snake. Already, after a single season, vegetation was beginning to take hold. Nettles would grow here, along with steeplebush and horsetail, purple loosestrife and joe-pye weed and Japanese knotweed. As the soil stabilized, alder, gray birch, sensitive fern, sycamore, cottonwood, black willow, and silky dogwood might move in. Birds would roost there; insects would flourish in the new growth.

24
The Ideology of Salmon

WHEN THE BIOLOGISTS FIRST RAISED THE IDEA of restoring salmon to the Naugatuck River, Cary Grant himself couldn't have done a more extravagant double-take. *Salmon?* In the *Naugatuck?* In fact, the proposal to put salmon in the river fulfilled two separate, and quite different, visions. One was historical and organic—restoring the Atlantic salmon, *Salmo salar,* to its rightful position as top predator in a comprehensively revived aquatic ecosystem; the other was more of a trope—the salmon as a recreational ideal, the sport of kings. In practice, the two ideas were often confused.

Restoring salmon to the coastal streams of New England has been a recurrent dream for 130 years, but one that has invariably ended in failure. Since the glaciers departed, the range of the Atlantic salmon has extended from northern Canada and Russia's Kola Peninsula in the north, to New England and the Iberian Peninsula in the south. As one-year-old smolts, six inches long, the salmon migrate to their feeding grounds. Those from North America and from Iceland head for the open ocean off southwestern Greenland. Most of those from Europe take off for the Faeroe and Lofoten Islands, although some also travel all the way to Greenland. On the feeding grounds, they fatten up on Arctic krill, other small crustaceans, sand eels, and an oily forage fish called the capelin.

Some of the salmon return to the river after their first year in the ocean. At this point they weigh about five pounds and are known as grilse. Most of the grilse are male, and the small number of females among them carry very few eggs. But the majority of the salmon stay on the ocean feeding grounds for two or three years, growing to ten or twenty pounds or more before they return, each fish tracking the distinctive chemical signature of its own native stream. These are the vital brood stock on which the species depends for its survival.

While every child knows the outlines of this story, and only the most hardened cynic could fail to be stirred by it, the quasi-religious fervor for salmon is actually a fairly recent development. The legends passed down about the abundance of Atlantic salmon during the colonial period, when it was said that descending smolts and arriving adults would create traffic jams on the Merrimack, pushing each other up onto the riverbanks, tell us more about late-nineteenth- and twentieth-century values than about historical realities. In colonial New England, Atlantic salmon were regarded as trash fish, and anyone netting a ten-pound fish in the Connecticut River in 1700 would have been lucky to get a penny for it in the Hartford market. Members of Lewis and Clark's expedition refused to eat the salmon of the Pacific Northwest, saying they were oily and gave them diarrhea.

But our values change, often radically. "Humans don't weigh species equally," Bob Orciari once remarked to me. "They have favorites, and salmon is a favorite. It's like, gee, if we've got salmon in our streams, we can't be all that bad."

THE PROBLEM is that we *don't* have salmon in our streams. But the larger, more perplexing question concerns the extent to which we ever *did*. Given the millions of dollars invested in Atlantic salmon restoration programs and the importance of the fish as a cultural symbol, this may sound like heresy. According to conventional wisdom, countless salmon swam in the rivers of precolonial New England, as far south as the Housatonic and perhaps the Hudson, before we wiped them out with our industrial revolution and our stupid dams and pollution; but now we know better, and as a society we are ready to atone for our historical guilt.

I had accepted this ideology as readily as anyone else. It felt so satisfyingly *right*. But then someone suggested that I read an article in an obscure scholarly journal, the *Annual Proceedings of the Dublin Seminar for New England Folklife*, by a British Columbia ichthyozoo-archaeologist named Catherine Carlson. Carlson was interested in the

Native American diet, and by excavating prehistoric middens along the Maine coast, she made the first ever archaeological analysis of fish bones. Her findings were a shock. Thirty thousand fish bones. No salmon.

As Carlson tried to square these discoveries with the historical record, she began to wonder how many of the accounts of the European settlers could be taken at face value. She found that one ingrained myth after another failed to stand up to serious scrutiny. She started with the old saw about agricultural laborers refusing to be fed salmon more than twice a week and found that no one could actually produce any historical documentation to substantiate the story. In those days before Linnaeus, species nomenclature was notoriously inaccurate, and Carlson became convinced that some of the primary references to "salmon"—a fish with which the Europeans were familiar—were actually references to shad. She also suspected deliberate embellishment, or "salmon inflation," knowing of the tendency of fishermen down the ages to tell tall tales. And naturally, early settlers wanted to boost the image of the new colonies, and exaggerating the presence of a fish with strong aristocratic associations in European culture—monarch of the oceans, sport of kings—was one way to do so. Or perhaps the salmon was just a temporary visitor to New England streams—absent during the precolonial period but briefly taking advantage of the cooler waters of the "Little Ice Age," which lasted from about 1550 to 1800—ending their stay, in other words, just as the industrial revolution and modern scientific record keeping began.

No one knows how many salmon migrated between the North Atlantic feeding grounds and the rivers of New England and Canada during this period. Some estimate 2.5 million; others say twice that number. Steve Gephard, who is in charge of the Connecticut restoration program, thinks it likely that, of all the rivers in New England, only the Penobscot in Maine would have had an annual run of one hundred thousand fish. In the past century, however, the numbers have dropped precipitously, and Carlson doesn't contest that fact for a moment. By the mid-1970s, the Atlantic salmon run numbered about eight hundred thousand. By 1991, it had fallen to three hundred thousand. In 1998, it was eighty thousand. Salmon now spawn in only nine New England rivers, all of them in Maine, and the total annual return is about three hundred fish.

The reasons for this decline are a mystery. Worst of all, the sharpest rate of decline is among the older, egg-rich brood stock. There are enough clean rivers nowadays to produce good numbers of young fish, but it isn't happening. Nor, contrary to widespread belief, is commercial overfishing to blame. As the result of international agreements and government buyouts of nets and licenses, the free-for-all that devastated the North Atlantic feeding grounds from the 1960s to the early 1990s has ended. All that we know, in the words of Bill Taylor, president of the Atlantic Salmon Federation, is that "something terrible is happening in the ocean." The salmon are disappearing into an "ecological black hole."

Three basic theories have been advanced to explain this phenomenon—and at this point none has yet been proven true. Theory number one is climate change, which stipulates that the rising temperature of the North Atlantic, whether as a cyclical phenomenon, a function of global warming, or both, is melting the polar icecap, chilling the feeding grounds so that forage species have been depleted. Theory number two is increased killing of salmon by a growing population of seals and other natural predators. Some people refer to this as the "Brigitte Bardot effect," dating the decline to the French actress's campaign against the clubbing of baby seals. Theory number three is disease and genetic contamination by salmon farming. Most store-bought salmon today has never been closer to the ocean than the edge of its holding pen. But there is no such thing as an escape-proof cage, and some recent Canadian studies have found as many as eight salmon-farm Houdinis to every wild fish. Obviously, these escapees compete for habitat and food in the ocean, just as hatchery trout compete with wild fish in rivers. The farmed fish are also blamed for introducing diseases and parasites that flourish in their crowded pens, such as brown sea lice and an unpleasant ectoparasitic worm called *Gyrodactylus,* which can strip all the skin from a fish.

At least as a contributory factor in the decline, the genetic theory seems highly plausible, perhaps because we have become sensitized—to the point of cynicism—to the parade of disasters resulting from our earlier rationalist attempts to engineer the world. Reading the publicity materials from Atlantic Salmon of Maine, a $65 million a year aquaculture business, sets off alarm bells. The industry's main motivation seemed clear from one handout, which began by quoting the management guru Peter Drucker—his drift being that although e-commerce was pretty interesting, the real growth opportunity of the twenty-first century was in fish farming. Another comment, in a speech by an aquaculture executive to the Rotary Club of Augusta, Maine, brought some spooky echoes of past folly: "We produce salmon more efficiently than Mother Nature. On our ocean farm, it takes only 1.3 pounds of feed to produce one pound of salmon. In the wild, salmon must eat about five pounds of fish to produce one pound of salmon." I had read similar claims, almost verbatim, in the nineteenth-century reports of the Connecticut fish and game commissioners, as they declared imminent victory over the profligate ways of nature.

Like hatchery trout, farmed salmon are bred for uniform genetic characteristics of docility and rapid growth. These qualities may be desirable in a pen or a restaurant, but they are all wrong for the ocean, especially if the farm-raised fish interbreed with wild salmon. "We salmon farmers need our own melting pot to ensure that there are no genetic misfits among our salmon," the executive told the Rotarians. But whatever other reasons may explain the decline of the Atlantic salmon, we do know one thing without a doubt—a decrease in genetic diversity means a decrease in the survival of a species.

In THE PACIFIC NORTHWEST, the decline of native salmon populations is totally bound up with the loss of adaptive diversity. The Northwest used to be home to hundreds of distinct salmon populations, with a long evolutionary history of adaptation to specific lakes and rivers. There's little question that dams and hatcheries are responsible for the change.

One should, however, be a little wary of overstating the parallels between salmon on opposite coasts. The historic runs of Pacific salmon dwarfed those on the Atlantic seaboard. Even though their evolutionary divergence is quite recent, Pacific and Atlantic salmon are in fact two distinct species. It's actually misleading to talk about Pacific salmon in the singular, since it's no more than a catchall term for six separate species that share the same territory. Five of these—the chinook or king, the sockeye, the chum, the coho, and the pink salmon—spawn in North American rivers. The sixth, the cherry salmon *(Oncorhynchus masou)*, sticks to Asian waters. Chinooks are the only one of the six that, like Atlantic salmon, can survive the act of spawning. For every other Pacific salmon, once it is done with reproduction, nothing remains but to die.

I had never witnessed this phenomenon, but a chance November business trip to Vancouver gave me the opportunity to steal a free week-end and cross over to Vancouver Island to visit the home of the great fly-fishing writer Roderick Haig-Brown, on the Campbell River. It was something I'd wanted to do for years.

I arrived in Nanaimo on a late-evening ferry and drove north in the darkness along the coastal highway, through driving rain and tawdry lit-tle pebble-dash settlements that reminded me of small towns on the coast of Scotland. All night the surf boomed, and the windows of the Mo-tel Six rattled, but when I awoke in the morning the sun was shining and I could see the snow-covered summits of the coastal range across the Strait of Georgia.

In the house on Campbell River, I sat in Haig-Brown's chair, leafed through his books, smelled his long-dead pipe smoke, and threw sticks for the caretaker's Labrador retriever in the orchard where Haig-Brown had his fatal heart attack in 1980. After lunch, I drove to the shore of his beloved Buttle Lake, walked among the sun-bleached deadfalls in the huge silence, and watched the clouds as they first covered the mountain peaks and then parted to reveal them again. Waterfalls glittered on the slopes.

On the second morning, I hiked in through moss-covered Douglas firs and red cedars to the falls on the Englishman's River. I found a cedar limb at the water's edge, stripped off its remaining shreds of bark, and found it made a fine wading staff. I had brought a fly rod with me, but it was too late to fish for the coho. The run was over, but there were more fish in the river than I thought possible. Even though the water was transparent, I didn't see them at first, in the first deep pool below the falls. Then I saw a movement of white, and a salmon of seven or eight pounds flashed away beneath my feet. Its flanks were mottled with death; it resembled an ornamental *koi* carp in a Chinese hotel pond.

As I walked downstream, through the most beautiful riverscape I had ever seen, I began to count the salmon. I counted to a hundred, to five hundred, but before I reached a thousand I stopped, realizing that it was pointless. Many of the fish had come onto the beach before dying, and they were lying ten, fifteen, even twenty feet from the water. Some were piled together in the shallows like cordwood. Others were splayed across exposed tree roots, like World War I soldiers shot down as they came out of the trenches.

At the edge of a pool on the Englishman's River, I sat on the dark gravel beach and propped my fly rod against a tree. A large cock fish was beneath the tree roots, finning almost imperceptibly. All the skin was gone from one side of its body, and the exposed flesh was a pale orange-gray. I slid a hand under the fish, and it didn't resist. It was heavy and still in my hand. I judged it was ten pounds. I held the fish that way for a long time, under the red cedar, until the finning stopped. Words came into my head. Mystery, wonder, dread, awe, reverence. Words to say that the death of the big coho was filled with gravity and wild meaning. Words to say that neither I nor anyone else would ever fully decipher that meaning, and in the end that was no bad thing.

Back in New York, I came across an article in the journal of the American Fisheries Society. It helped me better understand what I had seen that day on the Englishman's River and what it means when biologists speak of salmon as a keystone species, one on which every part of the ecosystem to some extent depends. The three authors of the article, all scientists from the Pacific Northwest, showed how, when the salmon's numbers decline, the ecosystem as a whole is threatened. They argued that salmon act as a huge natural recycling agent, transporting organic nutrients from the ocean, storing them in their bodies, and then leaving their carcasses to feed insects, bears, plants, trees, and other fish. They concluded that only about 5 percent of the historical biomass of salmon is now returning to the fish's native watersheds. As a result, they wrote, "Just five percent to seven percent of the marine-derived nitrogen and marine-derived phosphorus once delivered annually to the rivers of the Pacific Northwest is currently reaching those streams."

Using new technologies that can identify individual isotopes of nitrogen, phosphorus, and carbon, scientists in the Northwest have found high levels of ocean nutrients in leaves, plants, the bones of grizzly bears, and above all in young salmon. These nutrients could have come from only one place. The die-off of the salmon may in fact be an elaborate survival strategy, which originally evolved because the cold, crystal waters of the Pacific Northwest were so lacking in other nutrients. So the spawned-out body of my coho would nourish the trees. When the trees died, their leaves and branches would fall into the water and decompose, providing food and shelter for the benthic invertebrates, which would be consumed by the fish. Thus the coho's carcass would be eaten by a generation of

Taking Milt from the Male Salmon

younger salmon, improving their chances of surviving the ocean migration. As a result, more would return to spawn in their native streams. And when they died, their bodies would repeat the cycle.

THE NAUGATUCK VALLEY is a long way from the Englishman's River, yet the issues it presents are not dissimilar. In New England, the adaptive diversity of the salmon population has shrunk to a much more serious extent than it has in the Pacific Northwest. In the eighteenth century, the annual run of salmon in the Connecticut River is thought to have contained at least two dozen distinct genetic stocks. Now they're all gone, and the state's biologists—working, as they did in the 1870s, with genetic material from Maine's Penobscot River—are trying to create a simulacrum from scratch.

It's been a painful saga, marked by the unfounded optimism that people tend to display when they have to justify the use of public funds to a frustrated and demanding constituency. Just another ten years—you'll see; they'll be back. If not by 1990, then by the end of the century. The more the promises fall short, the more the pressure mounts. And the greater the pressure, the more flustered the promises.

The first smolts that the Connecticut hatcheries produced did not survive. They were fat, finless little creatures that bore only a passing resemblance to *Salmo salar,* with no tolerance for saltwater. They sat in the Connecticut River until they were eaten. So the state turned to stocking fry instead. The biologists knew that this would mean massive mortality rates, but at least the fish that survived to become smolts would have gone through a brutal process of natural selection. It was argued that this would deliver more bang for the buck.

More of a whimper, as it turned out. Each spring, the biologists waited by the fish ladders at the Rainbow Dam in Enfield, Connecticut, and counted the salmon that returned. In 1981 they counted 513 fish. This made them ecstatic, and they began to predict annual runs of 5,000, even 10,000, within a decade. In 1983, they counted 39 fish. No one knew the reasons for the drop. The optimistic predictions were withdrawn.

Each year, the returning fish were taken from the dam, anesthetized, weighed, tagged, vaccinated, and placed in hatchery tanks. By fall, the cock fish had been relieved of their milt, and the hens stripped of their eggs. The resulting fry, as many as ten million a year, were returned to the Connecticut River, to take their chances on the long swim to the Greenland coast. That left only the brood stock, whose purpose had been accomplished and whose utility was therefore at an end. At this point, said Steve Gephard, "We give them a gold watch and kick them out the door." For the first twenty years of the program, some of the brood stock were sent to be displayed in aquariums. Some went to the State University of New York for research in genetics, endocrinology, and immunology. Some were released in the estuary of the Connecticut River, where they almost certainly expired without further ado. Some were donated to the state Veterans Home at Rocky Hill, until it became clear that they were providing a source of illicit income for the guards, who were selling the salmon on the side.

For all the mystique of trout and salmon, fisheries management is a prosaic business, its priorities dictated by money and politics. As long as the promised salmon runs failed to materialize, the angling lobby would make complaints—complaints that needed to be answered, since anglers pay license fees and are not without influence. Someone suggested creating a salmon fishery by stocking the surplus brood stock in a couple of selected rivers. This would give the anglers some immediate gratification and perhaps buy time and free publicity for the beleaguered salmon restoration program. The DEP brass liked the idea, the angling lobby loved it, and the program began in 1992. Gephard described it unsentimentally as "taking a waste product from one project and turning it into a valuable asset for another."

The state looked for two rivers, one in the east and one in the west, with the right characteristics: suitable habitat, decent water quality, proximity to urban areas, good public access, and what the Fisheries Division called "aesthetics consistent with a traditional salmon fishery." In the east, they settled on the Shetucket River. In the west, they looked at the Housatonic but rejected it because of the PCBs. With some misgivings, they chose the Naugatuck instead.

BOB GREGORSKI was given the honor of planting the first of the salmon in the Naugatuck. "I have to say the first five years of the program were very successful from a fishing point of view," he told me. "I'd fish three or four times a week, a couple of hours each time. It took me the first year to get the system down, but when I did the fishing was great. I must have taken two hundred fifty salmon in five seasons."

But as the popularity of the program grew, so did the conflicts. Flyfishers against spin fishers; releasers against harvesters. "I have mixed feelings about the project now, to be honest," Bob said. "As soon as we'd done that first stocking, I left town. I had to get away from my phone, which was ringing off the hook with newspapers wanting to talk about the salmon program. It called attention to the river, all right, but it brought hundreds of people flocking, and there were some slobs among them. In the northern section of the river, up by Campville, you'd find people using illegal methods like snagging and lifting, people chumming the water with corn, people fishing with shiners and worms, and zero enforcement."

"That's a beautiful part of the river," I said.

"Well, there you go," Bob said. "That's the reason. Because the area is so secluded, people know they can get away with it."

Like everything else in the Naugatuck Valley, the hidden injuries of class pulsed beneath the surface of these clashes. The Naugatuck was primarily a blue-collar meat fishery. Half the anglers on the Shetucket were releasing the fish they caught, but only one in four on the Naugatuck. When Trout Unlimited asked for special regulations, the bait fishermen responded with a petition accusing them of snobbery. Since everyone paid the same license fee, why shouldn't everyone benefit equally? The fly-fishers retorted that bait fishing would violate the intent and spirit of the fishery; their method was the only legal one in North America, and anything else was a betrayal of the noble traditions of the sport. (Not strictly true—since time immemorial, English country gentlemen have liked nothing better than to catch their salmon on an artfully rigged dead prawn.)

I said to Bob that although I was a fly-fisherman to my marrow, it seemed a little perverse to insist on a catch-and-release regulation for creatures that the state had already placed on death row. He looked up at me sharply, then smiled.

He said, "I know everyone says these fish are finished. But you know what? We've found that salmon can breed in this river. Natural reproduction has now been documented twice. We found a parr-marked four-inch salmon at Beacon Falls, and a seven- or eight-inch smolt up at Torrington. When the dams are down, there'll be a shad run in the springtime, sea-run brown trout in the fall. And then maybe one day, salmon. Who knows?"

If that happened, I had to acknowledge, it would be correct to call the Naugatuck a salmon river, and not just a river with salmon in it.

25
A Fully Fought Case

O NE MORNING IN EARLY NOVEMBER, as I waited for the Shepaug trial to begin, Bob Orciari called to say that a couple hundred brood-stock salmon had just been planted in Campville. The Kensington hatchery had finally completed the census of its breeder fish, finding out which of them had, as Bob put it, "viable sex products." I had never fished for the Naugatuck salmon, but suddenly I wanted to see these fish and find out whether they were a benign imitation of nature or just a parody.

The hemlock gorge at Campville is a sparkling anomaly on the upper Naugatuck; Waterbury's derelict brass mills seemed as distant as another planet. However, a good proportion of the city's male population seemed to have made the journey, hearing that the salmon were in the river. At least a dozen vehicles had clustered around the Campville bridge, most of them big, gas-guzzling SUVs. The pool below the bridge was in effect a barrel, and the salmon swam in it, waiting to be shot. Fly-fishermen were not immune to the circus, but most of them had staked out one side of the river. The spin fishermen stood on the other, keeping a wary distance. Six or seven anglers of both persuasions had lined up along the banks of the bridge pool, a gorgeous piece of water with tumbling falls at its head and a long, deep, shelving midsection: a salmon pool from central casting.

I walked downstream through the forest, away from the crowds. It was November, but it could have been April. The sky was the color of cornflowers. Downstream, the river curved away into deep shade. I walked in that direction, past some pieces of broken pipe and the over-grown rubble of an old dam to a silent stretch of long pools, with riffled tongues, deep runs, and bedrock walls. A tiny rill trickled down the hill-side into the Naugatuck. It ran through a deep, narrow crevice lined with icicles and then dropped beneath a solid sheet of ice before entering the river. I fished for half an hour. Once I thought I had a strike, but it was only my fly hanging up against a rock.

The sun was high in the sky now, and most of the anglers had called it a day, packing up their gear and stripping off their boots and waders. Like me, most seemed to be empty-handed. But then I saw one middle-aged man walking across the Campville bridge, carrying a salmon in the folds of his net.

"You got one, I see," I said.

"Well, my buddy did," he said, gesturing to the stocky man be-hind him.

"What did you take it on?" I asked.

The first man held up his rod to show me a red and yellow Mickey Finn streamer. It's an old standby fly from Maine that salmon fishermen a hundred years ago would have recognized.

His friend caught up with him and took the net from his hand. He held it up for me to see. The fish was nineteen, perhaps twenty inches long, compressed into an S in the cheap twine netting. The sides of the salmon were a sad-sack, blackish-greenish-grayish sort of color. It was covered with dust and road grit. The man looked vaguely ill at ease, as if he knew something was not quite right about the picture.

Two spin fishermen were still working the pool below the bridge with their jangling metal lures. One raised a hand, and I waved back in farewell. I climbed into the car, turned the key in the ignition, snapped my seat belt shut, and pulled away. Granite chips flecked with mica flew up under my wheels. All along Route 8, down as far as the old Plume and Atwood brass mill, waterfalls of ice clung to the sheer rock faces of the Naugatuck Valley.

WATERBURY V. WASHINGTON began two weeks later. As a result of the city's tactical maneuverings, the Shepaug advocates bore the initial burden of proof. They had to show that Waterbury had "impaired" their river. If Judge Beverly Hodgson was persuaded by this argument, then the burden of proof would shift to Waterbury. The city would have to demonstrate that it had no "prudent and feasible alternatives" to its traditional way of operating its water supply system.

As Ed Matthews had promised, the lawyers for Washington conducted a "fully fought case," calling a parade of expert witnesses. Several were state officials from Hartford, although the state itself—meaning the attorney general's office—kept out of the argument, waiting to see how the six-week trial would play out.

At the heart of the dispute were the two words that had jumped out at me from the 1893 Special Law Authorizing the City of Waterbury to Increase Its Water Supply. Had the city used the Shepaug to meet its "necessities" or merely its "convenience"? As William Pape had written almost a century earlier, the physical development of Waterbury, in its narrow, rocky valley, was "essentially an engineering problem." Washington's legal team sought to show that the river had offered the city engineers a neat solution, free of charge.

The expert testimony showed that since the 1940s, Waterbury had been using the diverted water from the Shepaug to power the turbines that supplied electricity to the hilliest neighborhoods in the city—without

The Branch Dam, from where Waterbury gets her Water. Waterbury, Conn.

S. 882 Published by Geo. N. Ells, Waterbury, Conn.

paying a dime for the privilege. This was one source of Dimitri Rimsky's anger at outsiders coveting the "hydraulic force" of the river. But it was not the only one. The problem of low flow had grown worse, everyone in Washington agreed, since about 1988. The testimony showed that this was when Waterbury had built its new water purification plant to comply with federal standards. The plant was situated on the Morris Reservoir, second in the chain of three that received water from the Shepaug tunnel. It was gravity-fed, in other words. But if the city wanted to bring the quality of the Wigwam Reservoir up to federal standards (this being the third and lowest-lying of the impoundments), that would mean pumping it uphill to the purification plant. And that would have cost money. So the water in the Wigwam was neither used to generate electricity nor purified to provide drinking water. On some days, the city's own figures showed that it was using water from the Shepaug to meet 90 percent of its demand. Meanwhile, the unused water in the Wigwam flowed over the spillway and into a brook, which carried it into the Naugatuck River.

The testimony of Rick Jacobson, a garrulous and good-natured biologist for the state of Connecticut, showed beyond a doubt that the numbers of trout in the Shepaug were nowhere near what one would expect to find in this habitat, even though its tributaries were teeming with native brookies. Yet the question of the trout, and how they were affected by low flows, seemed to have become marginal to the dynamics of the case. In a way this was a relief to me. Fish were a matter of biology, while fishing was a human concept driven by economics, politics, and cultural preferences. No matter how sound their science or how pure their motives, anyone who appeared to press the case too hard for trout, or for fly-fishing, was going to come off as a self-interested elitist.

Then there was the testimony of an expert witness for Washington named Bo Shelby, from the University of Oregon. Shelby is a theorist of recreation and aesthetics. He advises the National Park Service, for example, on how varying flow levels in the Colorado River, or the Snake, affect the ability of visitors to derive satisfaction from the experience. His stock-in-trade, if you like, is to quantify the unquantifiable. In that sense, his work is a little reminiscent of those medieval theologians who were charged with calculating the height and weight of angels and the acreage of heaven, even though faith told them these things were ineffable.

Shelby had asked people using the Shepaug to say how much water was necessary for them to derive enjoyment from their own particular activity—fishing, canoeing, swimming, hiking, horseback riding, whatever. No one thought of the river in terms of millions of gallons per day, but everyone could point to his or her particular rock and say, in essence, there's enough water for me when that rock is covered. Starting with that rock, the hydrologists could do a transect, and so quantify, in millions of gallons per day (mgd), just how much water that was. This was exactly what I had seen Ed Matthews do when we were rooting around in the rocks for caddis cases.

Bo Shelby's testimony went right to the heart of Judge Hodgson's dilemma. If she found for Washington, what remedy could she order? Just saying "more water" wouldn't do. She would have to specify, in mgd, and for each month of the year, what the natural, unimpaired Shepaug River should look like—a river free of "anthropogenic manipulation." It was one thing to show that the Shepaug was not the river that nature intended. But could the "real" river even be visualized? Could it be re-created by historical analogy? Could it be modeled on a computer by hydrologists, who were the first to acknowledge that such modeling was still an imprecise science? On these central questions, there were as many methodologies as there were experts, and the state of Connecticut had no established law to draw upon.

A former chief hydrologist for the U.S. Geological Survey used something called "watershed ratio transform" to come up with one set of numbers. A stochastic hydrologist called to testify by Waterbury used a statistical approach called the QPPQ method and came up with another. Waterbury posited 4.9 mgd, the maximum amount the dam had been designed to release; that was the natural flow of the Shepaug. Washington's experts argued that the benchmark should be something called the August median flow, which they said was 10.5 mgd. Waterbury retorted that the August median flow was a meaningless abstraction. These competing theories all depended on analogy with a surrogate stream that shared the same broad characteristics as the Shepaug—drainage area, gradient, rainfall, land use. But the two sides couldn't even agree on a particular surrogate. One said the Pomperaug; the other said Salmon Creek, which enters the Housatonic near Falls Village.

Rick Jacobson explained that state law wasn't much help. The only flow standards that Connecticut had ever enunciated were those that governed stocked trout streams, which dated back to the 1970s. I assumed these were irrelevant, since their only purpose was to make sure that enough water flowed in a river to cover the backs of the trout until Memorial Day, by which time most of them would have been yanked out and turned into a fisherman's breakfast. In any case, only a small section of the Shepaug, down in Roxbury, was stocked by the state. When Rick Jacobson told the court that no ecological rationale existed for the stocked stream standards, I paid them no further mind, especially since so many other sets of figures were kicking around the courtroom, all of them envisioning much higher flows.

THE FINAL DAY of the trial dawned bitterly cold, and a wind that had gathered its energy in northern Ontario whipped down the Naugatuck Valley. Sharp splinters of winter light bounced off the rocks and the bare trees. By the time I had run the hundred yards from the car park to the Waterbury courthouse, my cheekbones and eye sockets were numb with pain. Inside, at the security desk, a sullen parade of teenage Latino kids from the South End were checking their stereo headsets through the metal detector, on their way to court appearances.

I found an empty seat next to Ed and Patricia Matthews and glanced over at the Waterbury attorneys. They were huddled together, talking in urgent whispers, and they looked angry. Judge Beverly Hodgson entered the courtroom. She had a severe manner and eyes sharp with intelligence. You felt there was humor beneath the surface, although it might be as dry as the Shepaug in August. Later in the day, when one of the Waterbury lawyers complimented her on being a quick study on some technical matter, she shot him a look that could have withered a magnolia tree, a look that said, "Don't *ever* patronize me."

The clerk called the court to order, and one of the Waterbury lawyers rose to his feet. Now we found out why they were angry. At the eleventh hour, the state of Connecticut had come off the fence. The precedents in this case were too important to ignore. Earlier that morning, the attorney general and the DEP commissioner had jointly filed an injunction backing the river advocates in every key particular. They called for the Shepaug to receive ten million gallons a day in summer—almost seven times the minimum laid down in the 1921 contract—and more than thirty-two million gallons a day in winter.

"They've given absolutely no notice," the Waterbury attorney fumed. "We just got this at a quarter to eight this morning."

The judge gave him a cool look and overruled the objection. The outcome of the trial, in a sense, was decided in that moment. Nonetheless, I have to confess to a certain morbid fascination with watching Waterbury go under.

As I listened to Christopher Rooney, the city's lead counsel, deliver his closing argument, I found myself thinking of a squirrel that had run under the wheels of my car a few weeks earlier on Route 47 in Washington. The squirrel would alternately freeze and then dart back and forth, first one way, then the other. But whichever way it darted was wrong and only made the eventual impact more inevitable.

Rooney invoked God and Nature with every breath, generally not a good move for a lawyer or a politician. He quoted First Selectman Titus of Washington to the effect that the 1921 agreement had given the Shepaug what God intended the river to have. He said that Waterbury's current releases from the dam were the same thing as the natural flow of the river.

He said, "This river is not the Mississippi. The river *always* ran dry. The most graphic depiction is Exhibit 42."

I looked for Exhibit 42 in the book. It was a photograph from the early twentieth century, before the Shepaug Dam was built. It showed a horse standing midstream in the river. The Shepaug was indeed dry; it had obviously been a bad drought year. But as a standard of legal proof, I found it less than compelling. I half expected someone from Washington to leap up in court with a photograph of the '55 flood, as proof that the river had always run wet.

Rooney said, "The fact of the matter is, we have a natural phenomenon. . . . When the rain stops, the flow stops. That's just the way it is. What these people believe to be a flow problem produced by us is actually tied to nature. The evidence is it is a natural phenomenon. We are being blamed for it, but it is natural, and it is difficult, I hope, to enter an order asking us to alter what nature is, because that is not what CEPA is about."

BILL BRIGHT, the lead counsel for the Shepaug advocates, was up next. He did not offer a long closing argument, and in truth, it was probably superfluous to do so. Bright said that the case boiled down to a conflict between old ways and new ways of looking at the value of flowing water. CEPA had grown from an understanding by the legislature that "the air, water, land and other natural resources taken for granted since the settlement of this state are now recognized as finite and precious. It is now understood that human activity must be guided by and in harmony with the system of relationships among the elements of nature."

Bright went on:

> Your Honor, I think I started this case by saying that what this was all about is need, and whether Waterbury needs the water. The answer to that is no. They don't need it. They take more than they need because it's convenient, because it saves them some money. Under CEPA, that's not a good justification. If Waterbury had come into this case and said, look, we can't do anything else, we have these dams here, there's no other water, we've conserved everything we can and we've maximized our releases down the river, I'm not sure I'm left with much to say. But that's not what you've heard from them at all. There are a slew of feasible and prudent alternatives out there. . . . Their system is in their control. It's been in their control for sixty years. Because they've abused it, because they've misused and ignored this river, that's why they're in the position they're in today.

As BILL BRIGHT stacked his papers and sat down, I had little doubt which way Judge Hodgson would ultimately rule. Yet it was much less clear how she would translate her decision into quantifiable terms. The truth of the matter was that everyone—Washington, Waterbury, the court—was being asked to put a figure to something that was, by its nature, unquantifiable. Judge Hodgson seemed to grasp this clearly, and perhaps that was why she had seemed to show particular interest in Bo Shelby's testimony, which she brought up again now.

Rooney thought Shelby's work was horsefeathers. Yes, he allowed, he had listened to "the sort of recreational expert" but decided that "there is not much science to what he does." Rooney went on: "It is not as if people say, boy, this is an ugly mud flat and I don't want to be anywhere near it; it gives me no joy. They say, I'd like it better if there were more water."

Judge Hodgson looked at him sharply for a moment and asked, "Do you think that the statutory standard would be there's no impairment unless the thing becomes so unattractive that it totally precludes use?"

Squirrel-like, Rooney darted straight under the wheels of Judge Hodgson's oncoming car. "I think that's right," he said. "An impairment, in an aesthetic sense—I don't know of any case law that recognizes that. . . . It's an abstraction. And the law does not protect abstractions."

It may be too much to say that a river is an abstraction, but it is certainly something greater than the sum of its quantifiable parts. What happened to the Naugatuck shows what can happen to a river reduced to its constituent elements, which are then measured by their utilitarian value. In relation to the body of its towns, the Naugatuck had ceased to be a vital artery and became instead an excretory canal. It had ceased, in this sense, to be a river at all.

Staring hard at the Waterbury lawyer, Judge Hodgson said—with some feeling, I thought: "Beyond the quantifiable things that can be studied in a quantifiable way, I assume that some claim is being made here that it is an impairment to a river to reduce it to a point that it isn't a river, and that it basically is eliminating all of the things that come with . . ."—she hesitated for a second, searching for the right word—*"riverness."*

Riverness. Yes, I had to agree with Judge Hodgson, that was the right word.

WE WENT TO DINNER that evening at Diorio's, the fanciest of the old Waterbury restaurants. Sitting at a long banquet table under the embossed tin ceiling, with the lamplight reflecting off the polished mahogany bankers' booths and the crystal wineglasses, I suppose we felt that in some sense we were thumbing our noses at the princes and captains of industry who had come here in the good old days to celebrate their business triumphs. I wondered if Robert Cairns had eaten here to mark the completion of the Shepaug tunnel. We drank a toast to the lawyers, drank another to Ed Matthews, and then drove off in our separate directions to await Judge Hodgson's decision.

26
Riverness

Almost two years had passed since the trial. There had been trout caught and trout lost. Insects had hatched, mated, and died. A book was almost written. Before another winter set in, I wanted to see each of my rivers again, these streams that had insinuated themselves so deeply into my life: Furnace Brook, the Naugatuck, the Shepaug and its stairstep tributaries, one stream at a time flowing inexorably to the big river.

Driving north from Manhattan in the predawn darkness, I pulled over at intervals to stare up at the sky, which was clear and brilliant with stars. The earth was passing through the tail of the Leonids, and the night sky brought a display of celestial pyrotechnics on a scale not seen in years.

Waterbury's new wastewater plant had been on line for more than a year now. When the last of the dams came down, the Naugatuck River would not only flow freely again; it would flow cleanly. The dam removal program was far behind schedule, however, as the best-laid plans usually are. Anaconda was gone, of course, and so was the Union City Dam. So was the sleeping policeman at Freight Street in Waterbury, for all the difference that made. Elsewhere difficulties had emerged. At the Tingue Dam at Seymour, the problem was cost overruns. An access ramp here, a fish-viewing platform there, and legal complications over the relocation of the skateboarding park had driven up the original $1 million estimate to $4.5 million and counting. At the Bray's Buckle Dam on the Mad River, other factors caused the delay. Community groups in the South End had lobbied for the structure to remain, on aesthetic grounds. Others might call it an eyesore, but in this ravaged neighborhood it was considered a thing of beauty, especially when the falls were floodlit at night. So the Bray's Buckle Dam was to stay in place, with the addition of a fish way.

At the dam at Platts Mills, below the Waterbury treatment plant, an eighty-foot section had been removed, enlarging an existing breach. A hardy late-season canoeist came through the opening as I stood on the riverbank, and we exchanged waves. The man was riding a rush of white water through the gap; the flow was carving out deep runs and pockets that would make great holding water for trout and salmon. It was possible, standing on the rocks at Platts Mill, to imagine a future in which shad, alewives, blueback herring, perhaps one day even Atlantic salmon, would again run freely up the river each spring. The returning fish would bring back the predatory birds, too—gulls and egrets, eagles and ospreys, kingfishers and great blue herons.

The new wastewater plant was only half a mile upstream, yet the river smelled sweeter than ever. It didn't smell that way to the feds, however. Both the Federal Bureau of Investigation and the Internal Revenue Service thought the contract for the plant, and the mayor of Waterbury's financial dealings with Joe Pontoriero of the Worth Corporation, smelled very bad indeed. They began to watch Giordano closely, even as the mayor announced his intention to run for the U.S. Senate against the incumbent Democrat, Joseph Lieberman, who would be Al Gore's running mate in November 2000.

Giordano ended up as a footnote to that year's bizarre presidential election, losing badly to Lieberman. Yet if the U.S. Supreme Court had not intervened in the disputed race in Florida, Al Gore, already the winner of the popular vote, might have become the nation's forty-third president, Joe Lieberman would have become his vice president, and the governor of Connecticut, the Waterbury native John Rowland, would have had to designate someone to fill Lieberman's vacant seat in the Senate. And that someone, more than theoretically, could have been Mayor Phil Giordano, since the Republican Party had found no one else willing to run against a popular incumbent.

Yet Giordano's career headed in the opposite direction. In February 2001, shortly after George W. Bush's inauguration, the FBI began to monitor calls on the mayor's city-issued cell phone, looking to gather evidence of corruption. The following month, after Giordano was at last forced to acknowledge the extent of Waterbury's fiscal crisis, a state-appointed oversight board took control of the city's finances. In April, Bush visited Waterbury, but his aides took care to keep the president and the mayor well apart: no handshakes, no photographs.

Phil Giordano seemed to be addicted to his cell phone, speaking with Joe Pontoriero as often as six times a day. Yet as the evidence of corruption piled up, the federal investigators found that they were spending even more time listening to evidence of a different sort—what one of the mayor's political associates decorously referred to later as his "alternative lifestyle." There were frequent calls to "companionship and massage" services. There were phone blitzes to young women—twenty-seven calls to a married woman in Waterbury; thirteen calls to a twenty-year-old in New Haven; thirty-three calls to a sixteen-year-old high school kid looking for a summer job with the city. But the heaviest volume of calls went to a pair of prostitutes whom Giordano liked to visit on the streets above the abandoned brass mills in Waterbury's North End.

In July 2001, federal agents were listening to a conversation between Mayor Giordano and an African American prostitute and crack addict. Giordano told her that he was in the mood for sex. He wondered if she could maybe bring along the same girl she'd brought before, the one who'd taken part in their sessions at Giordano's home, his law office, a friend's condo, and city hall. Not sure, the woman said, it's her birthday. Oh really, said the mayor, how old is she going to be? Nine, the woman answered.

There were two young children, in fact, according to the subsequent federal indictment, which charged Phil Giordano with using an interstate device—the cell phone—to arrange his malignant sexual encounters. The other victim was the prostitute's eleven-year-old niece. A third child was also in the picture, though not as a victim of sexual abuse. He was a seven-year-old boy of mixed race who was said to bear a striking physical resemblance to Phil Giordano. This was not surprising since, as investigators learned later, the mayor was the boy's father.

"Shocking even by Waterbury standards"—that was the phrase everyone used to convey the enormity of the Giordano scandal. But was it too much, I wondered, to say that the mayor's downfall was not only a tale of personal squalor but also the end of a causal chain that had begun with the rocks and water of the Naugatuck River? If the geology had been more forgiving, if the valley had flooded less, no brass industry would have flourished there. With no brass industry, no economic boom would have occurred, no chronic water shortages, no schemes to raid the water of the Shepaug, no civic culture of patronage and corruption. If brass had not been allowed to exercise such a choking monopoly, the post-Vietnam crash might have been less brutal; a more diverse economy might have shielded the most recent immigrants—the South End Latinos who kept their pit bulls chained under the Holy Land U.S.A. cross, an unskilled African American woman who became a crack addict—from their descent into the black hole of drugs and prostitution. If Waterbury's political elite had been more accountable, they might have more speedily cleaned up the river that industry had turned into a cesspit. If a corrupt mayor had not given the cleanup contract to a construction company with suspected Mafia ties, it would never have occurred to the feds to tap his cell phone. And without the wiretaps, they might never have found out about Phil Giordano's predatory serial pedophilia. I found myself asking, Did all that history come down to this?

I ALSO WONDERED whether ex-mayor Giordano, sitting in his federal jail cell, ever thought about the battle over the Shepaug. Six weeks after our dinner at Diorio's, Judge Hodgson had ruled in favor of the river advocates on virtually every point. She found that Waterbury's "chosen method of operations imposed on the flow of water down the Shepaug River constitutes an unreasonable impairment of the public trust in this natural resource" as well as a breach of the 1921 agreement with Washington. She ordered the city to retrofit the Shepaug Dam so that it would release more than six million gallons of water a day to the river during the summer months of lowest flow and as much as thirty-four million gallons a day in the springtime. Phil Giordano had vowed angrily that Waterbury would appeal.

The city *had* appealed—and it had won. The reason—foreseeable enough in hindsight, I suppose—was the Slinky-like character of the law. Rick Jacobson's testimony had put the problem in plain view. As he'd said, the regulations governing the minimum flow in stocked trout streams had absolutely no ecological foundation, no relationship to the larger public purpose expressed in CEPA. However, the appeals court judges pointed out that they were the only flow standards on the books, of any kind. It seemed that no one had ever spotted the anomaly or updated the regulations so they made sense. That being the case, Judge Hodgson had no other statutory basis on which to prescribe a remedy. Her figures, as far as the appeals court was concerned, might as well have been plucked from the air. I had to admit there was a certain logic in this, since the measure of a healthy river had to be found somewhere deeper than in the arbitrary numbers concocted to give anglers a make-believe trout stream. The issue was remanded for a fresh trial.

BY THE TIME I reached the Shepaug, the sky had clouded over. November brings a change in the palette, from color to monochrome. It brings a change in light, the sun pale and yellowed, with a milky nimbus around it, the trees skeletal, their last leaves hanging like scraps of old wallpaper. It brings a change in sound, which travels farther and resonates more sharply through the newly opened spaces in the forest. It brings a change in sensation: the skin feels somehow tighter and drier, the senses more alert.

I parked at the dogleg corner on Sabbaday Lane and hiked down the old fire road to the river, past the ghosts of abandoned farms. Crows cawed in the trees. The air was soft but chilly, and a few tentative drops of rain were falling. The streamside bushes were decorated with a silver filigree, the work of late-hatched spiderlings. My clothes were covered with burs from the edge of the farmer's field: cockleburs like miniature hand grenades, the brown burs of enchanter's nightshade, the green triangles of tick trefoil. The river flowed silently at the foot of the hill. Water, too, seems to change its character in November, seeming to run darker, more uniform. The flow has an almost viscous quality.

The Shepaug is still a wounded river, at least during the summer months. But I felt a certain serenity, despite the appeals court ruling, that one day its flow would be restored. With Phil Giordano gone, it was hard to imagine either side having the appetite to go back to court. Ed Matthews would find saner interlocutors on the Waterbury side. And when this happened, the Shepaug would be a river again, a real trout stream, something complete.

Whether or not it can be tabulated or reduced to statistics, I think we know what trout water is when we see it. It means a richness of benthic life, tiny elegant insects that emerge through the surface film and rise into the sky at certain times of year, setting the calendar as surely as the blossoming of certain flowers. It means a flow that delivers an abundance of oxygen. It means water of a certain depth, canopied by trees. It means water you can *hear* as well as see. Trout water can't be manufactured. In the Netherlands, where people fish in slow-moving canals for pike and bream and zander, there are no native salmonids, but there is a hunger for the meanings they provide. I have read that there is a swimming pool in the Netherlands that is stocked for recreation. Dutch anglers walk up and down the sides of the pool and cast with fly rods. The water is full of trout. But it is not trout water.

I imagined the Shepaug in springtime, running full from the dam at Woodville. I imagined one of the fly-fishing magazines extolling the river as a new mecca. I imagined an anxious editorial in the *Litchfield County Times*, lamenting the invasion and asking if perhaps the Steep Rock Association shouldn't reconsider Ehrick Rossiter's original charter, with its promise of unlimited public access to the river for everyone in the county.

NEXT MORNING I drove to Furnace Brook, stopping on the way at Harold MacMillan's fly shop. Harold said he had some interesting new stuff in, and I walked over to the display case to take a look. In the middle of the case was a Bogdan salmon reel. It was engraved "J. L. Pool." In the window, I found an old Wheatley fly box filled with beautifully tied salmon flies. The box, too, was marked "J. L. Pool." When I thought of Larry parting with his fishing tackle, I experienced the same sadness I'd felt when my father, who had grown up a three-iron shot from the Old Course at St. Andrews, turned eighty and sold his golf clubs. The last thing I needed was another fly box, but I bought this one and placed it on a shelf in my study.

Above the old ironworks on Furnace Brook, new DEP signs were posted on the trees, announcing special regulations for the stream. The state's trout management plan had been approved, and it called, among other things, for the establishment of seven new wild trout management areas in the Housatonic watershed. We'd seen the last of the hatchery rainbows in Furnace Brook.

Farther upstream, I had planted hemlock seedlings in the springtime with Mike Piquette, and I wanted to see how many had survived. All summer, the vegetation had been impenetrable, but now it was possible to push through the tangled brush to reach the brook. Branches heavy with pokeberries slapped at my face. The berries were violently purple on red stems.

The brook was full and clear, and its sandy bottom looked as if it had been scrubbed clean. A single crosshatching of branches lay in the middle of a deep pool. It looked like a Chinese ideogram. As I waded closer to it, through chest-deep water, a small brown trout streaked from its shelter and flashed away under my feet. Where the brook divides, beneath an overgrown log dam, I found one of my hemlocks. It was gray-green, a little bedraggled, fighting for space and food with the alders and marsh grasses. But it was there, and it had taken root in the sandy soil.

AT WEST CORNWALL, the last of the leaf-peepers had moved on. All through October, they had swarmed over the river, snapping my picture as I cast over trout in the pocket water below the covered bridge, trying to capture a printed memory of the red and orange blaze of the maples that are spreading relentlessly across our northeastern forests. Now the tourists were off somewhere preparing for the winter, like the trout in the river and the late migrant hawks riding the cold air currents south from Canada.

It had been a good year for the Housatonic. In August 2000, the DEP had issued its final 401 Water Quality Certificate, mandating natural flows—"run of the river"—at the Falls Village and Bull's Bridge plants, as a condition of the hydropower relicensing. FERC had reservations about the plan, asking whether the proposals went far enough to protect the river. For that reason, the final certification included a "reopener" that would allow the federal agency to reconsider the license in light of later scientific evidence—for example, findings about the effect of natural flows on the health of aquatic insects and the movement of impounded PCBs.

Then, on October 27, in the U.S. District Court in Springfield, Massachusetts, Judge Michael Ponsor approved a consent decree that compelled the General Electric Company to clean up its PCB contamination of the Housatonic. Estimates put the cost to GE at anything from $150 million to $300 million. Already the backhoes were at work, tearing down the GE powerhouse in Pittsfield, scouring out the sediments from Woods Pond. More than $15 million in damages, split between Massachusetts and Connecticut, would help to restore damaged wildlife habitat along the river.

None of these victories was permanent, I realized. They would have to be modified, defended. There would be challenges, reverses, shifts in political power. This good news did not constitute a happy ending to the saga any more than Judge Hodgson's ruling on the Shepaug did. They were only way stations, chapters in the unending story of what we do to rivers and what rivers do to us.

THE FIRST HARD FROST of the season had left a film of ice around the edges of the Carse Pool. It had formed on the surface in discrete plates, a translucent quilting of perfect triangles and rhomboids, no more than an eighth of an inch thick. I climbed onto a boulder. The rocks around me were outlined in concentric rings of white, where the mild current of the eddy had frozen in place. When I stepped off the boulder, the felt soles of my wading boots came free with a gentle tearing sound, like a tongue off cold metal, leaving behind a white trace footprint.

I waded through the ice quilt toward deeper water. The water that I displaced bulged under the ice ahead of me, causing the ice rings around each rock to squeak and grate and the area of whiteness to expand. The temperature was close to freezing, and the wind-chill effect of casting quickly froze the line guides on my rod, coating each one with a beard of ice crystals. By the fifth or sixth cast, each flick of the line was slowed by the friction of the ice, causing a gentle tug that felt like the take of a small fish. I had to free the ice buildup with my fingernail and warm the guides in my cupped hands.

When a fat end-of-season trout abruptly snatched my fly, I was so startled that I set the hook with an instinctive snap that was much too fierce. The fish showed briefly at the surface, rolling broad-shouldered and golden brown in the clear water, and was gone. Four more heavy trout took my fly that morning, but I lost every last one of them.

At last, though, one fish held. It snatched a black stonefly nymph and ran with panache, using the pressure of the current against me. But at last it tired and came to hand. It was beautiful, a sleek, shining, eleven-inch fallfish. A Shepaug salmon, *Semotilus corporalis*. A minnow, in other words.

I wondered, as I released the fallfish, what made it inferior to a trout. Was it the appearance? The fallfish was beautiful, and who is to say that gold is preferable to silver? Saltwater fish are prized for their identical platinum sheen.

Was it the fish's ease of capture, or the vigor of its fight? No, because until I saw it, I was convinced by its strength that the fish was a brown trout.

Was it that the food value of the fallfish was less than that of the trout? No, because I was not intending to eat either of them.

Was it what the presence of the fish said about the general health of the river? I thought not. This was not a buffalo or a mooneye, one of those species that grub around in the polluted bottom waters of the South and the Midwest. On the contrary, the biologists had declared that there was no better barometer of the river's health than the population of young fallfish we had found in August, as we electroshocked the Sand Hole. Nor was the fish deficient in wildness; it was, in every respect, wilder than the trout and truly indigenous to the river.

That left me with nothing but the cultural attributes of the fish, the value we assigned to it for being not-a-trout. The trout is a "game fish"; the other is a "trash fish." No one sells baseball caps imprinted with the image of a fallfish. When you hang out with the guys in the fly shop, no one will be impressed when you tell them you just landed a hell of a fallfish. I've seen angry anglers take a "trash fish" and smash it on a rock when they realized it wasn't a trout, as if the fish had betrayed them in some fashion.

I WAS QUITE ALONE in midstream. The hillsides were dark. Inexplicably, a solitary maple still had its leaves, which were the color of clementines. But the oaks occupied the stage now. For a month, they had been inconspicuous, passing through subtle stages of magenta and bronze, overshadowed by the fire of the maples. But now that the forest floor was carpeted with wet maple leaves, the oaks emerged, slow and stubborn, still dense with leaves that were leathery with tannins.

My fingers had grown numb with the cold, and ugly storm clouds were assembling over the Litchfield Hills. The road was out of sight, and the hard granite walls of the valley channeled the flow into two successive bends, one to the north of me and another to the south, so that the prospect of the river was blocked in each direction by a curtain wall of forest and mountain. I felt enclosed in a tunnel, where the only sounds were the soughing of the wind in the trees and the steady sibilant whisper of the water. It was a wild and solemn place, but it was not wilderness. On the contrary, humans had shaped it and worked it and changed its smallest particulars, and I found it oddly satisfying to think that we could continue to do so and that the river would do the same to us.

As I stood there, waist-deep in the Housatonic, the wind picked up and gusted down the valley, bringing a sudden chill, a message of winter from the Arctic. The force of the squall shook loose an uncountable volume of oak leaves, and they filled the air with a great whirring sound, like a rain stick as long as the valley. For a full minute, the dense, rattling cloud of leaves darkened the sky. Then the wind dropped as suddenly as it had begun, and the air crackled with ozone. The first large drops of rain splashed onto my face, and the whole unending hydrologic cycle—precipitation, percolation, evaporation, transpiration, precipitation—began all over again.

ANNE AND THE KIDS were waiting for me at Stillmeadow, the first time we had been back to the house in more than a year. The lot on the corner of Jeremy Swamp Road had been sold and cleared, and a half-million-dollar McMansion had sprung up there like an overnight mushroom. Our neighbor, the Lithuanian farmer's wife, had died, and the hundred-acre farm on the hill was up for sale. Developers wanted to put up two dozen new houses to replace cornfields and meadows and patches of old-growth forest. If their plans succeeded, the road would be paved, and Jeremy Brook would disappear into a cement culvert.

David and Julia had grown, and their summer horizons had expanded. We spent our Augusts in Canada now, in a small pink house on the Moon River in Ontario. We lived on the water there, in canoes and kayaks, and in the early mornings I paddled out onto the river and fished the rocky points for smallmouth bass. At night we toasted marshmallows, told ghost stories, and lay on our backs on the striped rocks of the Precambrian shield, listening to the cry of loons and the faraway whistle of Canadian Pacific freights and counting shooting stars as the earth moved through the path of the Perseids.

As I drove to meet them, I wondered how David and Julia would think about rivers as they grew older. They were, after all, the stakeholders in waiting. At school, they watched earnest videos about the destruction of the Amazon rain forest. They learned that we are stewards of the planet. Recycling was hard-wired into their brains. I only hoped that all this orthodoxy, though admirable in its intent, would not lull them into thinking that we now had the measure of the problem. It seemed to miss the restless dynamic of our relationship to the natural world, in which we never start with a clean slate, but with the complex legacy of past actions. There would be new Shepaugs, other Naugatucks, and each would force us to make choices. How we made them, and how much power we had to make them freely, would say a lot about the world that David and Julia would inherit and what kind of rivers would run through it.

I took my family to see the ruins of the old milldam among the hemlocks on Battle Swamp Brook, where my questions had begun. We drove south over the hilly, winding roads, and I talked to the kids about the trout pool paradox. I told them about Judge Hodgson and riverness. I told them about Lynn Werner saying she was two-thirds water.

But I could tell that they were tuning me out, that I was being tedious and didactic, as fathers often are. So we switched gears and sang 1950s doo-wop songs as we drove past Jack's Brook, through Tophet Hollow, and over Good Hill, where we paused at the top to look out over the valley of the Pomperaug, seeing essentially the same unbroken panorama that Zachariah Walker and his small band of pilgrims had contemplated from this spot more than three hundred years earlier.

As we drove down into Woodbury, a turtle crossed the blacktop in front of us. It was a long way from home; no pond, no wetland, no turtle habitat was within sight. It was a painted turtle, and his underside was edged with flaming scarlet. David and Julia begged to take him back to Alfaro.

I suppose I had known we would go back to the brook in the end. No one had been there all year, and the path that we had cut with machetes had disappeared under a tangle of alders and vines and wild roses. Julia frowned and said this wasn't how she remembered it.

But she came readily enough, cradling the painted turtle in her hands, when we had cleared the worst of the brush and reached the foot of the hill, where the brook tumbled through its series of miniature pools to the Thorn Fortress. In the damp ground around it were water plantain

and crested wood fern, arrow arum and swampcandle loosestrife, swamp
pine and bluejoint grass, flattened by fall rains. As Julia took in the scene,
I heard her singing softly:

> Who put the bomp in the bomp bah bomp bah bomp?
> Who put the ram in the rama lama ding dong?

Anne helped my daughter across the boulders, and she knelt down
by the water and placed the turtle gently in the edge of the current. I
couldn't see David for a moment, but then I heard his voice calling from
farther upstream.

He said, "Dad, can you bring me some rocks?"

I called back to him, "What for?"

David said, "I need to build a dam."

Notes on Sources

A large part of this book is based on several dozen personal interviews conducted between 1998 and 2003. The following are some of the primary and secondary written sources I found especially useful, accompanied here and there by some random suggestions for readers interested in particular topics.

1. THE TROUT POOL PARADOX

Colonel Albert L. Hodge's handwritten daybook (p. 9) is in the Minor Memorial Library in Roxbury, Connecticut. Tocqueville's comment on the "innumerable multitude of small [undertakings]" (p. 13) is taken from Chapter XIX of Book II of his *Democracy in America* ("What Causes Almost All Americans to Follow Industrial Callings"). Book II, Chapter V ("Of the Use Which the Americans Make of Public Associations in Civil Life"), expands on this notion.

2. THE EDGELANDS OF ALFARO

Gladys Taber's books (p. 15) have been out of print for many years. Much of her best work is collected in *The Best of Stillmeadow: A Treasury of Country Living*, edited by Constance Taber Colby (Philadelphia: J. P. Lippincott, 1976). Taber still has a loyal following, whose doings can be tracked at geocities.com/Athens/Acropolis/5612/taberfriends.htm.

In addition to my own amateurish observation, and some well-thumbed field guides, I've enjoyed the diaries of former *New York Times* nature editorial writer Hal Borland, especially his book *Twelve Moons of the Year* (New York: Knopf, 1979), a useful guide to the calendar of appearance of the various plant, insect, and bird species of the Housatonic Valley, where Borland lived.

Roderick Haig-Brown's remark about small streams, "I can lie for an hour at a time . . ." (p. 17), is from his essay "Why Fish?" Widely regarded as the finest twentieth-century angling writer, Haig-Brown deserves a broader audience. Two essays from his collection *A River Never Sleeps* (New York: Morrow, 1946)—"Why Fish?" (pp. 266–274) and "To Know a River . . ." (pp. 343–352)—are a good place to begin to get a flavor of this accomplished and deeply humane writer.

3. FOUNDATION STONES

Timothy Dwight's four-volume *Travels in New England and New York* (New Haven: S. Converse, 1822) remains an incomparable guide to the region's history in the period immediately following the American Revolution. It contains many remarkable insights into the intertwined natural and social landscapes of New England.

For basic facts on geology, and in particular the geology of glaciated streams in the northeastern United States, I have relied heavily on Michael Bell's classic *The Face of Connecticut: People, Geology, and Land* (Hartford: Department of Environmental Protection, State Geological and Natural History Survey of Connecticut, Bulletin 110, fourth printing, 1997, now available in full-text form at g3.tmsc.org/face_of_ct/); and James Grant MacBroom's *The River Book: The Nature and Management of Streams in Glaciated Terranes* (Hartford: DEP, Natural Resources Center Bulletin 28, 1998).

My sources on David Humphreys (pp. 25–28), in addition to Dwight's *Travels,* include several biographies of Thomas Jefferson, notably *The Lost World of Thomas Jefferson,* by Daniel J. Boorstin (Chicago: University of Chicago Press, 1981). My reconstruction of Jefferson's relationship to Humphreysville and its impact on his thinking about industrialization is drawn less from established sources on Jefferson than from local archival materials in the towns of Seymour, Derby, and Ansonia, Connecticut, supplemented by my reading of Jefferson's correspondence; see *Papers and Correspondence,* edited by Julian P. Boyd et al. (Washington, D.C., 1950–). There is no modern biography of Humphreys himself. Frank Landon Humphreys's two-volume *Life and Times of David Humphreys —Soldier, Statesman, Poet* (New York: G. P. Putnam's Sons, 1917) was reprinted in 1971, but a more recent biography is long overdue. Humphreys deserves one.

In trying to discover more about Benjamin Silliman, I consulted *Benjamin Silliman: A Life in the Young Republic,* by Chandos Michael Brown (Princeton, N.J.: Princeton University Press, 1989), and *Benjamin Silliman and His Circle: Studies in the Influence of Benjamin Silliman on Science in America,* edited by Leonard G. Wilson (New York: Science History Publications, 1979).

In addition to dating the creation (p. 29), Archbishop Ussher used similar methods to establish that Adam and Eve were allowed only two and a half weeks of freedom in the Garden of Eden before God expelled them on Monday, November 10, 4004 B.C. Noah's ark, according to Ussher, washed up on Mount Ararat on Wednesday, May 5, 1491 B.C. I have omitted one detail, however, that appears in most popular accounts of Ussher's chronology—namely, that he placed the moment of the creation at exactly 9:00 in the morning. This detail seems to have been added by Sir John Lightfoot, a seventeenth-century vice-chancellor of Cambridge University.

John Rodgers's *Bedrock Geological Map of Connecticut* (p. 31) was published in 1985 by the Connecticut Geological and Natural History Survey in cooperation with the U.S. Geological Survey (two sheets, 1:125,000 published scale). There are several solid biographies of Louis Agassiz (p. 32). The one I relied on most was *Louis Agassiz: A Life in Science,* by Edward Lurie (Baltimore: Johns Hopkins University Press, 1988).

4. SUBDUE THE EARTH

The general outlines of the Dudleytown story (p. 35) appear in a number of works of local history, including a useful short pamphlet written by Paul H. Chamberlain Jr. and published by the Cornwall Historical Society (7 Pine Street, Box 115, Cornwall, Conn. 06753). A large number of psychics have latched on to the Dudleytown story, with some claiming that it was the inspiration for the popular movie *The Blair Witch Project.* A recent book by the Reverend Gary P. Dudley, *The Legend of Dudleytown (Cornwall, CT): Solving Legends Through Genealogical and Historical Research* (Bowie, Md.: Heritage Books, 2001), sets out to debunk these myths. Connoisseurs of the more bizarre corners of the Internet may enjoy Rev. Dudley's Web site, legendofdudleytown.com.

For details of life in the Housatonic Valley during the colonial period, I consulted a large number of individual town histories. In 1999 the

University Press of New England reprinted a facsimile edition of the 1836 classic *Connecticut Historical Collections: Containing a General Collection of Interesting Facts, Traditions, Biographical Sketches, Anecdotes, Etc., Relating to the History and Antiquity of Connecticut,* which contains profiles of scores of Connecticut towns and almost two hundred engravings by the amateur historian, printer, and engraver John Warner Barber. The thirty-odd books written and illustrated by Eric Sloane, who was a longtime resident of Warren, Connecticut, are also well worth browsing. They offer an extremely detailed if sentimental portrait of New England life, but if you want to know the difference between various kinds of eighteenth-century privies, this is the place to start. Fans of Sloane, whose personal collection of antique tools is housed at the Sloane Stanley Museum in Kent, Connecticut, have recently established a Web site, ericsloane.com.

The nineteenth-century revisionist historian mentioned on p. 38 was a Dr. Hildreth of Ohio, who is cited by William Cothren in his *History of Ancient Woodbury, Connecticut, from the First Indian Deed in 1659 to 1854, Including the Present Towns of Washington, Southbury, Bethlehem, Roxbury, and a Part of Oxford and Middlebury* (Waterbury: Bronson Brothers, 1854).

Naturalist Walt Landgraf (pp. 39–46) continues to lead wonderful guided hikes through the People's State Forest in the Farmington River valley of northwestern Connecticut. Regularly updated information about schedules is available at stonemuseum.com. Be prepared for some energetic climbing.

5. The Cheering Rays of Civilization

Wallace Nutting's hand-colored photographs (p. 47) were regarded as an essential part of the decor of middle-class American homes before World War II. Produced in vast quantities, they can be found for reasonable prices in almost any antiques mall in New England (as can large numbers of forgeries and knockoffs by lesser artists). *Connecticut Beautiful* (Framingham, Mass.: Old America Company, 1923) is part of Nutting's ten-book States Beautiful series. *Connecticut Beautiful,* together with its companion volumes on Massachusetts, Maine, Vermont, and New Hampshire, depicts Nutting's idealized (and highly commercial) view of rural New England in the early part of the twentieth century.

For the details of the Reverend Zachariah Walker's journey up the Housatonic and the Shepaug (pp. 49–51), I have mainly used the account in Cothren's *History of Ancient Woodbury*. Accounts by later authors, including Chard Powers Smith, in *The Housatonic: Puritan River* (New York: Rinehart & Company, 1946), to which I refer frequently in these pages, appear largely to derive from Cothren.

William Wood's description of the cruelty of the Mohawks (p. 52) is taken from his classic 1634 work, *New England's Prospect*. The Institute for American Indian Studies (formerly the American Indian Archaeological Institute), is located at 38 Curtis Road, Washington, Connecticut (telephone: 860-868-0518); its reconstruction of an Algonquin village is well worth a visit, especially for kids. My description of Indian fishing techniques (pp. 59–60) is largely drawn from materials in the institute's collection.

William Cronon's principal writings, which have influenced me enormously, include *Changes in the Land: Indians, Colonists and the Ecology of New England* (New York: Hill and Wang, 1983); *Nature's Metropolis: Chicago and the Great West, 1848–1893* (New York: W. W. Norton, 1992); and the edited collection *Uncommon Ground: Rethinking the Human Place in Nature* (New York: W. W. Norton, 1995).

The list of manufacturing towns on p. 57 is included in *Yankee Dreamers and Doers,* by Ellsworth Strong Grant (Chester, Conn.: Pequot Press, n.d.). Of all the "wild and shaggy names" mentioned by Odell Shepard, the most celebrated is without a doubt Lake Chargoggagoggmanchauggagoggchaubunagungamaugg (known to most people, understandably, as Lake Char or Lake Webster), which is situated on the Connecticut-Massachusetts border. Numerous scholars, including the distinguished geologist Michael Bell, author of *The Face of Connecticut,* have written that this name means "You fish on your side—I'll fish on my side—no one fish in the middle." It took an article in the April 2003 *Reader's Digest* ("True or False?") to enlighten me: the name was concocted as a spoof by a local newspaper editor in the 1920s, who later said that its real "meaning" was something like "Englishmen at Manchaug at the fishing place at the boundary." Moral of this story (like that of Bishop Ussher and the 9:00 A.M. creation): don't believe everything you read in books.

Paul Schullery's reference to the absence of books on sex and fishing in the colonial period (p. 59) is taken from his exemplary work *American*

Fly Fishing: A History (New York: Lyons & Burford, 1987, © The American Museum of Fly Fishing).

Bill Cummings (pp. 60–62) is the author of *A Master's Guide to Atlantic Salmon Fishing* (New York: McGraw-Hill, 1995).

6. FIRE ON THE MOUNTAIN

There are several good general histories of the iron industry in northwestern Connecticut. J. Lawrence Pool's *America's Valley Forges and Valley Furnaces* (Dalton, Mass.: Studley Press, 1982) is one of the most complete and also contains a useful overview of the development of the iron and steel industry nationwide after the Connecticut furnaces fell silent. Another excellent source is Ed Kirby's *Echoes of Iron in Connecticut's Northwest Corner* (Sharon Historical Society, 1998). What makes Kirby's book especially useful is its detailed field guide to the Housatonic Valley Iron Heritage Trail. Much of the region's industrial history is documented at the recently opened Museum of Mining and Mineral Science at the restored iron furnace in Kent, Connecticut. The museum is open during the summer months only (telephone: 860-927-0050).

Walt Landgraf's description of the charcoal hearths (p. 68) ("As soon as the first leaves . . .") is taken from a talk to the annual meeting of the Housatonic Valley Association at the White Hart Inn, Salisbury, Connecticut, December 1999. For other details of the life of the colliers, I enjoyed the account by *New Yorker* writer Christopher Rand, who spent two and a half months alone in a cabin on Mount Riga in an effort to replicate the collier's experience. His experiences are recounted in *The Changing Landscape: Salisbury, Connecticut* (New York: Oxford University Pres, 1968).

7. YDAWAIX AND OLDPHOGIZ

The epic story of American railroads in the nineteenth century, which provides essential context for understanding the growth and decline of the Housatonic and other local lines in Connecticut, is well told in David Haward Bain's monumental book, *Empire Express: Building the First Transcontinental Railroad* (New York: Penguin, 2000). Several books offer detailed histories of Connecticut's local railroads. The most complete, with some wonderful archival pictures of the early branch lines, is

Gregg M. Turner and Melancthon W. Jacobus's *Connecticut Railroads: An Illustrated History* (Connecticut Historical Society, second revised edition, 1989). The story of the Housatonic line (and the failed Housatonic Canal) is on pp. 47–66. The Shepaug Valley Railroad is discussed on pp. 111–114 and the Naugatuck Railroad on pp. 87–98.

The classic early history of the brass industry in the Naugatuck Valley is William G. Lathrop's *The Brass Industry in the United States: A Study of the Origins of the Brass Industry in the Naugatuck Valley and Its Subsequent Extension over the Nation,* revised edition (Mount Carmel, Conn.: William Lathrop, 1926). The Timexpo Museum, located in the mall that now occupies the site of the old Scovill Manufacturing Company in Waterbury, has an interesting permanent exhibit on the history of the clock-making industry, although it glosses over inconvenient details such as the death of dozens of young women in the industry who were poisoned by radium they ingested in the course of painting luminous watch dials. Ann Quigley's article "After Glow" (*Waterbury Observer,* September 2002) is a valuable corrective.

Unfortunately, few of Major Edwin McNeill's personal papers have survived. Those that have—including his original plans for the Shepaug Valley Railroad—are housed in the library of the Litchfield, Connecticut, Historical Society. Major McNeill's standoff with the local farmers is described in a number of local histories, including Fred H. Barnes's "The Old Shepaug Railroad—Slow, Late and Noisy" (*The Lure of the Litchfield Hills,* n.d.), on file at the Litchfield Historical Society. William C. Bader's *An American Village: The Light at the North End of the Tunnel* (Washington Depot, Conn.: Design to Printing, 1998) contains many old photographs of the Shepaug Valley Railroad and is a great example of the importance of publishing local history while residents can still remember it. For details of the Mine Hill operation and the Shepaug Spathic Iron and Steel Company, the best single source I have seen is Michael Bell and Diane Mayerfeld's *Time and the Land: The Story of Mine Hill* (Roxbury Land Trust, 1982).

In addition to Bill Bader's book, the town of Washington, Connecticut, has been well served by local historians and scholars. Alison Gilchrist Picton's booklet *Return to Arcadia: Ehrick Rossiter's Washington—The Architect, His Clients and Their Houses* (Washington, Conn.: Gunn Memorial Library and Museum, 1998) provides a valuable picture of

Washington society in the late nineteenth and early twentieth centuries and describes the most important residences in the town designed by Rossiter.

8. There but for Fortune

Kenneth T. Howell and Einar W. Carlson's *Empire over the Dam* (Chester, Conn.: Pequot Press, 1974) is the single most comprehensive account of the failed industrialization of the Housatonic Valley. It contains useful passages on several of the topics I have dealt with in earlier chapters, including the mill economy, the iron industry, and the railroads.

The iron master Alexander Lyman Holley's possibly apocryphal remark about the preservation of Salisbury (p. 91) is reported in virtually all local histories, including Ed Kirby's *Echoes of Iron*, p. 74. Although Holley is a largely forgotten figure, a statue of him can still be seen in Manhattan's Washington Square.

9. Dark Satanic Mills

The description of Waterbury in the 1930s on p. 95 ("Black iron and yellow firebrick . . .") is taken from the Works Progress Administration's *Connecticut: A Guide to Its Roads, Lore and People* (Boston: Houghton Mifflin, 1938). On the same page, I may be a little harsh on *Stanley and Iris,* which rates two and a half stars from Leonard Maltin and is worth watching if only for Robert De Niro's performance.

My discussion of Waterbury's neighborhoods has been enriched by my conversations with a number of town residents, including Raechel Guest, assistant curator of the city's excellent Mattatuck Museum, and by many published and unpublished materials in the museum's archives. Cristina Mathews's unpublished manuscript, "An Italian Hill Town with a Neon Cross: The Short-Lived Alchemy of Holy Land U.S.A." (Yale University, Senior Essay in Religious Studies, 1991, on file at the Mattatuck Museum) has been an indispensable source on Holy Land U.S.A. and the Pine Hill/Abrigador neighborhood.

Waterbury has been the subject of a number of semiofficial civic histories. I have relied mainly on William J. Pape's *History of Waterbury and the Naugatuck Valley* (Chicago and New York: S. J. Clarke Publishing Company, 1918). Pape also catalogues (in mind-numbing detail) the growth of specialized brass-related industries in the other seven towns of the Naugatuck Valley corridor.

A revised and updated edition of Jeremy Brecher's history of the U.S. labor movement, *Strike!* was published by South End Press in 1997. *Brass Valley: The Story of Working People's Lives and Struggles in an American Industrial Region,* edited by Jeremy Brecher, Jerry Lombardi, and Jan Stackhouse (Philadelphia: Temple University Press, 1982), is a model of the kind of oral history that flourished twenty years ago but has sadly fallen out of fashion. On the Italian immigrant experience, there is no substitute for Sando Bologna and Richard M. Marano's *Growing Up Italian and American in Waterbury: An Oral History* (Portland, Conn.: Waverly Printing Company, 1997). John Fusco's novel *Paradise Salvage* (Woodstock and New York: Overlook Press, 2002) is a wonderful evocation of Italian American life in the city in the 1970s, after the decline of the brass industry. It's also a terrific thriller.

10. THE HIGH COST OF BRASS

The discussion of occupational hazards and injuries in the brass industry (pp. 108–109) is largely drawn from various sections of *Brass Valley.* The lyrics of Michael "Faker" Sullivan's song "Scovill's Rolling Mill" (p. 109) are taken from the same source.

I was able to consult the reports of the Connecticut State Water Commission in the State Library in Hartford. For the Board of Agriculture's remark about the "diabolical bondage" of water pollution (p. 111), I am again indebted to a conversation and correspondence with Jeremy Brecher.

The Connecticut State Library also helped me locate a number of obscure materials by and about Robert Cairns, the Waterbury city engineer. These included Cairns's own account of the building of the Shepaug tunnel in a speech to the American Society of Civil Engineers, April 10, 1929. The story of the "mole men" and the Dempsey-Tunney fight is taken from Sando Bologna, "Water for Waterbury Through the Shepaug Connection" (*Waterbury Republican-American Sunday Magazine,* October 24, 1976). The basic outline of Cairns's biography is drawn from E. Robert Stevenson's *Connecticut History Makers* (Waterbury Republican-American, 1929).

11. FOUNDLINGS OF THE FINNY FAMILY

For the history of the town of Cornwall, I relied mainly on the second edition of the 1926 book by Edward C. Starr, *A History of Cornwall, Connecticut: A Typical New England Town* (Torrington, Conn.: Rainbow Press, 1982).

The work of Thaddeus Norris (p. 123), a singularly important figure in the nineteenth-century sporting and conservation movement, is discussed in various sections of Schullery's *American Fly Fishing: A History.* A more recent article on Norris was written by Jerry Girard: "Thaddeus Norris: America's Izaak Walton" (*American Fly Fisher* 29, no. 2, Spring 2003, pp. 3–7). Norris's own book, *The American Angler's Book: Embracing the Natural History of Sporting Fish and the Art of Taking Them* (Philadelphia: E. H. Butler, 1864), is a classic. A limited-edition facsimile reprint was published by the Derrydale Press (Lyons, Miss.: 1994).

On the brook trout, the most detailed work available is Nick Karas's *Brook Trout: A Thorough Look at North America's Great Native Trout— Its History, Biology, and Angling Possibilities* (New York: Lyons and Burford, 1997). The true fanatic may wish to consult pp. 66–67 for the arcane formula devised in the 1890s by a Canadian biologist to see why Cothren's giant brook trout (p. 126) was a physical impossibility. Until recently, the gold standard for books on the biology of trout in general was edited by Judith Stolz and Judith Schnell: *Trout* (Harrisburg, Pa.: Stackpole Books, 1991). All earlier volumes have now been trumped, however, by Robert J. Behnke's *Trout and Salmon of North America* (New York: Free Press, 2002). As a scientific reference Behnke's book is indispensable, and the species illustrations by Joseph L. Tomelleri make it a thing of beauty.

For the discussion of trout species in Connecticut, I have used Neal T. Hagstrom, Michael Humphreys, William A. Hyatt, and William B. Gerrish's *A Survey of Connecticut Streams and Rivers: Statewide Summary* (Hartford: DEP, Bureau of Natural Resources, Fisheries Division, Federal Aid in Sport Fish Restoration: F-66-R Final Report, 1987–1995). Bob Orciari and several of his DEP colleagues kindly made available to me much of the raw research data on which this report was based.

12. THE MAGIC BULLET

Behnke's *Trout and Salmon of North America* has discussion throughout on hatcheries, sport fishing regulations, and related questions of genetics. His regular column in *Trout*, the magazine published by Trout Unlimited, also frequently discusses these topics.

Herbert Hoover (p. 136), who knew a thing or two about inequality, once remarked that "fishing is great discipline in the equality of men, because all men are equal before fish." Hoover was not the only U.S. president to have been a fly-fisher, although the presidents' levels of skill varied widely. Jimmy Carter was undoubtedly the most passionate, tying his own flies and writing widely on the subject. More than any other president, he took advantage of the fact that the Camp David retreat lies just fifteen minutes from Big Hunting Creek, a renowned Maryland trout stream, where he went to take refuge from the Iranian hostage crisis. Dwight Eisenhower, on the other hand, famously failed to catch any of the hatchery trout that had been dumped into a Vermont river for his pleasure the night before his arrival. These and other adventures are recounted in Bill Mares's *Fishing with the Presidents* (Harrisburg, Pa.: Stackpole Books, 1999).

The early controversies surrounding the newly arrived brown trout are recounted in numerous sources, especially books dealing with the Beaverkill River and other famous streams in the Catskills. Of these, the best are Ed Van Put's *The Beaverkill: The History of a River and Its People* (New York: Lyons and Burford, 1996) and two books by Austin M. Francis, *Catskill Rivers: Birthplace of American Fly Fishing* (New York: Lyons and Burford, 1983) and the lavishly illustrated coffee-table book *Land of Little Rivers: A Story in Photos of Catskills Fly Fishing* (New York: Beaverkill Press, 1999).

13. ARE LOCUSTS KOSHER? ADVENTURES IN ENTOMOLOGY

I first learned of Wil Downs's work on caddis flies (p. 151) from a reference in Jeff Passante's *Housatonic River: Fly Fishing Guide* (Seattle, Wash.: Frank Amato Publications, 1998). There are literally thousands of books on fly-fishing and fly tying, and several hundred on the bugs that trout eat. Like most fly-fishers, my shelves groan under the weight of such volumes. The most relevant for typical fishers are the few classic volumes of "angler's entomology"—as opposed to the real science. I would include Louis Rhead's *American Trout Stream Insects* (New York: Frederick Stokes, 1916), Preston Jennings's *A Book of Trout Flies* (New York: Derrydale, 1935), Art Flick's *A Streamside Guide to Naturals and Their Imitations* (New York: Putnam, 1947), Ernest Schweibert's *Matching the Hatch* (New York: Macmillan, 1955), Al Caucci and Bob Nastasi's *Hatches* (New York: Comparahatch, 1975), Gary LaFontaine's *Caddisflies* (New York: Nick Lyons Books/Winchester Press, 1983), and Dick Pobst's *Trout Stream Insects* (New York: Lyons and Burford, 1990). I list these in chronological order of publication, since that reflects the rapid evolution of scientific knowledge on the subject. Starting with LaFontaine, the more recent angler's entomologies (with the honorable exception of Pobst) display a tendency to gigantism and frankly tell me more than I would ever want to know. I would trade all these books for my well-worn copy of Art Flick's *Streamside Guide,* which has the additional merit of fitting into a vest pocket.

Glenn Wiggins's description of tube-case making on p. 155 is from his *Larvae of the North American Caddisfly Genera* (Toronto: University of Toronto Press, 1977).

14. THE PILGRIM ROAD

The green drake mayfly is discussed in several of the volumes listed above and in innumerable articles in fly-fishing magazines. Most of the prose in these articles is purple to within an inch of its life. Various pieces by Art Lee, the editor of *Fly Fisherman,* are probably the most useful. Alvin Grove's book *The Lure and Lore of Trout Fishing* was originally published in 1951 by Stackpole Books (Harrisburg, Pa.). It was reprinted by the Freshet Press, Rockville Center, New York, in 1971, with a new introduction by Charles K. Fox.

15. TOXIC POLITICS

I consulted a variety of scientific and popular sources on PCBs; three were especially concise and useful: *PCBs: What Are They, Where Did*

They Come From, and What Are We Doing About Them? (Cornwall, Conn.: Housatonic Valley Association, n.d.); *A History and Status Report on PCB Contamination in the Housatonic River* (HVA, n.d.); and *PCB Concentrations in Fishes and Benthic Insects from the Housatonic River, Connecticut, in 1984–94* (Report #95-3F, prepared for the General Electric Company by the Environmental Research Division, Academy of Natural Sciences of Philadelphia, May 1995). Bioaccumulation in polar bears—which are particularly vulnerable because of their heavy consumption of seal blubber and other fatty foods—is discussed in many general accounts of PCBs.

The *New York Times* columnist mentioned on p. 171 was Elizabeth Kolbert, whose article "The River," dealing with PCB pollution of the Hudson, appeared in the December 4, 2000, issue of *The New Yorker*. The exchange between Jack Welch and Sister Patricia Daly was published in the August 1998 issue of *Harper's*. Welch's most recent book (with John A. Byrne) is *Jack: Straight from the Gut* (New York: Warner Books, 2001). A biography of Welch—or perhaps *hagiography* is a better word—is Robert Slater's *Jack Welch and the G.E. Way: Management Insights and Leadership Secrets of the Legendary CEO* (New York: McGraw-Hill, 1998). I confess I haven't read either of these, and Welch's star seems to have fallen somewhat since his messy divorce led to revelations of the extravagant perks he received as CEO of General Electric. This lurid media coverage had the bad taste to coincide with a wave of other corporate scandals and a seriously sluggish U.S. economy.

16. ROW V. WADE

The membership-based Housatonic Valley Association has a Web site, hvathewatershedgroup.com, which is probably the best single resource for following developments in the valley and its towns. It includes, among other things, regular updates on the cleanup of PCBs in the river, as well as background information on FERC and hydropower relicensing issues.

Although this chapter may suggest otherwise, I have nothing against canoeists or kayakers—unless they distort the flow of their preferred rivers in a way that harms the ecosystem. Natural rainfall often allows for serious white-water paddling on the Housatonic (and, in springtime at least, on the Shepaug), and information on this is available from the Housatonic Area Canoe and Kayak Squad (HACKS) in Falls Village, Connecticut. A useful guidebook is Bruce Lessels's *Classic Northeastern Whitewater Guide: The Best Whitewater Runs in New England and New York—Novice to Expert* (Boston: Appalachian Mountain Club Books, 1998). For those with a slower metabolism, I recommend Alex Wilson's *Quiet Water Canoe Guide: Massachusetts/Connecticut/Rhode Island* (1993), from the same publisher.

The Deerfield settlement is discussed in "PG&E Agrees to Acquire New England Power Plants" (*Wall Street Journal,* August 7, 1997). The Web site of American Rivers maintains a useful digest of information on hydropower reform disputes nationwide; see americanrivers.org/hydro powerdamreform/runoftheriver.htm.

17. Reading the Water

Unfortunately there is very little nonspecialist literature on trout genetics or the particular strains mentioned in this chapter. A general overview is given in the opening chapters of Stolz and Schnell's *Trout,* which includes two good short articles—Robert J. Behnke's "The Ancestry of Trout" (pp. 2–9) and Charles C. Krueger's "Genes—The Code Word" (pp. 10–15).

18. The Call of the Wild

William Cronon's comment on p. 206 ("What we mean when we use the word 'nature' . . .") is taken from his introduction to the edited collection of his essays, *Uncommon Ground,* p. 25. In the same passage, Cronon also quotes a famous remark by the British critic Raymond Williams: "The idea of nature contains, though often unnoticed, an extraordinary amount of human history." See Williams's *Problems in Materialism and Culture* (London: Verso Books, 1980), p. 67. The second quotation from Cronon in this chapter (p. 215) is also taken from the introduction to *Uncommon Ground,* p. 26.

Ray J. White, author of the article that Mike Piquette uses for his "wild trout road show" (p. 212), has also written widely on the disruptive effect of hatchery fish on wild populations. A group of scholars including White recently surveyed almost a thousand articles on the subject, dating back to 1900. An interesting summary of their findings and recommendations is available at ortrout.org/for/hatcheryreform.htm. The comment on cultural and behavioral adaptation by Van R. Potter (p. 216) is cited in "Natural Workings: The Adaptive Advantage," one of the many columns by Ray J. White available at flyfishamerica.com/Conservation/WildFish.

19. STAKEHOLDERS

The headline quoted on p. 219 is from Terry Corcoran's "Mayor Says Exciting Times Just Around the Corner" (*Waterbury Republican-American,* October 31, 1999). Mayor Phil Giordano was sentenced to thirty-seven years in prison by a federal judge in June 2003, on a variety of charges relating to the sexual abuse of minors. As this book went to press, Giordano also faced separate state sex-crime charges as well as federal corruption charges. For those who have the stomach for it, the basics of the Giordano scandal are summarized in David Howard's "Betrayal" (*Connecticut,* March 2002) and in an extended article by Edmund Mahony, Bill Leukhardt, et al., "Unmasked: The Depravity Within" (*Hartford Courant,* December 16, 2001). The *Waterbury Republican-American,* showing hitherto unsuspected investigative zeal, at last began to cover the story effectively after Giordano's arrest in July 2001. See, for example, Darlene McCormick's "Too Little Time Spent Minding the Store: Downfall—Sex, Inattention Let Woes Grow" (*Waterbury Republican-American,* December 31, 2001).

A detailed summary, with maps, of the state of Connecticut's Naugatuck River Restoration Project is available online at dep.state.ct.us. I am grateful to Lynn McHale for providing me with documents relating to the Waterbury wastewater treatment plant.

The story of Henry Kissinger and the blueberries (p. 230) is recounted in Ron Power's book *Far From Home* (New York: Random House, 1991), which paints a vivid picture of the impact of weekenders and new development on the town of Kent, Connecticut. My notes on Washington real estate are based mainly on the hyperventilations of the *Litchfield County Times,* supplemented by numerous conversations with local residents, while the comments from real estate brokers are taken from Robin Stansbury's "Beverly Hills of the East: Why the Stars Love Litchfield County" (*Hartford Courant*, December 16, 2001).

20. Fer Fightin' Over

On the downfall of David Brower (p. 238), see John McPhee's *Encounters with the Archdruid* (New York: Farrar, Straus & Giroux, 1971). An interesting supplement to the book is Daniel Coyle's "The High Cost of Being David Brower" (*Outside*, December 1995). Another dimension of Ed Matthews's remarkable career is his extensive pro bono work on death penalty cases. While it is not directly relevant to this book's story, I highly recommend Alec Wilkinson's profile of Ed Matthews, "A Night at the Beast House" (*The New Yorker*, September 27, 1999). Wilkinson's piece concentrates on Matthews's defense of Don Paradis, an Idaho man wrongfully convicted of murder and sentenced to death. Paradis was freed in 2002 after Matthews had spent sixteen years working on the case. See Bob Simon's "The Lawyer and the Biker" (60 Minutes II/ CBSNEWS.com, June 5, 2002).

21. Floodwaters

I drew on both interviews and contemporary sources for my account of the 1955 flood, including unpublished manuscripts in the Gunn Memorial Library in Washington, articles in the *Waterbury Republican-American,* and relevant portions of Bader's *An American Village.* I am grateful to Bill Bader for Ingersol Townsend's memorable cry of "Great Caesar's ghost!" which I quote on p. 247.

For the discussion of Taylorism in the Naugatuck Valley mills, and the fate of the Seymour Specialty Wire Company, I was greatly helped by Jeremy Brecher's "The Naugatuck Valley Project: Canst Thou Draw Out Leviathan with a Fishhook?" (Grassroots Policy Project/Civic Practices Network, 1995, available at cpn.org).

23. Old and in the Way

A recent general book on the subject of dam removal, published after this chapter was completed, is Elizabeth Grossman's *Watershed: The Un-*

damming of America (Boulder, Col.: Counterpoint Press/Perseus Books Group, 2002).

The removal of the Edwards Dam in Maine, which is discussed in Grossman's book, has also been the subject of a number of good articles. These include John McPhee's "Farewell to the 19th Century: The Breaching of Edwards Dam" (*The New Yorker*, September 27, 1999) and Jim Yuskavitch's "Rivers of the Dammed" (*Trout*, Summer 1999). On the specifics of small-dam removal, see the joint report by American Rivers, Trout Unlimited, and Friends of the Earth, *Dams That Don't Make Sense* (January 2000).

The specific technical data on pollution problems uncovered at particular sites on the Naugatuck are drawn mainly from publications by Milone & MacBroom, Inc.: *Phase I Preliminary Design Report: Anadromous Fish Restoration—Naugatuck River Basin*, Volume I: *Group A Dams* (December 1997) and Volume II: *Group B Dams* (March 1998). These are supplemented by reports on individual dams produced by the same consulting firm and additional materials supplied to me by Tom Morrissey and other officials of the Connecticut DEP.

The bypassing of the Tingue Dam in Seymour is a classic illustration of the unforeseen delays and cost overruns that can beset small-dam removal projects. Groundbreaking on this part of the Naugatuck Restoration Project, originally scheduled for completion in 2000, had still not begun by the middle of 2003. According to Tom Morrissey, director of planning and standards for the Connecticut DEP Water Management Bureau, the cost of the modifications to Tingue had risen by then from an initial estimate of $1 million to approximately $4.5 million, as a result of a variety of legal and regulatory considerations. The information is based on a telephone interview with Tom Morrissey (November 8, 2002).

24. THE IDEOLOGY OF SALMON

The literature on Atlantic salmon is quite extensive. As far as books are concerned, a good starting place is Peter Bodo's *The Atlantic Salmon Handbook* (New York: Lyons Press, 1997), although, like many, it concentrates more on the fishing than on the fish and its biology. A good summary article on the enigma of the decline of the Atlantic salmon is

William K. Stevens's "As a Species Vanishes, No One Can Say Why: Wild Stocks of Atlantic Salmon Plummet" (*New York Times,* September 14, 1999). See also Ted Williams's "Last Stand of the Yankee Salmon" (*Trout,* Autumn 1996) and Robert J. Behnke's "The Perils of Anadromy: What Have We Learned from History?" (*Trout,* Summer 1998).

A straightforward critique of the cost of restoring Atlantic salmon, and the meager results achieved, is Ezra Bowen's "The Million Dollar Fish" (*Connecticut,* May 1994). Of the specific articles discussed in the text, Catherine Carlson's essay (p. 276) first appeared in *New England's Creatures 1400–1900* (vol. 18 of the *Annual Proceedings of the Dublin Seminar for New England Folklife,* Boston University, June 1996) and was reprinted as "The [In]significance of Atlantic Salmon" in *History Through a Pinhole* (National Park Service Archaeological and Ethnographic Program 8, no. 3/4, Fall-Winter 1996); the speech on salmon aquaculture (pp. 278–279) was given by Brian Leavitt, administrative production coordinator for Atlantic Salmon of Maine, to the Rotary Club of Augusta, Maine (March 14, 2000); and the discussion of organic nutrients provided by salmon to the ecosystem of the Pacific Northwest (p. 281) is Ted Gresh, Jim Lichatowicz, and Peter Schoonmaker's "An Estimation of Historic and Current Levels of Salmon Production in the Northwest" (*Fisheries* 25, no. 1, January 2000). Lichatowicz's book *Salmon Without Rivers: A History of the Pacific Salmon Crisis* (Washington, D.C.: Island Press, 2001) may be the best overview of the subject.

The Haig-Brown House (p. 280) in Campbell River, Vancouver Island, was the writer's home from 1936 to 1975 and was dedicated as a historic site by the province of British Columbia in 1990. It is now a unique mixture of museum, seminar center, and bed-and-breakfast. See britishcolumbia.com/Attractions/attractions/haig-brownhouse.html.

25. A FULLY FOUGHT CASE

For descriptions of the *Waterbury v. Washington* trial, I relied on personal attendance, interviews with lawyers, and regular news coverage in the *Washington Republican-American,* the *Litchfield County Times,* and the *Hartford Courant.* Attorneys at the law firm of Cummings & Lockwood were especially helpful. For legal analysis of the trial and its broader impact on environmental litigation in New England, I was helped greatly by the work of the Rivers Alliance of Connecticut and the Connecticut Fund for the Environment (which appeared as amicus curiae).

Byron Bruce (Bo) Shelby (p. 289) is coauthor, with Thomas A. Heberlein, of *Carrying Capacity in Recreation Settings* (Eugene: University of Oregon Press, 1986).

As the Shepaug trial makes clear, the complicated question of instream flow, which I discuss briefly in this chapter, is one of the next and trickiest frontiers of environmental regulation and litigation. Rick Jacobson patiently answered my questions on the subject, and pointed me in the direction of some basic resources. I started with the condensed version of the U.S. Geological Survey's Instream Flow Incremental Methodology (IFIM), and recommend that anyone interested in the subject do the same. You can find this on the USGS Web site: mesc.usgs.gov/products/software/ifim/ifim.asp. American Rivers also has useful information on the subject, at amrivers.org/instreamflow/. I also found it helpful to look at the Connecticut DEP's *Report to the General Assembly on State Water Allocation Policies Pursuant to Public Act 98-224.*

26. RIVERNESS

As I feared (p. 302), shifts in political power have affected the decision to restore natural flow to the Housatonic as a condition for relicensing hydropower facilities on the river. In the final year of the Clinton administration, the objection raised by the Federal Energy Regulatory Commission (FERC) was that the state-level Water Quality Certificate might not go far enough to protect the Housatonic. Under the Bush administration, FERC's position is quite different. The agency's Draft Environmental Impact Statement, issued in July 2003, rejects run of the river in favor of seasonal peaking flows that would favor the recreational boating lobby. The impact of these recommendations is far from clear, since the federal government is legally obligated to incorporate the state's water quality certification into its hydropower relicensing. The saga continues.

Acknowledgments

For help, advice, and encouragement way beyond the call of duty, special thanks to Cornelia Bessie, Whitney Ellsworth, Ed Matthews, and Larry Pool.

For pieds-à-terre and well-timed R & R, thanks to Peter Canby, Anne and Connie Colby, Betsy and Steve Howard, Judith and Harry Moses, and Val Ross, Morton Ritts, and the collected Ritts-Rosses.

For their insights on the Housatonic, thanks to Ed Kluck, Mike Piquette, and Lynn Werner. On the Shepaug, thanks to Bill Bader, Dana Gibson, Edwin and Patricia Matthews, Gerry Mullen, John Osborne, Curtis Read, and Dimitri Rimsky. On the Naugatuck, thanks to Jeremy Brecher, Bob Fumire, Bob Gregorski, and Jon Ploski. On the Pomperaug, thanks to A. Hunter Brawley, Bill Cummings, and Dick Leavenworth.

For helping me navigate the arcana of mayflies, caddis flies, and assorted creepy-crawlies, thanks to Drs. Rodrigo Andrade, Bill Krinsky, Leonard Munstermann, Vernon Nelson, Ray Pupedis, and Charles Remington.

For some wonderful hands-on experiences of aquatic biology and environmental policy, thanks to Neal Hagstrom, Mike Humphreys, Bill Hyatt, Jerry Leonard, Ed Machowski, Jim Moulton, and Bob Orciari.

For their patient answers to my questions about the technical aspects of river restoration, thanks to Steve Gephard, Rick Jacobson, and Tom Morrissey.

For reaffirming the integrity of so many public servants in the city of Waterbury, thanks to Don Carver, Dada Jabbour, Mayor Michael Jarjura, and Lynn McHale.

For reinforcing my long-standing view that many of the nicest people in the world are librarians, thanks to Sarah Griswold and her colleagues at the Gunn Memorial Library and Historical Museum in Washington, Connecticut; Sean Sonderman at the American Museum of Fly Fishing in Manchester, Vermont; Ruth Mallins at the Housatonic Valley Association in Cornwall Bridge, Connecticut; Raechel Guest at the Mattatuck Museum in Waterbury, Connecticut; Mike DeLeo at the Bronson Memorial Library in Waterbury; and the staffs of the New York Public Library; the Connecticut State Library; the Minor Memorial Library of Roxbury, Connecticut; the Oliver Wolcott Library in Litchfield, Connecticut; the Connecticut State Historical Society; and the Historical Societies of Cornwall, Falls Village, Litchfield, Roxbury, and Southbury.

For photography much finer than the subject deserved, my gratitude to my good friend Bill Foley.

For assistance in more small ways than I can enumerate—a factoid here, a couple of beers and a sympathetic ear there—thanks to Bill Abrams, Coale Anderson, Doug Barnard, Burkhard Bilger, Susan Branson, Phil Demetri, Maya Dollarhide, Pam Edwards, Rachel Ellner, Hart Fessenden, Jan Fumire, Clare Gold, Jehv Gold, Steve Grover, Alistair Highet, Judy Jacobs, Cameron Jones, Kathy Jones, Marty and Lillian Keane, Walt Landgraf, Harold MacMillan, Margaret Miner, Hank Moses, Jennifer Nelson, Mary Osborne, Brint Ostrander, Dan Pool, Cara Rubinsky, Reggie Taylor, Lauren Westbrook, and Jim Zug.

Wendy Wolf has given me many gifts of friendship over the years, but none greater than the suggestion that Henry Dunow would be the ideal agent for me. She was right. Henry hasn't put a foot wrong, starting with the decision to offer this book to Anton Mueller at Houghton Mifflin and his able assistant, Erica Avery. One of the pleasures of writing the book has been the conviction that its subject matter, the clear eye and sharp intellect of my editor, and the editorial mission of one of America's great publishing houses have been in such close alignment.

As always, my deepest debt of gratitude is to Anne, David, and Julia, for their constant love and support and their willingness to indulge—if not always share—my outlandish fascinations.

Manhattan
June 2003

DATE DUE

36261

Greetings from NAUGATUCK, CONN.